COLLECTED STUDIES SERIES

Union, Revolution and Religion in 17th–Century Scotland

David Stevenson

Union, Revolution and Religion in 17th–Century Scotland

VARIORUM
1997

This edition copyright © 1997 by David Stevenson.

DA
803
.S74
1997

Published by VARIORUM
    Ashgate Publishing Limited
    Gower House, Croft Road,
    Aldershot, Hampshire GU11 3HR
    Great Britain

    Ashgate Publishing Company
    Old Post Road,
    Brookfield, Vermont 05036–9704
    USA

ISBN 0–86078–642–0

British Library CIP Data
    Stevenson, David.
    Union, Revolution and Religion in Seventeenth-Century Scotland.—
    (Variorum Collected Studies Series: 570)
    1. Scotland—Church history—17th century. 2. Scotland—Politics and
    government—17th century. 3. Scotland—History—17th century.
    I. Title. II. Series: Variorum Collected Studies Series: CS570.
    941.1'06

US Library of Congress CIP Data
    Stevenson, David.
    Union, Revolution and Religion in Seventeenth Century Scotland / David
    Stevenson.
       p. cm. — (Variorum Collected Studies Series: CS570) Includes index.
    1. Scotland—Politics and government—17th century. 2. Christianity and
    politics—Scotland—History—17th century. 3. Presbyterian church—
    Scotland—History—17th century. 4. Church and state—Scotland—
    History—17th century. 5. Church of Scotland—History—17th century.
    6. Scotland—Church history—17th century. 7. Covenanters. I. Title.
    II. Series: Collected Studies: CS570.
    DA808.S74 1997   96-40400
    941.106—dc21   CIP

The paper used in this publication meets the minimum requirements of the
American National Standard for Information Sciences - Permanence
of Paper for Printed Library Materials, ANSI Z39.48-1984. ∞ ™

Printed by Galliard (Printers) Ltd
    Great Yarmouth, Norfolk, Great Britain

VARIORUM COLLECTED STUDIES SERIES CS570

CONTENTS

RELIGION

PRINTING

vii

This volume contains xiv + 334 pages

PUBLISHER'S NOTE

The articles in this volume, as in all others in the Collected Studies Series, have not been given a new, continuous pagination. In order to avoid confusion, and to facilitate their use where these same studies have been referred to elsewhere, the original pagination has been maintained wherever possible.

Each article has been given a Roman number in order of appearance, as listed in the Contents. This number is repeated on each page and quoted in the index entries.

PREFACE

When I began research on seventeenth century Scotland, concentrating on the covenanters, back in the late 1960s I had few specific preconceptions as to what I would find. My ignorance of Scottish history was awesome. But I was motivated by having studied and become fascinated by the histories of England and Ireland in the period. They experienced complex wars and revolutions, and many experiments (mostly disastrous) in thought and government. But Scotland appeared as a hazy figure on the sidelines in the context of the British Isles – primarily as a nuisance, interfering in English affairs. No-one studying the upheavals of the period (with the honourable exception of C.V. Wedgwood) seemed to take any interest in what went on in Scotland and why the Scots meddled in both England and Ireland. The assumption seemed to be that there was no need to study Scotland, because the answer was so well known. The Scots were an unruly, backward lot, and insofar as their actions made any sense at all, they resulted from religious fanaticism.

Turning to specifically Scottish historians brought only limited enlightenment as to motivations. To many, it seemed, presbyterianism was Scottish identity. Scottish history was church history – and of course this applied to the Reformation and the Covenanters in particular. The story of the covenanting period was of noble – though rash in worldly terms – attempts to impose the true religion throughout Britain. The appearance of Gordon Donaldson's *Scotland: James V to James VII* in 1965 brought much refreshment and scholarship. But still the emphasis was on religion, though given a sharp edge through his own episcopalian inclinations.

It seemed, to the beginner, that England and Ireland had fascinating complexity, rebels seeking to create new political and governmental structures, struggling with political problems of credibility, gaining support, finding resources, raising armies. Scotland had Religion. Now religious motivation and conflict were of course of central importance in the other two kingdoms as well, but in Scotland it was the be all and end all. It explained everything. The Scots (from an English perspective) behaved stupidly, irrationally, self-destructively. They were infected with virulent religion.

No doubt I exaggerate. But my starting point in research was to try to take a fresh look at the covenanting movement without assuming that religion was the only thing worth studying. Secular history for a secular age, perhaps, but I was well aware that it would be folly to take that too far. Obviously religious motivation was central to what had happened. But I wanted to ask what else there was. Was the Scottish nobility, not in the past noted for high, unselfish principles, suddenly set on self destruction through religious zeal? Or blind stupidity? How was power seized, political organisation established, revolutionary government formed, tax raised, formidable armies brought to the field? Such things are not explained by invoking the magic word 'religion'.

So, I set out in a sense to 'modernise' the historical approach to the covenanters, and to the whole century. In two books, *The Scottish Revolution, 1637–44* (1973) and *Revolution and Counter Revolution in Scotland, 1644–51* (1977), I sought to chart and analyse the early covenanting movement. Many of the papers in the present volume seek to add to this the study of specialist topics relating to government, both of church and state, during these years, and to set the period in wider contexts.

As the first paper in this collection indicates, the century has long been unfashionable among Scottish historians. But in recent years the situation has changed. Numbers of talented of scholars are active in the field, greatly widening the areas that are being properly research. The picture emerging is of a country where religious considerations were indeed often of paramount importance, but where political rivalries, greed, ambition, nationalism, folly and other human concerns have their part. Scotland is no longer to be explained away by saying it was a theocracy, and I hope my own writings have made a contribution to such changing perspectives.

St Andrews   DAVID STEVENSON
October, 1996

ACKNOWLEDGEMENTS

The author and publisher would like to acknowledge copyright and express their appreciation for permission to reproduce the articles in this volume to the following: The Saltire Society (I); John Donald Publishers Ltd (II & III); Addison Wesley Longman Ltd (IV); *History Today* (V); *The Scottish Historical Review* Trust (VI & VIII); Cambridge University Press (VII & XII); W. Green Ltd, The Scottish Law Publisher (IX); The Stair Society (X); The Scottish Church History Society (XI & XIII); The American Society of Church History (XIV); The Council of the Bibliographical Society (XV); The Scottish Group of the University, College and Research Group of the Library Association (XVI).

For Wendy
Who has endured being married to me since
the first paper in this book was published

I

Twilight before night or darkness before dawn? Interpreting seventeenth-century Scotland

The seventeenth century in Scotland has had few friends. Traditionally, since the eighteenth century, it has been interpreted as a peculiarly unhappy age in Scotland's turbulent story, marked by cultural failure, religious fanaticism, economic decay, political violence and corruption, lacking any clear positive identity to offset these negative characteristics. This is all the more marked as the century is sandwiched between two which have strong identities. The sixteenth is dominated by Reformation and Renaissance, the eighteenth by Improvement and Enlightenment. The seventeenth often seems the awkward bit in between, with no similar dominant theme to give it unity. In popular history, the sixteenth and eighteenth centuries are illuminated respectively by the dazzling flares of Mary Queen of Scots and Bonnie Prince Charlie and their lost causes. The seventeenth century offers linking symbols of romantic failure in the persons of the Marquis of Montrose and Viscount Dundee, but they are pale and shadowy by contrast, casting only fitful light.

Yet though Scotland's seventeenth-century experience is frequently seen as repellent, this does not mean there is agreement about its significance – or lack of it – as a sort of grotesque interlude between the great ages of Reformation and Enlightenment. Historians of the two diametrically opposed main-line traditions in interpreting Scotland's past have, indeed, found common ground in rubbishing the seventeenth-century – though for very different reasons.

Historians use centuries as convenient shorthand terms for distinctive periods in the past, often taking considerable liberties with precise dates in the process. But Scotland's historical seventeenth century conforms fairly closely to the chronological one: it runs from the Union of the Crowns in 1603 to the Union of the

Parliaments in 1707. Differing attitudes to the latter event often influence or even determine attitudes to the whole century. To those in the nationalist tradition the age preceding 1707 in Scotland is discredited by that great betrayal, by the willingness of a majority of members of the country's political and social élites (as represented in the last Scottish Parliament) to vote away her sovereignty. In this perspective the seventeenth century becomes the age in which the traditional rulers of the country were corrupted by close links with England under the Union of the Crowns. It was the twilight of Scottish independence, in which her élites came to take English dominance for granted, and which culminated in their dereliction of duty in surrendering the country's hard-won independence. They failed the Scottish people by refusing to take account of the latter's patriotic hostility to the new incorporating Union. Thus the century of the Union of the Crowns was Scotland's dim twilight age before the long black night of Union fell, a grim age in which the forces of élite perfidy prepared themselves for the final treachery.

Historians in the rival unionist tradition have agreed on the blackness of the age. For them, the seventeenth century in Scotland was one of increasing poverty, oppression and violence, a century in which, if anything, these traditional badges of the country's backwardness and barbarism were even more marked than in previous centuries. But salvation was at hand, for the gloom of this age was the intensified darkness which precedes the dawn. The dawn was, of course, the incorporating Union with England, bringing archaic Scotland into a modern world of progress so that she could blossom into a new era of better and more stable government, economic improvement and Enlightenment. And looking further ahead, as the low morning sun rose higher in the sky, Scotland was – through 1707 and the rejection of her discredited past – freed to play a full part in the glories of the British world-empire on which the sun never set. She had achieved her destiny, not as a struggling independent state doomed to insignificance, but through acceptance of a British and imperial rôle.

As the Union of 1707 has lasted (up to the present at least), the unionist distortion of Scotland's seventeenth century has generally prevailed over the nationalist one, and its tentacles have spread to all aspects of Scotland's past in ways designed (though usually unconsciously) to reconcile Scots to the decision made in

1707. In considering subsequent positive or 'progressive' developments in the Scottish experience, there has been a strong tendency
to take 1707 as a starting point, the unexamined assumption being
that everything creditable in eighteenth-century Scotland flowed
from the Treaty of Union, directly or indirectly. Agricultural
improvement, the eventual flourishing of trade and industry,
political stability, parliamentary government, the rule of law,
Enlightenment: all have more often been seen in terms of breaks
with Scotland's past than as developments evolving from that
past. Study of pre-1707 Scotland, in this perspective, is little more
than antiquarian indulgence, for the burden of her past was excess
baggage sensibly jettisoned so that Scotland, as part of a new
Britain, could embrace England's historical experience as more
relevant to the future. Above all else perhaps, English constitutional history was transformed into British constitutional history.
In theory in 1707 both Scottish and English Parliaments were
abolished, a new institution, the British Parliament, created. In
reality, of course, the English Parliament continued to exist, its
traditions, powers and procedures unchanged except that a few
new members representing Scotland were added to it. Scotland
contributed nothing to the new state's constitution: her native
parliamentary tradition was a discredited irrelevance. Surely, therefore, it was obvious that when Scots were taught constitutional
history it should be the 'English' constitution they lived under
that was explained to them.

Scotland's seventeenth century: dark, repellent, irrelevant, worth
nothing more than a hasty glance to demonstrate how awful life
had been before the Scots wisely embraced Union? Or a sad age of
creeping betrayal of national destiny? Does Scottish History,
1603-1707, really matter no more than this?

The answer is a resounding denial of this suggestion, and this
must be whether the personal perspective is unionist, nationalist
or couldn't care less. At last in recent decades the seventeenth-
century experience has begun to be re-assessed, and the century
turns out to be vastly more diverse, exciting and interesting than
it had previously seemed. It remains in many respects a pro-
foundly unhappy century for Scotland, but her attempts to cope
with the problems she faced emerge as fascinating, and it is now
clear that 1707 does not mark the point at which the Scots wrote
off their past and began new history within Britain, based on

adoption of England's historical legacy. Culturally, it is true, the century was far from distinguished; anglicisation largely destroyed much of the native literary tradition, and the dominance of narrow and gloomy religious literature tends to repel. Yet historians of the Enlightenment now reach far back into the century in seeking to trace its origins, and find plenty of evidence of modest cultural and intellectual achievement as fanaticism gradually declines and men's interests broaden out into new secular fields.

In the economy there is considerable development in trade and industry in the course of the century. This is sporadic, and serious trading problems appeared in the last decades of the century, making a major contribution towards forcing the Scots to accept Union with England in 1707; but nonetheless, the slow, piecemeal changes which were taking place were preparing the way for the massive expansion that was to begin in the mid-eighteenth century. In agriculture the picture is similar. Many of the types of reform which were eventually to transform the Scottish countryside were already under discussion and even being put into practice in the seventeenth century. They were not implemented on a large scale, but nonetheless did contribute to a significant if unspectacular rise in agricultural productivity – though again this continuity has been disguised by short-term problems at the end of the century – a massively demoralising series of catastrophic harvest failures resulting from bad weather in the later 1690s, which caused the worst famine to hit the country for generations.

Changes in agriculture obviously reflected changing priorities in Scotland's dominant landed élites, moves away from the old 'lordship' society dominated by ties of kinship and feudalism in which manpower gave status, to a more commercial ethos in which money revenues came first. The involvement of many landlords in industrial and trading ventures confirms the trend. Along with commercialisation came anglicisation: under the Union of the Crowns Scots landlords had the choice of either retaining their distinct identity, but paying the price of being reduced to a provincial nobility, or assimilating to the English landed classes. Eventually, though often reluctantly, they chose assimilation, an anglicisation of attitudes and culture that they hoped would gain them status at court in London. Though little studied as yet, it is clear that this slow, unspectacular process of assimilation was central to the coming of political Union in 1707. It was (from the nationalist perspective) an insidious process that alienated them from the mass of the population of Scotland, and made their great betrayal of the country possible – or (switching to a unionist viewpoint), it was the rational acceptance of the superiority of things English that allowed the Scots élites to abandon narrow, outmoded national prejudices and set their country on a new course.

This brings us to what is perhaps the most central of the many themes of seventeenth-century Scottish history, and indeed perhaps of all Scottish history since the early kingdoms within the island of Britain had coalesced into two dominant political systems: the question of relations with England. Here, study of Scottish history is of significance not merely to Scots: it is vital to the understanding of England's political evolution in the course of the century, and of the development of the concept (and, eventually, the reality) of Britain.

Two kingdoms uneasily sharing one island, differing greatly in population and wealth. The generalisation applies that, whether considering individuals or nations, quarrels with neighbours are more likely than with anyone else, because neighbours have most contacts with each other and thus most possible occasions for conflict. If they had been left to fight it out between themselves, it is quite possible that a solution would have been found in English conquest and absorption of Scotland. Scotland escaped through the obvious strategy of a lesser power threatened by a great neighbour: ally with another neighbour at odds with your enemy – in this case, France. Thus Scotland preserved a precarious independence. By the sixteenth century, however, some Scots were wondering if the price was too high. Alliance with France was intended to protect them from English aggression, but if the French were to aid the Scots, the Scots in turn had to aid them: Scotland found herself involved in disastrous military enterprises – culminating in shattering defeats at Flodden (1513) and Solway Moss (1542) – more as a pawn in French wars with England than through protecting her own independence. Unease at increasing French domination of Scottish affairs peaked in the 1550s when the country was ruled by a French regent and her Crown seemed destined to be united with that of France. Fear of becoming a French province was central to the 1559-60 Reformation/Revolution which brought to power a Protestant, pro-English régime.

But escape from a French frying-pan was possible only through risking immolation in an English fire. The overthrow of the French was made possible through English military intervention. In 1573 the English intervened again, to support a tottering Protestant regency, and on other occasions during the minority of the young James VI English influence was exerted against threatened Counter-Reformation. Even when James achieved adulthood he was both financially and politically dependant on the good will of Elizabeth of England, and though he strove to be his own man there is, in late sixteenth-century Scotland, more than a whiff of clientship – of Scotland, in spite of her formal independence, becoming informally a client or satellite state. This was made bearable to James and his subjects by two considerations: first, through recognition that friendship with England was central to the survival of a Protestant régime, the two countries having a common interest in resisting Catholic threats: second, and more positively, by the likelihood that James would succeed Elizabeth on the English throne. To have a Scot seated on the throne of England, the throne of Edward I and Henry VIII whose attempts to conquer Scotland had ended in failure, would be an ironic historical achievement for which it was well worth putting up with temporary humiliations.

This great hope achieved fruition in 1603. Edward I might have hijacked the symbol of the Scottish monarchy, the Stone of Scone, but now a Scotsman sat on the English throne that enclosed it. But what was Scotland's future to be in the new dual monarchy? In constitutional terms there were, basically, three alternatives.

The first option was that England and Scotland should remain separate in government, politics, religion, culture, etc. Accident of inheritance meant that the two kingdoms shared the same monarch, and this would insure peace and stability in their relations with each other. This was what most Scots wanted and expected: two equal partners under one monarch.

The second choice was that the kingdoms should remain distinct, but the dominance of England – based on wealth and population as well as on historical claims to the overlordship of Scotland – would be recognised. Scotland's relationship with England would come to have many similarities to that of Ireland – a separate but subordinate and dependent kingdom to be anglicised and to be ruled in England's interests. Not surprisingly this was an option that appealed to the English, but not to the Scots.

The third choice was that the two kingdoms could be completely merged to form a new, single, state.

These issues were commonplaces in European history. Most existing states of any size had grown out of the amalgamations of smaller political units in the past, brought together by conquest or the results (accidental or intended) of dynastic marriages in earlier generations. And these provided many precedents and parallels relevant to what Britain was now beginning to experience. Most of them should have led thoughtful Scots to fear for their country's future. Certainly it had been common for centuries for rulers of composite states and multiple monarchies to accept diversity, that formerly independent units could retain their own institutions, laws, languages, customs. Nonetheless, smaller units which became attached to larger ones almost invariably found themselves ruled in the interests of the greater. Moreover, by this time emerging absolutist theories of political authority were tending to stress the advantages of uniformity in territories under a single ruler – and obviously the model for such uniformity tended to be the greater unit which formed the core of the monarchy. Imposing greater uniformity was intended to make provincial revolts less likely – but in the short term it often provoked them.

So dynastic ambition was realised in 1603: as far as James was concerned, the destiny of Scotland's ancient race of kings had at last been fulfilled in the divinely ordained Union of Britain under his rule. Yet surely some people saw the ominous relevance of one continental precedent to Scotland's case. The Burgundian dynasty which ruled the Netherlands had inherited the crown of Spain. It was taken for granted that the dynasty would rule from what was now its greatest territory, Castile, at the heart of the Spanish monarchy – just as nobody questioned that King James would rule Britain from London. An alien dynasty took over Spain, but within a generation it had 'gone native', and was coming to be seen as alien by its Dutch subjects: it was regarded as ruling them in Spanish interests. The result was the great Revolt of the Netherlands, beginning in the 1560s: and in 1603 the Dutch were still fighting to gain independence from absentee rule from Spain.

The attitude of King James himself was that Union of the kingdoms and people should logically, and indeed automatically, follow from the Union of the Crowns, and he devoted much wordy rhetoric (though it was distinctly vague about details) to trying to persuade his subjects of this. He failed. Mutual suspicions between the two peoples were too strong: Scotsmen feared absorption into England; Englishmen feared being dominated by Scots favoured by their royal compatriot. Though James's attempts at 'complete' Union were thwarted, the fact that he made them suggests that he foresaw difficulties in trying to rule the kingdoms separately in ways which would keep both happy. Events were to prove him right – but the alternative policies he adopted when his Union plans failed contributed greatly to this outcome. Since he had to rule the kingdoms separately, he resolved to seek to make them as like each other as possible. Conflict between them would become less likely as they became more alike, and perhaps eventually they would be so similar that objections to political Union would collapse. In practice uniformity meant no change for England, but anglicisation for Scotland. This was most clearly seen, and most resented, in religion. The two kingdoms might be bound together by common Protestantism, but simultaneously they were held apart by the different ways in which their national churches had developed. Resentment in Scotland intensified when James's son, Charles I, accelerated his father's policies, greatly increasing the demands he made on his Scottish subjects for obedience to unpopular and frequently anglicising policies.

The result was the great national revolt which began in Scotland in 1637 – and which had many similarities with the revolts of Catalonia and Portugal against Castilian domination in 1640. Religion legitimised revolt, providing an ideology that united Scots at all levels of society against their native, but now alien, dynasty. Their defiance, aimed at the king and his advisers and not at the English, was remarkably successful: for once the English sympathised with the Scots and obstructed his attempts to fight them.

By 1641 the Scots had achieved religious and constitutional revolution, creating a presbyterian Church and a Parliament free from royal control. King Charles had to accept being reduced to a figurehead. But the Scots rebels, the Covenanters, now had an even more challenging role to perform, one that verged on the impossible. They accepted continuing political links with England – not least because these seemed unbreakable unless the dynasty was dethroned north of the border, and this was inconceivable: it might be anglicised, but it was Scots in origin, and central to the country's national identity. Therefore instead of rejecting the Union of the Crowns, the Scots set out to remodel it so that Scotland could play her rightful rôle within it. What was envisaged was a loose federal arrangement, with royal power strictly limited by Parliaments in each kingdom, and a joint body of an equal number of commissioners from each kingdom supervising matters of joint concern – such as relations between the kingdoms, and foreign policy. From the Scottish perspective a fair Union with England involved equal partnership of this sort.

Inevitably, however, and understandably, from an English perspective such a partnership seemed most unfair. It would give the fewer than one million Scots the same power in joint affairs as the more than five million Englishmen and Welshmen: and the discrepancy in wealth between the two nations was much wider still. The Scots were, it seemed, trying to follow up victory over the king by seizing a totally disproportionate power in British affairs. Other aspects of Scottish ambitions emphasised this further. In religion, they demanded the Scotticisation of England and Ireland – the imposition of presbyterianism. Just as much as James VI and Charles I, they took it for granted that politics and religion were inseparable, and that stable friendship in the former sphere necessitated uniformity in the latter.

Yet at first the prospect for what amounted, in English eyes, to Scottish domination of Britain, seemed good. After defeating the king in England the Covenanters forced him to summon parliament in England, to give his English enemies a forum in which to attack his power. Thus the famous Long Parliament, which was to push through an English constitutional revolution and then defeat the king in a bloody civil war, was summoned at the behest of the Scots: and a number of the most important constitutional reforms it introduced were based on recent Scottish legislation. English parliamentarians admitted that they owed their liberties to the Scots, and their dependence on the Scots was such that they were willing to make promises – if rather vague ones – to reform religion and the Union on Scots lines.

The Scots fancied themselves as controllers of events, ring-masters of Britain's three-kingdom three-ring circus, but the performers were soon spinning wildly, beyond anyone's control. First

Ireland and then England, destabilised by the destruction of royal power by the Scots, collapsed into civil war. At the request of the English parliament the Covenanters sent armies into both kingdoms. Though this was an immense drain on Scotland's resources, the Covenanters reconciled themselves to it with the argument that it increased the English Parliament's dependence on the help of the Scots, and thus would strengthen their ability to impose the Scots variant of equal Union on Britain.

They were deluding themselves. Predictably, once the Scots had helped the English Parliament win the civil war, that Parliament forgot the promises the Scots had exacted from it as the price of military aid. Bitterly disillusioned, the Scots sought repeatedly and increasingly desperately to force the English into a Scots-dominated settlement. The result was, eventually, to exasperate the English under Oliver Cromwell into invading and conquering Scotland (1650-1) and imposing what they understood to be equal Union: a political Union with a single British Parliament in which only a small proportion of the members were Scots. As England had many times the population and wealth of Scotland, this had to be reflected in the membership of a joint legislature if power was to be justly distributed between the two nations.

By revolting against anglicisation the Scots thus ended up with amalgamation with England, and far more thorough anglicisation under Cromwell's republican régime than they had ever suffered under Charles I. Monarchy was soon restored, it is true, in the person of Charles II in 1660, and the hated 'incorporating' Union disappeared as Union of the Crowns returned. But the great mid-century upheaval had deeply seared the Scots' psyche. In 1637 they had had the confidence to take their destiny in their own hands, and seek to re-model Britain to their liking. The result had been years of bloodshed and destruction culminating in the utter disaster of conquest. The national myth that Scotland was the never-conquered nation had frequently given Scots heart in hard times in the past: now it had been shattered for ever. So too, for the great majority, had the awe-inspiring belief, which had reached its apogee under the Covenanters, that the Scots were the successors to the Jews as a chosen people of God, to whom he would bring victory, whatever the odds, in doing His work on earth. Harsh reality had proved that in Britain the tail could not wag the dog – or at least only very briefly, when the English dog had been thrown off-balance by internal illness. The lesson was learnt well. Scotland followed England's lead both in restoring monarchy in 1660 and in overthrowing a tyrannical and incompetent ruler – James VII – in 1688, rather than risk taking the initiative herself. And though the Scots did try again to assert their vision of their rightful place within the Union of the Crowns after 1688, when this led to a situation in which open conflict with England was likely, they gave way to an essentially English-dictated, incorporating Union (sweetened with concessions on free trade, law and religion).

Seen in one context, Scotland's experience in the seventeenth century is a classic example of the problems of a small state within a multiple monarchy. In another, understanding of it is essential to understanding the emergence of the kingdom of Great Britain. A nation *is* its past, and to comprehend what it means to be British it is necessary to take seriously the pasts of Scotland, Ireland and Wales as well as of England – as British historians, encouragingly, are increasingly accepting. Perhaps one day 'British' history, meaning 'English history, with some mention of the tiresome Scots Irish and Welsh when they are making a nuisance of themselves' will finally be buried. Finally, just as it is entirely legitimate for the English and others to study English history in its own right – provided it is not called British – so equally it is important to study Scottish history to understand what it means to be Scots, and how to place the country in wider British and European historical contexts.

For some, whose political hearts rule their historical perceptions, the seventeenth century in Scotland will remain stereotyped: darkness before dawn or twilight before night. They are missing a lot. This complex century has many inter-twined themes, most of which cannot find space for even a mention in this short essay. The real darkness comes not from the nature of developments in the century, but from lack of modern historical research. To put this positively, the opportunities for research are many and exciting, and the probing torch-beams of specialist studies are beginning to criss-cross and merge into wider illumination of broad areas.

II

The English Devil of Keeping State:
Élite Manners and the Downfall of Charles I in Scotland

> And learn to fly, to shun and hate,
> This English devil of keeping state.[1]

In the late 1640s an elderly Aberdeenshire laird, Patrick Gordon of Ruthven, mused on the causes of the overwhelming disasters which had struck his country in the previous decade. First had come the great rebellion of the covenanters against King Charles I, a disaster in the eyes of the royalist Patrick Gordon because it had been successful. Then had followed the outbreak of civil wars in Ireland and England, civil wars in Scotland in which the royalist cause suffered catastrophic defeat, and great epidemics of plague. How were these great and painful upheavals to be explained?

Gordon's explanation was that they were the work of God, who was reacting to the corruptions of the age. But God was acting not — or not only — to punish a corrupt generation, but to cure its ills. The sufferings which seemed to be tearing Britain, and in particular Scotland, apart were the side effects of supernatural medical intervention. According to the principles of physic, the divine physician was treating the land with blood-letting for the liver, vomiting for the stomach, and purging for the belly. Scotland's nobility and gentry were her liver, and were suffering blood-letting by the sword; the merchants and craftsmen of the towns, the main victims of the plague, were the land's purged belly. If this treatment did not cure the infirmity, famine, analogous to vomiting as it emptied the stomach, was sure to follow. However drastic the successive treatments prescribed might seem, the illness was so serious that they were necessary — and resort to alternative medicine was not an option: the Scots must continue to trust their doctor.[2]

In keeping with his cosmic medical framework of explanation, Gordon entitled his observations on the troubles *Ane Short Abridgement of Britane's Distemper*. A more appropriate title might have been *On some Side-Effects of*

II

Divine Medical Treatment, since strictly speaking in his analogy the actual events of the decade which he describes were not themselves the distemper, but symptoms produced by the treatment designed to cure it. Gordon himself, however, was distinctly ambiguous on this point, for he also called the momentous events he was living through "this dreadful and never to be matched distemper".

Patrick Gordon was a modest and scholarly man, whose career was of such exemplary obscurity that virtually nothing is known of it. But events had

> found an unwonted motion in my soul to leave a memorial to posterity of such observations as I have noted ... although I cannot but confess my own weakness, there being so many judicious, learned, and able spirits who can and will go in hand with the business. This only shall be my best encouragement, that as I carry spleen nor hatred to no man, so shall my relation go always accompanied with the truth; and therefore, I could wish that it were buried in oblivion till I were in my grave, for well I know that the truth shall never be gracious whilst the actors are on life; and, therefore, true histories are usually written in succeeding ages.[3]

In this Gordon got his way: his history was not published until 1844. Since then it has been widely used by historians of the civil wars for details of campaigns in north-east Scotland, and it has been recognised that it was written partly as an attempt by Patrick Gordon to rescue the name of the head of his own kin, George Gordon, marquis of Huntly, from denigration by supporters of the rival royalist leader, the marquis of Montrose. But the author would have been saddened that later ages have shown virtually no interest in his explanations of the causes of events. Drastic cures by divine doctors are out of fashion as modes of historical explanation, and Gordon's supporting evidence of old prophecies, great comets and threatening conjunctions of the planets have not added to his credibility with modern historians.

Yet there is one sub-theme of *Britane's Distemper*, a specific corruption of the age which Gordon saw as contributing to disaster in Scotland, which deserves serious attention. Indeed, so this essay will argue, it merits wider application than Gordon himself gave it, for whereas he applied it to some members of the Scottish nobility, it applies above all to King Charles I himself. It is hard to believe that Gordon did not realise this. Doubtless he did, but forbore to criticise royalty — while perhaps expecting posterity to read this additional application between the lines.

The sub-theme emerges as Gordon pondered the problem of why his own lord, Huntly, was so uniformly unsuccessful in his efforts to serve the king, arousing very little support or enthusiasm, while Montrose, by contrast, aroused passionate loyalty and dedication from his followers, and won a great reputation as a military leader and cavalier hero in royalist circles. The puzzle was all the greater as Montrose was ultimately defeated conclusively, and had never won united support from Scottish royalists.

Much lay in the general differences of character and ability between the two men, but Gordon focused on one contrast between them: the way they treated their social inferiors. For Gordon, Montrose represented the virtues of traditional Scottish manners, while Huntly displayed the corrupting influences of English manners, alienating those who were his natural followers. Huntly, in terms of property and kinship, was potentially a vastly greater noble than Montrose, but he, like some others amongst the Scottish nobility, suffered the fatal defect of infection by "the English devil of keeping state".

Montrose was a man who by his manner and bearing won the respect due to him from inferiors naturally, without having to ask or demand it. He seemed

> to scorn ostentation and the keeping of state, and therefore he quickly made a conquest of the hearts of all his followers, so as when he list he could have led them in a chain to have followed him with cheerfulness in all his enterprises; and I am certainly persuaded, that this his gracious, humane and courteous freedom of behaviour, being certainly acceptable before God as well as men, was it that won him so much renown, and enabled him chiefly, in the love of his followers, to go through so great enterprises, wherein his equal had failed, although they exceeded him far in power, nor can any other reason be given for it, but only this that followeth.[4]

Gordon then launched into an attack on keeping of state which in its bitterness and sarcasm suggests that he himself had at some point felt personally humiliated by how Huntly, his own lord with new-fangled ways, had treated him:

> For once that English devil, keeping of state, got a haunt amongst our nobility, then began they to keep a distance, as if there were some divinity in them, and gentlemen therefore must put off their shoes, the ground is so holy whereon they tread; but as he is an evil bred gentleman that understands not what distance he should keep with a noble man, so that noble man that claims his due with a high look, as if it did best fit his nobleness to slight his inferiors, may well get the cap and knee, but never gain the heart of a freeborn gentleman.

— or at least not in Scotland, for

> It is true that in England the keeping of state is in some sort tolerable, for that nation (being so often conquered) is become slavish, and takes not evil to be slaves to their superiors.
>
> But our nation, I mean the gentry not the commons, having never been conquered, but always a free-born people, are only won with courtesy, and the humble, mild, cheerful, and affable behaviour of their superiors.... . And because

II

they have never been brought to bow their necks under the yoke of bondage, nor were they ever slaved with the awful tyranny of a conqueror, nor forced to yield respects as the English do, to him that keeps, or rather seeks to keep, great state... , looking for observance so greedily as he cannot stay [stop] till it is given him, but with a lofty look claiming as is due his own awful reverence from all; this I say only, this our Scots nation cannot endure, but are ever found with secret murmurings and private grudges to repine at. And, therefore, although their leader be their chief, their master, of whom they hold their lands or their being, yet was it never found abroad nor at home that a leader of such stately and reserved carriage could, with our nation, perform any great enterprise.[5]

Therefore, Gordon urged, nobles should take heed of the lines of verse about the "English devil" printed at the start of this essay. Montrose was naturally inclined to humility, courtesy and freedom of carriage:

He did not seem to affect state, nor to claim reverence, nor to keep a distance with gentlemen that were not his domestics; but rather in a noble yet courteous way he seemed to slight those vanishing smokes of greatness, affecting rather the real possession of men's hearts than the frothy and outward show of reverence; and therefore was all reverence thrust upon him, because all did love him.[6]

"He that exalteth himself shall be humbled" concluded Gordon piously, and it served them right for failing to make a difference in how they treated free-born gentlemen and servile or base-minded slaves.

In all this adulation of Montrose the contrast was being made with anonymous other nobles. Even the comparison with Huntly was left implicit, perhaps because Gordon at this point was writing before Huntly was executed in 1649. But later in his work, writing after Huntly's death and seeking to explain his abysmal failure in the traditional noble role of war-leader, Gordon was more candid. Self-will, obstinacy, and refusal to take advice contributed to Huntly's failure. So did the fact that, when he experienced difficulties, "Service done... was forgotten, and old servants, for whom there was no use, must be brushed or rubbed off, as spots from clothes". But Gordon remained to the end ambivalent about Huntly, for as the head of the Gordon kin his reputation should be upheld, so he hastily added that this was a truly noble fault, for all nobles were ungrateful! Nonetheless, "the hard construction which was made of this did more harm to himself than to those castaways, for it did, by little and little, insensibly alienate the hearts of his followers". Moreover,

with a certain kind of reserved inclination, he seemed desirous to keep a distance with his inferiors, without distinction of quality; for friends and followers were equalled with domestics ... unless his affairs required it, and then [he] could be both familiar and obsequious. This got him but an outward and constrained obedience.

Consequently, when Huntly planned risings in the king's name, some of his followers simply retired to their homes – and, even more damningly, others went and served Montrose instead. Again ambivalent, Gordon condemned this desertion of Huntly because of his "one fault". Nonetheless, the moral was there to be underlined yet again:

> Thus we may see how far the inward tie of the heart prevaileth against the strong bond of nature, or the duty they owed to their chief, or obedience to their lord and master or superior; and this truly should be a warning to our nobility, letting them see how great an antipathy there is betwixt the genius of our nation and the English keeping of state.

Yet still Gordon tried to excuse his master. His

> keeping of distance, and the proud show of affecting state, was no part of his natural inclination; he was known to be both affable, courteous, and sociable before he was called to court; his breeding in England, the habit and long custom he got there, overcame and wholly changed his natural inclination.[7]

There is a most striking historical irony here. James VI had insisted that the young heir to the Gordon empire in north-east Scotland be brought up in England, with the deliberate intention of cutting him off from his roots, from the Gordon power-base which had enabled his father so frequently to defy the crown. The policy was entirely successful, for when Huntly returned to his estates after his father's death in 1636 he was an Anglicised stranger. But this meant that, though he had been inculcated with loyalty to the crown, he was unable to mobilise Gordon resources to help the king effectively against the covenanting rebels in the years ahead. The great Gordon interest, potentially one of the very greatest in the country, had been successfully tamed by the crown just at the moment when the crown had desperate need of it.

The increasing insistence of the Scots nobility on formality in dealing with inferiors had been lamented long before Patrick Gordon's time. In 1607 James Cleland had advised a degree of humility in dealing with men of all sorts:

> because I see so many of our young nobles deceive themselves herein, thinking that we are bound to respect and honour them in all devotion and service, and that they are not tied to any reciprocal courtesy, as if it were possible that they could stand of themselves, and uphold their imaginary and fantastical greatness without us. For my part I can neither honour nor respect such persons.[8]

II

In another fine example of historical irony Cleland dedicated one of the books of his work to the future marquis of Huntly – and the whole work to the future Charles I.

* * *

Patrick Gordon ended *Britane's Distemper* with a comparison between Huntly and Charles I, who had been executed just a few weeks before him, pointing out the similarities between them. The comparison was however confined to their merits: no criticism of the "superlative" martyr-king or his "unparalleled" servant was appropriate.[9] But by inference a question lurked beneath the surface: did the two men also share defects which contributed to their downfalls?

The answer is undoubtedly in the affirmative. The manner in which Charles I treated most members of the élites of society of Scotland in the course of personal contacts was frequently regarded as insulting, leading ultimately to alienation and reluctance to support him even by his natural supporters when crisis came — exactly what Huntly experienced in his much smaller sphere. Inferiors were shocked by being treated by superiors in ways which were not traditional and were interpreted as degrading. But the superiors concerned were equally upset: as they interpreted what was happening, it was their inferiors who were behaving with appalling lack of courtesy, failing to behave with the deference necessary to indicate respect and reverence. Social relationships were being destroyed by conflicting codes of manners.

The Scots prided themselves on a degree of robustness and informality in relations between men of different rank. Society might be intensely hierarchical in structure, but nonetheless men of differing rank could indulge in informal interactions, partly indeed because this hierarchy was fairly secure and confident: great emphasis on outward display of differences was unnecessary. As Patrick Gordon indicated, gentlemen knew how to treat a noble with respect, and nobles did not feel that any great show of boot-licking was necessary to re-assure them of their status. The monarchy itself before the union of the crowns in 1603 had frequently been informal in style. James VI might theorise on divine right in grandiose terms but saw no incongruity in addressing a Scots earl as "My little fat pork" or, after 1603, an English earl as "My little beagle".[10]

Such informality might be acceptable in Scotland, but it grated in England, where the trend was towards greater formality of manners, more rigid behaviour, more emphasis on outward show of deference from inferiors, and towards haughty, withdrawn coldness from superiors determined to exact such deference. Tracing this development is not easy — hardly surprisingly, for few contemporaries were likely to comment directly on changing nuances of manners over time, and modern works concerned with the history of manners are usually based largely on published treatises on conduct (often translations of European originals) which tell more about ideals than practical realities. And indeed such treatises generally recommended something like Patrick Gordon's ideal of behaviour towards inferiors rather than "keeping state". A man may "winneth with a look to subdue all the world" and when a noble shows "a gentle and familiar visage" the hearts of lesser men "leapeth for gladness" and they are happy to obey freely.[11]

However, by the later sixteenth century actual English élite manners seem to have come under unusually strong influence from stoic concepts stressing the importance of entirely suppressing strong emotions in outward demeanour,[12] leading to coldness and formality. In addition, insecurity among nobles about their position in society made them touchy and liable to insist on deference, seeing any lack of such formal show of inferiority as threatening to their status. Having lost their role as military leaders, threatened by wealthy gentry, the "most visible feature" of their counter-attack "was an over-weaning arrogance symptomatic of their insecurity" and a withdrawal into inaccessibility.[13]

"Keeping state" was no monopoly of the nobility, however: it was partly copied by them from the crown, and its influence spread quickly down the social ladder. If nobles demanded more explicit deference from lesser men, then they in turn would tend to feel the need to exact it from their inferiors. In 1578 Barnaby Rich lamented that:

> For the most in number of our young country Gentlemen think that the greatest grace of courting [courtesy, manners] consisteth in proud and haughty countenances to such as know them not.

Significantly, Rich linked this to the loss of military power of the nobility, a loss which had led men to seek new ways of bolstering their status: his work was entitled *Alarme to England, for eschewing what perils are procured, where people live without regarde for martiall lawe.*[14]

In some respects the "distancing" effects of keeping state were one aspect of a centuries-long change in life-styles which was transforming élite behaviour in Europe: an emerging emphasis on personal privacy, as monarchs, lords and gentlemen withdrew from the semi-communal life of the great hall to eat, socialise and do business in the privacy of personal or family rooms.[15] In time the domestic servants came to be banished to their own world of servants quarters; and where villages or hamlets of common folk had grown up round castles or country houses, they were banished, pushed out of sight, sound and smell of their betters — or alternatively, the old castle with its distressingly lowly neighbours was abandoned as gentry retreated to splendid isolation on greenfield sites. Thus a "gradual distancing took place between great lords and the social inferiors they dominated".[16] Even when venturing out of their residences, the lords moved towards travelling in increasing privacy, with "the withdrawal on journeys from the equestrian cavalcade to the privacy of the coach or sedan-chair".[17]

In such developments England played a prominent role, and from the late fifteenth century distancing in the interests both of privacy and of enhancing status was given a lead by the example of the crown itself. Monarchs "elevated themselves unapproachably above even the greatest of their lords". Under Henry VII the king withdrew into the privacy of his privy chamber, to which access was strictly regulated.[18] Francis Bacon (writing in 1621) was to identify the key to Henry's style of kingship as being "keeping of distance, which indeed he did towards all".[19] This style, once established, endured as the English court norm until the mid-seventeenth century, though it was modified by the personal character of monarchs.

The greatest shock the style experienced was the arrival of a Scottish king in 1603, inheritor of a very different monarchical tradition. By English standards James VI had remarkably little privacy at his Scottish court, with access to his person being very open — and though restrictions were placed on access to his bedchamber in 1601, it still remained generous. The "English court was designed for the preservation of distance; the Scots for the management of relatively free and open access. Or to put it differently: the English etiquette was English, while the Scottish was French".[20] An English observer in 1601 noted that "anyone may enter the king's Presence while he is at dinner, and as he eats he converses with those about him" in a typically French way.[21]

The clash of these two styles in the years after 1603 was inevitably painful: "no king, I am sure, in Christendom, did observe such state and carried such a distance from the subjects as the kings and queens of England did", whereas "there was no such state observed in Scotland".[22] In terms of institutional structure James was happy to accept the English court model, though with the bedchamber door being the key filter in restricting access to him, rather than the privy chamber, to which access was much more open than in the past. And James's vanity and ideals of kingship made him happy to accept the court ceremonial and excessive (in Scots eyes) deference usual in England: he seemed to the Venetian ambassador to be being corrupted out of his "French familiarity"[23] — a comment echoed by the alleged mutterings of a Scot as the king had travelled south to take up his new inheritance: that the obsequious grovellings with which the English welcomed him would spoil a good king.[24] Much of the personal abuse heaped on James in England reflected, it has been plausibly argued, the depth of anti-Scottish feeling,[25] and one aspect of this was undoubtedly revulsion at aspects of James's manners which were specifically Scottish — especially the familiarity with which he treated his Scots friends. Such informality of kingship was not for the English.

Once one leaves the rarefied circles of the court and delves more generally in society for the influence of the unusual English emphasis on formality, privacy and "distance" emanating from the court, evidence not surprisingly becomes much harder to find. The best witness is the anthropologically-inclined English traveller of the 1590s, Fynes Moryson.[26] The "French use great liberty of conversation and small reverence to superiors" and — like Patrick Gordon — despised English gentlemen for giving so much deference to great lords. In English inns, gentry insisted on eating in rooms shared only with other gentry — or at the very least demanded a separate table for gentry use, whereas in France and Germany it was customary for commoners to sit at the same table — though lower down it. Germans might treat their wives like servants, but they behaved to their servants like companions. Servants served food at table with their hats on, and similarly "continually talk with their masters without any reverence of the cap or like duty". In Scotland in a knight's house Moryson found that the servants served food at their master's table without removing their blue bonnets, "and when the table was served, the servants did sit down with us" — though while the servants ate from "great platters of porridge, each having a little piece of sodden meat", the gentry had "a pullet with some prunes in the broth". Germans did not exact humility or respect from their children, who treated their parents familiarly and talked to them with their hats on. When German children went to bed at night their fathers shook hands with them, a sign of familiarity, whereas English fathers made their children kneel before them to ask a blessing.[27]

These anecdotes from Moryson's vast and rambling work are straws in a wind of cultural change that he, with his interest in comparative codes of manners, was one of the few to comment upon. Another was the abusive anti-Scots English writer, Sir Anthony Weldon, who denounced the Scottish lack of "complimental courtesy", and the fact that that "their followers are their masters, their wives their slaves". Weldon's comments were written in the same year (1617) that Fynes Moryson's work was first published, and his remarks about the relative attitudes of Scotsmen to their servants and wives are so close to what Moryson says about the Germans that there must be a strong suspicion that Weldon was copying Moryson's anecdote. But that he thought it appropriate to apply it to the Scots is significant: as the report of another traveller, in 1629, confirms, one of the things Englishmen felt peculiar enough to be worthy of comment was Scottish servants serving food and dining in presence of their master while wearing their hats.[28]

There is plenty of evidence in writings on the behaviour of individual English nobles at this time of the key importance of the concept of "distance" — the pride they took in preserving distance from men of different status.[29] However, though it is clear that there was a difference between English distance and Scottish familiarity, it is important to stress that such differences

II

were relative, and fluctuated from individual to individual, and circumstance to circumstance. The relative informality of Scots élite manners is clear, and can be linked to their close traditional links with the French court and French culture, and to her nobility enjoying a much greater confidence in their own role and status in society than their English counterparts. Yet a Scots noble could react with the same rage as an English one at what seemed behaviour designed to derogate from his status,[30] and by the late sixteenth century financial problems and changes of perceptions of their role in society, stemming from the teachings of the Reformed Church and the suppression of the honourable violence of the feud, were contributing to producing the first signs of a sense of insecurity in some Scots nobles which paralleled that of the English and elicited the same response — a demand for greater deference.[31] The union of 1603 brought them into much closer contact with English codes of deference just at a time when some at least were likely to find them appropriate to their emerging anxieties.

* * *

England's élites, from the crown downwards, had taken the lead in Europe in the "distancing" inherent in keeping state and demanding greater privacy. King Charles I carried these tendencies to new extremes which even disconcerted many of his English subjects, used as they were to formality. He created the most ceremonially obsessive and ritualistic court etiquette ever seen in Britain, and added to the barriers separating the monarch from the vast majority of members of the court. While maintaining and extending the exclusiveness of the bedchamber, he re-established the exclusiveness of the privy chamber, which had lapsed when James VI had established the former.[32] The court was to be "a shrine of virtue and decorum",[33] with a king at the centre accessible only to a small group of the most privileged. Inter-personal behaviour was to be rigidly formal and deferential.

If the king's extreme ideals of distancing raised English eyebrows, they caused far more shock when they came into contact with traditional Scottish informality. This was demonstrated dramatically when the king came to Edinburgh in 1633 for his coronation. The visit was in many respects a public relations disaster. The king behaved in accordance with his rigidly formal and subtly nuanced codes of manners, whereas some at least of the Scottish nobility blithely sought to relate to him in a friendly informal way that he found deeply offensive. The impression given is that the king returned south convinced that the Scots were boors who did not understand civilised norms of behaviour, and in particular the deference due to a ruler. The Scots were left with bitter confirmation that their native dynasty had "gone native" within a generation of its move to England, and that they were faced by a king who not only was insisting on policies deeply threatening to Scottish noble power, religious traditions and national identity, but who treated them with haughty contempt, expecting them to grovel in a manner which might be acceptable to Englishmen but certainly was not to free-born Scots.

It was an Englishman, Edward Hyde, the later earl of Clarendon, who recorded and analysed this clash of codes of conduct. When the Scottish parliament met, with the king present in person, some nobles dared to speak out against royal policies. Charles took action which he assumed would make clear the extent of his displeasure and break their spirit: he displayed "a little discountenance upon those persons". But unfortunately, continued Hyde, the Scots

> have naturally an admirable dexterity in sheltering themselves from any of those acts of discountenance which they have no mind to own ... when it hath been notoriously visible, as it was then notorious, that many of the persons then, as the earl of Rothes and others, of whom the King had the worst opinions, and from whom he most purposely withheld any grace by never speaking to them or taking notice of them in the Court, when the king was abroad ... when the greatest crowds of people flocked to see him, those men would still be next him, and entertain him with some discourse and pleasant relations, and which made those persons to be generally believed to be most acceptable to his majesty.

The thick-skinned and informal Scots either failed to notice the royal hints that their company was unwelcome, or — in Hyde's opinion — were damned if they were going to admit to noticing them and slink off with tails between their legs like (as Patrick Gordon would have put it) slavish Englishmen. Another Englishman (in spite of his Scottish title) in Scotland with the king, Lord Falkland, commented on his monarch's discomfiture:

> "that keeping of state was like committing adultery, there must go two to it;" for let the proudest or most formal man resolve to keep what distance he will towards others, a bold and confident man instantly demolishes that whole machine, and gets within him, and even obliges him to his own laws of conversation.[34]

As Falkland's seventeenth-century version of "it takes two to tango" stressed, the problem for Charles was that keeping of state rested on mutual observance of a relationship by two parties. As James Cleland had warned a generation before, the imaginary and fantastical greatness of a superior could not be maintained "without us", without the co-operation of inferiors. English subjects would play their part in the game: some Scots at least were determined to show the king that when he was in Scotland they expected him to behave in accordance with their own traditions.

In seeking from the start of his reign to push the show of deference and formality to extremes, Charles I doubtless saw himself as repairing the

II

damage done by his father's often informal style, and by the disorders and scandals at court which had accompanied James's declining years. To attempt to restore the dignity and grandeur of monarchy made sense from the crown's point of view. But the king's motivation (whether he realised it or not) was in some respects highly irrational and potentially damaging to the future of the monarchy, and arose from his personal limitations and weaknesses. His exalted vision of monarchy, his withdrawal into grandiose privacy, his belief in his God-given mission, and his determination to impose his will, were all linked, it seems clear, to fears of inadequacy, perhaps intensified by his smallness of stature, and symptomatised by his stutter and by the inflexibility that sometimes reflected stubborn refusal to face reality rather than confident strength. It has been remarked that "his image-building, unlike that of modern commercial operators, was not based on any consumer research. He neither knew nor cared what prejudices, what traditions, what passions he might antagonise",[35] for the image of remote, indeed almost invisible majesty, distanced even from most of his greatest subjects, resulted largely from his shy and introspective nature. The well-established tradition of keeping of state in England could be seen as combining conveniently with exalted theories of monarchy to justify the creation of protective ramparts around the king to insulate him from stressful contacts with his subjects.

> His deportment was very majestic; for he would not let fall his dignity, no not to the greatest foreigners that came to visit him and his court; for though he was far from pride, yet he was careful of majesty, and would be approached with respect and reverence

testified Sir Philip Warwick.[36]

An article by Judith Richards has illuminated the ways in which Charles's new codes of monarchical behaviour damaged rather than enhanced the prestige of monarchy in England, as they amounted to a remarkably irresponsible abandoning of traditional roles expected of a king.[37] His concern for image was genuine, but the image projected seemed to be intended for consumption largely within the confines of the court. There were deliberate restraints on projecting it more widely, and even within the confines of the court the number of subjects who had an opportunity to experience the image first-hand was limited by policies aimed at the exclusion of members of the public who wanted to petition the king, or even merely to see their sovereign. The latter were informed graciously but bluntly that while their zeal was appreciated, the king wished to dispense with public displays of it. Petitioners would face his majesty's displeasure unless they had matters of great urgency to present. This 1625 proclamation against unnecessary and disorderly resort to court ordered such inconvenient subjects to keep at least twelve miles away. When the king was travelling, the poor were not to flock to him for alms. Instead his almoner would give alms to local overseers of the poor for distribution.[38] Charles's "progresses" were very limited geographically, and anyway were not traditional occasions stage-managed to let subjects see their ruler and observe him at work and recreation. Instead they were often largely private hunting trips, and both on them and on other journeys deliberate attempts were made to discourage people from hastening to see him. On his way to Scotland in 1633 Charles travelled in closed coaches — except when switching to horseback to hunt.[39]

Thus there emerges the seeming paradox of a king at once intent on being treated with great formality and reverence, and on the other going to considerable lengths to prevent most of his subjects from having any opportunity of displaying their awe and loyalty. And if personal feelings of inadequacy and insecurity provide much of the explanation for such strange behaviour, there may also be added laziness. For all his concern to project an exalted concept of kingship, Charles refused to accept that successful authoritarian monarchy required immensely hard work. His tendency to issue orders and assume they would be obeyed automatically reflected naive concepts of what absolute monarchy meant — but it also provided a convenient excuse for not overseeing the nitty-gritty of implementing policies.[40] Theoretical arguments about order were used to justify barring as many subjects as possible from his presence, and this also saved him from a lot of work.

Thus "distancing" was carried so far that the king deliberately remained invisible to as many of his subjects as possible — at which point distancing instead of inspiring reverence was in danger of coming to inspire indifference, or even hostility. Here was a king who evidently did not want the affection of, or personal contact with, his subjects, a king who showed strong distaste for the age-old function of receiving petitions, who sought to depersonalise the royal function of largesse for the poor, who (like the nobility) sought to hide himself from subjects when travelling.

The passion for order and decorum — in part at least pretexts for indulging the royal priority given to privacy — applied within the court itself, with strict regulation of access to the king's presence of members of court as well as exclusion of outsiders, creating the most formal court in Europe. Of all monarchs only Charles kept state to such an extent that those serving his food had to kneel to do so.[41] When the king washed in his private chambers, a groom of the bedchamber had to observe which parts of the royal towel actually touched the royal body, and make sure to carry those parts above the level of his head when he took it away.[42] Thus a fastidious and retiring king, cocooned in self-exalting rituals, gave up or devoted only the minimum time necessary to many of the traditional functions of kingship, and "the result was a personal monarch who for nearly fifteen years [1625–40] withdrew from the vast majority of his subjects to a degree unprecedented

II

for generations".[43] That alienation from Charles's monarchy in Scotland was partly caused by absentee monarchy has long been recognised, but in some respects Charles managed even to create absentee monarchy in England by distancing himself from his subjects, a strange variant of internal exile in which the ruler exiled himself from subjects anxious to display their loyalty.

Significantly, once the Scots had revolted and open dissent became widespread in England, Charles consciously sought to revive in England the traditional and public roles of kingship he had deliberately suppressed, at last taking heed of the expectations of his subjects.[44] North of the border it was too late even to try. But it is worth noting that when in 1638 Charles sent the marquis of Hamilton to Scotland to negotiate with the covenanter rebels, one contemporary remarked that "Truly I have known him keep greater state when he was not the King's Commissioner".[45] Had a deliberate decision been taken that a change in style in dealing with the Scots was expedient, with less keeping of state for fear of antagonising them? Hamilton, like Huntly, was one of the minority of the Scots nobility who were more used to court life than to their native land, and who had fully adopted English state to win acceptance at court. But Hamilton evidently had the flexibility to change his ways when in Rome.

Was Charles I's downfall in Scotland that of the marquis of Huntly writ large? The parallels are most illuminating, demonstrating how loyalty could be eroded by differing codes of manners leading to mutual misunderstanding. Obviously as a cause of the outbreak of rebellion in Scotland, keeping of state was far subordinate to matters of policy and machinery of government. But it was a contributory element, and was inextricably linked with them — not least by Charles's personal traits of stubborn determination and total lack of realisation of how subjects reacted to his actions (or, if he had glimmers of realisation, rejection of this as irrelevant to true monarchy). Moreover, if it was principally the king whose keeping of state offended the Scots, his example, and indeed the general example of English formal state, was inevitably spreading to other Scots under the union of the crowns, as Scots courtiers and officials realised they had to adjust to English norms if their careers at court were to flourish. The English scornfully noted their role in thus "civilising" the barbarous Scots:

> Bonny Scot, we all witness can,
> That England hath made thee a gentleman.[46]

However, though Anglicised court nobles might win favour in the south, the price they had to pay was alienation from their Scottish power-bases. Not only Huntly but others of his ilk found difficulty in rallying their resources to aid the king: there is no direct evidence that their Anglicised manners contributed to this, but this may be suspected. Scottish bishops appointed by

Charles I were said to have increased discontent among parish ministers by "too much slighting of them" and by "carrying themselves so loftily".[47] And, of course, the fact that the formal ceremony of keeping state was the secular counterpart of the widely unpopular reforms in worship that Charles was seeking to impose on the Church of Scotland was so obvious that opposition to the latter was likely to go hand in hand with hostility to the former.

* * *

Matters of precise definition become difficult in discussing manners. Where does offence at generally autocratic attitudes, copied from the king by his servants, shade into offence more specifically at "keeping of state"? Sources are frequently too imprecise to tell us with certainty. The same problem arises with a number or references which occur after the Scottish troubles began to occasions on which contacts between king and subjects became acrimonious not merely about matters of substance, but about manner of address. Edward Hyde recorded that

> The Scots had from the beginning practised a new sturdy style of address, in which, under the licence of accusing the counsel and carriage of others, whom they never named, they bitterly and insolently reproached the most immediate actions and directions of his majesty himself; and then made the greatest professions of duty to his majesty's person that could be invented.[48]

A specific instance concerned the earl of Rothes – the same man Hyde had singled out in 1633 as refusing to play his part in enabling the king to keep state. In 1639 the earl was one of the Scots commissioners who negotiated personally with the king. The meeting got off to a disastrous start when the Scots, in Charles's eyes, insulted him by neglecting to kneel before him. His response was to ignore them, hoping (as in 1633) that such discountenancing would bring the Scots (literally, in this case) to their knees.[49] Not surprisingly the debates which followed were heated. Later Rothes complained about the king's attitude to him:

> I am ... taxed for speaking with less respect to sovereignty than I ought. God bear witness to the true respect of my heart to authority, and of my particular regard to his majesty's sacred person; but his majesty was put on to affront me, calling me twice a liar and twice an equivocator. Those with whom I live know me to be free of both ... The honesty of my heart to speak to my prince that truth which was entrusted to me by so many of his faithful subjects, getting so hard construction made me to exceed, and would have tempted any honest man; but I will not be ashamed to beg his majesty's pardon for any rudeness of my carriage there, and humbly to beseech never to be so used again.[50]

II

In other words, being a loyal subject did not mean that a free-born Scot had to accept insult from the king: and though Rothes apologised, this was linked with a suggestion that the king mind his mouth in future!

More generally, a covenanting propaganda pamphlet of 1640 replied to complaints from the king of lack of ceremony in his treatment by Scottish commissioners by stating that Charles "knoweth well that the Scottish Nation glorieth more in kindness and realities than in expressions by word or gesture".[51] Part of the Scottish self-perception was of a plain-speaking folk, whose words were more honest and sentiments more sincere for not being wrapped up in courtly coding and the irrelevances of ceremony.

Charles I, by keeping such high state, made a significant contribution to losing his thrones, and appropriately resistance began in Scotland where his imperious manner was seen as much more offensive than in England. In keeping state Charles responded to the dictates of his own personality, but also reacted against his father's laxity of manners. Charles's own son swung the pendulum of formality back the other way — in spite of English courtiers' attempts to prevent this. While the young Prince Charles was in exile in Jersey during the English civil war, Lord Jermyn reported with horror that, in his make-shift court, there was at first "no distance kept, but all suffered to be as familiar with him as if they were his fellows". This was soon rectified and "the English were kept at a great distance". But there remained a problem: in exile Charles spent much time at the French court, or at least closely connected to it, and adopted French standards of taste and conduct. His entourage included many Frenchmen, and while the English distanced themselves from the royal boy they served "the French were as familiar with him as could be imagined".[52] This experience, coupled with a very different personality and, doubtless, realisation of the part excessive keeping of state had played in his father's downfall, persuaded the future Charles II that majesty was compatible with a degree of informality with subjects.

This doubtless worried the duke of Newcastle, who had urged Charles to keep up ceremony, as familiarity bred contempt: "show yourself gloriously, to your people; like a god ... certainly there is nothing keeps up a king, more than ceremony, and order, which makes distance, and this brings respect and duty".[53] That Charles II failed to follow this advice might, from a Scottish point of view, sound like a happy ending, Scots informality triumphing over English state. In fact even after the Restoration of monarchy English élite manners were far from relaxing to correspond to anything like Scottish traditional informality and lack of ceremony. England remained, relatively speaking, a land of keeping state. Before the troubles, most of the Scots nobility had held out against English formality, determined to retain their own identity within Britain's élite. After the Restoration, horrified by the disastrous quarter century which had followed their defiance of the king, they hastened towards assimilation with their English counterparts: the trend towards the Scottish noble being characterised by English education, attitudes and accents accelerated rapidly, developments which would have reduced that sturdy old free-born Scottish gentleman, Patrick Gordon of Ruthven, to despair. High-born Scots now looked to their English rather than their French counterparts for role-models — and in any case, though the English court had relaxed from its peak of "distancing" formality, the French court, for so long regarded as the model for Scots informality, was reaching for a Charles I-like ritualism and keeping of state under the Sun King, Louis XIV.[54]

* * *

Trying to trace so intangible and ephemeral a topic as the history of the etiquette of inter-personal relations is at once frustrating and fascinating, and this paper has left a lot of questions unanswered. The contrast between English codes of formality and Scots informality clearly reached a peak in the time of Charles I. But how far back can traces of such differences be traced? When English descriptions of the Scots in almost ritual fashion commented on the latter's rude and barbarous ways, how far was an element of this the response to a perceived lack of refinement (formality) in Scottish manners? Or, looking forward rather than backwards, how far did Scottish informality survive, increasingly abandoned by the great but preserved lower down in society? The Scots like to pride themselves today on a greater warmth and informality in treating acquaintances and strangers than the colder English. If this is not entirely national myth, perhaps we have here the last bastion of Scots resistance to keeping state. A related myth — or reality — lauds a "democratic" element in Scots society not evident south of the border, referring to greater informality in social relations of men of different classes. Another survival of the distant days of Scottish independence and of a relatively stable and confident hierarchical society in which formality was not seen as necessary to preserve structure?

The sad meanderings of an obscure old laird can lead the historian a long way.

Notes

1. Patrick Gordon of Ruthven, *Ane Short Abridgement of Britane's Distemper, from the yeare of God MDCXXXIX to MDCXLIX*, ed. J. Dunn (Spalding Club, 1844), 77. The spelling of all quotations has been modernised. I have previously touched on the main theme of this essay in *The Scottish Revolution, 1637–44* (Newton Abbot, 1973), 22. It is not clear whether or not these lines of verse were composed by Gordon himself.
2. *Ibid.*, 3–5.

II

3. *Ibid.*, 4.
4. *Ibid.*, 76.
5. *Ibid.*, 76–7.
6. *Ibid.*, 77.
7. *Ibid.*, 229, 230.
8. J. Cleland, *The Instructions of a Young Noble Man*, ed. M. Molyneux (New York, 1948), 171. Cleland's work is often assumed to be an English manual of behaviour, as it was published in Oxford. But Cleland was a Scot and repeated references make it clear that he is thinking primarily of the Scottish nobility – most obviously when he devotes a whole chapter to supporting James VI's denunciation of the bloodfeud. When the book was reissued in 1607 the point was made by re-titling it *The Scottish Academie*, with the original title relegated to subtitle.
9. Gordon, *Britane's Distemper*. pp. 231-2.
10. G.P.V. Akrigg (ed.), *Letters of King James VI and I* (Berkeley, 1984), 95, 278.
11. R. Kelso, "The Doctrine of the English Gentleman in the Sixteenth Century", *University of Illinois Studies in Language and Literature*, xvi (Urbana, 1929), nos. 1, 2, pp. 79–80.
12. W.L. Ustick, "Changing Ideals of Aristocratic Character and Conduct in Seventeenth Century England", *Modern Philology*, 30 (1932-3), 147–52.
13. L. Stone, *The Crisis of the Aristocracy, 1558–1641* (Oxford, 1965), 750.
14. Kelso, "Doctrine", 81.
15. See Stone, *Crisis*, 583–4.
16. T.K. Rabb, *The Struggle for Stability in Early Modern Europe* (Oxford, 1975), 93.
17. Stone, *Crisis*, 584.
18. D. Starkey, "Court History in Perspective", in D. Starkey (ed.), *The English Court: from the Wars of the Roses to the Civil War* (London, 1987), 3–4.
19. Quoted in *ibid.*, 7.
20. N. Cuddy, "The Revival of the Entourage", in Starkey (ed.), *The English Court*, 178–80.
21. Sir Henry Wotton, *The Life and Letters of Sir Henry Wotton*, ed. L.P. Smith (Oxford, 1966), i, 314–15, quoted (translated from the Italian original) in Cuddy, "Revival of the Entourage", 180.
22. G. Goodman, *The Court of King James I*, ed. J.S. Brewer (London, 1839), i, 30, quoted in Cuddy, "Revival of the Entourage", 178.
23. *Ibid.*, 182.
24. Cited in J. Wormald, "James VI and I: Two Kings or One?" *History*, 68 (1983), 190.
25. *Ibid.*, 190–2.
26. Moryson himself never uses the term "keeping state", but it is interesting that it is at precisely this time that it makes its first recorded appearance in English, in 1599 in a play by Ben Jonson, *Oxford English Dictionary*.
27. Fynes Moryson, *An Itinerary containing his Ten Yeeres Travell* (Glasgow 1907-8), iv, 141, 183, 324–5; Fynes Moryson, *Shakespeare's Europe: A Survey of the Condition of Europe at the end of the 16th century. Being unpublished chapters of Fynes Moryson's Itinerary* (1617), ed. C. Hughes (2nd. edn., New York, 1967), 290; J.P. Cooper, "General Introduction", *New Cambridge Modern History*, iv (Cambridge, 1970), 27.
28. P.H. Brown (ed.), *Early Travellers in Scotland* (Edinburgh, 1891), 102; C. Lowther, *Our Journall into Scotland* (Edinburgh, 1894), 18.
29. Eg, B. Manning, "The Aristocracy and the Downfall of Charles I", in his *Politics, Religion and the English Civil War* (London, 1973), 40–1, cited in K.M. Brown, "Aristocratic Finances and the Origins of the Scottish Revolution", *English Historical Review*, 104 (1989), 48n.

30. See, eg, Brown, "Aristocratic Finances", 46, and Stone, *Crisis*, 750.
31. Brown, "Aristocratic Finances", 46–8, 52–3.
32. K. Sharpe, "The Image of Virtue: the Court and Household of Charles I, 1625–42", in Starkey (ed.), *The English Court*, 228, 233–4, 239.
33. *Ibid.*, 236.
34. E. Hyde, earl of Clarendon, *The History of the Rebellion and Civil Wars in England*, ed. W.D. Macray (Oxford, 1888), i, 108–9.
35. R. Ollard, *The Image of the King. Charles I and Charles II* (London, 1979), 39.
36. *Ibid.*, 28.
37. J. Richards, " 'His Nowe Majestie' and the English Monarchy: the Kingship of Charles I before 1640", *Past and Present*, 113 (1986), 70–96.
38. *Ibid.*, 77–8; C. Carlton, *Charles I. The Personal Monarch* (London, 1984), 62.
39. Richards, " 'His Nowe Majestie' ", 83–6.
40. Carlton, *Charles I*, 62, 64, 107–8, 109, 113, 124.
41. Richards, " 'His Nowe Majestie' ", 78–9; Carlton, *Charles I*, 129–30.
42. Sharpe, "The Image of Virtue", 243.
43. Richards, " 'His Nowe Majestie' ", 93.
44. *Ibid.*, 93–4.
45. Sir James Turner, *Memoirs of his own Life and Times* (Bannatyne Club, 1829), 234. For differing reactions of Scots courtier-nobles after 1603 to Anglicising influences, see K.M. Brown, "Courtiers and Cavaliers: Service, Anglicisation and Loyalty among the Royalist Nobility", in J. Morrill (ed.), *The Scottish National Covenant in its British Context* (Edinburgh, 1990), 155–92.
46. Quoted in B. Galloway, *The Union of England and Scotland. 1603–1608* (Edinburgh, 1986), 140.
47. H. Guthry, *Memoirs* (2nd edn., Glasgow, 1748), 17.
48. Hyde, *Rebellion*, i, 160.
49. Carlton, *Charles I*, 205–6.
50. S.R. Gardiner, *The Hamilton Papers* (Camden Society, 1880), 99–100. See Carlton, *Charles I*, 185.
51. *True Representation of the Proceedings of the Kingdom of Scotland* (1640), pt. 2, p.74.
52. Quoted in Ollard, *Image*, 63–4.
53. T.P. Slaughter (ed.), *Ideology and Politics on the Eve of the Restoration: Newcastle's Advice to Charles II* (Philadelphia, 1984), 45.
54. It is worth noting that as early as 1607 James Cleland had recommended as the model for salutations the "old manner" of the French, "for we have too many new French toys", indicating that he felt that deplorable developments were already taking place in French manners, Cleland, *Instructions*, 177.

III

The Early Covenanters and the Federal Union of Britain

Much has been written about the question of the union of Scotland and England in the period 1603–1707. But the problem has been largely ignored for one crucial period, that of 1637–51 when the covenanters ruled Scotland.[1] This is partly the result of attention being concentrated on the attempts of the covenanters to achieve religious unity. It is understandable that this should be the case, for it was religious issues which aroused most controversy, but exclusive concentration on them has tended to hide the fact that for the covenanters religious unity was intended only to be one of the strands of a wider union.

The purpose of this paper is to demonstrate that the question of union was of central importance to the covenanters, and that they undertook a sustained attempt to redefine the terms of the union of Scotland with England in order to protect Scotland's interests. Problems, however, arise from the word 'union' itself. Firstly, it could be used in the seventeenth century to mean no more than alliance, co-operation, or friendship. Can we be sure that the covenanters did not use the word merely in this sense? Secondly, historians looking at the union problem in Britain under the Union of the Crowns know that ultimately a solution is to be found in a parliamentary, incorporating, union; they therefore tend to ignore proposals that would have led to other forms of union, either dismissing them as insignificant or refusing to allow that 'union' is an appropriate word to use in discussing them.

On the first point, the convenanters certainly used the word 'union' at times to denote alliance and friendship; but it is clear that they also frequently meant more than this, as is seen by the contexts in which they used the word and by the concrete proposals they made under the heading of 'union'. Doubtless in their minds the distinction between alliance and political union was not clear cut, one definition merging imperceptibly into the other and the same word being used of both: frequently they used it to cover close alliance and political union simultaneously. Turning to modern definitions of union, with reference to states, 'formation or incorporation into a single state, kingdom or political entity, usually with one central legislature'[2] does not include what the covenanters sought. But the definition of federal union as 'that form of government in which two or more states constitute a political unity while remaining more or less independent in their internal affairs' seems to describe accurately what the covenanters were seeking.

The essentials of the union sought by the covenanters were:

a) The continuation of the Union of the Crowns.
b) Autonomy for each kingdom in most internal affairs, and the retention of separate parliaments in England and Scotland.
c) Close consultation and co-operation between the two kingdoms in matters of joint concern, institutionalised through meetings of commissioners of both parliaments, or (after 1647) through strong representation of each nation on the privy council of the other and at court. The covenanters saw this at first as primarily a way of checking royal power, but later as a way to limit the power of the over-mighty English parliament.
d) Joint control of action in foreign affairs and trade, making the kingdom of Britain a single political unit so far as foreign nations were concerned.
e) The establishment of free trade between Scotland and England.
f) Uniformity in religion, with each kingdom retaining its separate church, though these were to be uniform in government.

These attempts to add other elements of union to the personal Union of the Crowns are clearly in one sense moves towards closer union between the kingdoms. But of course in one important respect the covenanters, up to 1647 at least, were seeking to weaken the union which already existed. The 1603 union had united executive power within Britain in the hands of a single monarch, whereas the reforms proposed by the covenanters were designed to check and limit this power, partly by strengthening the internal political institutions of the two kingdoms and partly by creating new links between these institutions. Thus the covenanters wished to weaken some aspects of union, and strengthen others.

Why did the covenanters seek such radical changes in the type of union that bound the kingdoms together? The problem of union in Britain was that of geographical neighbours with many similarities and common interests, already linked by the Union of the Crowns. Few could contemplate complete separation. Yet the two kingdoms differed too much in history and traditions, in customs and manners, in society, constitution, law and religion for complete amalgamation.[3] What type of union, in these circumstances, would best serve the interests of both kingdoms? The Union of the Crowns was of course merely personal, the result of dynastic accident — though some hailed it as a happy dispensation, indicating the divine will for the future of Britain as well as being of practical value to both kingdoms.[4] Early efforts by James VI and I to bring about closer union had failed. But as James and Charles I became increasingly Anglicised, they began to unite the kingdoms more closely not by any formal act of union but by Anglicising Scotland. Seeing differences between kingdoms with a common ruler as anachronistic, they worked to lessen them. Inevitably they chose England as the model. Not only was England by far the larger, the richer, the more populous and the more powerful of the two, it had much else to lead a monarch to prefer it: the rule of law was more firmly established, the king more readily obeyed.

Scotland undoubtedly gained by the Union of the Crowns, above all in security, by being united with a major power. Scots were flattered to see their fellow countryman on the English throne, and hoped for an era of peace and prosperity. But as James and Charles became English in manner, outlook and policy, satisfaction with the union tended to give way to suspicion of the policies and methods of government it had introduced. Scotland's identity was threatened with absorption by her great neighbour. Instead of helping to protect Scotland the union seemed to be slowly destroying her. Union had deprived many of the nobility of the centre of their social and political life, and of opportunities of influencing the king and his policies, by depriving Scotland of her royal court. Union was enabling absentee kings to introduce foreign influences and institutions, undermining especially her religion. It was such Anglicising policies in religion and contempt for the feelings of the nobility that were mainly responsible for driving Scotland to rebellion in 1637.[5]

One might have expected the covenanters simply to denounce the union, since by strengthening the hand of the monarchy and Anglicising the king it had led to the introduction of unpopular policies in Scotland. But the covenanters were well aware of Scotland's weakness; they could not hope to defy Charles I successfully if he had England united behind him. The covenanters therefore appealed to the people of England, trying to win their support by arguing that Scotland's cause was the same as that of the king's English opponents. To demand the breaking of the union would have been widely regarded in England as a threat to her interests, and thus aroused hostility to the Scots. In any case, the covenanters never seem to have considered any alternative to continued union in some form. No doubt this was partly because, from their point of view, a breach of the union was simply impossible. They were committed to monarchy in principle, and could not conceive of any alternative to Charles I continuing to rule in Scotland (whatever limitations might be placed on his power). The continuation of the Union of the Crowns was therefore taken for granted. The Union of the Crowns had failed to protect Scotland's interests, but the cure for this was not no union but a different union.

The implications of the covenanters' revolt for the future of the union emerged only gradually. The demands they made for reforms grew steadily as it emerged that the king's word was not to be trusted. As was to happen later in England, demands for change in royal policy broadened into demands for some control over policy making and implementation, and over the king's advisers, through constitutional changes in both church and state. But for the covenanters such changes in Scotland alone could not be sufficient. Similar changes would have to be made to control royal power in England before they could feel safe. Thus the king's obstinacy and untrustworthiness, and his willingness to use English resources against his native kingdom, drove the covenanters to rethink the union to guarantee their position. If presbyterianism was to be safe in Scotland, bishops would have to be abolished in England. Constitutional changes in Scotland would have to be safeguarded by similar ones in England, and by new links between the countries at other levels than that of the monarchy.[6]

In 1639, as war between king and covenanters approached, royalist propaganda tried to present the quarrel as a national one. This the covenanters vigorously denied. They insisted that they had no quarrel with the English; the two nations in one island were 'once at variance, but now happily reconciled and tied together by the most strict Bonds, which We desire rather to encrease than diminish'. Thus the covenanters declared their faith in union, and they went on to appeal for the first time beyond the king to the English parliament, expressing their confidence that if it was summoned and judged their cause it would find in their favour.[7]

When, after a brief truce, it became clear late in 1639 that a new military confrontation with the king was all but inevitable, the covenanters again turned to explaining their standpoint to the English. They had no wish to break ties with England; on the contrary, it was to them 'a ground of many hopes, that the two Nations so long, and so far divided before, are in our time straitly joyned, not only by naturall union in one Iland, but also spirituall in one Religion, civill under one Head, morall in the mutuall interchange of so many duties of love: And domesticall, by marriages and allyances'.[8] A remonstrance to the parliament of England, issued in April 1640, was more explicit about union. Of all the great blessings that God had bestowed on the island, next to Christian faith 'the Union of the two Kingdomes, under one Head, doth by many degrees exceed all other that fall in the reckoning'. But union and the strength it brought had not been used to the best advantage, and wicked men worked to divide king from people and one kingdom from the other. The cause of the Scots was not theirs alone; if they submitted to servitude this would be dangerous to England's liberties, as both countries were under one king. Therefore the covenanters expected support from England so 'that in our Union they [the enemies of both kingdoms] may be crushed who in our division have builded their hopes'. Enemies were trying to stir up a national quarrel; the covenanters were acting to prevent this and 'by a seasonable remeidy, provide for the safetie of our selves and posteritie. The readiest meane for the present that come in our consideration in [sic, for 'is'] this, that as when the treatie of the Union was intended [in 1604–7], but did not take effect, the two parliaments did sit, and did appoint their commissioners to treat thereanent (with expresse reservation of their own Lawes and Liberties) and to report their proceedings back againe to them that sent them'. The covenanters therefore suggested that the king appoint English parliamentary commissioners to meet Scots ones to judge the equity of their demands.[9] Thus a quarrel betwen the kingdoms was to be averted by contacts between the two parliaments. This is the first mention of one of the main ways in which the covenanters were to press for closer union in the coming years; links between parliaments through 'conservators of the peace' or 'militia commissioners'.

When in the summer of 1640 the covenanters resolved to march into England to force the king to agree to their demands, they worked hard to justify their 'expedition'. Again it was emphasised that the covenanters sought to strengthen the links between the nations.[10] But by now the covenanters were determined that any settlement should include changes in England as well as Scotland: 'We put little doubt bot we shall get for our selves fair enough conditions; bot it will be to our great regrate, if we gett not all the King's dominions to our happinesse'.[11]

The motives behind the demands for changes in England were mixed, but above all was the belief that they were necessary for Scotland's future security. Priority was given to religion, but here to genuine religious zeal and belief that the threat to Scotland's religion had originated in the English bishops was added the consideration that interfering in religion in England was easier to justify than interfering in civil affairs, as religion obviously transcended national boundaries. Moreover, demands for religious change south of the border were partly politically motivated, as the covenanters were to indicate in December 1640 when they began their charges against Archbishop Laud by stating that 'Novatiouns in religioun ... ar vniuersallie acknoulegit to be the mane causs of commotiouns in kingdoms and states'.[12]

When negotiations opened at Ripon in October 1640, after the covenanters had occupied the north of England, they made it clear that they would insist on changes in England and in the relations between the two countries. They negotiated with English peers, not with the king himself, and demanded the summoning of the English parliament 'which is conceived to be the only mean of settling both Nations in a firm Peace',[13] and they would only agree to a temporary cessation of arms, insisting that a peace treaty be transferred to London so it could be negotiated with parliament.

Scots commissioners arrived in London in November 1640. They at first concealed the demands that they intended to make concerning union in a vaguely worded final demand, that the king agree to all particulars necessary to establish a stable peace, without fear of 'molestation and undoing from year to year, as our Adversaries shall take advantage'.[14] Secret instructions listed demands to be made under this clause once other articles had been settled. Parliaments were to meet in each country at least every two or three years to try wrongs committed by either country against the other; they would appoint commissioners to consider such disputes and to try differences between the king and his subjects. Between meetings of the parliaments *Conservatores pacis* were to preserve the peace between the nations. Neither kingdom was, without the consent of its parliament, to raise an army against the other, and neither was to make war on the other without giving three months' notice. Scots were to serve about the king's person, some of them in chief places. The prince of Wales was not to marry without the consent of both kingdoms. A common confession of faith for both kingdoms was to be agreed upon.[15]

It had not yet, it seems, been decided to demand full unity of religion and uniformity of church government, though the ministers among the Scots commissioners in London preached outspokenly against bishops and other corruptions.[16] Within a few months, however, the covenanters widened their demands; the treaty negotiations were proceeding successfully and this led them to believe they could achieve more than they had originally hoped for. By February 1641 all their first seven demands had been settled and they were ready to proceed to the eighth, 'for ane happie and durable peace which is the cheefest of all our desyres And wnto which all the former sevine articles being now agreid wpon are as many preparations'.[17] But before their new demands were made public there occurred a crisis which damaged their chances of having them conceded.[18] The Scots had at first been hailed as giving England the chance to assert her liberties, but in time many got tired of the Scots. Rumours began to circulate in London that, having got what they wanted, they would desert their English allies, taking no further interest in prosecuting Laud and the earl of Strafford or in attacking episcopacy.[19] To counter this the Scots commissioners drew up bitter attacks on episcopacy and the two 'firebrands'.[20] Not only did this infuriate the king, it also roused the indignation of many members of parliament. They felt the Scots were openly interfering in purely English affairs, and the feeling was growing that it was disgraceful for reformation in England to be dependent on a Scottish army.[21] The Scots were taken by surprise by such reactions, but they responded by explaining that as to English affairs they desired 'to have no further hand but in so far as they may concern us and the peace betwixt the two Kingdoms'. But they also promised to present proposals 'for settling of a firm and happy peace and nearer union betwixt the two Kingdoms'.[22]

Thus even in disclaiming any intention of interfering in purely internal English matters, the covenanters laid claim to a say in matters which concerned Scotland, so their reassurances did little to decrease suspicion of them. Nonetheless, the commissioners proceeded in March to make their eighth demand, seeking redefinition of many aspects of the relationship between the two kingdoms. Their first proposal was for unity in religion and uniformity in church government. In the present context what is most interesting is that the demand was presented 'as a speciall meane to conserve peace in his Majesties Dominions'. Religion should be a bond of unity. The Scots wanted not a 'cessation of armes for a time, but peace for ever; and not peace onely, but a perfect amity and a more neere union than before'. They acted 'not from any sauciness, or presumptious intentions to reform England' but to prevent their own reformation being destroyed from England, and to please God.[23] Union in church matters was thus seen as an aid to union in general, as contributing to national security, as well as being justified on purely religious grounds.

The covenanters' religious proposals met with a cool response. The king told them not to meddle with reformation in England; they replied that this was necessary if there was to be a durable peace,[24] uniformity of church government being 'one principall meanes of a continued peace between the two Nations'.[25] As for the English parliament, it long put off any reply, and the Scots were forced in the end to be content with a very vague undertaking that conformity of church government was desirable and would be proceeded with 'in due tyme'.[26]

The covenanters' demands for union in civil matters were also now much more extensive than those of November 1640. Most of the proposals then made were repeated and amplified, and new ones were added. Scots of respect, entrusted by Scotland, were to hold places about the king, the queen and the prince of Wales. Neither country was to declare war on a foreign state without the consent of the other. Citizens of one country were to be regarded as naturalised in the other. Free trade was to be established between England and Scotland, and they were to co-operate in commercial matters.[27]

In moving towards such a civil union the covenanters were only slightly more successful than in religious matters. In the peace treaty Charles and the English parliament agreed that commissioners (conservators of the peace) should be appointed by the parliaments of the two countries to discuss matters of mutual interest and prevent disputes between them. Neither country would, without the consent of its parliament, raise forces against, or make war on, the other. Three months' notice would be given of any such breach between the nations. Each country would assist the other against common enemies. Provision was made (though only in vague terms) for the employment of Scotsmen about the king and his family, and for frequent visits to Scotland by the king and the prince.[28] But other proposals intended to bring the countries into a closer relationship met with a less favourable response. Suggestions that foreign war and alliances should require joint consent, that each country should assist the other in case of invasion, were left unsettled. So were Scots requests for free trade and commercial co-operation. Instead these matters were referred to further consideration by commissioners of both countries.[29]

Settlement of such matters was thus delayed partly because there had not been time to discuss them fully, but the main reason was clearly that the English parliament was not interested in the Scots proposals. Revising the union seemed vital to the covenanters, but parliament saw little point in it for England. So the first major attempt of the covenanters (1640-1) to reform the union was largely a failure. The English parliament was interested in friendly relations with Scotland, but not in a revision of the terms of the union. The covenanters followed up the peace treaty by promptly appointing conservators of the peace and commissioners to negotiate on the articles referred to further consideration.[30] The English parliament failed to appoint conservators and showed little interest in further negotiations.

Yet events continued to prove to the covenanters how essential to Scotland's security a new union was. As England drifted into civil war in 1642 it was impossible for the covenanters to regard it as being no concern of theirs. If the king was victorious their position in Scotland would be precarious, while victory for parliament would probably bring them security. The covenanters at first tried to avert, and then to end, the English civil war by offering to mediate. Parliament thanked them; the king told them to mind their own business.[31] But the Scots persisted, doubtless encouraged by a declaration from the English parliament read to the general assembly of the kirk in August 1642 which played skilfully on Scots desires for reform of the union. It talked of the kingdoms being already 'united by so many and so near bonds and tyes, as well Spirituall as Civill', and of hopes of a settlement in England out of which 'there will also most undoubtedly result a most firme and stable Union between the two Kingdomes of England and Scotland, which ... we shall by all good wayes and meanes, upon all occasions, labour to preserve and maintain'.[32]

Later in August, at the request of the commissioners of the kirk, the Scots privy council summoned the conservators of the peace to meet for the first time.[33] They assembled on 23 September and declared that they had power to try to mediate in

England.[34] The English parliament accepted the conservators' offer; the king would give no direct answer, though he was now ready to appeal to the covenanters for help. To gain such help both sides were now prepared to declare their intentions of furthering religious unity and uniformity of church government. The English parliament first appealed openly for military aid in November 1642, stressing that the Scots had 'invited us to a nearer and higher Degree of Union' in religion and church government and holding out hopes that this would be achieved.[35] A positive response from Scotland was delayed by the fact that the conservators were still trying to mediate. Only after it became clear in April 1643 that the king would not recognise their right to intervene in English affairs did the covenanters turn to negotiations with the English parliament.[36]

The convention of estates met in Edinburgh in June, primarily to negotiate an alliance with the English parliament (though this was not admitted). But a treaty with the English was delayed by the reluctance of the house of lords to send commissioners to Scotland, and by political divisions over the conduct of the war. The Lords did agree to appoint commissioners to conserve the peace and commissioners to complete the 1641 treaty,[37] as a gesture of goodwill to the Scots. Similarly the request which both houses sent to the convention in June inviting it to send commissioners to attend the assembly of divines (the Westminster Assembly, which was to advise parliament on reformation of religion) helped to prepare the way for military alliance.[38]

At last in July the Lords agreed to send commissioners to Scotland to negotiate a military alliance. The commissioners were also given power to consider articles for the security and defence of the religion and liberties of both kingdoms, 'whereby the Assistance and Union betwixt the Two nations may be made more beneficiall and effectual'.[39] But while parliament gave its commissioners detailed instructions about military matters, nothing specific was said about the other articles, and the ambiguities of the word 'union' meant that the English could claim only to mean 'alliance'. What parliament would have liked was simply a military treaty. Provision for reworking the union was made only because it was likely that the Scots would insist on it.

That such concessions were necessary the English commissioners found immediately on their arrival in Scotland. Robert Baillie's comment 'The English were for a civill League, we for a religious Covenant'[40] has often been quoted, and the Scots did indeed insist on agreement on the Solemn League and Covenant before they would negotiate a military treaty. Yet Baillie's comment is misleading if it is taken to mean that the new agreement was solely concerned with religion. In fact, as its title clearly indicates, it was a civil league as well as a religious covenant.

The Solemn League and Covenant states its aims as the glory of God, the honour and happiness of the king, and the liberty, peace and safety of the two kingdoms. Of its six articles only two (admittedly the first two) are solely concerned with religion; they include a declaration in favour of 'the nearest conjunction and uniformity' of religion, church government and worship. The other four articles are mainly concerned with constitutional matters and relations between the kingdoms. Article five binds signatories to preserve the peace lately concluded between the kingdoms so that they 'may remaine conjoyned in a firme peace and unione to all posterity'. By article six they were never to agree 'to be divided and withdrawn from this blessed Union and conjunction'.[41]

Thus the Solemn League and Covenant mentions union, but in general terms and without much emphasis. If, as has been argued, negotiations on union were so important to the covenanters, why does this not figure more prominently here? The answer probably lies in the nature of the new league and covenant as a compromise. It is well known that ambiguity was allowed to creep into the clause dealing with religious reform in England, such changes being designed to commit the English parliament less closely to reformation on Scottish lines than the covenanters intended. It seems likely that in a similar way the English commissioners sought to avoid any specific commitments about union. In the draft Solemn League and Covenant clause five had been a promise to 'inviolablie observe the articles of the late treattie of peace . . . to the end that this blissed peace may be perpetuall to all posteritie'.[42] This specific reference to the 1641 treaty, with its provision for conservators and negotiations on other aspects of union, was watered down in the final version approved by the English parliament to the vague reference, cited above, to preserving the peace lately concluded.

The covenanters were willing to accept such changes since they were confident that their army would quickly win the English civil war for parliament, and that this would enable them to dominate any peace settlement. Believing that this was necessary for Scotland's security, they made no allowance for English resentment at such interference. Robert Baillie hoped that Scots commissioners in London 'would get the guiding of all the affairs both of this State and Church'[43] — which was exactly what many English feared. As in 1640-1, the Scots soon found that the English had little interest in new forms of union. The commissioners of the kirk attending the Westminster Assembly found that there was little hope of immediate action on uniformity of church government, though at first both English and Scots were willing to avoid confrontation on the issue as both realised that winning the war against the king must have the first priority.[44] The Scots civil commissioners had been instructed to work jointly with the English parliament for peace 'And for the better effecting heirof ye shall by all meanes strengthen the happie begune vnione',[45] but they found little enthusiasm for this. There was much controversy over the running of the war and the part the Scots should have in it. Eventually a committee of both kingdoms was set up with power to order and direct the war. But even though the Scots commissioners were greatly outnumbered by English, many in the English parliament had opposed giving even this nominal role to the Scots, as they wished to 'avoid the Scots' power over us'.[46] However, the covenanters remained confident that once their army brought victory they would have everything their own way. This was why the failure of their army to win any dramatic victory was so bitter to them.[47] Too much had been expected of the Scots army; though it played a major part in winning the war for parliament, its achievements were regarded as disappointing, and the successes of Montrose's royalist rising in Scotland soon forced the covenanters to weaken their army in England, further diminishing their reputation there.[48]

Even in 1644, the first year of their intervention in England, the covenanters began to be disillusioned with their allies. Whereas to parliament the first priority in negotiations lay in obtaining constitutional concessions from the king, the Scots seemed to be more interested in religious ones. The reasons for this emphasis by the Scots were the same as in 1640–1 — religious arguments; the needs of security based on religious unity; the fact that parliament needed no encouragement in seeking concessions in constitutional affairs. In addition a new motive slowly emerged. The achievement of constitutional liberties by parliament did not seem to be guaranteeing a regime in England which sympathised with the demands of the Scots for redefinition of the union. They had assumed too easily that once the power of parliament was firmly established in England the evils of the Union of the Crowns would be quickly rectified, the king's power to abuse the union being removed. Might it now turn out, as disputes with the English parliament grew, that too little power in the hands of the king in England would be just as dangerous to Scots' interests as too much had been? Would not some compromise peace with the king, which did not give parliament unlimited power in civil matters, be safer for Scotland?

The growing differences between the allies became clear in debates over peace proposals. The more the Scots pressed their views, the more they found themselves disliked. And of course the more they were disliked, the more they felt that Scotland's security required that they insist on their demands. But as yet there was no hint of a quarrel between the two nations; the war still had to be won. Parliament was therefore ready to humour its Scots allies, and agreed on opening negotiations with the king. Peace proposals sent to Charles in November 1644 reflected the wishes of the Scots. There was strong emphasis on the need for 'union'. As well as asking for unity and uniformity in religion and church government, the proposals laid down that the raising and commanding of armed forces in England and Scotland were to be controlled by commissioners appointed by the respective parliaments. Up to one third of the Scots commissioners were to sit and vote with the English ones in matters concerning Scotland, and vice versa. All the commissioners of the two kingdoms would meet together to settle matters concerning the preserving of the peace between them and the king, breaches of the peace between the two kingdoms, resisting of invasion or rebellion in either kingdom, and directing the war in Ireland. The making of war or peace with foreign states was to require the joint consent of both parliaments. Tutors and governors for the king's children were to be chosen by both parliaments, who would supervise their education and marriage. Agreement was also to be reached on the matters which had not been settled by the 1641 treaty.[49]

Thus the conservators of the 1641 treaty were to be transformed into joint militia commissioners of both kingdoms, and given control of all armed forces. The Scots proposals of 1641 for a united British foreign policy were accepted, while free trade and commercial co-operation were to be considered again. Negotiations on these propositions were held at Uxbridge early in 1645, but broke down as the concessions offered by the king satisfied neither the Scots nor parliament. In the months that followed, tensions between the allies continued to increase. By mid-1645 it was obvious that Scots influence and power was declining. The English New Model Army had been created and was dominated by Independents with no love of the Scots and their religion; at Naseby in June it won a decisive victory. Meanwhile, in Scotland, Montrose's victories continued; the covenanters began to fear that credit for winning the war in England would go entirely to the Independents.[50] For fear of this they again began to press for a negotiated peace with the king.[51]

Relations between the nominal allies were by this time so strained that some parliamentarians were said to have rejoiced at Montrose's victory over the covenanters at Kilsyth,[52] hoping this would 'rid England of "our brethren" [the Scots army], who otherwise might not so easily be got out of England'.[53] When the covenanters requested English help against Montrose,[54] many Englishmen hoped that the Scots would instead withdraw their whole army from England to deal with him.[55]

By now rumours were circulating that the Scots intended to make a separate peace with the king, without consulting the English parliament.[56] By March 1646 such negotiations had gone far enough for the Scots to promise to receive the king in honour and respect if he came to their army, provided he accepted the propositions of Uxbridge.[57] Alliance with parliament had failed to bring about the close links, amounting to loose federal union, which would provide Scotland with security within Britain. Parliament no longer seemed to have any interest in military co-operation and other aspects of joint action by the kingdoms as had been provided for in the propositions of Uxbridge.[58] The Scots had therefore concluded that it might be better to turn to the king to gain terms which would give Scotland security. Now he had been defeated in war, might he not prove more flexible than the victorious parliament?

For the moment, however, the Scots continued also to negotiate with parliament. On 3 February 1646 the Scots commissioners in London were urged to continue with the work of settling religion and peace, and preserving the 'union' with England. The Uxbridge propositions were to be the foundation of a well-grounded peace and 'a firme vnioune betuixt the kingdomes'. The proposition on the militia was to be urged as 'the best and surest way for conservation of a dureable peace and vnitie betuix the king and his kingdomes and of each kingdome with other'. If this was not acceptable to the English parliament, it was to be proposed that the militia should be settled by the king with the advice of the parliaments of the two kingdoms separately. In other words, if there was not to be direct co-operation between the two parliaments in controlling armed forces, then the covenanters wanted the king to be involved in their control, rather than to leave it in the hands of the two parliaments separately.

Moreover, if the English parliament insisted on altering the Uxbridge militia article, the Scots commissioners were then to ask that one third of 'places of trust and offices' about the king and his family should be held by Scotsmen; that one third of the English and Irish privy councils should be composed of Scotsmen; and reciprocally one third of the Scots privy council be English. Scots should be declared capable of holding all offices in England. Free trade between the two

174

kingdoms should be established, and foreign treaties negotiated jointly. Illogically, the Scots parliament then added that these extra demands were to be made even if the militia article was not altered.[59] Some of these demands are merely revivals of old ones, but those guaranteeing Scots representation in offices and on the privy councils are clearly (like the proposal that the king be involved in control of the militia) indicative of the covenanters' conclusion that, if Scots interests were to be protected, a renegotiated union between the kingdoms might have to be based more on the king and his councils than on links between parliaments.

A few weeks later the English parliament at last produced its new peace proposals. These justified the worst fears of the Scots, and thus their turning towards the king. The proposals claimed to uphold the 1641 treaty and the Solemn League and Covenant, but no specific proposals were made for reform of the union. The Scots commissioners complained on 16 March: 'we cannot bot observe, that the most materiall Additions, Omissions, and Alterations . . . betwixt these and the [Uxbridge] Propositions formerly agreed upon doe trench upon the joynt Interests of both Kingdomes, and tending to the lewsing of the Bands, and weakening of the Sinewes, of our happy Union'. Control of the militia was to be in the hands of the two parliaments separately. Nothing was said of conservators, or of joint consultation over making war or peace with foreign states, or of joint control of the education and marriage of the king's children.[60]

Pleas by the Scots for the peace terms to be changed had little effect. They argued that 'our greatest security and saifty is in the conjunction of our counsels and forces'; 'that which may Unite ws most, is to be preferred'. Provision must be made for mutual security. The English replied that they would never make war on Scotland; the Scots aptly retorted that the king had raised an English army against them in 1640. The English claimed that the less intermixture of counsel there was, the less occasion there would be for discord between the kingdoms: 'the keeping the Governments distinct, is better than intermixture'. If there was 'a full Union' (presumably an incorporating one in which Scotland would, in effect, surrender her parliament), then co-operation over militia would be best. But while the kingdoms 'are not totally one', it was best to keep their counsels separate. Unavailingly the Scots denied the logic of this. If full union was desirable (as all admitted), then surely partial union was the next best thing, and certainly better than nothing.[61]

Disagreements came to a head after papers concerning the peace proposals were published with a preface by a Scot, David Buchanan, demonstrating how the new proposals differed from the propositions of Uxbridge.[62] The English parliament reacted strongly, ordering that the preface be burnt by the common hangman.[63] The Commons then issued an outspoken declaration showing they had no intention of compromising with the Scots. No mention was made of union, and it was made clear that no right by the Scots to interfere in English affairs would be admitted. As to the Solemn League and Covenant, 'no Interpretation of it (so far as it concerns the Kingdom of England) shall by any be endeavoured to be imposed on us, other than we ourselves do know to be suitable to the first just Ends for which it was agreed'.[64] The Scots commissioners gloomily concluded that there was no possibility of agreeing satisfactory peace proposals with parliament.[65]

So it came about that in May 1646 the king fled to the Scots army in England. The covenanters at first greeted this as a major triumph; once they and the king agreed on terms for a peace, parliament would be forced to make concessions. But it soon became obvious that they had miscalculated. The king would not make the concessions in religion which the covenanters regarded as essential, and parliament reacted with fury to their receiving him in their army. The Commons voted that the disposal of Charles was a matter for the English parliament alone, and that parliament had no further need for the Scottish army in England.[66] In these circumstances the covenanters had little choice but to try to patch up relations with parliament. To do this they, not parliament, were forced to make concessions over peace proposals,[67] though the marquis of Argyll still pleaded for a new union: 'lett us hould fast that Union which is soe happily established betwixt us; and lett nothing make us againe Two, who are soe many Wayes One; all of One Language, in One Island, all under One King, One in Religion, yea, One in Covenant; soe that in Effect wee differ in nothing but in the Name (as Brethren doe), which I wish were alsoe removed ... for I dare say, not the greatest Kingdome in the Earth can prejudice both, soe much as One of them may doe the other'.[68]

The propositions agreed with parliament, soon to be presented to the king at Newcastle, had at least been altered in some ways from those the Scots had found so offensive in February. Conservators of the peace were revived and were to meet jointly. Control of the militia was to be in the hands of each parliament separately, but only for twenty years, not indefinitely. Negotiations would be held on the matters referred to further consideration by the 1641 treaty.[69] The king, however, would give no satisfactory answer to the new propositions, so the Scots reluctantly abandoned him to parliament and withdrew their army from England in January 1647.

The covenanters continued to insist that Charles, now the prisoner of the English parliament, accept the propositions of Newcastle, but in September 1647 he indicated that he found the New Model Army's peace terms, the Heads of Proposals, more acceptable.[70] This horrified the Scots;[71] a peace dominated by an English army hostile to both Scots and presbyterianism was anathema to the covenanters. Proposals put forward by the English parliament in December, the Four Bills, were no more attractive to the Scots,[72] who rejected them as prejudicial to religion, the crown, union and the interests of both kingdoms.[73]

By this time an alliance of moderate covenanters and royalists was emerging in power in Scotland, as disillusionment with the English parliament led to growing sympathy for the king. In December 1647 they negotiated a secret treaty with him, the Engagement. Presbyterian church government was to be established in England for three years only in the first instance; although most of the Engagers undoubtedly intended that it would then be made permanent in a final settlement, this was a major concession to the king. In return the Engagers got the assurances which the Scots had long sought about union: 'His Majesty, according to the intention of his father, shall endeavour a complete union of the kingdoms, so as they may be one under His Majesty and his posterity; and, if that cannot be speedily effected, that all liberties, privileges, concerning commerce, traffic, and manufactories peculiar to the subjects of either nation, shall be common to the subjects of both kingdoms without distinction; and that there be a communication of mutual capacity of all other privileges of the subject in the two kingdoms'. In return for such concessions the Scots agreed to help the king implement the treaty, sending an army into England if necessary.[74]

Additional articles, separate from the main treaty, were based on part of the instructions of February 1646 to the Scottish commissioners in London. Scots were to be employed equally with English in all foreign negotiations and treaties. Scots were to sit on the English privy council, and English on the Scots one. One third of those in places of trust and offices about the king and his family were to be Scots. The king and Prince Charles, or at least one of them, were to reside in Scotland frequently.[75]

Thus the Engagers tried by agreement with the king to settle a new union with England which would protect Scotland. Yet of course the first result of the treaty was the severing of the remaining ties which 'intermixed' the governments of the two kingdoms. In January 1648 the English parliament abolished the committee of both kingdoms;[76] its power and influence had long been insignificant but its abolition was nonetheless important, being symbolic of the failure of Scots attempts to develop alliance between the two parliaments into a new form of permanent union.[77]

The attempt of the Engagers to impose a new union collapsed with the defeat of their army at Preston in August 1648. In Scotland the extreme covenanters who had opposed them, the kirk party, seized power. Ideally they would no doubt have liked to continue to seek union through increasing links with the English parliament, but the political and religious complexion of the latter made this unrealistic. The English now insisted that the invasion had nullified all treaties between the two countries. The only formal link between the two was now the Union of the Crowns; and that was soon broken by the execution of Charles I and the abolition of monarchy in England.

Thus the last link of union between the two countries was destroyed. Partly through outraged nationalist sentiment at the execution, partly through determination to continue the union, the Scots parliament at once proclaimed Charles II not just king of Scotland, but of England and Ireland as well. But this revived Union of the Crowns was to be based not on royal power, but on the institution of monarchy, for though the Scots were prompt to proclaim Charles II they stipulated that before he be admitted to the exercise of his royal dignity he must give satisfaction concerning security of religion, the union between the two kingdoms, and the peace of Scotland, all according to the Solemn League and Covenant.[78]

The arrival of Charles II in Scotland (after signing the covenant) in 1650 immediately provoked English invasion. Thus the Scots at last got a new union, but one which was much closer than they had ever bargained for, in the form of the

Cromwellian Union following English conquest. The covenanters had at last forced England to accept their argument that union was vital to mutual security, but only by themselves threatening England's security. But instead of a union designed to protect Scotland's interests within Britain, they got a union based on subjection to England. The wheel had come full circle. The covenanters had revolted (in part at least) to prevent what they saw as an unequal union leading to the Anglicisation of Scotland. They had tried to add to the Union of the Crowns other strands of union, based on links between the two parliaments. When this failed in the face of English indifference (1640-1, 1643-6) they had turned rather desperately to the king for help in redefining the union (1647-51). The failure of this in turn led to complete incorporating union arising from English conquest.

At times the covenanters had talked of complete union, of abolishing all distinctions, even of name, between the two countries. Yet in the specific proposals they made they never went nearly so far. Thus they demanded unity of religion, but only uniformity of church government. The two countries were to have the same kind of church government, but the two churches were nonetheless to remain separate. Similarly in civil affairs the covenanters never specifically proposed an 'incorporating' union in which the two parliaments would become one. Closer union would provide security for the constitutional and religious revolutions they had achieved in Scotland. But too close a union would destroy their security. The two countries involved were so unequal in size, in population and wealth that England and her interests would inevitably predominate in an incorporating union. Therefore Scotland had to retain her own parliament and church, however close links were to be with their English counterparts. In other words, it was to be a loose federal union.

That the covenanters should propose a federal political structure for Britain was hardly surprising, given Scotland's grievances and the fact that federal ideas formed a long-established strand in European political thought. In the context of Switzerland, Calvin had favoured the federation of city-republics for 'self defence and other common purposes'. At the beginning of the seventeenth century Johannes Althusius, a German Calvinist, had built on Calvin's ideas to interpret all political relationships in terms of bonds of contractual union,[79] and in 1638 Archibald Johnston of Wariston, the fanatical ideologue of the covenanting movement, was busy studying the work of Althusius.[80] Religion and politics clearly go hand in hand here; Calvin had favoured federations of churches, as well as of states, and the ideas of covenants between God and man and between a man and his fellow men which inspired the covenanters are obviously closely related to such political ideas. Indeed the Latin for 'covenant' is *foedus*, a treaty or compact creating a 'federal' relationship.[81] The federal union of Britain was to be the civil equivalent of the covenanted Britain the covenanters also sought to achieve, and the examples of the United Provinces (which had won their independence from Spain, the greatest European power of the day) and of Switzerland indicated that federal systems could successfully resist royal protagonists of sovereign power and centralisation such as Charles I.

Unfortunately, however, while federal union, close but not too close, recommended itself to the Scots, the English parliament showed no interest in it — except as a means to gain the help of the covenanters. What seemed equal union to the covenanters seemed most unequal to the English, since the two countries differed so much. Would not an equal union be one in which England predominated by right of her superior wealth and population? What seemed equal union to the Scots seemed (with some justification) to the English to be Scottish interference in English affairs.

In the 1640s and again at the end of the century Scots wishes for partial, federal, union met with English demands for all or nothing. Eventually Scotland accepted that she could not impose her concept of union on her neighbour. They were only to get the security and the commercial privileges they sought once they were ready to accept full parliamentary union and abandon their plans for religious union. Moreover, in order to bring about a new union the Scots not only had to modify their terms, they had to make England interested enough in union to act, and events showed that this was only brought about when Scotland presented a threat to England's security. Full union was only achieved in the 1650s when the threat posed by Scotland provoked English conquest. Similarly in 1707, though in very different circumstances, full union was only achieved because the weakness of the position of Scotland led her to accept full union, while the threat to England's security posed by Scotland's actions forced the English into giving priority to redefining the relationship between the kingdoms. Throughout the seventeenth century Scotland's position had been too weak to impose federal union; only in the 1650s and after 1700 was it so weak that she would accept full union as better than nothing, and the 1640s had seen the most sustained attempt of the century to bring about an 'equal' union (as she saw it) by Scotland.

NOTES

1. An exception to this generalisation is provided by the work of C. L. Hamilton. In several short notes he has stressed that the covenanters were primarily seeking security in their negotiations with the king and English parliament: 'The Basis for Scottish Efforts to Create a Reformed Church in England, 1640-1', *Church History*, xxx (1961), 171-8; 'The Anglo-Scottish Negotiations of 1640-1', *SHR*, xli (1962), 84-6; 'Anglo-Scottish Militia Negotiations, March-April 1646', *SHR*, xlii (1963), 86-8. For my own views on the topic, see D. Stevenson, *The Scottish Revolution, 1637-44* (Newton Abbot, 1973), *Revolution and Counter-Revolution in Scotland, 1644-51* (London, 1977), and 'The Century of the Three Kingdoms', *History Today*, xxxv (March 1985), 28-33.

2. Definitions quoted in this paragraph are taken from *The Oxford English Dictionary* under 'Federal' and 'Union'. For a suggestion that the covenanters' ideas on reform of the union were very similar to those put forward by the Liberal Party in the Devolution debate of the 1970s, see D. Stevenson, 'When British Federalism Failed', *The Scotsman*, 6 Nov. 1976.

3. For some increasing similarities between the two countries, see G. Donaldson, 'Foundations of Anglo-Scottish Union', in his *Scottish Church History* (Edinburgh, 1985), 137-63.

4. For some of the most important contributions to the union debate in the early seventeenth century, see B. R. Galloway and B. P. Levack (eds.), *The Jacobean Union: Six*

Tracts of 1604 (SHS, 1985) and Sir Thomas Craig, *De Unione Regnorum Britanniae Tractatus* (SHS, 1909). W. Ferguson, *Scotland's Relations with England: A Survey to 1707* (Edinburgh, 1977), 99, dismisses the pro-union literature as merely sycophantic propaganda inspired by James VI, but there was clearly much more to it than this — an ideal of a united Britain which had its roots deep in the past. For discussion of some important aspects of this, see A. H. Williamson, *Scottish National Consciousness in the Age of James VI* (Edinburgh, 1979) and 'Scotland, Antichrist and the invention of Great Britain', in J. Dwyer and others (eds.), *New Perspectives on the Politics and Culture of Early Modern Scotland* (Edinburgh, 1982), 34–54, though unfortunately in both works the style renders the argument difficult to follow.

5. For some of the stresses caused by union and attitudes to it, see C. V. Wedgwood, 'Anglo-Scottish Relations, 1603–40', *TRHS*, 4th series, xxxii (1950), 31–48, and Ferguson, *Scotland's Relations with England*, 97–116.

6. H. Trevor-Roper, 'Scotland and the Puritan Revolution', in his *Religion, the Reformation and Social Change* (London, 1967), 392–4, 399–411, has stressed that what made the Scots interfere in England time after time in the 1640s was the desire to export their revolution and thus gain security, but he interprets this entirely in religious terms. For an attack on his ideas concerning Anglo-Scottish relations in this period, see D. Stevenson, 'Professor Trevor-Roper and the Scottish Revolution', *History Today*, xxx (February 1980), 34–40. For other accounts of relations between the kingdoms in the 1640s, see Ferguson, *Scotland's Relations with England*, 113–36, and L. Kaplan, *Politics and Religion during the English Revolution: The Scots and the Long Parliament, 1643–1645* (New York, 1976). For the importance of Irish issues in Anglo-Scottish relations (a matter not considered here), see D. Stevenson, *Scottish Covenanters and Irish Confederates* (Belfast, 1981).

7. J. Rushworth (ed.) *Historical Collections* (London, 1659–1701), II, i, 798–802.

8. *A True Representation of the Proceedings of the Kingdome of Scotland since the Late Pacification. By the Estates of the Kingdome . . .* ([Edinburgh], 1640), pt. 2, 51.

9. *A Remonstrance Concerning the present Troubles, From the Meeting of the Estates of the Kingdome of Scotland, Aprill 16 unto the Parliament of England* ([Edinburgh], 1640), 1, 2–3, 4–5, 22, 25–6.

10. Rushworth, *Collections*, II, ii, 1223–7.

11. R. Baillie, *Letters and Journals* (Bannatyne Club, 1841–2), i, 258.

12. J. Spalding, *Memorialls of the Trubles* (Spalding Club, 1850–1), i, 363–4.

13. G. Burnet, *The Memoires of the Lives and Actions of James and William Dukes of Hamilton* (London, 1677), 177.

14. *Ibid.*, 177.

15. *Calendar of State Papers, Domestic* [*CSPD*], *1640–1* (London, 1882), 244–6; Hamilton, 'Anglo-Scottish Negotiations of 1640–1', 84.

16. J. D. Ogilvie, 'Church Union in 1641', *Records of the Scottish Church History Society* [*RSCHS*], i (1926), 149. See also W. S. Hudson, 'The Scottish Effort to Presbyterianise the Church of England during the Early Months of the Long Parliament', *Church History*, viii (1939), 255–82.

17. T. Thomson and C. Innes (eds.), *Acts of the Parliaments of Scotland* [*APS*], (Edinburgh, 1814–75), v, 340.

18. Baillie, *Letters*, i, 275–6.

19. *Ibid.*, i, 305; D. Dalrymple, Lord Hailes (ed.), *Memorials and Letters relating to the History of Britain in the Reign of Charles the First* (Glasgow, 1766), 107–9.

20. Spalding, *Memorialls*, ii, 9–10.

21. S. R. Gardiner, *History of England*, (London, 1883–4), ix, 297.

22. J. D. Ogilvie, 'The Story of a Broadside of 1641', *Proceedings of the Edinburgh Bibliographical Society*, xii (1921–5), 81.

23. Hamilton, 'The Basis for Scottish Efforts to Create a Reformed Church in England,

180

1640-1', 174-5; W. M. Hetherington, *History of the Westminster Assembly of Divines* (Edinburgh, 1843), 376-84.
24. Ogilvie, 'Church Union in 1641', 156.
25. Ogilvie, 'Story of a Broadside', 83.
26. Ogilvie, 'Church Union in 1641', 157; *APS*, v, 340.
27. *CSPD, 1640-1*, 513-14.
28. *APS*, v, 340, 341, 342-3.
29. Hamilton, 'Anglo-Scottish Negotiations of 1640-1', 84-5; *APS*, v, 344-5.
30. *Ibid.*, v, 404-5.
31. *Register of the Privy Council of Scotland [RPCS], 1638-43* (Edinburgh, 1906), 163, 198, 248-51, 256-9, 260-5.
32. A. Peterkin (ed.), *Records of the Kirk of Scotland . . . from the year 1638* (Edinburgh, 1838), 323-4.
33. *RPCS, 1638-43*, 316; Burnet, *Hamilton*, 195, 197-9, 200-1.
34. SRO, PA.14/2, Proceedings of the Scots Commissioners for Conserving the Articles of the Treaty, 1642-3, pp. 1-6; *The Proceedings of the Commissioners . . . for Conserving the Articles of the Treaty and Peace . . .* ([Edinburgh], 1643), 5-10.
35. *Journals of the House of Lords [LJ]*, v, 430-1.
36. SRO, PA.14/2, 13-15, 20, 26-36, 41-4; Baillie, *Letters*, ii, 66-7; Rushworth, *Collections*, III, ii, 399-406.
37. *Journals of the House of Commons [CJ]*, iii, 66, 92, 110, 113, 121, 132; *LJ*, vi, 25, 32, 38, 55-6, 60, 97, 99; Baillie, *Letters*, ii, 79.
38. *APS*, VI, i, 13-14.
39. *LJ*, vi, 140-2.
40. Baillie, *Letters*, ii, 90.
41. *APS*, VI, i, 150-1.
42. *Ibid.*, VI, i, 42.
43. Baillie, *Letters*, ii, 106.
44. L. Kaplan, 'Presbyterians and Independents in 1643', *EHR*, lxxxiv (1969), 251-2; Baillie, *Letters*, ii, 117.
45. *APS*, VI, i, 70-1.
46. V. Pearl, 'Oliver St John and the "Middle Group" in the Long Parliament', *EHR*, lxxxi (1966), 494, 498, 508-9, 513, 514; W. Notestein, 'The Establishment of the Committee of Both Kingdoms', *American Historical Review*, xvii (1912), 477-95; Baillie, *Letters*, ii, 141-2. For the Scots members of the committee, see L. Mulligan, 'The Scottish Alliance and the Committee of Both Kingdoms, 1644-6', *Historical Studies*, xiv (1970), 173-88.
47. Baillie, *Letters*, ii, 156, 166.
48. *Ibid.*, ii, 234; C. V. Wedgwood, 'The Covenanters in the First Civil War', *SHR*, xxxix (1960), 10-12.
49. S. R. Gardiner (ed.), *Constitutional Documents of the Puritan Revolution* (3rd ed., Oxford, 1958), 275-86.
50. Baillie, *Letters*, ii, 294.
51. *LJ*, vii, 442-3.
52. [D. Buchanan], *Truth its Manifest: or a short and true relation of divers main passages of things . . .* (London, 1645), 110-11.
53. *CSPD, 1645-7* (London, 1892), pp. xviii, 130.
54. *A Speech of the . . . Earle of Louden . . . to a Grand Committee of both Houses of Parliament, upon the 12 of September, 1645* (London, 1645).
55. M. W. Meikle (ed.), *Correspondence of the Scots Commissioners in London, 1644-6* (Roxburghe Club, 1917), 117-19.
56. *Ibid.*, 82-3; *LJ*, vii, 639.
57. J. G. Fotheringham (ed.), *The Diplomatic Correspondence of Jean de Montereul . . .*

III

(SHS, 1898–9), i, 163–4; Gardiner, *Civil War*, iii, 73–6.

58. Hamilton, 'Anglo-Scottish Militia Negotiations', 86; Baillie, *Letters*, ii, 348; Meikle, *Correspondence*, 139.

59. *APS*, VI, i, 575–9. For additional Instructions of 10 February, see SRO, PA.13/4, Register of Instructions to the Scots Commissioners in London, 1644–6, fos. 42–43v.

60. *LJ*, viii, 217–19; Hamilton, 'Anglo-Scottish Militia Negotiations', 86–7; Baillie, *Letters*, ii, 348.

61. SRO, PA.13/5, Register of Negotiations, 1643–7, fos. 301–303; Hamilton, 'Anglo-Scottish Militia Negotiations', 87–8.

62. *Some Papers of the Commissioners of Scotland, given in lately to the Houses of Parliament concerning the Propositions of Peace* (London, 1646), 1–4.

63. Meikle, *Correspondence*, 173–4, 176; *LJ*, viii, 272, 274, 276, 277, 281; Baillie, *Letters*, ii, 366–7.

64. *CJ*, iv, 513–15.

65. Meikle, *Correspondence*, 175, 177.

66. *CJ*, iv, 537–8, 551.

67. SRO, PA.13/4, fo. 44v; Meikle, *Correspondence*, 194–6; Baillie, *Letters*, ii, 376; *LJ*, viii, 393–4.

68. *Ibid.*, viii, 392–3.

69. Gardiner, *Constitutional Documents*, 290–306; *LJ*, viii, 237–9.

70. Gardiner, *Constitutional Documents*, 326–7.

71. *Ibid.*, 316–26.

72. *Ibid.*, 335–47.

73. *CSPD, 1645–7*, 582–3.

74. Gardiner, *Constitutional Documents*, 347–52.

75. *Ibid.*, 353.

76. *CJ*, v, 416.

77. Baillie, *Letters*, iii, 32–3.

78. *APS*, VI, ii, 157, 161.

79. F. S. Carney (ed.), *The Politics of Johannes Althusius* (London, 1965), viii–xi.

80. G. M. Paul (ed.), *Diary of Sir Archibald Johnston of Wariston, 1632–1639* (SHS, 1911), 348 & n., 408.

81. When the Solemn League and Covenant was printed in Latin in 1643, 'league and covenant' was translated simply as *foedus*.

Abbreviations

APS   Acts of the Parliaments of Scotland
BL   British Library
BIHR   Bulletin of the Institute of Historical Research
EETS   Early English Text Society
EHR   English Historical Review
HMC   Historical Manuscripts Commission
IR   Innes Review
JMH   Journal of Modern History
NLS   National Library of Scotland
PRO   Public Record Office
PSAS   Proceedings of the Society of Antiquaries of Scotland
SHR   Scottish Historical Review
SHS   Scottish History Society
SRO   Scottish Record Office
STS   Scottish Text Society
TRHS   Transactions of the Royal Historical Society

IV

Cromwell, Scotland and Ireland

When Britain collapsed into civil wars in the years around 1640 the crisis began in the periphery, first in Scotland and then in Ireland, and then spread to England as failure to crush revolts in these out-lying kingdoms discredited Charles I's regime. A decade later the process was reversed, the power of government centralized in London being first asserted in England, then applied to Ireland, and finally to Scotland where the breakdown of power had begun. And just as failure in the periphery had discredited Charles I, so the asser-tion of English power in it was central to the prestige of Oliver Cromwell.

In one respect Cromwell's basic attitude to the two outlying kingdoms was the same. They posed threats to England, not just in that they had overthrown control from London, but more actively in that they sought to impose their wills on the central kingdom. The security of England thus necessitated their conquest. Yet in other ways his attitudes to the two differed fundamentally. Whereas from 1641 onwards he can have had no doubt that Ireland would have to be reconquered, until late in the day he hoped it would not be neces-sary to conquer Scotland.

Where the Irish were concerned, doubtless Cromwell's starting point was the simple view of the Irish as barbarous papists who, through their religion, were potentially disloyal as well as being a standing reproach to the protestant Crown of England. In the later 1630s, however, Cromwell's perceptions of Ireland would have begun to change. The 'thorough' policies of Lord Wentworth as Lord

* I am grateful to John Morrill and Sarah Barber for their comments on a draft of this paper.
Reprinted by permission of Addison Wesley Longman Ltd.

Deputy suggested that in the short term a threat from Ireland might not be presented by native Irish, but through Ireland being deliberately made into a bastion of arbitrary royal power, a test-bed for policies later to be introduced in England. Then, after the Scottish revolt of 1637 broke out, Ireland assumed a new threatening role, when a largely catholic army was raised for use against protestant Scots, a worrying precedent that might later have an application in England.

Yet of course when Ireland did suddenly become a major threat to English interest, it was in a traditional way – by the revolt of the native Irish in October 1641. This revolt, the real suffering inflicted on protestant settlers, and the vastly exaggerated rumours of catholic atrocities hardened and fixed attitudes to the Irish for most Englishmen, Cromwell among them. He took an active part in planning to restore English control of Ireland, and was a substantial subscriber under the 1642 Adventurers' Act, by which parliament raised money for a campaign there by promising repayment in land confiscated from the Irish.[1] But with the approach of civil war in England later in 1642 Cromwell's attention, like that of parliament as a whole, was diverted to problems closer to home: Ireland would have to wait until England's destiny had been decided.[2]

After the First Civil War was over parliament had resources free to devote to Ireland, and Cromwell's commitment to reconquest was emphasized by his offer in March 1647 to invest arrears of pay due to him plus up to £5,000 in the Irish venture.[3] In the event a major campaign in Ireland was delayed by the need to deal with the Scottish invasion and English royalist rebellions of 1648. But in 1649 attention swung back to Ireland. With rebellions defeated, Charles I executed and monarchy abolished, the new commonwealth regime was at last free to deal with the threats to its authority presented by Ireland. In all we know of Cromwell's attitude to Ireland and the Irish up to this point, there is no sign of any distinctive outlook, any special insights into the Irish problem. He simply shared the attitudes of most Englishmen. Ireland had to be reconquered, as historically subordinate to England, as a potential strategic threat, and as the home of barbarous papists whose crimes must be punished, whose religion must be suppressed.

1. See K. S. Bottigheimer, *English Money and Irish Land. The 'adventurers' in the Cromwellian settlement of Ireland* (Oxford, 1971).
2. See Abbott, I, 147–8, 160, 162, 172, 182.
3. Ibid., I, 588

Cromwell, Scotland and Ireland

By contrast, Cromwell's attitude to the Scots was – or became – more subtle, and he showed a readiness to modify stereotyped attitudes based on prevailing English prejudices. From an English viewpoint the Scots shared some of the characteristics of the Irish: they were poor and backward, even barbarous, and not to be trusted. On the other hand, they were protestants, and by the 1630s traditional perceptions of the Scots were being modified in the eyes of those who, like Cromwell, were worried by Charles I's policies in England, by sympathy for the Scots as a people suffering from the same misguided religious and other policies as Englishmen. Such an attitude would have been strengthened, in Cromwell as in so many other Englishmen, into positive respect and support for the Scots when their open resistance to royal policies demonstrated the brittleness of the king's power in and after 1637. It is said that Cromwell told some officers of the army the king was gathering against the Scots that he disliked the war.[4]

Yet once the Scottish covenanters had defeated the king, their ambitions for a peace settlement protecting their interests seemed to many Englishmen to amount to interference in English affairs. There is, however, no direct evidence of Cromwell's changing attitude to the Scots until after parliament negotiated the Solemn League and Covenant and a military treaty with the covenanters in the autumn of 1643. Like most parliamentarians Cromwell accepted the necessity for gaining Scottish military help against the king; but he also resented and feared the price the Scots demanded in return. Cromwell's attitude was indicated by his long delay in signing the new covenant,[5] and he quickly emerged as the leader of those parliamentarians opposed to Scottish pretensions on all fronts: in religion he opposed their demands for a religious monopoly for presbyterianism; in the conduct of the war he opposed their demands for a compromise, negotiated peace with the king; and in constitutional affairs he was opposed to what he saw as their attempt to determine England's future.

The hostility of Cromwell to Scottish pretensions came into the open after the battle of Marston Moor in July 1644. The Scots, who had fought alongside parliamentary armies in the battle, claimed the victory as largely a Scottish one, but they found that in London it was widely presented as a victory won above all by Cromwell. As the independents and other opponents of the Scots tried to exploit

4. Ibid., I, 107–8.
5. Gardiner, *Great Civil War*, I, 262, 310–11.

the victory for propaganda purposes, the embittered Scots found that 'their' victory had greatly increased the prestige of Cromwell and others determined to limit their influence.[6]

The Scots fought back, winning considerable English. backing. They seized on evidence that Cromwell had 'spoken contumeliouslie of the Scots intention in coming to England to establish their Church-government, in which Cromwell said he would draw his sword against them' – as readily, indeed, as against any in the king's army.[7] The Scots therefore proposed in December 1644 that he should be impeached under the terms of the Solemn League and Covenant as 'an *incendiary*' who was kindling 'coals of contention and raises differences in the state to the public damage'. The attempt failed, but that it was made at all showed how Cromwell was by this time clearly recognized as the leader of opposition to their ambitions in England.[8]

As anti-Scots attitudes spread among parliamentarians, so Cromwell's prestige grew, he being regarded as 'the first to incense the people against the Scots' nation'.[9] The frustration of the Scots, betrayed (as they saw it) by their English parliamentarian allies, led them to sign the secret Engagement treaty with the imprisoned Charles I in December 1647. But the convenanters were now deeply divided. The dominant faction, the Engagers, was an alliance of moderate covenanters, with royalists, determined to help the king, while the more extreme covenanters, supported by most of the parish ministers, felt there was no justification for a war between the kingdoms.

The split among the Scots into Engagers and their opponents, soon to be known as the Kirk Party, was seen by Cromwell as corresponding to the dichotomy present in his own attitude to the Scots, and this dictated his conduct in the 1648 campaign against the Scots and its aftermath. He accepted that in the past decade the Scots had been essentially agents of God's work, and that in their theology, worship, Church organization at the local level, and generally sober and 'puritan' outlook they had much in common with him and his

6. D. Stevenson, *Revolution and Counter-Revolution in Scotland, 1644–51* (1977), p. 12; R. Baillie, *Letters and Journals* (3 vols, Bannatyne Club, Edinburgh, 1841–2), II, 203, 209.
7. Baillie, *Letters*, II, 245; Gardiner, *Civil War*, II, 23
8. Baillie, *Letters*, II, 245; Stevenson, *Revolution and Counter-Revolution*, p. 15; Gardiner, *Civil War*, II, 87–8.
9. E. Hyde, earl of Clarendon, *The History of the rebellion and Civil Wars in England*, ed. W. D. Macray (6 vols, Oxford, 1888), IV, 307.

English allies. Yet in their insistence on a strongly centralized system of Church government and in its complete separation from the state, and in their political ambitions, the Scots were enemies of both God and England. Now the Scots had split. The Engagers were clearly enemies of God and England, while the Kirk Party was revealing the essentially godly nature of its supporters by opposing the Engagement. Thus at this point there was no question of a war to conquer Scotland. The war was to defeat the Engagers and help godly Scots gain power in their own country. A new Kirk Party regime, once established in Scotland, would be bound in· firm friendship to whatever godly regime emerged in England, tied to it by gratitude (as English intervention had brought it to power), by political expediency (as it had shown that it had the power to make or break a regime in Scotland), and by common godliness. The Scots would recognize that Cromwell's victory was a demonstration that he was indeed an agent through whom God was revealing His intentions.

The Engagers' invasion of England was routed by Cromwell at the battle of Preston in August 1648, and he then advanced north, confident that the Scots would see his victory as overwhelming proof of whose side God was on, as 'The witness that God hath borne against your army'.[10] The Kirk Party now staged a *coup d'état*, and Cromwell believed that it was God's will that he treat the new Scottish regime not as representing an enemy nation, but as an ally with which he should cooperate. One of God's motives in allowing the Engagers and English royalists to rise in arms was to show the necessity for friendship between the kingdoms.[11] Enthusiastically he reported that 'I do think the affairs of Scotland are in a thriving posture, as to the interest of honest men.'[12] The godly now ruled the land, and he was eager to discuss the future with both politicians and ministers. One account survives of him trying to persuade godly Scots of his sincerity. At a meeting with some ministers he 'had a long discourse to them, with a fair flourish of words, and sometimes tears, taking God to be a witness of their sincerity and good intentions'. On leaving one minister was impressed: 'I am very glad to hear this man speak as he does'; but a harder-headed colleague retorted

10. Abbott, I, 650.
11. Ibid., I, 653.
12. Ibid., I, 669.

And do you believe him. If you knew him as well as I do, you would not believe one word he says. He is an egregious dissembler and a great liar. Away with him, he is a greeting [crying] devil.[13]

As this indicates, the success of Cromwell's 'hearts and minds' campaign in Edinburgh was in reality very limited. Godly though it might be in many respects, the Kirk Party remained implacably opposed to him on matters of Church government and toleration.

Nor was Cromwell's conduct popular in London. Instead of teaching the Scots a harsh lesson by following up victory at Preston with further military action, Cromwell had offered them friendship. Thus the man notorious for years as a hater of the Scots now came to be suspected of undue leniency to them. This provoked Cromwell into defending his attitude to the Scots. He had prayed and

waited for the day to see union and right understanding between the godly people (Scots, English, Jews, Gentiles, Presbyterians, Independents, Anabaptists, and all). Our brothers of Scotland (really Presbyterians) were our greatest enemies. God hath justified us in their sight; caused us to requite good for evil, causing them to acknowledge it publicly by acts of state, and privately, and the thing is true in the sight of the sun. It is an high conviction upon them. Was it not fit to be civil, to profess love, to deal with clearness with them for removing of prejudice, to ask them what they had against us, and to give them an honest answer? This we have done, and not more. And herein is a more glorious work in our eyes than if we had gotten the sacking and plunder of Edinburgh, the strong castles into our hands, and made conquest from the Tweed to the Orcades; and we can say, through God we have left by the grace of God such a witness amongst them, as if it work not yet there is that conviction upon them that will undoubtedly bear its fruit in due time.

Conquest 'was not very unfeasible, but I think not Christian' – and anyway parliament had not ordered a conquest. By requiting evil with good Cromwell hoped he had put the Scots under an unbreakable moral obligation to live in friendship with England.[14]

Just as the Scots were, Cromwell hoped, ready to learn from him, he was ready to learn from them. The Kirk Party (which only formed a minority in the Scottish parliament of 1648), had, after seizing power, disqualified the Engager majority from sitting in the 1649 and later sessions of parliaments. Cromwell was deeply impressed:

. . . a lesser party of a Parliament hath made it lawful to declare the greater part a faction, and made the Parliament null, and call a new one, and do this

13. T. M'Crie (ed.), *The Life of Mr Robert Blair, Minister of St Andrews, containing his autobiography* (Wodrow Society, Edinburgh, 1848) p. 210; Abbott, I, 665–60.
14. Abbott, I, 677–8.

Cromwell, Scotland and Ireland

by force . . . . Think of the example and of the consequences, and let others think of it too.[15]

A month later 'Pride's Purge' saw the army expel most of the members of the House of Commons. Cromwell claimed not to have known of the planned purge, but it is hard to believe he did not have a part in inspiring it, through drawing the attention of 'others' to a useful Scottish precedent.

Cromwell was soon disappointed by the Scots. The trial and execution of the king turned uneasy alliance between the revolutionary regimes of the two kingdoms into hostility. Again Cromwell argued with them, seeing their attitudes as tragically misguided rather than totally ungodly. He even, in an argument the irony of which must have been evident to all, cited the very article of the Solemn League and Covenant under which the Scots had once tried to impeach him as justification for acting against the king: Charles was an incendiary![16]

It was all to no avail. When Charles was executed the Scots immediately proclaimed his son Charles II as king – and king of England and Ireland as well as Scotland. Cromwell at last admitted that his policy of leniency towards the Scots had failed. In the new Council of State on 23 March 1649 he explained his understanding of the situation:

In the kingdom of Scotland, you cannot too well take notice of what is done nor of this; that there is a very angry, hateful spirit there against your army, as an army of sectaries, which you see all their papers do declare their quarrel to be against. And although God hath used us as instruments for their good, yet hitherto they are not sensible of it, but they are angry that God brought them His mercy at such an hand.

The ungrateful Scots had spurned England's proffered friendship, and the godly Kirk Party, like the ungodly Engagers before them, were seeking, through links with royalists, 'the ruin and destruction of those that God hath ordained to be instrumental for their good'.[17]

England having been lost to Charles II, it was obvious that any attempt to restore monarchy would come through Scotland or Ireland. He at first favoured Ireland as the base for an attempt to regain his thrones, and Cromwell told the Council that the Irish might soon be able to land their forces in England. Given the deep divisions in Ireland he probably exaggerated, but his statement showed where

15. Ibid., I, 678.
16. Ibid., I, 746.
17. Ibid., II, 37.

he believed England's priorities lay. An informal aside confirmed this:

I confess I have had these thoughts with myself, that perhaps may be carnal and foolish. I had rather be overrun with a Cavalierish interest than a Scotch interest; I had rather be overrun with a Scotch interest, than an Irish interest; and I think of all this is most dangerous. [18]

Ireland presented the most immediate threat, so action against Ireland was the first priority. Moreover the adventurers, with their claims to land in Ireland in return for their investments, were clamouring for action.

The political situation in Ireland was chaotic. Most of the Irish who had originally rebelled in 1641 had, by 1649, joined themselves to protestant royalists under the marquis of Ormonde, uniting in an uneasy alliance as this seemed to offer the only hope of resisting the attack which would clearly come from the armies of the English parliament – which indeed already held Dublin. But minorities of both protestants and catholics rejected such an alliance based on political expediency, so there also existed forces of Irish catholics which refused to work with royalists, and disaffected protestant royalist forces which were moving towards acceptance of the authority of the English parliament rather than ally with catholics. In Ulster the situation was further complicated by the presence of many thousands of Scots presbyterians whose political sympathies lay with Scotland rather than England.

Cromwell landed in Dublin on 15 August 1649. Just two weeks before parliament's commander there, Michael Jones, had won a remarkable victory at Rathmines over Ormonde's combined Irish and royalist army, a disaster to the Irish which was so complete and demoralizing that they never again dared face the English army in the field. Instead they concentrated on garrisoning towns and castles. Cromwell's campaign was therefore one in which the only large-scale fighting took place at the storming of such strongholds, though there was a good deal of mopping up of small bands of Irish to be done as their armies disintegrated.

Cromwell hailed Rathmines as 'an astonishing mercy; so great and seasonable as indeed we are like them that dreamed. What can we say! The Lord fill our souls with thankfulness.'[19] He told Dublin's inhabitants – mainly protestant – that he intended with divine aid to

18. Ibid., II, 38.
19. Ibid., II, 103.

restore them to their just liberty and property.[20] Thus some in Ireland were to be able to win the favour of the commonwealth: but the vast majority of the country's inhabitants were not offered such hopes. It was not just the catholic Irish (who were now taken to include the 'Old English' – catholics of English descent – as well as native Irish) who could expect no mercy. Protestant royalists who were now allied to the Irish were regarded as sharing in their crimes. Even among protestants who had not joined the Irish there were few who had not at some point in the chaotic events since 1641 collaborated with Irish or royalists, and the Scots in the north were suspect as collaborators with their misguided countrymen in Scotland. There was, therefore, no possibility of military action in Ireland giving way to a compromise settlement negotiated with some existing faction in the country, as had happened in Scotland the year before.

The Cromwellian conquest of Ireland is associated above all else with the names of Drogheda and Wexford. Brutal though the massacres in these towns are in the British context, in a wider context of European warfare they are not outstanding. Indeed they can be taken as examples of the two most common types of massacre after the fall of a stronghold. At Drogheda Cromwell summoned the governor to surrender, adding that 'If this be refused you will have no cause to blame me' for the consequences.[21] According to the accepted conventions of warfare (see page 111–2 above), if a garrison inflicted casualties on a besieging army after refusing a summons to surrender, and it was then taken by storm, the victors were justified in exacting retribution for the unnecessary losses they incurred. Cromwell applied this convention: it was his bitterness at the losses of his army in the storm of Drogheda that provoked him into sanctioning indiscriminate massacre. But though this provides an explanation, it does not provide an excuse: and undoubtedly the fact that his enemy was 'Irish', representing a people whose blood guilt was regarded as putting them almost beyond the bounds of humanity, contributed to his readiness to sanction the deed. In reality, most of the garrison was composed of English royalists, under an English commander, but in Cromwell's eyes as they had allied themselves to the Irish they shared the blood guilt of the latter.

Cromwell felt no need to excuse his conduct at Drogheda, but he did feel it needed explaining: 'And truely I believe this bitterness will save much effusion of blood, through the goodness of God', as it

20. Ibid., II, 107.
21. Ibid., II, 118.

would frighten other garrisons into surrendering without a fight. Thus it was 'a marvellous great mercy',[22] a 'righteous judgment of God on these barbarous wretches, who have imbrued their hands in so much innocent blood', and this and the hope of preventing later bloodshed 'are the satisfactory grounds to such actions, which otherwise cannot but work remorse and regret'.[23]

At Wexford Cromwell again summoned the town, but he agreed to negotiate terms for a surrender. The massacre took place in confused circumstances when the captain of Wexford castle suddenly surrendered while negotiations about the town's fate were still in progress, and parliamentary troops broke into the town from the castle and began killing and looting indiscriminately. Drogheda was an officially sanctioned massacre: Wexford was one which took place when a sudden and unexpected development led to soldiers acting outside the direct control of senior officers. Cromwell was probably being honest when he said he had wished to avoid the sack of the town. Yet his conduct at Drogheda had given his men a terrible example to follow, and Cromwell believed that at Wexford his intention to be merciful had been overruled by God's determination to impose justice instead. Cromwell had

intended better to this place than so great a ruin, hoping the town might be of more use to you and your army, yet God would not have it so; but, by an unexpected providence, in His righteous justice, brought a just judgment upon them.[24]

Cromwell's belief that the bloodbath at Drogheda would limit later bloodshed was probably correct; news of the massacre, and of that at Wexford, led to the rapid collapse of resistance, and town after town surrendered as Cromwell approached.

Not until May 1650, when the back of Irish resistance was clearly broken, did Cromwell return to England and turn his attention to the Scots, who were now replacing the Irish as the main threat to the Commonwealth. Ironically, the very fact that he had been successful in Ireland increased the threat from Scotland, for it had led Charles II to despair of help from Ireland, and this had driven him back to negotiations with the Kirk Party. By the end of April 1650 he had reached agreement with the Scots, and they invited him to Scotland. There could be little doubt that this would mean war with

22. Ibid., II, 124.
23. Ibid., II, 127.
24. Ibid., II, 142.

England, and by June 1650 the Council of State had resolved that a pre-emptive invasion of Scotland should be launched. Cromwell had no doubts as to the justice of this: the Scots had invaded in 1648 and were preparing to do so again. This being the case, it was obviously best from England's point of view that the war should be fought on Scottish rather than English soil, and that England should seek to strike before the Scots were fully prepared.[25] Yet Cromwell regretted having to fight the Scots. Once again godly – or potentially godly – Scots had been deluded into fighting for an ungodly cause. A declaration issued by his army on its march to Scotland in July spelled out his attitude. England hoped bloodshed could be avoided. She was willing to discuss religious and other differences, in attempting to reach agreement on the interpretation of the Word of God. The English had displayed Christian love to Scotland in 1648, and were willing to do so again.[26]

After the army had crossed into Scotland Cromwell maintained the pressure, though with increasing frustration at the lack of response. He wrote to the Church of Scotland expressing sadness at its attempts to prejudice those 'who do too much (in matters of conscience, wherein every soul is to answer for itself to God) depend upon you' against the English. He accused the Church's leaders of suppressing the English declarations offering love to the Scots, and invited them to send as many of their papers to his army as they liked: 'I fear them not.' Were they really sure they spoke infallibly for God? 'I beseech you, in the bowels of Christ, think it possible you may be mistaken.' To their repeated appeals to the covenants he replied 'there may be a Covenant made with death and hell. I will not say yours was so . . .'.[27] But the bald reply of the Church showed a confidence of righteousness equal to his own: 'would yow have ws to be scepticks in our religion?'[28] Cromwell reported to parliament that 'Since we came in Scotland, it hath been our desire and longing to have avoided blood in this business, by reason that God hath a people fearing His name, though deceived':

We have been engaged on a service the fullest of trial ever poor creatures were upon. We made great professions of love, knowing we were to deal with many who were Godly, and pretended to be stumbled at our invasion; indeed, our bowels were pierced again and again; the Lord helped us to sweet

25. Ibid., II, 265–70.
26. Ibid., II, 283–8.
27. Ibid., II, 302–3.
28. Ibid., II, 305.

words, and in sincerity to mean them. We were rejected again and again, yet still we begged to be believed that we loved them as our own souls; they often returned evil for good.[29]

These expositions of Cromwell's attitude to the Scots were contained in dispatches announcing the turning point of the Scottish war. A decisive battle had been fought near Dunbar on 3 September. God had arisen and his enemies had been scattered. But even among those who had fought for the enemies of God there were many godly people, and it was his duty to try to reclaim them for the Lord. Thus when Edinburgh was occupied after the victory Cromwell redoubled his propaganda assault on the Scots.[30] Surely, now that God had shown His will so openly, they could not continue to shut their eyes to the truth?

The propaganda was indeed having an effect on the morale of the more 'godly' Scots, and this worked to Cromwell's advantage – but not quite in the way he had hoped, for only a tiny handful of Scots gave up the fight against him. Many of the more extreme supporters of the Kirk Party, however, concluded that they were suffering defeat because they were offending God: their offence lay not in fighting Cromwell, but in fighting him in the king's name. Remedying this became a matter of urgency after Dunbar, for defeat destroyed the already tottering Kirk Party regime, as worldly arguments convinced most Scots that all men, including royalists or Engagers, should be recruited to face the enemy. Even more clearly than in the past Scotland was fighting for an ungodly king. The godly extremists, concentrated in the western Lowlands, reacted by establishing what amounted to a separate administration and godly army under the name of the Western Association (its very name reflecting grudging admiration for Cromwell and his Eastern Association). In the event, however, God's mysterious failure to bring godly Scots victory continued, and the Remonstrants (so called from the Western Remonstrance in which they set out their attitudes to the war) devoted much of their energy to agonizing over precisely what they were fighting for. It became clear that some of them at least found it increasingly hard to justify fighting Cromwell, whose repeated appeals to them helped to sow dissention in their ranks. Thus though he was disappointed that he could not persuade the Remonstrants to submit peacefully, the speed with which their resis-

29. Ibid., II, 325, 327–8.
30. Ibid., II, 335–41.

IV

tance collapsed after their defeat at the battle of Hamilton (1 December 1650) indicated the extent to which he had undermined their resolve. Yet Cromwell was sad they had had to be defeated in battle: 'Those religious people of Scotland that fall in this cause, we cannot but pity and mourn for them, and we pray that all good men may do so too.'[31]

Cromwell's efforts to conquer Scotland with words rather than bloodshed continued. Since the occupation of Edinburgh he had debated with ministers there. He visited Glasgow to persuade the godly of the west of his sincerity, hoping to win them over by his conduct and arguments.[32] But the majority of those he believed godly remained stubborn in adhering to their errors, and the main enemy, Charles II's army north of the Forth, would not succumb to his rhetoric. It took hard fighting to out-manoeuvre it, push it into a despairing invasion of England, and finally rout it at the battle of Worcester on 3 September 1651. Thereafter Scots resistance collapsed – and Cromwell could relax and admit something that he had not hinted at while the war was still to be won: of all the regime's actions, justifying the Scots war had caused him 'greatest difficulty', 'by reason we have had to do with some who were (I verily think) godly, but, through weakness and the subtlety of Satan involved in interests against the Lord and His people'. He had therefore proceeded carefully, making sure that his every action was fully justified: and as a result of this care, 'The Lord hath marvellously appeared even against them.'[33]

In 1649–51 Cromwell had conquered two kingdoms for the English commonwealth. But what was to be done with these prizes? How were they to be governed? Ireland presented few problems as to her status once conquered: she was an English dependency in which a great rebellion had been crushed. When the English parliament had abolished monarchy in England and established the republic, it had done the same in Ireland: the new commonwealth was that of England and Ireland. When Cromwell landed there in 1649 he held the traditional office of Lord Lieutenant as well as that of commander-in-chief. But his ambitions for Ireland's future were far from traditional, for he brought ideals as well as an army with him, and he believed that Ireland offered an unrivalled opportunity

31. Ibid., II, 365; D. Stevenson, *The Covenanters and the Western Association* (Ayrshire Archaeological and Natural History Society: Ayrshire Collections, 11, no. 1, 1982).
32. Abbott, II, 352–7, 360–72, 408; Stevenson, *Western Association*, pp. 160–3.
33. Abbott, II, 483.

for implementing these ideals. It had long been an irritation that in England even though power had been seized, introducing radical reform in such matters as law and religion was proving unexpectedly slow and difficult. The dead weight of tradition, of existing legal and administrative frameworks and of strongly entrenched vested interests was almost impossible to overcome. But in Ireland nearly a decade of chaos had virtually destroyed all previous frameworks. The structure of society and authority had collapsed. The opportunity to build a new godly society, and a legal system and government guaranteeing liberty and equality before the law, should not be missed. Thus the Cromwellians, like Wentworth back in the 1630s, saw Ireland as a test site for policies ultimately to be introduced in England.

Cromwell's vision of unlimited possibilities is explained in a letter written at the end of 1649. When his army had landed in Ireland

there was a dissolution of the whole frame of Government; there being no visible authority residing in persons entrusted to act according to the forms of law, except in two corporations [Dublin and Londonderry] under the Parliament's power, in this whole Land.

This vacuum provided immense opportunities. It would be possible to establish

a way of doing justice amongst these poor people, which, for the uprightness and cheapness of it, may exceedingly gain upon them, who have been accustomed to as much injustice, tyranny and oppression from their landlords, the great men, and those that should have done them right, as, I believe, any people in that which we call Christendom . . . . they having been inured thereto. Sir, if justice were freely and impartially administred here, the foregoing darkness and corruption would make it look so much the more glorious and beautiful; and draw more hearts after it.[34]

A few months later he talked of the exciting possibilities of Ireland to Edmund Ludlow. In England the law encouraged the rich to oppress the poor, but the strength of lawyers' vested interests and fears for social stability prevented reform. Ireland, by contrast was 'as a clean paper',

capable of being governed by such laws as should be found most agreeable to justice; which may be so impartially administered, as to be a good precedent even to England itself; where when they once perceive propriety preserved at an easy and cheap rate in Ireland, they will never permit themselves to be so cheated and abused as now they are.[35]

34. Ibid., II, 186–7.
35. Ibid., II, 273

That parliament shared at least some of this vision is indicated by the abolition of the office Lord Lieutenant (and the subordinate office of Lord Deputy) in May 1652: Ireland was to be governed instead by parliamentary commissioners.[36] The old offices, associated with monarchy and the old relationship between Ireland and England disappeared now that they formed a single commonwealth. But many questions remained unanswered. It was evidently intended from the first that the Irish parliament would be abolished, Ireland instead sending representatives to parliament at Westminster, but public confirmation of this did not come until March 1653, when the number of such representatives was fixed at thirty. Not until 1656 was a bill introduced in parliament for the union of England and Ireland – and though it was revived in 1656–57 it never completed its passage through parliament.[37]

In Scotland's case explicit definition of the country's place in the political system was required more urgently than Ireland, for here England had conquered an independent State, not re-asserted control over a dependency. But whereas in Ireland's case England had sought complete conquest and union into one commonwealth from the start of Cromwell's campaign, this was not so in Scotland. The aim of the Scottish war was to remove the threat the alliance of the covenanters with Charles II presented to the commonwealth: quite how this would be achieved was secondary, dependent on how the situation developed. Thus when Cromwell wrote to the Scots on 9 October 1650, all he said was needed to end the war was for the Scots to give the English 'satisfaction and security for their peaceable and quiet living by you'.[38] Only when it became clear that such satisfaction would not be forthcoming did conquest become the goal.

Not having planned to conquer Scotland, the English had no ready-made plans for what to do with their prize. At first the areas under English control were treated as conquered territory, and many felt that Scotland as a whole deserved no better. But more moderate counsels prevailed. England should offer Scotland union with England and Ireland to form one commonwealth.[39] Expediency suggested that generosity to the defeated would help to reconcile them

---

36. Ibid., II, 556–7; T. C. Barnard, *Cromwellian Ireland. English government and reform in Ireland, 1649–60* (Oxford, 1975), pp. 13–15, 18.
37. *C. J. VII, 263, 415, 452–50 passim*, 519; P. J. Corish, 'The Cromwellian regime, 1550–60', in T. W. Moody, F. X. Martin and F. J. Byrne (eds), *A New History of Ireland*, III, *Early Modern Ireland, 1534–1691* (Oxford, 1976), p. 354.
38. Abbott, II, 350.
39. F. D. Dow, *Cromwellian Scotland, 1651–60* (Edinburgh, 1979), pp. 30–1.

to the new order. Moreover, how could a regime which claimed to stand for liberty and justice justify rulirtg its neighbour by brute strength alone? In Cromwell's mind the Scots were already basically godly: treating them justly and removing the forces which had lèd them astray (king, feudal landlords and bigoted ministers) would convert them into active supporters of the commonwealth.

This policy was fully expounded in a declaration 'concerning the Settlement of Scotland' compiled in October 1651 though not published until February 1652. Parliamentary commissioners for the administration of Scotland were appointed (as they soon were to be for Ireland). Their first priority was to be the advancing of the word of God, protection being given to all who worshipped according to His revealed word. Such toleration would not only allow the spread of Independency in Scotland but would undermine the power over the people of the ministers of the kirk, whom Cromwell believed had misled them. Concerning the 'freedome to be established to the people there', and for future security, Scotland was to be incorporated into one commonwealth with England. To help pay for the wars of 1648 and 1650–51 the estates of all those involved in resistance to the English were to be confiscated (with exceptions for those who had submitted after Dunbar or who had served the commonwealth). Those not liable to punishment who, having at last discovered their true interests, agreed to cooperate with the commonwealth would be taken into parliament's protection and enjoy the liberties of the free people of the commonwealth of England. Vassals and tenants of the nobles and gentry 'the chief Actors in these invasions and wars against England', drawn into participation in the wars by their superiors, would be pardoned if they put themselves under parliament's protection, and would be freed from their former feudal dependences, becoming instead tenants of the State on such easy terms that they could live 'like a free People, delivered (through Gods goodnesse) from their former slaveries, vassalage, and oppressions'.[40]

Thus the English would bring to Scotland not just the sword, but godliness, liberty and prosperity. Apart from the upper classes virtually all stood to gain. Further, not only was Scotland offered all these benefits: she was to be allowed to choose whether she wanted

---

40. C. S. Terry (ed.), *The Cromwellian Union* (Scottish History Society, Edinburgh, 1902), pp. xix, xxi–xxiii; Dow, *Cromwellian Scotland*, pp. 31–2; L. M. Smith, 'Scotland and Cromwell. A study in early modern government' (unpublished D.Phil. dissertation, Univ. of Oxford, 1979), pp. 55–6.

Cromwell, Scotland and Ireland

them. A forcible union would be an unjust union, based on conquest. Thus after the commissioners for the administration of Scotland had issued the declaration of England's intentions, delegates of the shires and burghs were summoned to receive a 'tender' or offer of union. In reality, of course, the English were making an offer that could not be refused. It was made clear that the alternative to accepting the union was to be treated as a conquered people, and under English threats most of the delegates reluctantly declared their acceptance of the offer.[41] To maintain this stage-managed picture of two countries freely entering into union some of the delegates were then sent to London to negotiate details with parliament, but their presence was merely cosmetic. The process of consultation was a solemn farce, but it revealed the English ideal of what the union should be, insisted on in the face of almost universal hostility in Scotland. That the Scots remained stubbornly suspicious of Englishmen bearing gifts was ignored.[42]

The English sincerely saw themselves as acting generously: they were pressing on the Scots the inestimable gift of being treated as Englishmen. As Ludlow remarked, 'How great a condescension it was in the Parliament of England to permit a people they had conquered to have a part in the legislative power.'[43] Cromwell himself had taken no direct part in the moves towards a peace settlement in Scotland, but his approval of it may be assumed: it was entirely consistent with his attitude to the country in previous years. However, as a result of his quarrels with successive parliaments, it was a long time before the new union was formalized: in April 1654 Cromwell (by now Lord Protector) and his Council of State issued an Ordinance of Union, but a parliamentary act did not come until 1657. As in the case of Ireland, however, it was assumed from the first that union was in operation. Scots and Irish representatives were summoned to 'Barebone's Parliament' in 1653 and the Instrument of Government in December which created the Protectorate referred to the Commonwealth as being that of England, Scotland and Ireland, with Scotland (like Ireland) being represented by thirty members of parliament.[44]

---

41. Terry, *Cromwellian Union*, pp. xxvii–xxix; Dow, *Cromwellian Scotland*, pp. 38–41.
42. Dow, *Cromwellian Scotland*, pp. 46–51; Smith, 'Scotland and Cromwell', pp. 57–60.
43. Quoted in Terry, *Cromwellian Union*, p. xv.
44. Ibid., pp. xlvii, xlix–l, lxxiv; C. H. Firth and R. S. Rait (eds), *Acts and Ordinances of the Interregnum, 1642–60* (3 vols, 1911), II, 814, 818–19, 871–5.

IV

Cromwell dreamed of an ideal new society in Ireland, but in reality there were major constraints on the freedom of action of the new regime there. What was the place of the catholic Irish in the new Ireland? Cromwell wrote as if 'the people' of Ireland would benefit from equality before law and good justice, but policies to which the commonwealth was already committed made it almost inevitable that the Irish themselves would be brushed aside as an irrelevance, if not indeed an impediment, to the new just society. Harsh punishment was what was planned for the Irish, and that this would include massive confiscations of land had been made clear by the 1642 Adventurers' Act and further legislation in 1643 and 1649 which provided for payment of the arrears due to soldiers in land in Ireland.[45]

Scotland at least was given a pretence of choice about joining the Commonwealth; Ireland was not consulted. The sorts of benefit and privilege that were offered to most Scots, were only promised in Ireland in vague and general terms, and restrictions and exceptions meant that few if any native Irish would benefit from commonwealth idealism. The October 1651 declaration concerning the settlement of Scotland had been mainly concerned with offering advantages; the 1652 Act for the settlement of Ireland was almost exclusively concerned with punishment. In Scotland the upper classes were to be swept aside to adapt existing society to new ideals; in Ireland almost an entire society was to be destroyed to build a new one, for the guilt of shedding innocent blood was believed to be almost universal. The act was a blueprint for the destruction of the nation – though the preamble of the act denied any design to extirpate 'the entire nation'. All those of rank and quality would be treated according to their 'respective demerits', a phrase which at once indicated that it was assumed that none had merits. Among these classes in society many individuals and categories were singled out for execution. Other landowners, somewhat less guilty, would forfeit their estates, but would receive land elsewhere worth one-third of their value, or in some cases two-thirds. Those whose only crime was that they had not been actively loyal would have one-third of their existing estates confiscated, but would retain the rest. To most of the 'inferior sort' pardon would be granted, sparing their lives and property.[46]

One estimate suggested that if the act had been fully implemented up to half the adult male population of Ireland would have been ex-

45. Corish, 'The Cromwellian regime', p. 360.
46. *Acts and Ordinances*, II, 598–603; Corish, 'The Cromwellian Regime', pp. 357–9.

ecuted. In the event no more than a few hundred were killed, and while this seeming 'leniency' can partly be explained by the fact that many of those liable to execution went into exile – there was an exodus of about 34 000 Irish soldiers and a further 10 000 or so Irish were transported to the West Indies – it also reflects both inefficiency and a gradual moderation of desire for revenge.[47]

The place of the former Irish landowners was to be taken by godly protestants, adventurers whose investments in 1642 had at last matured, and former soldiers. These, and other protestant colonists, would form the basis for the new Irish society. Quite what the fate of the Irish landowners was to be in practice was at first uncertain, with many differences of opinion as to how harshly they should be treated and whether any deserved a degree of mercy through only having been marginally or passively involved in the rebellion or through having shown signs of repentance. Eventually, in 1653, the views of those favouring indiscriminate punishment prevailed: catholic Irish landowners in general would have their estates confiscated, the partial compensation due to them being land in Connaught and County Clare.

The site for this vast Irish penal settlement was not chosen because of its lack of resources (Connaught was regarded as a richer province than Ulster) but for strategic reasons. Penned in between the sea and the River Shannon, with a belt several miles wide of protestant soldier-settlers along the coast and the line of the river surrounding them, in an area remote from the centres of commerce and government in the east, it could be ensured that never again would the Irish present a threat to protestant and English interests.[48]

The scheme to transplant the Irish was vastly ambitious. In addition, it was planned to break up the predominantly Scottish population of parts of Ulster, resettling landowners in other parts of Ireland intermingled with English proprietors, so they would no longer be a political threat.[49] Once Scotland was conquered the schemes for moving the Ulster Scots were shelved: but the transplantation of the Irish went ahead. It proved a major millstone round the

47. Corish, 'The Cromwellian regime', pp. 359–60, 362, 364; R. C. Simington (ed.), *The Transplantation to Connacht, 1654–8* (Irish Manuscripts Commission, Dublin, 1970), p. xxiv.
48. Corish, 'The Cromwellian regime, p. 364; Simington, *Transplantation* pp. vii, x; N. Canny, *From Reformation to Restoration: Ireland, 1534–1660* (Dublin: 1987). p. 220; Barnard, *Cromwellian Ireland*, pp. 10–11.
49 D. Stevenson, *Scottish Covenanters and Irish Confederates* (Belfast, 1981), pp. 285–90.

neck of the regime, for processing the claims of thousands of adventurers and soldiers to land, moving Irish landowners to Connaught, and allocating them land there, represented a huge and complicated administrative burden. Moreover, fundamental flaws and ambiguities in the transplantation and resettlement scheme soon emerged. First, there simply was not enough land available for all the adventurers and soldiers who had valid claims. As a result, much of the land originally assigned to transplanted Irish, including whole counties, was withdrawn from the scheme, while simultaneously the decision not to execute many held to deserve death swelled the numbers of Irish claimants, for those spared were regarded as entitled to land in Connaught. The basic sums for the resettlement of Ireland simply did not add up. As for the ambiguity of the scheme, were all Irish to be transplanted? Or only landlords and their families? The intention at first was probably that virtually all should go: when landlords left, the assumptions was that their tenants, dependants and followers would go with them. But in practice in the great majority of cases this did not happen. In time this was tacitly accepted. As the difficulties of resettling even landlords became clear, limiting the numbers transplanted became expedient. Another argument was even stronger: if the common people were transplanted to Connaught, who would work the land for the new protestant landlords? Hopes for large-scale immigration from England of farmers, farm workers and tradesmen soon faded, so the removal of the Irish labour force would have been a recipe for economic disaster. They were too useful to be uprooted. By the time of the 1657 Act for the attainder of rebels in Ireland it was accepted – though still only tacitly – that only landlords would be forcibly transplanted. But at least where Irish landlords were concerned the transplantation policy was (on its own terms) ultimately fairly successful. Before the troubles catholics had owned about 59 per cent of Irish land: by the 1660s they only owned 20 per cent largely in Connaught. But if concentrating and limiting Irish landownership was accomplished, the attempt to build a new protestant society in the rest of the country failed. Some 12 000 soldiers settled, but most of those entitled to land grants in Ireland, whether soldiers or adventurers, preferred to sell their rights rather than settle in Ireland.[50]

The contrast with Scotland is striking. There too it had originally been planned to disinherit many native landowners, though there had

---

50. Corish, 'The Cromwellian regime', pp. 360–2, 365, 368–70, 373; Simington, *Transplantation*, pp. xx–xxv; Barnard, *Cromwellian Ireland*, p. 11.

been no thought of uprooting whole populations. Virtually all the larger landlords had been involved in making war on England, and it was intended to destroy them – even more thoroughly, indeed, than their Irish counterparts, since there was no provision for compensation in some Scottish Connaught. And what was to happen to confiscated lands in Scotland? Talk of lands being leased on easy terms to those supporting the regime indicated an intention of keeping land in the hands of the State, but in 1651 parliament ordered land grants in Scotland to be made as rewards to senior army officers,[51] and the duke of Hamilton's estates passed into the hands of such officers for some years.[52] In 1654 trustees for confiscated estates were appointed,[53] but their significance was limited as most estates were either returned to their former owners (on payment of fines) or handed over to their creditors.

Confiscating the lands of most great landowners was supposed to secure the stability of the new regime in Scotland, by removing the powerful elements in society hostile to it. In practice the policy had the opposite effect, for it left such men nothing to lose. The result was the incoherent rebellion of 1653–55 known as Glencairn's rising, based on the Highlands and reducing much of northern and central Scotland to chaos.[54]

The rebellion was crushed, but it forced a rethink of policy, and this was reflected in the 1654 Act of Grace and Pardon. Instead of blanket disinheritance of all tainted with war guilt, it listed twenty-four individuals (mainly nobles) who were to lose their estates, and seventy-three other landlords who were only to retain their lands on payment of heavy fines. Other landlords (except any found to have supported the rebellion) were to retain their estates. Further, in the event those excepted from pardon were shown leniency. In the years that followed fines were often substituted for confiscation, and most of the fines were eventually reduced or cancelled altogether. Thus though at first virtual extinction of Scotland's greater landlords had been threatened, in the end they escaped with lighter punishment than English royalists.[55]

51. *C.J.* VII, 14.
52. R. K. Marshall, *The Days of Duchess Anne* (1973), p. 26; *Register of the Great Seal of Scotland, 1652–9* (1904), nos 188, 453, 568; *Register of the Privy Council of Scotland, 1665–9* (1909), pp. 27–8.
53. *Acts and Ordinances*, II, 885–8.
54. Dow, *Cromwellian Scotland*, pp. 42, 53, 57–8.
55. C. H. Firth (ed.), *Scotland and the Protectorate* (Scottish History Society, Edinburgh, 1899), pp. xxvii–xxxi; *Acts and Ordinances*, II, 875–83; Dow, *Cromwellian Scotland*, pp. 77, 112, 117, 122–3, 157.

Clearly the commonwealth had watered down its plans in Scotland. It had accepted that seeking to destroy the great landlords was more trouble than it was worth: it was expedient to try to reconcile them to the regime. This was all the more necessary as by the mid-1650s the regime had to admit that it had not won the support it had hoped for among the common people of Scotland. As the people had failed to respond with loyalty to offers of liberty, it made sense to attempt to recruit their former social superiors to influence and control them. There was no question of restoring the feudal powers and jurisdictions of the mighty, but there was an admission that the exercise of their traditional influence would help stabilize the regime.[56]

This change of emphasis was not, of course, an isolated phenomenon. In other aspects of policy in Scotland, and in England and Ireland as well, Cromwell was turning away from ambitions of radical change to concentrate on more immediate problems of maintaining stability and winning support for a regime which was deeply unpopular throughout Britain, back-peddling on some of the policies which alienated powerful interests. The acceptance of the title of Lord Protector by Cromwell at the end of 1653 was symptomatic of this change, and the change in form of government at the centre was soon reflected in Ireland and Scotland. In 1654 the office of Lord Deputy was revived, and a Council of State was established in Dublin.[57] Scotland did not receive a deputy – such an appointment would have been regarded in Scotland as implying subordination to England. But she received a Council of State, with a president who was Lord Deputy of Scotland in all but name, in 1655.[58] The establishment of two outlying councils, replacing former parliamentary commissioners in both cases, seemed to imply a degree both of decentralization and of recognition that more permanent and formal arrangements than in the past should be made for governing Ireland and Scotland separately from England. Further, just as executive power had been to some extent concentrated in the hands of one man at the centre, the Lord Protector, so such individuals, subordinate to him, should be established in the peripheral capitals.

With changes in policies and in machinery of government went changes in personnel. The majority of the parliamentary commissioners in Ireland, and after them the Lord Deputy (Charles

---

56. Dow, *Cromwellian Scotland*, pp. 159–60; Smith, 'Scotland and Cromwell', pp. 209–10.
57. Barnard, *Cromwellian Ireland*, pp. 19–20; Corish, 'The Cromwellian regime', p. 354
58. Dow, *Cromwellian Scotland*, p. 160; Smith, 'Scotland and Cromwell', pp. 77, 83.

Fleetwood) and his council, had been radical in their religious and political outlooks. Like Cromwell in 1649–50, they saw Ireland as a land where a new godly society could be built. So far as the future was concerned, the native Irish were brushed aside. Even Ireland's 'Old Protestants' – those there before the Cromwellian influx – were excluded from the new design, being suspect through their political actions in the past and for their episcopalian religious inclinations. Thus the 'Old Protestants' found their advice was not needed. The presbyterian Scots in the north were equally anathema to the sectaries who now prevailed in Dublin. But by the mid 1650s the excessive zeal of the Protectorate's representatives in Ireland was becoming an embarrassment to Cromwell in London, for it alienated many unnecessarily. As in Scotland, one of parliament's first priorities in Ireland was to cut costs so the massive subsidies provided by English tax-payers could be reduced. This meant that reconciling as many as possible to the regime so that the expensive armies of occupation could be reduced and encouraging the recovery of the economy so local tax revenue would increase were now given priority.

The anabaptists and other sectaries in power in Dublin in 1652–55, with their exclusive policies and insistence on pushing ahead with harsh transportation policies, seemed almost to be going out of their way to minimize support and maximize disruption. A lead in attacking such policies was taken by Cromwell's son Henry, who was appointed a member of the Irish Council of State in December 1654.[59] Fleetwood remained Lord Deputy in name until late 1657, when Henry replaced him, but Henry was in practice acting deputy from September 1655 as Fleetwood was then recalled to England, leaving Henry as the dominant force on the Irish council. With Henry's rise came more moderate policies. The still powerful Old Protestant interests increasingly found their advice listened to, their support sought. It was in part their arguments about the economic consequences of wholesale transportation of the common Irish to Connaught that led to the policy being tacitly abandoned. Willingness to show favour to presbyterian ministers in the north reconciled many to the regime.[60] Even catholics benefited: while there could be no question of official acceptance of the presence of priests in Ireland, the lessening of repression allowed their numbers to increase significantly in the later 1650s.[61]

59. Abbott, III, 558; Barnard, *Cromwellian Ireland*, pp. 20–1, 98, 102–5, 300, 302.
60. Barnard, *Cromwellian Ireland*, p. 14, 22, 52, 58.
61. Corish, 'The Cromwellian regime', p. 355.

In Scotland the same general process can be observed. The replacement of Robert Lilburne as commander-in-chief in Scotland by George Monck in 1654 substituted a presbyterian and former royalist for an independent, a gesture that was conciliatory – though in fact Lilburne had already begun to urge moderation. It went hand-in-hand with the move away from attempting to destroy the greater landlords and instead making it worth their while to accept the regime. The part played by Henry Cromwell in Ireland was shared in Scotland by Monck and Lord Broghill. The son of the earl of Cork, Broghill had played a prominent part in Irish affairs, helping win over his fellow Old Protestants to support the Commonwealth and seeking to persuade Cromwell that they should be treated better. His views finally prevailed in the mid-1650s, but though Old Protestants were increasingly favoured by the regime it was politically inexpedient to promote one of them to high office in Ireland, so reward for Broghill's services and abilities came through his appointment in 1656 to be president of the Council of State in Scotland. Experience gained in dealing with one outlying territory was thus applied in the other. Under the clear-headed and amiable Broghill, progress was made on two fronts: winning the acceptance, if not the active support, for the regime of the landowning classes; and at least partly solving the religious problems which plagued the regime. Broghill left Scotland in August 1656, but he had set the regime on the course it was to follow until after Cromwell's death.[62]

The number of Scots converted to sectarianism under English- imposed toleration was very limited, though handfuls of Anabaptists, Independents and Quakers can be traced.[63] But this was not seen as necessarily disastrous, for the Church of Scotland was regarded as providing a godly alternative. The problem, as before, was that though Cromwell would tolerate the Presbyterian Church, it would not tolerate him. In any case, the Church was deeply divided. The split which had emerged when the Remonstrants virtually disowned Charles II had spread and solidified. The Protester minority, successors to the Remonstrants, squabbled endlessly with the Resolutioner majority, which supported the exiled king. The split meant that the Church could not unite against the English, and this obviously was to their advantage in some respects, but continued disruption in the church was seen as interfering with the general settlement of the

---

62. Dow, *Cromwellian Scotland*, pp. 162, 210.
63. G. D. Henderson, 'Some early Scottish Independents', in *Religious life in Seventeenth-Century Scotland* (Cambridge, 1937), pp. 100–16.

country. At first the English favoured the Protesters: they had refused to fight for the king, so at least they were not tainted by royalist malignancy. The English hoped to win the Protesters' support by giving them control of the Church and helping them against the Resolutioners. In fact there was no real possibility of this: the Protesters would not accept the legitimacy of a regime which insisted on State supervision of the Church and on toleration.[64]

Broghill swiftly broke the religious deadlock. Seeing that the Resolutioners' hostility was partly a reaction to the regime's support for the Protesters, he decided to see what could be done by offering a share of favour to the Resolutioners. In return he did not ask for promises of loyalty to the Protectorate, but simply that ministers should live quietly under the regime and give up their public prayers for Charles II. It is a mark of Broghill's charm and skill as a negotiator that most Resolutioners accepted this tacit bargain in 1656.[65] But further hopes, of reconciling the two factions in the Kirk and winning their positive support for the regime, failed. Representatives of both parties debated the matter with Cromwell in London in 1657, but he found Scots ministers as reluctant as ever to accept his ideas, and threatened that if they could not reform themselves 'an extraordinary remedy' should be employed.[66] But in reality he knew that any attempt to impose unity on the Kirk would cause massive resentment which would be politically dangerous. He could defeat the Scots in war, but not in debate.

Nonetheless, at least a settled parish ministry preached godly doctrine throughout most of Scotland, and in this the country was in a much more satisfactory condition than Ireland. The organization and ministry of the Church of Ireland had been destroyed by the wars since 1641. The commonwealth sought to build a new Church, but there was never any official decision as to precisely what form it should take. At first the anabaptists prevailed, but the efforts of their officially sponsored sectarian preachers were concentrated on newcomers – English soldiers and administrators – with little attempt to cater even for other protestants. The best organized Protestant ministry in the country, that of presbyterian ministers in Ulster, was regarded as an alien Scots intrusion to be repressed. Many had expected that propagation of the Gospel in Ireland would mean

---

64. Abbott, IV, 399–400
65. Dow, *Cromwellian Scotland*, pp. 195–8, 206; J. Buckroyd, 'Lord Broghill and the Scottish church, 1655–6', *Journal of Ecclesiastical History*, XXVII (1976), 359–68.
66. Abbott, IV, 399–404, 618–19.

primarily an attempt to persuade the catholic Irish of the error of their ways, but this was neglected: at heart, it seems, the country's rulers believed trying to convert them was a waste of time. That many wanted transplantation to Connaught to involve Irish commons as well as landowners seemed to reflect such despairing attitudes to the redemption of the Irish, for such a policy would have created an entirely catholic population in much of the province. Those who came to argue against transplanting the commons added to economic arguments a religious one taking a more optimistic view of the potential of the Irish: if the commons were allowed to remain scattered through the country, where most would have protestant landlords and (hopefully) preachers and neighbours, there might be a real chance of converting them.[67]

However, though in the later 1650s a few gestures were made towards concern for the spiritual welfare of the Irish,[68] the emphasis remained on providing a ministry for existing protestants. Henry Cromwell, alarmed by the divisive and exclusive policies of the anabaptists, switched official favour to the independents instead. But they proved just as intolerant of rivals, trying to impose their own monopoly of influence, and eventually Henry swung round to supporting the presbyterians. In 1655 he reached an agreement with the dominant (as in Scotland) Resolutioner party among the presbyterian ministers, whereby they would receive government salaries without having to make any political commitment which would interfere with their loyalty to Charles II. The policy was unpopular both in England and with new protestants in Ireland, but it worked – and formed a precedent for the similar 1656 agreement with the Resolutioners in Scotland. The numbers of State-sponsored ministers rose from about 110 in 1655 to about 250 in 1658, but this was still a remarkably low total – and it was achieved largely by the inclusion of existing presbyterian ministers rather than by provision of new preachers. Overall the efforts of the regime to spread the Gospel in Ireland were a humiliating failure.[69] There was little more success in education. Many had hoped that encouragement of education would convert Irish children. But by 1659 there were only thirty-five State-supported parish schoolmasters – and they mainly served English garrisons.[70] If things were better in Scotland it was, again, because

---

67. Barnard, *Cromwellian Ireland*, pp. 12–13, 91–6, 102–21.
68. Ibid., pp. 135, 171–82, 297–8.
69. Ibid., pp. 122–9, 143, 146–7, 155–7, 168.
70. Ibid., pp. 97, 183, 186–8, 194, 206.

the existing established Church there had not been destroyed by war and continued to support schools and universities. As in Ireland, Cromwellian attempts to increase the resources devoted to education were welcome, but very limited.[71]

Propagation of the Gospel was almost invariably the first priority in commonwealth declarations and instructions to officials in both Scotland and Ireland. Good intentions were frustrated in Ireland by lack of money, indecision about what sort of religious settlement should be made, and despair about the unregenerate Irish. In Scotland they were frustrated by failure to establish a relationship based on mutual trust with either faction in the Church. Another high priority repeatedly stated by the commonwealth was the spread of justice and liberty. People must be treated equally by the law, whatever their social status. Justice should be impartial, cheap, and reasonably swift. But as in so many other spheres, early reforming zeal soon gave way to expediency. The judicial system had collapsed in Ireland, so there was an opportunity for a new start. But though the building of a largely new systems of courts began, it was soon abandoned. In 1655 the traditional Four Courts were revived, and soon the legal system became almost indistinguishable from that which had existed in 1641. Not only was reverting to old ways convenient, especially when there was much disagreement about what should replace them, but the speedy justice of those zealous for new ways had often turned out to be summary justice, making reverting to old procedures welcome.[72] In any case, as far as the great majority of the population was concerned, talk of liberty was a mockery, for justice as applied to them was a euphemism for punishment.

Scotland differed from Ireland in that instead of largely conforming to English law she had her own law and procedures.[73] The general assumption among Scotland's conquerors was that in law (as in many other matters) things English were superior to things Scots. Thus, paradoxically, while the existing legal system in England was under strong attack for its many defects, north of the border it was presented as a model for Scotland. There was, however, no attempt at immediate wholesale introduction of English law. The old feudal jurisdictions vanished along with the old central courts (the Court of Session and Court of Justiciary), which were replaced by commis-

---

71. Dow, *Cromwellian Scotland*, pp. 58–60; Abbott, III, 395, 874; IV, 794–5, 582–3, 825, 852–3.
72. Barnard, *Cromwellian Ireland*, pp. 249–61, 267–8, 274–7.
73. Ibid., p. 250.

sioners for civil and for criminal justice. But the new courts continued to work, with a few exceptions, in accordance with existing Scots law. Parliament's instructions in 1652 were that English law was to be introduced only 'as to matters of government', and even then only as far as 'the constitution and use of the people there' and circumstances permitted.[74]

The quality of justice provided by the Cromwellian regime in Scotland is often cited as a major achievement,[75] but the praise heaped on it appears to be exaggerated. Glowing tributes by Englishmen to their achievements among the benighted Scots should not be accepted uncritically, for obviously they are likely to be biased, and the one Scottish source supporting them is no more convincing. In his *Diary* John Nicoll writes enthusiastically of how fast and impartial English-administered justice was, and how delighted litigants were with it in comparison with old Scottish justice.[76] However, Nicoll requires to be used with great care, for he himself explained that what he wrote was not what he believed, but 'the reall wordis, deidis and actiones' of those in power at the time.[77] Thus the views he expressed changed according to what regime was in power, and he is not a reliable witness.

It would, however, be going too far to say English rule brought no benefits in the administration of justice in Scotland. It seems very likely that the English judges were more impartial than their predecessors, less influenced by vested interests and the power of great men. But above all what contributed to making the courts popular was the simple fact that they sat regularly and gave judgments at all. Scotland had experienced nearly fifteen years of turmoil, during which much had happened that tended to increase the amount of litigation, while the meetings of courts had frequently been interrupted. Thus for many, any settled system of justice which resolved cases was welcome. The commonwealth worked hard and honestly

---

74. Firth, *Scotland and the Protectorate*, p. 395. H. R. Trevor-Roper, 'Scotland and the Puritan Revolution', *Religion, the Reformation and Social Change* (1967), p. 420, erroneously cites this as a general attempt to introduce English law into Scotland.

75. Trevor-Roper, 'Scotland and the Puritan Revolution', pp. 418, 421; Dow, *Cromwellian Scotland*, 56; A. R. G. McMillan, 'The judicial system of the Commonwealth in Scotland', *Juridical Review* (1937), pp. 232–55, Smith, 'Scotland and Cromwell', pp. 120–1, 244.

76. J. Nicoll, *A diary of public transactions and other occurrences, chiefly in Scotland, from January 1650 to June 1667* (Bannatyne Club, Edinburgh, 1836), pp. 64, 66, 69, 104.

77. Ibid., pp. ix–x; D. Stevenson, 'The covenanters and the court of session, 1637–51', *Judicial Review* (1972), pp. 244–5.

to improve justice in Scotland, and the number of cases settled is impressive. But the evidence for this being perceived as a major benefit by Scots is unconvincing.[78]

The other main benefits that the Cromwellian regime sought to bring to the people of Scotland were freedom from feudal and clerical oppression. Again there is virtually no evidence of a positive response to this. The abolition of feudal jurisdictions and superiorities appears to have been greeted with indifference.[79] Moreover, the regime never even got round to the formal abolition of feudal tenure in Scotland,[80] and even some regality and baron courts seem to have continued to meet on a feudal basis (rather than in the guise of the new 'courts baron' introduced in 1654 to replace them).[81] In religion few Scots had a real chance to exercise their new liberties, for the intolerant Kirk remained dominant in most parishes. It is doubtful if the vast majority of Scots noticed that they had new liberties, civil or religious, and as the regime moved towards reconciliation with landlords and with the Resolutioner majority of ministers the possibility of such liberties meaning anything in the future declined.

By the time of Cromwell's death in September 1658 there was in Scotland a growing feeling of returning normalcy – or acceptance of a new normalcy for the time being as there seemed no immediate prospect of anything better. At least the regime was now trying to make itself attractive to powerful interests such as landowners and ministers. It still had to be based on an army of occupation, but its numbers were declining – from about 18,000 in 1654 to an establishment of about 10,500 in 1657.[82] Increasingly English civilians were taking over from soldiers in civil offices, though their numbers remained small. The numbers of Scots prepared to hold office or sit in parliament grew – though again progress was slow.[83] Relations

---

78. Smith, 'Scotland and Cromwell', pp. 106–21, 244; Dow, *Cromwellian Scotland*, p. 221.
79. Trevor-Roper, 'Scotland and the Puritan Revolution', p. 418, cites enthusiastic Scots in 1651 crying 'Free the poor commoners and make as little use as can be either of the great men or clergy'. But though the cry did come from Scotland the context makes it clear that it was in fact the cry of the English conquerors. See C. H. Firth, *Scotland and the Commonwealth* (Scottish History Society, Edinburgh, 1895), pp. 339.
80. See C. J. VII, 407, 427 for attempts to do so.
81. Smith, 'Scotland and Cromwell', pp. 205–7.
82. C. J. Firth, *The Last Years of the Protectorate* (2 vols, Oxford, 1900), II, 87–8.
83. Dow, *Cromwellian Scotland* pp. 149–50, 177, 179–81, 185–8, 221–2; P. J. Pinckney, 'The Scottish representation in the Cromwellian parliament of 1656', *Scottish Historical Review*, XLVI (1967), 95–114.

with English officers and officials were often good. Broghill in particular won a good reputation through both personality and policies, and Geneal Monck was respected.[84] Yet the repeated themes of Robert Baillie's summaries of the state of the country from 1654 to 1659 are negative – military occupation, deep poverty ('the English hes all the moneyes'), high taxes, nobility broken, commons oppressed.[85] Monck's reports were little more optimistic: things were 'well' in that Scotland was quiet, but at heart the Scots were still malignant.[86]. Cromwell himself, just months before his death, described Scotland as 'a very ruined nation'.[87] The mood seems one of desolation. If Cromwell had not quite made a desert, he had created something that Scots found hard to think of positively as peace.

That the great and idealistic ambitions of Oliver Cromwell for Scotland and Ireland were thwarted, that he remained conqueror rather than a liberator, is of course no surprise: the same is true in England, where his regime was endured rather than loved. Next to lack of positive support from the populations concerned, the most basic of all problems was money. Visions for reform often failed because they were expensive in themselves, or because they entailed alienating powerful interests – which in turn meant that increased military expenditure was necessary. Even after radical policies were abandoned Ireland and Scotland showed no prospect of becoming self-supporting. In 1659 Scotland's regime needed a subsidy from England of £164,000 – 53 per cent of total public expenditure.[88] Ireland at least covered 75 per cent of her own costs of government, but even here the expected deficit for 1658 to be met by England was anticipated as £96,000.[89] There was no realistic possibility of either nation being able to pay its own way until the armies of occupation were very greatly reduced in size – and there seemed little prospect in the near future of it being safe to do that.

Another major problem concerned the personnel of government. Who was to adjudicate and administer in Scotland and Ireland? There were three constraints that made this a problem. First was acceptability to the regime. In Ireland almost the whole population was disqualified from office, and the same was true of Scotland's ruling

84. Nicoll, *Diary*, p. 183; Baillie, *Letters*, III 315, 321.
85. Baillie, *Letters*, III, 249–50, 252, 287, 289, 317, 357, 387.
86. Dow, *Cromwellian Scotland*, p. 228.
87. Abbott, IV, 718.
88. Dow, *Cromwellian Scotland*, p. 219.
89. Barnard, *Cromwellian Ireland*, pp. 26–7.

élites at first. In the early years civil government was very much subordinate to military, and leading officers held civil offices, later being joined by English civilians. Soon, particularly in Scotland, office was opened to those inhabitants regarded as suitable, the plan being for offices to be divided between natives and Englishmen. But here the second constraint appeared: many to whom the privilege of office was offered declined it, not being willing to serve the regime. And the final constraint was that the number of Englishmen of ability willing to accept office in the outlying countries of the commonwealth was very limited. The results were continuing involvement of army officers in civil affairs – since they were qualified and on the spot – and that the small numbers of English civilian administrators often held several positions at once, leading to inefficiency. And though the loyalty of English administrators might be certain, their experience of the countries they were helping to rule often limited their effectiveness.[90]

Another problem lay in uncertainty as to where power in making decisions and appointments lay – in Dublin and Edinburgh, or in London? Frequently those unable to get their way in the sub-capitals of the Commonwealth by-passed them and got favourable decisions from Cromwell or parliament, thus undermining the authority of those struggling to rule in Edinburgh and Dublin.[91] Further, decisions based on ignorance of circumstances were often made in London which were difficult or impossible to implement in the peripheral nations of the commonwealth. Before the troubles Scotland and Ireland had suffered from being governed by a system of absentee monarchy. The 1650s experiments proved that absentee republican government could be just as blundering, ignorant and insensitive, with just as little time or priority for their concerns. That an act of union for Ireland was never passed; that Ireland was left without a civil government for two months in 1657 through delays in commissioning a new Lord Deputy, that Scotland was ordered to set up new courts baron based on 'manors' (which did not exist in Scottish land law) were all examples of the 'haphazard processes of the Cromwellian regime'.[92] In both countries news of Cromwell's death was greeted with apprehension, for it opened up worrying

90. Ibid., pp. 12–13, 19–20, 25, 284, 287; Dow, *Cromwellian Scotland*, pp. 162–4; Smith, 'Scotland and Cromwell', pp. 102, 134.
91. Barnard, *Cromwellian Ireland*, p. 25; Smith, 'Scotland and Cromwell', pp. 99, 101.
92. Barnard, *Cromwellian Ireland*, pp. 21–2, 98, 294; Smith, 'Scotland and Cromwell', p. 102; *Acts and Ordinances*, II, 883.

questions of what would follow, but in neither country was there much sorrow except among the members of the English armies and administrations of occupation. With the restoration of monarchy in 1660 the parliamentary unions with Scotland and Ireland were dissolved: not until 1801 were the three legislatures again to be united.

One final observation on Cromwell's attitude to the outlying kingdoms within the British Isles is called for. He conquered them and incorporated them into a single State. But it retained a tripartite name: the Commonwealth of England, Scotland and Ireland. Cromwell might rule the entire archipelago, but its periphery had only been conquered to protect England, and for 'God's Englishman' the name of England was sacrosanct, the concept of 'Britain' an unwelcome intrusion associated with the ambitions of the Stuarts and the covenanters which had threatened England's identity. He had dreams of just and godly futures for Ireland and Scotland – through making them little Englands; but England would remain England.

Abbreviations

Abbott: W.C. Abbott, *The Writings and Speeches of Oliver Cromwell* (4 vols., Cambridge, Mass., 1937–47)

Gardner, *Great Civil War*: S.R. Gardner, *History of the Great Civil War, 1642–9*, (4 vols., London, 1893)

V

Professor Trevor-Roper and the Scottish Revolution

1 April, 1976 Professor Hugh Trevor-
.oper, now Lord Dacre of Glanton, lent
1e authority of the Regius Chair of
1odern History at Oxford to the remark-
ɔle statement that the Scottish political
ʳstem before the Act of Union of 1707
ʳas simply 'political banditry'. He then
ʳoceeded, in the same article in *The
'imes*, to the even more extraordinary
ssertion that this tradition was not yet
ead, as 'we have seen it at work in the
cotch province of Ulster from 1922 till
had to be suspended there, too, in
972'. Trevor-Roper's article was written
ʂ a contribution to the debate on
ʲevolution, and he was trying to show
ɪat any attempt to undo the Union of
ʲ07 would lead to disaster for the Scots,
ʂ history had proved that they were
tterly incapable of governing them-
ʲlves competently.

From this context one might conclude
ɪat these statements should be ignored
ʲ historians on the grounds that they
ɛre wild and ill-considered assertions
ade in the heat of the moment during a
ʲssionate political controversy. But in
ɪt they are more than this, being per-
ɪps the most extreme of many arguments
ʲd assertions made over many years by
ʳevor-Roper, which appear to be based
1 a commitment to the 1707 Union
hich is so strong that nothing interest-
g or creditable can be admitted to have
me from Scotland before that date.

Trevor-Roper's most sustained exposition of this interpretation of Scottish
history first appeared in 1963 in the
form of an essay on 'Scotland and the
Puritan Revolution'. The essay undoubtedly contains some profound insights, and it has proved influential
through making sense of complex and
seemingly chaotic events by elegantly-
stated and superficially persuasive
arguments. But these arguments rest on
a caricature of the society, economy,
politics and religion of seventeenth-
century Scotland.

Before considering his arguments, let
us look briefly at the complicated relations between England and Scotland in
the mid-seventeenth century.

In 1603 James VI of Scotland had
succeeded to the English throne as James
I. In this Union of the Crowns the two
kingdoms maintained their separate
identities, being joined only by the fact
that they had a sovereign in common.
Accession to the English throne greatly
increased James' power and prestige as
King of Scotland, enabling him to speed
up his work of restoring royal power
there in both church and state. In the
church the demands of the presbyterians
for a kirk free from royal control and
without a clerical hierarchy were defeated;
the powers of bishops were restored, and
through them the King governed the
church. But royal policies and the effects

of the 1603 Union led to increasing discontent in Scotland. Scots came to believe that their country was being ruled in England's interests, and that official policies were designed to make Scotland as like England as possible. Such feelings were already evident in the later years of James VI, and after his death in 1625 they grew fast under his inflexible and politically incompetent son, Charles I. This discontent culminated in open resistance to the King in 1637, and in the signing of the National Covenant in 1638. The occasion of the Covenanters' revolt was religious – opposition to innovations in worship imposed by the King – and it was religion that was used to justify resistance to the King and to give unity to those who opposed him; but constitutional and other secular grievances also contributed powerfully to the revolt.

In the 'Bishops' Wars' of 1639–40 Charles I, facing increasing opposition in England, failed in his attempts to use the resources of that kingdom to crush the Covenanters, and in 1640 they successfully invaded England. In negotiations in 1640–41 Charles was forced to accept the establishment of presbyterian church government in Scotland and severe limitations in his power in the state.

The Covenanters may have triumphed in Scotland but as England drifted into civil war in 1642 between King and Parliament, the Scots felt they had to intervene. In the early stages of the war it looked as though the King was going to win, and it was obvious that if he was successful in asserting his absolute power in England, he would then turn to destroying his opponents in Scotland. In 1643, therefore, by the Solemn League and Covenant and a military treaty, the Covenanters agreed to send

an army to help the English Parliament In return Parliament promised religiou reforms in England on Scottish pres byterian lines, and other reforms designe to protect Scotland's interests.

The Scottish army which fought i England in 1644–46 played an essentia part in bringing about Parliament' victory over the King. But tension gre between the allies, for it seemed to th Covenanters that Parliament had a cepted their help, but then refused t carry out the promises in return fc which that help had been given. Di illusionment with the English Parliamer ultimately led many Covenanters to cor clude that they should ally themselve with the now defeated King and, throug him, impose a settlement in Englar which would safeguard Scottish inte ests. As a result of this, in 1648 tl 'Engagers', an alliance of modera Covenanters and Royalists, invade England. But there they were prompt defeated by Cromwell, and with h approval and help the extreme pre byterian 'Kirk Party' regime seize power in Scotland and rigorously purge all Engagers from the Scottish Parli ment. But when Cromwell proceeded execute Charles I and abolish monarcl in 1649, the Kirk Party refused to acce this unilateral action by the English matters which clearly concerned bo kingdoms. The Scots therefore pr claimed Charles II King of England well as Scotland, and sought to resto him to his English throne. This provoke English retaliation, and in 1650–5 Cromwell conquered Scotland.

In interpreting the complicated inte actions of these two kingdoms, Trevo Roper acutely concentrated on revealir the consistency that underlies the supe ficial confusion of events. In the 164(

he Scottish covenanters tried repeatedly o export their revolution to England, but failed because it proved unacceptable to the English. Eventually this interference in English affairs forced the English into the conquest of Scotland, and in the 1650s the process was reversed; the English sought to export heir revolution to Scotland. But they in urn found that their revolution was unacceptable to their neighbours.

Thus far Trevor-Roper's arguments are interesting and persuasive. But when he proceeds to examine the differences between the two kingdoms his arguments become highly misleading. Firstly, he Scotland depicted by Trevor-Roper s a land of truly remarkable backwardness, economically, socially and culturally. Secondly, while he emphasises the importance of Scottish intervention in England, he defines Scots influences on he English revolution far too narrowly. Repeated Scottish military intervention s rightly seen as having major effects on the course of events. And Scottish attempts to impose presbyterianism in England are seen as significant, though only because they provoke hostile reaction. Thus the ideals and aims of the Scots are seen purely in religious terms; and even these religious ideals are taken to have had no contribution to make to English ideals except through the strength with which they were rejected.

These two arguments are closely related, and both are central to Trevor-Roper's contention that the reason that he revolutions of the neighbouring kingdoms proved incompatible was that the two societies were at very different stages of development. Scottish society was so backward that the ideology of its revolution could have no relevance to England; and the ideals of the English revolution were equally irrelevant to Scotland.

That Scotland was backward at this time compared to England is clear. She was much poorer than her great neighbour, through limited natural resources, an inefficient agricultural system, and a relatively small share in international trade. Population was stagnant, economic growth slow. But Trevor-Roper pushes his argument about Scottish economic, and therefore social, backwardness to extraordinary extremes, asserting that the country was entirely free from the sort of economic strains that were leading to tensions and changes in other European societies. Scotland, we are told, was a land 'without merchants'; Edinburgh was 'devoid of mercantile spirit'. In fact, though Scotland's merchants were relatively few, and relatively poor, by no definition can it be said she had none. To take one outstanding example, Sir William Dick of Braid, the greatest Edinburgh merchant of his day, lent huge sums to the Covenanters to support their resistance to the King, and his son Lewis Dick subscribed far more as an 'Adventurer' for the reconquest of Ireland in 1642 than any Englishman, merchant or otherwise. Dick of Braid was of course far from typical, but all the larger Scottish burghs had plenty of merchants engaging in international as well as local trade. Even more extraordinary is Trevor-Roper's assertion that Scotland experienced 'no inflation'. The great sixteenth-century price revolution which caused economic and social strains throughout Europe evidently halted abruptly at England's northern border, considerately leaving Scotland's fossilised economy to slumber on undisturbed. Such a suggestion is inherently improbable, and even the most superficial examination proves its inaccuracy. The fact that the pound sterling was worth four pounds Scots in 1560 and twelve pounds Scots in 1600 demonstrates that the value of the Scots currency had collapsed relative to sterling, and there is plenty of evidence of fast-rising prices within Scotland. But Trevor-Roper, it seems, felt free to discuss the Scottish economy without apparently taking into consideration any of the works published on the topic.

When Trevor-Roper turns to the social structure of seventeenth-century Scotland one can sympathise with his complaint that so far as published work was concerned the subject was 'a blank'. Into this void he modestly proposes to offer some general suggestions 'with prudent caution' as he is a 'foreigner' rashly intruding. The apology is strange, implying the existence of a convention that only the natives of a country are really qualified to write on its history; and what undermines his contribution to Scottish seventeenth-century social history is not that he is 'foreign' but that, again, he appears not to have done his homework. Moreover, the promised 'prudent caution' is thrown to the winds in favour of dogmatic assertion. Scottish society is seen, like her economy, as static. Most important of all, Scotland 'lacked altogether the new class of educated laymen on which the greatness of Tudor England had been built'; for practical purposes the educated middle classes consisted of lawyers and clergy, 'the pillars of conservatism'. In England an educated laity had kept Calvinist clerics in their place; in Scotland the laity were not strong enough to do this, and the clerics were thus able to indulge their theocratic pretensions. The revolution which the Covenanters tried to export to England was essentially this theocratic revolution of the clerics.

This argument immediately raises difficulties, for it leads to two major inconsistencies. Firstly, Trevor-Roper has been insisting that Scotland was entirely free from the sort of major strains and pressures that had been transforming English society. But now another strand of his argument has led to the assertion that in one central respect, religious reformation, Scotland had seen much more radical change than England. This difficulty is seen, and is surmounted by a daring temporary reversal of previous assumptions. In all other matters lack of radical change has held back social change in Scotland; but in religion, it is asserted, it was the very fact that change *was* radical that *prevented* tensions arising and leading to social change! Because Scottish society had 'experienced a more radical religious reformation, it no longer felt certain ancient pressures'; whereas England's partial reformation had left elements of old and new to confront each other and thus create tensions. The argument is ingenious, but in the context smacks of special pleading. Further, it does not accord with the facts. Certainly there were Calvinist clerics in Scotland who would have liked to establish the theocratic, conservative tyranny that Trevor-Roper believes to have existed; but they did not get their way. They were out-manoeuvred and crushed in the first decade of the seventeenth century by James VI with the help of the independent lay elements that Trevor-Roper seems to believe did not exist. Scots nobles and lairds tended to be as hostile to the pretensions of the clergy as English nobles and gentry. For though Scottish society was not experiencing change at the same speed as English society, similar types of change were taking place, in response to similar types of pressure – inflation, the transfer of great areas of church lands into lay hands, reformation, and the emergence of the lairds (lesser tenants-in-chief) into a more active role in national affairs, independent of the nobility. Very little work has been done to chart and evaluate these changes; but this is no excuse for asserting that no change took place at all. The Scottish nobles like their English counterparts were suffering economic problems and challenges to their role in society, both from below, and from an increasingly powerful monarchy which sought to centralise power and (by its prodigality in creating new titles) seemed to threaten the older nobility through inflation of honours. Indeed in Scotland the challenge to the old ruling classes from an absolutist monarchy, bureaucratic and centralising, was in a sense greater than in England, for by the union of the crowns power was 'centralised' to the point at which it withdrew from Scotland altogether. The sort of alienation and tension expressed in 'country' versus 'court' divisions became intensified when the court was an absentee one. Yet Trevor-Roper does not see that Scotland suffered from any strains from such developments in monarchy and government, in spite of the fact that Scotland, of course, shared with England the kings responsible for such policies in England in the early seventeenth century.

The second inconsistency that arises from Trevor-Roper's picture of a Scotland dominated by a clerical tyranny concerns the position of the nobility. If Presbyterian ministers were the real masters of Scotland, clearly the nobility must have been subordinate to them. Yet to accept this would mean abandoning one of the main elements which appear in interpretations like Trevor-

Roper's which stress Scotland's remarkable backwardness – all-powerful nobles, acting oppressively towards those below them in society, feuding violently among themselves, and successfully defying the Crown. It is not surprising to find that such over-mighty subjects do appear in Trevor-Roper's interpretations; but their relationship with the clergy is left vague, for to discuss the matter explicitly would make it obvious that both groups could not simultaneously wield despotic power over the kingdom. Trevor-Roper does stress the great and arbitrary powers of the nobility both before and after the 1640s. Thus we are told of the 'great, incorrigible feudatories' of Scotland who made kings their 'playthings' before 1603 (which in itself is a very questionable assertion). Similarly, in dealing with the 1650s, Trevor-Roper argues that 'the despotism of the Church' in Scotland was 'hardly less formidable than the despotism of the great nobles'. Thus the nobles evidently had the edge on the clergy when it came to despotism. But what were these great feudal nobles doing in the 1640s? Nothing is said on this, for to mention them here would undermine the picture of Scotland in the 1640s as the plaything of clerics determined on theocratic revolution to which Trevor-Roper is committed. Only once is the role of the nobility hinted at, suggesting that perhaps after all it was not the clergy who were supreme. We are told that in backward, clerical-dominated Scotland 'those who wished to mobilise the people . . . had to use the tribunes of the people', the clergy. This was hardly uniquely Scottish. What about the role of Puritan preachers in England or Catholic priests in the 1640 revolt of the Catalans? But what is significant in this context is the suggestion that other interests, by implication lay ones, existed behind the clerics of Scotland and 'used' them. But these interests are never identified, and apart from this hint it is assumed that the clergy and their ambitions dominate Scotland.

The differences which led Trevor-Roper to conclude that Scotland and England were 'poles apart', that an 'immense social gulf' lay between them, thus turn out not to be so extreme after all. Clearly there were major differences between the two societies, but his analysis is based on a crude caricature of Scottish society. He suggests that to Englishmen of the 1640s 'Scotland . . . is not an intelligible society responding to intelligible social forces'; but the same charge can be made against his own approach, and indeed his views on Scotland bear a good deal of similarity to those presented by many English propagandists in the 1640s. It is remarkable that the author of a seminal essay on 'The General Crisis of the Seventeenth Century' could appear to believe that Scotland was entirely isolated from the forces and trends that shaped that crisis.

Turning to the nature and effects of Scottish intervention in England in the 1640s, Trevor-Roper rightly sees the Covenanters as seeking to export their revolution in order to bring it security. How could they be confident of retaining the concessions they had forced from the King if he retained full power in his other, much greater kingdom, England? But, having interpreted the revolution which had taken place in Scotland in purely religious terms, Trevor-Roper can only see the religious side of the changes that the Covenanters demanded in England. They tried to impose their church: theocratic, intolerant and tyran-

nical. The attempt inevitably failed, fo this church, though well suited to Scot land's backward society, was totall inappropriate to an English societ dominated by lay interests. 'Except fo a few clergymen, tempted by clericc power, there were no English presby terians.' But such innate abhorrence c presbyterianism was disguised by man English parliamentarians in 1640–4 and 1643–44 in order to buy Scottis military aid by a pretence of willing ness to accept such a church. Now it certainly true that many in England op posed presbyterianism on the Scottis model, and did so because they feare that a church which claimed indeper dence of the state would move on t demand theocratic domination over th state. But, ironically, many of these fea might have been stilled had the Englis looked at the Covenanters' religiou practice rather than at their theorie For in Scotland the lay Covenante had kept firm control over the churcl As Professor Gordon Donaldson h; written, 'all in all, the presbyterian syste proved admirably adapted to be an ir strument of the aristocracy and gentry Like their English counterparts, the la Covenanters had no wish to free then selves from the clerical tyranny bishops only to fall under the cleric tyranny of presbyterian ministers. In th light of Trevor-Roper's interpretatio there is irony in the fact that the close that Scotland even came to the theocrac he posits was in 1648–50 under th Kirk Party; for this regime, a minori faction of the extreme Covenanters, w helped to power by English interventic in Scotland.

But though in Scotland most la Covenanters of any status in society (a indeed many of the clergy) successful pposed presbyterian pretensions to ominate society and the state in practice, a theory they usually supported such retensions in order to maintain the nity of the covenanting movement. 'his tacit compromise benefited the covenanters within Scotland; but it roved a fatal obstacle to them in trying o sell their religious revolution in ngland. Having demanded the establishent of an autonomous church on resbyterian lines, it was impossible for em to add, reassuringly, that in ractice laymen could control this church y acting as elders. Thus however much ne Scots urged that presbyterianism epresented a happy medium between ne tyranny of episcopacy and the anarchy f independency, most Englishmen reained deeply suspicious of its theoratic implications.

Trevor-Roper has interpreted correctly ne of the major reasons for the refusal f the English to accept reformation on cottish lines (though 'Scots' presbyterianm did have a considerable number of nglish supporters, especially in London), ut he has misinterpreted the Scottish ackground that gave rise to the problem. Moreover, he makes this fear of lerical tyranny the only reason for nglish refusal to import Scotland's evolution. But there were other reasons, nd at times determination to reject cotland's religion through this argument vas little more than a rationalisation of general determination to reject all hings Scots. After their early triumphs, ne Covenanters urged their revolution religious and, as will be argued below, onstitutional) on the English with an rrogance and tactlessness which invitably provoked massive nationalistic esentment. Many Englishmen felt umiliated at having to rely on military

help from their despised northern neighbours, and at having to purchase this aid by agreeing (however insincerely) to consider making changes in England suggested – or dictated – by the Scots. One of those who led in expressing such patriotic determination to resist Scottish demands was Oliver Cromwell, who won much popularity by his attitude. Trevor-Roper tends to dismiss those who question his views on Scottish history as Scottish nationalists, but he ignores the existence of English nationalism.

Trevor-Roper succeeds in presenting the Scots in England as concerned solely with religion, by quoting only the ministers among the Scots Commissioners who negotiated with the English Parliament in 1640-41 and 1644-47. The lay Commissioners sent by the state are totally ignored. So, indeed, are the ministers when they stray off purely religious topics and display wider interests. Alexander Henderson, one of the most widely respected of the Kirk's ministers, produced the 'Instructions for Defensive Arms' (1639), listing constitutional as well as religious justifications for opposing the King in arms. This work was thought relevant enough to English preoccupations on the eve of civil war to be twice printed in London. Lex Rex, a major treatise on mixed monarchy by Samuel Rutherford (Professor of Divinity at St. Andrews, 1639-47), was first published in 1644 in London, and aroused much interest. But such indications that some ministers at least could see beyond the joys of clerical tyranny are ignored by Trevor-Roper. He frequently quotes, with a sort of fascinated contempt, Robert Baillie, 'the voluble, invaluable letter writer, that incomparable Scotch dominie, so learned, so acute, so factual, so complacent, so unshakably omniscient, so infallibly wrong'. Baillie (Professor of Divinity at Glasgow, 1642–61) is used to show how the Scots, obsessed with religion and incapable of interpreting events in a society so different from their own, misunderstood what was happening in England. However, though Baillie is held to be infallibly wrong about England, Trevor-Roper treats him as infallibly right about Scotland and the clerical nature of the Scottish revolution. But when Baillie was wrong about England he was at least as much wrong because he was a minister as because he was a Scot. Many English ministers, like Baillie, saw events in bigoted religious terms, and the narrowness of his vision, it is arguable, renders his interpretations of events in Scotland almost as suspect as his views on England. In 1648, when the Engagers defied the church in Scotland, raised an army and invaded England, Baillie was forced into realisation that his belief in the clerical nature of the Scottish revolution, which he assumed had left the church able to dominate the state, had been wrong. The covenanting state had shown, in its first open clash with the church, that it could prevail, leaving Baillie as bewildered about Scotland as he had been about events in England.

What then were the non-religious ambitions of the Scots in England? Firstly, having destroyed royal power in their state as well as in their church, they wanted to do the same in England. Not until the English Parliament had been put in a position to prevent the King using English resources against Scotland would their revolution in Scotland be safe. Secondly, to the personal union of the crowns the Covenanters wished to add permanent links between the Parliaments of the two kingdoms through joint meetings of English and Scottish Parliamentary commissioners This loose federal structure would be used to prevent quarrels between the kingdoms (and especially to prevent the King trying to use one against the other) and to ensure that Scotland had an equal say with England in matters of joint concern – foreign policy, commercial policy (free trade between the kingdoms was to be established) and the making of war and peace. In the Covenanters' eyes the Union of the Crowns had led to Scotland's interests being subordinated to England's, so they now demanded a new, truly 'equal', union.

Over union the Covenanters were thwarted by a mixture of indifference and open hostility on the part of the English. Few in England saw any real need for closer ties with the Scots; and none were ready to consider union on Scottish terms. Understandably, a union which gave about one million Scots as much to say in joint affairs as five million English seemed very 'unequal' south of the Border.

Yet, in spite of the Covenanters' failures over religion and union, the events and ideas of the Scottish revolution did have important effects on developments in England which went far beyond the implications of their military intervention and reaction against their religion.

It is of course recognised that the Scottish revolt of 1637, at a time when there was no sign of violent opposition to Charles I in England, began that King's downfall. But often the influence of the Scots revolt on England seems to be placed in the same category as the undermining of a régime by defeat in foreign war. In fact the Bishops' Wars were much more directly relevant to the attitudes of Charles' English subjects than this. The King's English subjects were certainly encouraged by seeing him defeated in war; but perhaps even more important for them was that they saw their King had been successfully resisted by his own rebellious subjects. From the first the Covenanters appealed to the King's English opponents by claiming to be motivated by grievances similar to theirs. The cause of the Covenanters was also the cause of the English. It was, therefore, not surprising that when open opposition to the discredited King grew in England the leaders of opposition tended to follow Scottish patterns and precedents. That Charles was forced to summon the Long Parliament in 1640 because the Scots had invaded England and threatened to advance south unless the King paid their army is well known. Parliament had to be summoned to vote the necessary taxes. But it was not chance that led the Covenanters to act in way that brought about the meeting of the English Parliament. They insisted that Parliament must meet before they would negotiate a peace with the King, and they then insisted that Parliament be a party to their treaty with the King. In a very real sense it was the Scots who ended the 'Eleven Years' Tyranny' in England.

Throughout his negotiations with the Covenanters, Charles I was worried that any concessions he made to them would lead to demands for similar concessions in England. When he reluctantly agreed to the abolition of bishops in Scotland in 1639 he tried, unsuccessfully, to insist that they only be abolished as contrary to the constitutions of the Kirk, as he held that the Covenanters' further demand that they be declared 'unlawful' would lead to claims that episcopacy must be unlawful in England as well. When Charles visited Scotland in 1641 he bitterly resisted demands that he surrender control of the executive (through agreeing to parliamentary approval of the appointment of all councillors, judges and officers of state), and he was encouraged in his stand by repeated reports from his English Secretary of State that English parliamentary leaders were preparing to make similar demands if he gave way in Scotland. They were resolved to act 'according to ye Scottish precedent'. Charles did give way in Scotland, and the English demands duly followed. Other constitutional demands already made in England had been in part copied from the Scots. The 1640 Scottish Triennial Act (stipulating that Parliament should meet at least once every three years) was followed by the 1641 English Triennial Act. In 1640 the Covenanters had removed the bishops from the Scottish Parliament by a redefinition of the traditional three estates of prelates, barons and burgesses. These estates now became nobles, shire commissioners or small barons, and burgesses. The following year Lord Saye proposed a similar way of removing bishops from the English Parliament while adhering to the tradition of three estates. Lords, bishops and commons should become King, Lords and Commons. The Bishop of Exeter at least was aware of the Scottish precedent here, for he remarked that Saye 'savoured of a Scottish covenanter'.

Robert Baillie was more accurate than usual when he reported that the King's English opponents admitted that they owed 'their religion, liberties, parliaments and all they have', under God, to the Scots. An English historian, Conrad Russell, has recently expressed this even more emphatically: 'The name of John Hampden is better known in the history of English liberties than the names of Lord Rothes, Lord Loudoun, and Lord Balmerino, but it does not deserve to be'. Such Scottish influence in England was strongest in and before 1641, but it can also be found at work later. In 1648 'Pride's Purge' of the English Parliament cleared the way for Cromwell's rise to power. A month before, Cromwell had written in wonder of the Kirk Party's purge of the Scottish Parliament: 'a lesser party of a parliament hath made it lawful to declare the greater part a faction, and made a parliament null, and call a new one, and to do this by force. . . . Think of the example and consequences'. It is hard to believe that this disreputable Scottish 'constitutional' precedent had no influence on the English purge that followed it so promptly.

These arguments and examples are, however, perhaps unlikely to persuade Professor Trevor-Roper that the Covenanters had anything positive to offer the English. When some of the Scottish precedents for the constitutional gains of the Long Parliament were noted in a book he was reviewing in the *Times Literary Supplement* as recently as 1977 he dismissed this as insignificant as, firstly, Charles was insincere in the concessions he granted in both kingdoms, and, secondly, that in Scotland the concessions had been forced from the King by 'great men' making use of the clergy. No concessions granted in such circumstances can, it appears, be taken seriously as constitutional gains. Unfortunately this type of argument directly contradicts a judgement which Trevor-Roper has made earlier in the same review. In discussing the 1707 Treaty of Union he asserted that the

value of a political act is not to be judged by considering the men who passed it and the means they used!

Scotland was a small, poor and in some respects backward country compared with England in the mid-seventeenth century; but nonetheless she had more to offer England than armies to be used for or against the King, and religious intolerance to be indignantly rejected. Presbyterianism was a form of Church government acceptable to many in England. Leading Scots Presbyterians and English Independents – including Cromwell – respected each other's godliness in spite of their disagreements. Political and constitutional ideas expounded by Scots Covenanters were accepted as relevant contributions to English controversies. When convenient, hatred of the Scots and their attempts to impose a settlement on England could easily be stirred up, but the appearance of such nationalistic prejudices hardly proves that the two kingdoms were totally incompatible. Indeed their relations in this period present a fascinating study of the problems of forming an acceptable union between two formerly independent states when they differ greatly in size, wealth and population. What seemed fair to the Scots, that each kingdom should have an equal say in matters of joint concern, naturally seemed most unfair to five times as many English.

NOTES ON FURTHER READING
Professor Trevor-Roper's essay 'Scotland and the Puritan Revolution' was first published in *Historical Essays, 1600–1750, presented to David Ogg*, edited by H. E. Bell and R. L. Ollard, A. & C. Black (London, 1963), and reprinted in *Religion, the Reformation, and Social Change*, Macmillan (London, 1967). Recent work on the relations of the Scots with English parliamentary parties is contained in D. Underdown, *Pride's Purge. Politics in the Puritan Revolution*, Oxford University

Press (Oxford, 1971) and L. Kaplan, *Politics and Religion during the English Revolution. The Scots and the Long Parliament, 1643-1645*, New York University Press (New York, 1976); M. J. Mendle, 'Politics and Political Thought, 1640-1642' in C. Russell (ed.), *The Origins of the English Civil War*, Macmillan (London, 1973), has some interesting comments on how English events were influenced by Scottish precedents. The quotation by Conrad Russell is from *The Crisis of Parliaments. English History 1509-1660*, Oxford University Press

(Oxford, 1971). My own views on the Scottish revolution are to be found in *The Scottish Revolution, 1637-44. The Triumph of the Covenanters*, David & Charles (Newton Abbot, 1973) and *Revolution and Counter-Revolution in Scotland, 1644-51* (Royal Historical Society, 1977). The wider Scottish background may be approached through G. Donaldson, *Scotland. James V to James VII*, Oliver & Boyd (Edinburgh, 1965) and T. C. Smout, *A History of the Scottish People, 1560-1830*, Collins (London, 1969).

VI

The 'Letter on sovereign power' and the influence of Jean Bodin on Political Thought in Scotland

In the 1830s Mark Napier (1798–1879), in the course of research for a biography of the marquis of Montrose, discovered among the papers of the historian Robert Wodrow (1679–1734) a transcript of a letter described by Wodrow as 'Montrose (Marquis) Letter about the soveraigne and supreme power'. The Letter (transcribed by Wodrow himself) takes the form of a letter addressed to an unidentified 'Noble Sir', and signed 'Montrois'.[1] Between 1838 and 1856 Napier published no fewer than four transcripts of the Letter,[2] and both he and subsequent biographers have stressed its importance in demonstrating that Montrose was a scholar as well as a man of action, and in illustrating the principles which led him to support Charles I against the covenanters. Yet there have been considerable differences of opinion among such writers as to quite what the message of the Letter is. Mark Napier, who has been described as a Jacobite 'of the old-fashioned fanatical type',[3] saw in the Letter support for his own horror of revolution, reform and democracy which threatened the Europe of his day, and therefore hailed it as of great contemporary relevance. It was, he claimed, indistinguishable in essence from the political ideas of Adam Sedgwick, Woodwardian Professor of Geology at Cambridge, as expounded in his *Discourse on the studies of the university*. 'Professor Sedgwick's sacred principle of obedience to civil government, and his views on the depravity of rebellion, are not to be distinguished, except by those who indulge in mere verbal disputes, from Montrose and [Lord] Napier's exposition of the divine and inviolable character of sovereign power upon earth.'[4] 'There is something extraordinary and startling', concluded Mark Napier, 'in this late discovery, that a young Scottish nobleman, only known to

---

1   M. Napier (ed.), *Memorials of Montrose and his times* (Maitland Club, 1848–50), i, 289n; N[ational] L[ibrary of] S[cotland], Wodrow MSS, Quarto XL, no. 2, fos. 3ʳ–5ᵛ. The letter on sovereign power will be referred to below simply as 'the Letter'.
2   M. Napier, *Montrose and the covenanters* (London, 1838), i, 397–409; M. Napier, *The life and times of Montrose* (Edinburgh, 1840), 509–16; Napier, *Memorials*, ii, 43–53; M. Napier, *Memoirs of the marquis of Montrose* (Edinburgh, 1856), i, 280–9.
3   *Dictionary of National Biography*, under Napier, Mark.
4   Napier, *Montrose and the covenanters*, i, xiii; Napier, *Memorials*, ii, 33–41. Sedgwick's *Discourse* was first published in 1833; see J. W. Clark and T. M. Hughes, *The life and letters of the Reverend Adam Sedgwick* (Cambridge, 1890), i, 399–405, ii, 187–93.

26

history as a daring cavalier who passed from his war-saddle to the scaffold, had, in the year 1640, pondered so deeply the problem of government, and prophesied so truely the issue of all violent democratic movements.'[1] To Mark Napier the Letter displayed Montrose's 'deeply cogitated principles' and the 'strong tendency of his genius towards letters and learning'.[2] It was a tract in favour of a balanced constitution in which royal power was upheld against rebellion and democracy, but was limited by the laws of God and nature and the just liberties of subjects. He admitted that parts of the Letter might seem to lead to other conclusions—that it was 'the extravagant tribute of a courtier to the divine hereditary right of Kings to do wrong'.[3] But he dismissed such interpretations; they could not be maintained after any study of the Letter which went beyond a 'cursory glance' at it.

Later writers have modified and adapted Mark Napier's interpretation to support their own precise political and historical convictions. Thus to Lord Glencorse, President of the Court of Session, the Letter was 'a very remarkable production, and enunciates with precision the constitutional doctrine on which the Covenant of 1638 is based. It reads almost like a direct defence of that Covenant in some of its parts', showing Montrose's 'moderate and conciliatory' views and certainly not lending any support to absolutism.[4] To William Law Mathieson on the other hand, the Letter demonstrated 'it need hardly be said', 'the true spirit of the English Constitution—the spirit of Magna Carta as opposed to that of the Declaration of the Rights of Man'. It showed Montrose to be 'surprisingly modern in spirit'.[5]

John Buchan made greater claims of originality for the Letter than previous writers. 'The seventeenth century saw no more searching political treatise, for it reveals a capacity for abstract thought rare at any time in a man of action.'[6] The Letter upholds constitutional monarchy and shows 'startling originality'; but then Buchan adds a note of caution by asserting that 'much in his creed is not new'.[7] Similarly, we are told that though Montrose's 'central principle' could be deduced from Bodin, 'Many philosophers of divers schools, like Hobbes and Milton, accepted his [Montrose's] doctrine of sovereignty.'[8] Needless to say, these philosophers did not 'accept' Montrose's theories, of which they could have had no knowledge.

1   Napier, *Memorials*, ii, 35–36; the passage is repeated in *Memoirs*, i, 290.
2   Ibid., i, 278.
3   Ibid., i, 291–2.
4   J. Inglis, 'Montrose and the covenant of 1638', *Blackwood's Magazine*, cxlii (July–December 1887), 617–18, 620.
5   W. L. Mathieson, *Politics and religion in Scotland, 1550–1695* (Glasgow, 1902), ii, 34n, and review of Buchan's *The marquis of Montrose* in *ante*, xi (1913–14), 107.
6   J. Buchan, *Montrose* (London, 1947; first published 1928), 136.
7   Ibid., 139.
8   Ibid., 140.

Moreover, these theories were not Montrose's own in the first place, for the Letter takes them wholesale from the work of Jean Bodin. Thus Buchan's passing reference to Bodin is at first sight puzzling. Had he actually read Bodin's greatest work he would have seen that much of the Letter is lifted directly from it; but if Buchan had not read Bodin how did he come to refer to him? The answer seems to be that Buchan had picked up and used (without acknowledgment) a reference in a somewhat bizarre and rambling article published in 1917 by Archdeacon William Cunningham, a well known economic historian. Cunningham held that Montrose's political thought tended to be overrated, pointing out that in the Letter's ideas on sovereignty can be seen 'the direct influence of Bodin'. Like Buchan, Cunningham made no attempt to follow up this brief comment, preferring to concentrate instead on comparing Montrose's ideas with those of Adam Sedgwick (thus, without acknowledgment, copying Mark Napier) and of Woodrow Wilson![1]

Cunningham, however, was the first to identify Bodin's influence on the Letter; Buchan took up the reference but failed to see its importance, a miscalculation which renders profitless his discussion of the relation between Montrose's ideas and those of other seventeenth-century writers. Nonetheless, Buchan had at least tried to set the Letter in the context of the general history of political thought. This was a move in the right direction, but subsequent biographers of Montrose have failed to follow his example, and none of them even mention Bodin. Ronald Williams, for example, relies heavily on Cunningham and Buchan, but on the origins of the Letter's ideas he contents himself with stating that Montrose 'may have been influenced by certain philosophers of his age',[2] which is not very helpful. E. J. Cowan has tried a different approach, interpreting the sentiments expressed in the Letter as the culmination of a long Scottish constitutionalist tradition. 'The letter's subjective eloquence entitles [Montrose] to a place with those who, through the centuries, grappled with and sought to define the vexed question of the Scottish constitution.'[3] In reality, however, the Letter is startlingly novel in the Scottish context; in its emphasis on sovereign power, its definition of such power, and its absolutist implications, it has no part in the tradition of the powers of the three estates.

The present writer must also plead guilty to having failed in the past to note Cunningham's reference to Bodin, but can at least claim to have stated that the Letter was in effect a justification of absolute

---

1   W. Cunningham, 'The political philosophy of the marquis of Montrose', *ante*, xiv (1916–17), 354–69. There is no reference to Bodin in Buchan's earlier work *The marquis of Montrose* (London, 1913), published before Cunningham's article.
2   R. Williams, *Montrose. Cavalier in mourning* (London, 1975), 97–99.
3   E. J. Cowan, *Montrose. For covenant and king* (London, 1977), 112; see also 41–43, 110.

royal power—and, in addition, to have argued that the Letter does not represent Montrose's own beliefs.[1]

This brings us to the obvious starting point for discussion of the Letter—its provenance and the evidence of its authorship. Mark Napier accepted Robert Wodrow's attribution of the Letter to Montrose, pointing out that there was no reason for deception on Wodrow's part; and it may be agreed that Wodrow acted in good faith, either (as Napier assumed) copying from an original letter signed by Montrose or (as will be argued below) taking his text from a draft which he assumed to be a copy of such an original though in fact no such original written by Montrose had ever existed. Further, Mark Napier argued, the Letter is 'curiously identified by the fact that some of the sentences are the very same that occur in Lord Napier's manuscripts'.[2] Lord Napier was Montrose's brother-in-law and former tutor, so his manuscripts undoubtedly help to prove that the Letter has some connection with Montrose's circle. But the argument that the fact that papers written by Lord Napier and the Letter are closely connected proves that Montrose himself wrote the Letter is obviously illogical. This, however, did not prevent Mark Napier developing his useful form of reasoning further. In 1840 he asserted that the fact that a draft letter to the king in Lord Napier's hand had similarities to parts of the Letter was grounds for attributing the former to Montrose.[3] In 1856 he triumphantly concluded that the Letter and some maxims on government in Lord Napier's hand 'authenticate each other', meaning that they must both have been the work of Montrose.[4] Yet on other occasions Mark Napier was more cautious, suggesting that Montrose probably drafted these documents in conjunction with Lord Napier.[5]

Thus Mark Napier claimed that these papers (and others related to them) were either entirely Montrose's work, or were the joint works of Montrose and Lord Napier. But there is a third alternative with strong evidence to support it that Mark Napier refused to entertain; that all the papers are entirely the work of Lord Napier. All survive only in Lord Napier's handwriting except one, the Letter itself, and that exists only in a later transcript. The only positive link with Montrose is that his 'signature' appears on the Letter in Wodrow's transcript. This might seem strong evidence, but taken as a whole the evidence points towards a different interpretation of these papers— that in 1640–1 Lord Napier prepared drafts of a number of papers and letters attempting to express the principles of the small family

1   D. Stevenson, *The Scottish revolution, 1637–1644. The triumph of the covenanters* (Newton Abbot, 1973), 225–7.
2   Napier, *Montrose and the covenanters*, i, 410; Napier, *Memorials*, ii, 33–35.
3   Napier, *Life and times*, 157n.
4   Napier, *Memoirs*, i, 289–90n.
5   Napier, *Life and times*, 157n; Napier, *Memoirs*, i, 314.

group branded by the covenanters as 'the Plotters' for their secret
approaches to the king—Napier himself, his brother-in-law
Montrose, his son-in-law Sir George Stirling of Keir, and Keir's
brother-in-law Sir Archibald Stewart of Blackhall. Among these draft
papers was the Letter, intended to be sent out in the name of
Montrose, as leader of the group and therefore bearing his name. It is
significant that the 'signature' on the Letter reads 'Montrois', for the
supposed author consistently signed himself 'Montrose' in this
period,[1] and the latter form is that generally used by Wodrow as well,
which strongly suggests that Wodrow was not transcribing an
original in Montrose's own hand. On this interpretation, the Letter
which Lord Napier prepared failed to meet with the approval of the
Plotters, and was therefore laid aside.

This conclusion, that Montrose and most of the other Plotters
rejected the Letter as a statement of their standpoint, is at variance
with the repeated assumptions of Montrose's biographers that the
ideas expounded in the Letter are also expressed in the public
statements and letters of Montrose. In fact there is no satisfactory
evidence of this. The emphasis of the Letter is on sovereign power,
and there is no evidence whatever—apart from the Letter itself—that
Montrose ever expressed his principles in such terms, centring on the
need for sovereign, supreme power held by a single individual in the
state.

A quick look at Mark Napier's *Memorials of Montrose*, the collection
of papers which has been the starting point for all subsequent research
on Montrose, seems to demonstrate immediately that this statement is
false, for printed there is a letter from Montrose to the king expressing
sentiments similar to those of parts of the Letter. But though
published as if it was a letter actually sent to the king, a footnote
reveals that it is a draft in Lord Napier's writing; the attribution of it
to Montrose is the work of Mark Napier. Similarly a paper published
as reasons for Montrose supporting the king in 1642 turns out to be a
draft by Lord Napier to which Mark Napier has given a title. A
petition (headed as being that of Montrose and his friends) arguing
that peace 'can never long continue if the Soveran power which unites
us together be weakened' is, yet again, only a draft in Lord Napier's
hand, without title or date.[2] The last of the papers putting forward
some of the ideas contained in the Letter, Lord Napier's own account
of the Plot which earned the group its name, seems to have been a
private document which was never circulated.[3]

Thus none of these papers can be attributed to Montrose with any

1   As a youth Montrose sometimes signed himself 'Montrois', but evidently
abandoned that form after *c.*1629, Napier, *Memorials*, i, 145 and n, 146, 149.
2   Ibid., i, 268–71, ii, 57–62, 63n.
3   Ibid., i, 285–7.

confidence. By contrast the declarations, statements, letters and justifications which are known to have been issued by the Plotters in 1640–2, and by Montrose in later years, show no interest at all in sovereign power as the basis of political theory and action. Mark Napier's facile assumption that papers drafted by Lord Napier must represent Montrose's ideas rests solely on their links with the Letter. By publishing these papers with misleading headings Mark Napier has been responsible for confusing both himself and subsequent writers about Montrose's ideas for over a century.

Apart from the Letter itself, there is no evidence that Montrose ever drew up any substantial paper on political theory or practice. Lord Napier, on the other hand, had long been in the habit of compiling papers on political controversies and theory, and on problems of government. One of these foreshadows the Letter's argument that a king is above civil law and is only punishable by God; 'Suffrance and obedience is our partes' as subjects.[1] Thus it is not surprising to find that Lord Napier, having adopted such ideas before the revolt of the covenanters began, failed for more than a year to join Montrose in supporting the rebellion. Even when he did come, temporarily, to join the covenanters he was not in full agreement with Montrose; on at least two occasions in 1640 he failed to follow Montrose's lead in politics.[2] Thus though the two men soon became 'Plotters', swinging back to supporting the king, the assumption of Montrose's biographers that he and Lord Napier must always have been in agreement does not stand up to examination.

The Plotters were seeking to persuade moderate covenanters that extremists were carrying resistance to the king too far and that, by depriving the king of much of his power, such policies would bring anarchy to Scotland. Men should, therefore, swing round to uphold the king and thus help achieve a balance between the liberties of the subject and the power necessary for a king to maintain order. Parts of the Letter are certainly compatible with this stand of the Plotters. But, on the other hand, the Letter's discussion of democracy and aristocracy as legitimate forms of government would have seemed to many completely out of place in such a context, and the Letter's ruling that under no circumstances was active resistance to a king by subjects justified was incompatible with the Plotters' claim that they remained loyal to the national covenant. In any case, such extreme assertions of absolute sovereign power were likely to . alienate moderate men—the very men whose support the Plotters were trying to gain. Again, it was hardly really politic, in trying to persuade covenanters that they could trust the king and should support him, to

---

1   Ibid., ii, 5–14, 22–7, 29–33, 45–59, 65–78.
2   Stevenson, *Scottish revolution*, 225.

state (as the Letter does) that most princes rule unwisely, many tyrannically!

The Letter, with its emphasis on sovereign power and cold calculation based on the lessons of history, must have seemed alien and offensive as well as inexpedient to Lord Napier's Plotter friends. Thus the argument that 'the probability that the letter was written by Lord Napier . . . does not invalidate the identification of its sentiments with those of Montrose'[1] is unconvincing. The evidence suggests that not only did Montrose not write the Letter, he did not accept its arguments either.

How was it that Lord Napier, a man deeply involved in the political controversies of his time and with long experience of politics, could produce a manifesto so inappropriate to the needs of the Plotters? How is it that a paper containing fundamentally absolutist arguments has generally been interpreted as a plea for constitutional monarchy? The answer to these questions turns out to be very simple. In its approach to political thought, its structure and its contents most of the Letter is a brief summary of perhaps the most influential work on political thought that had been published in the previous century, *Les six livres de la republique* by Jean Bodin (*c*.1530–96). First published in Paris in 1576, the book appeared in a revised Latin version *De republica libri sex* in 1586. An English translation, *The six bookes of a commonweale*, by Richard Knolles, was published in London in 1606.[2]

In turning to sixteenth-century France for his political ideas Lord Napier was doing what a great many men in both England and Scotland had been doing ever since the French religious wars had produced a remarkable ferment of political ideas. Both the Catholics of the Holy League and the Huguenots had produced religious justifications for resistance to kings who persecuted true religion or were not sufficiently zealous in upholding it. In reaction to the disastrous civil wars which such theories helped to justify some turned back to the monarchy as the only effective guarantor of law and order; only absolute monarchy, it seemed, could prevent anarchy. Some stressed the divine right of kings, thus continuing to rely on religious arguments. But Bodin made a radical break with the past. Recognising that the main problem of political authority in the post-Reformation world lay in that men claimed to be doing God's will but could not agree on what God's will was, Bodin largely separated politics from religion and sought to justify submission to the 'sovereign power' in the state (which in France lay in the monarchy) on grounds of practical necessity as revealed through the detailed

1   Cowan, *Montrose*, 110.
2   J. Bodin, *The six bookes of a commonweale. A facsimile reprint of the English translation of 1606. Corrected and supplemented in the light of a new comparison with the French and Latin texts*, ed. K. D. McRae (Cambridge, Mass., 1962), A. ix, 79–82. This edition is used for all references below.

study of the actual working of states. However, God was not entirely banished from the political scene; sovereign power is subject to divine law.

In Scotland and England the French religious wars and the political theories they gave rise to were followed with interest, but their practical impact was much greater in Scotland than in England. The course of the Scottish Reformation, originating in rebellion against the monarchy (represented by a French regent) was much more similar to the pattern of Reformation in France than to that in England. To similarities between political and religious developments in Scotland and France were added strong intellectual ties, and three of the best-known Scottish political theorists of the age, George Buchanan, Adam Blackwood and William Barclay, were as much at home in France as in Scotland.

Buchanan, 'by far the most radical of all the Calvinist revolutionaries',[1] owed much to Huguenot writers, but reached more radical conclusions than they did. His *De jure regni apud Scotos* (1578) argued in favour of limited monarchy, the power of monarchs being granted conditionally by the people.[2] Scots writers in France who denounced Buchanan's ideas turned to Bodin, thus countering constitutionalist secular theories with absolutist secular ones. Adam Blackwood's *Apologia* (1581) was 'little more than a reflection of Bodin's views on sovereignty'.[3] William Barclay's attempt to refute Buchanan, *De regno et regali potestate* (1600), was much wider ranging, for he undertook to bring together all arguments in favour of absolute and divine right monarchy; but again Bodin was a major influence, his definitions of sovereignty being accepted.[4]

Links between Scotland and France weakened after the 1603 union of the crowns, and increasingly Scots looked to England rather than to the continent for intellectual inspiration. Yet this development did not cut Scotland off from French influence in political thought, for French ideas were highly regarded in England. Englishmen 'looked to French precedents to elucidate their own dilemmas, and imported French ideas to provide theoretical solutions to them'.[5] Bodin's work was especially popular, and it has been said that in 1600–42 'there was no political writer cited in England more often or more favorably than Jean Bodin'.[6] But though Bodin's emphasis on sovereignty was

---

1   Q. Skinner, *The foundations of modern political thought* (Cambridge, 1978), ii, 343n.
2   Ibid., ii, 339.
3   J. W. Allen, *A history of political thought in the sixteenth century* (London, 1964: first published 1928), 378.
4   Skinner, *Foundations*, ii, 386–93.
5   J. H. M. Salmon, *The French religious wars in English political thought* (Oxford, 1959), 3.
6   Bodin, *Six bookes*, A63, the editor here quoting C. H. McIlwain, 'Sovereignty in the world today', *Measure*, i (1950), 110; Salmon, *French religious wars*, 24.

widely adopted, general acceptance of his whole approach to politics and its absolutist implications was rare in Britain. Instead his *Six bookes* was frequently treated as a great treasury of ideas, arguments, historical examples and illustrations from which each writer drew fragments which were relevant. Thus Sir Thomas Craig (1538–1608), the eminent Scots lawyer, tried to identify feudal superiority with Bodin's sovereignty, and occasionally turned to Bodin for historical examples to back up his own arguments.[1]

The outbreak of the Scottish rebellion against Charles I in 1637 inspired renewed interest in the French religious wars and the political thought that had arisen from them, for many believed that Britain was entering a period of religious civil wars similar to that formerly experienced by the French.[2] Late in 1637 Robert Baillie wrote with dread that 'The barricads of France, the Catholick league of France, is much before my eyes; but I hope the devill shall never finde a Duke of Guise to lead the bands' and carry out a massacre like that of St Bartholomew in Scotland.[3] Baillie thus feared that the king's supporters would form a new Holy League; but royalists were soon at work reversing the argument, seeking to discredit the covenanters by identifying them with the subversive principles of the League. Walter Balcanquhal, writing in the king's name, referred to the covenant 'or pretended Holy League (a name which all good men did abhorre in them of France)'.[4] This soon became a commonplace of royalist propaganda. John Corbet, a Scottish minister deposed by the covenanters, denounced their ideas on grounds based on Bodin and identical to the sentiments of parts of the Letter, arguing that tyranny was better than anarchy. 'It's no question, but great hurt may fall out to both Prince and people, while the Prince, pressing upon his authority, abuseth the same, and makes himself liable to the wrath of God. But much more hurt would follow upon the other hand, if the Prince's power were subject to the inferior subjects; that would breed great confusion, and turns all upside down.'[5] In the same tract Corbet implied that the covenanters were acting in ways similar to the Holy League, and the following year he extended this useful argument by claiming that the covenanters, for all their talk of protecting protestantism from the Catholic menace,

1   D. B. Smith, 'Sir Thomas Craig, feudalist', *ante*, xii (1914–15), 286, 288; T. Craig, *Jus feudale* (London, 1655), 13, 15, 113; T. Craig, *De unione regnorum Britanniae tractatus* (Scottish History Society, 1909), 12, 224; T. Craig, *The right of succession to the kingdom of England* (London, 1703), 129. The absolutist political writings of James VI and I show no interest in—or acquaintance with—the work of Bodin: cf. C. H. McIlwain (ed.), *The political works of James I* (Cambridge, Mass., 1918).
2   Salmon, *French religious wars*, 4, 80.
3   R. Baillie, *Letters and journals* (Bannatyne Club, 1841–2), i, 23.
4   [W. Balcanquhal,] *A large declaration concerning the late tumults in Scotland* (London, 1639), 2.
5   [J. Corbet,] *The vngirding of the Scottish armour* (Dublin, 1639), 20–21.

were behaving in exactly the same way as seditious Catholics. Corbet stressed this point by producing his pamphlet in the form of a letter supposedly written by a Jesuit to the covenanters, addressing them as 'most worthy Brethren of the Holy League' and congratulating them for acting on Catholic principles. With considerable ingenuity Corbet sought to demonstrate that the ideas on resistance to royal authority of Calvin, Beza, Knox and Buchanan were indistinguishable from those of Jesuit authors such as Bellarmine, Suarez, Mariana and Ignatius Loyola.[1]

As Robert Baillie's fears indicated, from the first covenanters as well as royalists had seen the French experience as relevant to their problems. Archibald Johnston of Wariston, the fanatical young lawyer who drafted many of the covenanters' declarations and petitions, and who was responsible for much of the national covenant, was reading the history of the French wars by Henri Lancelot Voisin de la Poplinière in early March 1638, just a week after the first signing of the national covenant.[2] A relation of Wariston lent him three volumes on the 'History of the Civill Warres of Fraunce', and it was said that Wariston took from them 'his modell for thes public papers' that he composed.[3]

As well as studying French histories Wariston was imbibing, indirectly, the ideas of Bodin. In May 1638 he was reading Joannes Althusius' *Politica methodice digesta* in preparation for answering opponents of the covenant. Althusius' work was based on Bodin but developed his ideas in order to use them to attack the absolutist theories Bodin had upheld. Bodin's definitions of sovereignty were correct, according to Althusius, but he had been wrong in his conclusions as to where sovereign power lay; it could not lie in a king, being vested inalienably in the community as a whole. The usefulness of Althusius, a German Calvinist who accepted many of Buchanan's ideas, to the covenanters is thus clear.[4]

In August 1638 Wariston turned to the study of another German work, Henninges Arnisaeus' *Doctrina politica genuinam methodum* (1606), and in January 1639 he was translating Arnisaeus' *De jure majestatis* (1610) into English. In the *De jure* Arnisaeus sought to remove some inconsistencies from Bodin's arguments to prevent his

1   *The Vngirding*, 6; [J. Corbet,] *The epistle congratulatorie of Lysimachus Nicanor* (1640), passim. See also [J. Maxwell,] *Sacro-sancta regum majestas: Or: The sacred and royall prerogative of Christian kings* (Oxford, 1644), 6–7, 133, and P. du Moulin, *Letter of a French protestant to a Scotishman of the Covenant* ... (London, 1640).
2   A. Johnston of Wariston, *Diary, 1632–1639* (Scottish History Society, 1911), 324 and n.
3   J. Gordon, *History of Scots affairs* (Spalding Club 1841), i, 33n.
4   J. Althusius, *Politica methodice digesta* (1603); Salmon, *French religious wars*, 40–50; F. S. Carney (ed.), *The politics of Althusius. An abridged translation of the third edition of politica methodice digesta* (London, 1964), xv–xxx; Skinner, *Foundations*, ii, 341–2.

absolutist theories being distorted and perverted by enemies of monarchy—among whom he included Buchanan. Simultaneously Wariston was translating Althusius and copying out extracts from the works of John Knox and Buchanan.[1]

Wariston evidently only came into contact with Bodin's ideas at second hand. The authors of the two major Scottish political treatises of the period, on the other hand, took ideas from Bodin directly as well as indirectly. In his *Sacro-sancta Regum Majestas* of 1644 John Maxwell (former bishop of Ross) introduced in his definition of sovereignty based on Bodin 'a new element soon to be found in many royalist works'.[2] He also demonstrated much more clearly than previous writers that theories of popular sovereignty predated the Reformation, and thus could not be held to be peculiarly protestant theories. Thus, according to Maxwell, the covenanters and others in justifying resistance to the king were drawing their doctrines from the 'polluted cisterns' of Catholicism. However, it seems that not all Catholic cisterns were equally polluted, for Maxwell singles out his Catholic countrymen Adam Blackwood and William Barclay for praise, along with Bodin.[3]

The other major Scottish writer of the period, Samuel Rutherford, wrote his *Lex rex* (1644) specifically to refute John Maxwell, but he also sought to discredit William Barclay and Arnisaeus.[4] Thus those whom he saw as his main opponents were all men who had relied much on Bodin; but the same is true also of Rutherford himself, for his work is based on Althusius' adaptation (or distortion) of Bodin's doctrines in order to uphold popular sovereignty, and Althusius too had singled out Barclay and Arnisaeus for denunciation. 'Among the writings of this turbulent period of English [*sic*] history, the anonymous book by Samuel Rutherford . . . comes perhaps closest to the Althusian position.'[5] John Buchan perceptively noted that *Lex rex* had similarities in its general approach to politics to the Letter on Sovereign Power,[6] but did not realise that this odd connection between two such different works, one advocating absolute monarchy and the other pleading for popular sovereignty, was due to the fact that they both derived from Bodin.

Bodin's great contribution to modern political thought was to

1   Wariston, *Diary*, 373, 408; Salmon, *French religious wars*, 50–52. Wariston also studied 'Brutus' on resistance (February 1639), *Diary*, 410. This was one of the most radical of Huguenot tracts, the *Vindiciae contra tyrannos* (1579) of 'Junius Brutus'—which is denounced in Gordon, *Scots affairs*, ii, 170, 203.
2   Salmon, *French religious wars*, 91–92.
3   G. J. Schochet, *Patriarchalism in political thought* (Oxford, 1975), 109–12; Skinner, *Foundations*, ii, 123; Maxwell, *Sacro-sancta*, 144.
4   S. Rutherford, *Lex rex* (London, 1644), title page.
5   Carney, *The politics of Althusius*, xii, xxii. Rutherford also, of course, relies much on Buchanan.
6   Buchan, *Montrose*, 140.

36

define the concepts of sovereignty and the state much more clearly than previous writers. It is this, and his analytical approach, that make the *Six bookes* 'arguably the most original and influential work of political philosophy to be written in the sixteenth century'.[1] Bodin was reacting both to the destabilising effect of the Reformation on European politics, and to the longer-term development of national monarchies determined to escape from even nominal subjection to any earthly authority such as the papacy.[2]

Sovereign power, according to Bodin, cannot be divided, but there are three forms of state, monarchical, aristocratic and democratic. Mixed constitutions Bodin saw as a contradiction in terms, for sovereignty cannot be shared; if a king 'shares' his power with his people he is not a sovereign king and the state is democratic. Wherever sovereignty lies in a particular state, subjects have no right to resist it, no matter how tyrannically it is exercised, for destroying the sovereign power leads to anarchy, the disintegration of the state and civil society. Certainly rulers are bound to obey the laws of God and nature, and certain fundamental laws of the state, but such seeming limitations on royal power are nullified in practice by the belief that if they fail to obey such laws only God could punish them. Thus in many ways Bodin was providing a charter for tyrants, for he left subjects helpless under their rule (provided they were legitimate rulers and not usurpers). Yet Bodin saw himself as an enemy of arbitrary rule, a defender of states against tyrants.[3]

It was Bodin's denunciation of tyranny, his repeated warnings of the fates of tyrants and his urging of the wisdom of moderate government, combined with his detailed investigation of the working of states of all sorts, which provided rich treasure to be mined by the opponents of absolutism. Bodin might in the last analysis support absolute monarchy in France and elsewhere, but he was no starry-eyed believer in the glories of kingship and did not hesitate to point out that kings were often as bad, or as stupid, as other men.[4] Thus it was possible to accept much of Bodin's analysis of the structure of states, and of how history showed the exercise of sovereignty in states working in practice, without accepting his conclusions.

The full extent of the debt of the Letter on Sovereign Power to Bodin can only be revealed by detailed comparison of the texts of the Letter and the *Six bookes*. The Letter[5] opens with a statement of what

1   Skinner, *Foundations*, i, 208.
2   Bodin, *Six bookes*, A13–14.
3   J. H. Franklin, *Jean Bodin and the rise of absolutist theory* (Cambridge, 1973), 49, 51; Bodin, *Six bookes*, A69–70.
4   Skinner, *Foundations*, ii, 284.
5   The version of the Letter most frequently used by later historians is probably that in Napier, *Memorials*, ii, 43–53, but comparison of this with Wodrow's transcript shows that Napier left out some phrases and misread a few words; and, inconsistently,

the author is trying to do. The anonymous (or fictitious) 'Noble Sir' has set him a difficult question concerning sovereign power. 'Nevertheless to obey your desire' he will give his opinion on the nature and practice of such power, how it may be strengthened or weakened, and what the effects of such changes are. Finally, the Letter will answer some false arguments 'mentioned' by impugners of royal power.

Sovereign power is then defined. Civil society and government cannot exist without some ultimate power to enforce obedience to law. This power is the truest image of God on earth, and is not to be 'bounded, disputed, medled with at all by subjects'. Yet this power is limited—by laws of God and nature, and some laws of nations and fundamental laws of the country. Such fundamental laws are those on which sovereign power rests, and those which secure to a good subject his life, honour, and 'the propriety of his goods'. All this is pure Bodin, and superficially appears to be upholding constitutional monarchy. For rulers to disobey the laws of God and nature is to make war on God. But the catch is, of course, that even if princes do break such laws subjects have no right to resist them; only God can punish holders of sovereign power who misuse it. Bodin also argues, like the Letter, that kings are bound by 'laws royall, upon which the soueraigne maiestie is stayed and grounded', the fundamental laws which defined where sovereign power in a state lay. Rulers may not treat free-born subjects as slaves, and must allow each subject 'the proprietie of his owne goods'. Rulers who do not accept such limitations are tyrants—but still are legitimate rulers who must be obeyed.[1]

The Letter next defines the 'essential points of soveraignty'. These are power to make laws, 'to creat principal officers'; to make peace and war; to pardon those condemned by law; and to be 'the last to whom appellation is made'. This again is copied directly from Bodin. The latter distinguishes nine essential points of sovereignty, of which the first five (and most important) are those listed in the Letter; and the Letter like Bodin gives primacy to legislative power. Even the language in which the points are expressed in the Letter is taken directly from Bodin, who wrote of power 'to create and appoint magistrats, . . . especially the principall officers' and of power 'of the Last Appeal'.[2] In the Letter the essential marks of sovereign power are 'inalienable, indivisible, incommunicable'; in Bodin sovereignty 'is alwaies indiuisible and incommunicable'.[3] Mixed government,

---

he partially modernises punctuation and spelling. Buchan, *Montrose*, 396–406 provides a rather better text, with modern punctuation and spelling. Quotations below are from Wodrow's transcript.

1   Bodin, *Six bookes*, 92, 95, 104, 210, 707.
2   Ibid., 159–62, 166, 168; Skinner, *Foundations*, ii, 289.
3   Bodin, *Six bookes*, 250.

38

theories of which were popular in Lord Napier's time as in Bodin's, is denounced by both men as an impossibility, and the Letter follows Bodin in explaining that those who may seem to be sharing the sovereign power of a prince, in fact only exercise power at the ruler's pleasure, and thus do not help constitute the mythical mixed constitution.[1]

Like Bodin, the Letter moves on from defining sovereign power to showing it at work in the three kinds of state. From Bodin's vast store of historical examples the Letter chooses a few. Republican Rome typifies popular states or democracies, though here the Letter adds a reference to Holland, a state which had not existed when Bodin wrote. Aristocracy is expounded through the Venetian example. Venice is held to be 'a pure aristocracy, laws, warr, peace, election of officers, pardon and appellation are all concluded and done in Conciglio Maggiore'. This clearly echoes Bodin's description of Venice as 'a pure Aristocracie' in which the great council 'hath soueraigne power to make and repeale lawes, to place or displace all officers, to receiue the last appeales, to determine of peace and warre, and to giue pardon vnto the condemned'.[2]

The Letter does not discuss specific examples of monarchies, presumably because this was the type of state likely to be most familiar to readers. Instead the ways in which sovereign power can be weakened and strengthened are discussed; and at this point the seemingly dispassionate discussion of all types of states is abandoned, for only monarchy and its problems are considered. This section is the most original part of the Letter, though the originality lies in expression rather than content. There is nothing new in the basic ideas and assumptions, but they are assembled in a straightforward, eloquent and persuasive manner that commands attention.

Sovereign power is strong and durable when it is used temperately and moderately, being exercised within the limits of the laws of God and nature and fundamental laws. It is weak if it is either extended beyond these laws, or if it is restrained by subjects. Wise princes use their power moderately, but alas 'most desire to extend it', fomented by ambitious advisers, courtiers and counsellors. This is in full agreement with Bodin, who had written that few princes were virtuous and most were polluted with vice through their education; and, moreover, that the exercise of sovereign power had in itself a tendency to corrupt. It made the wise foolish, the valiant cowards, the good wicked.[3]

Royal power extended by unwise princes, the Letter continues, leads to tyranny, 'which could never be any time endured by the

1   Ibid., 185, 194–5, 199–200, 250, 278, 280, 281.
2   Ibid., 190–1.
3   Ibid., 414, 713–14.

people of the western parts of the worlde, and by those of Scotland as little as any'. Power extended would thus provoke revolt by subjects against tyranny. But such attempts to restrain royal power, whether provoked by tyranny or not, only made matters worse, for rebellion led to the tyranny of some subjects over others, 'the most feirce, insatiable, and insupportable tyranny in the worlde'. Once again the language as well as the sentiments recall Bodin.[1]

Fear of popular tyranny and anarchy underlies much of the Letter and Bodin, and each has the same basic message to offer. To the prince the message is, rule wisely and moderately, for if you act the tyrant your subjects will rebel and God will punish you. For subjects the message is, submit to a tyrannical prince for only God can discipline him, and rebellion will only increase your suffering. Both Bodin and the Letter then seek desperately for arguments to help make such submission to injustice and oppression palatable to subjects (both had admitted, after all, that in practice subjects do tend to rebel under such circumstances) by suggesting that their suffering will only be temporary. The 'surest way and meane' to suppress tyranny, according to Bodin, is to do nothing, to wait until the tyrant dies; for, we are hopefully assured, it commonly chances that 'vnto the most cruell tyrants succeeded the most iust and vpright princes'.[2] The Letter grabs at straws of the same sort and is no more convincing; a tyrannical prince may be brought to 'the sense of his errors' by good advice, by satiety, by fear of infamy, or by some event, 'and when nothing else can doe it (seing the prince is mortall) patience in the subject is a soveraigne[3] and dangerless Remedy'. It is hardly surprising that a paper which could be interpreted as urging those who opposed Charles I's policies to reconcile themselves to his tyranny by looking forward to his death should have had little appeal to the royalist Plotters!

As an illustration of the folly of rebelling against tyranny the Letter points to Germany. Would it not have been better for Germany to have endured the 'encroachments' of the Emperor Ferdinand II 'and after his death rectified them' than, by resisting, to have brought about the horrors of the Thirty Years' War (1618–48)? Obviously this example is not taken from Bodin; but it reads very much like a simple updating of Bodin's argument about the ruin and destruction brought on Germany by unjustified resistance to the Emperor Charles V.[4]

From this point on the Letter is less directly derived from Bodin, though it is still based on his principles. Subjects are assured that they

1   Ibid., 700–1, 708, 717.
2   Ibid., 413, 475.
3   The pun is presumably intentional!
4   Ibid., 225.

have 'a fair and justifiable' way to procure moderate government, which is 'to endeavour the security of Religion and just Liberty' as contained in the laws; and 'parliaments (which ever have been the bulwarks of subjects liberties in monarchys) may advise new laws, against emergent occasions which prejudge their libertys'. This passage, torn out of context, has been much favoured by those who see the Letter as a manifesto for constitutional monarchy. Yet, even out of context, it makes it clear that parliaments can only advise; sovereign, law-making power resides wholly in the king.

Hastening past such awkward matters, the Letter turns to defining the 'perpetuall cause of the controversys' between princes and subjects as the ambitious designs of great men 'vailed with the plausible and speciouse pretext' of religion and the liberties of the subject. Suddenly the admission that most princes sought unwisely to extend their powers and thus destroyed moderate government is forgotten, and the whole blame for controversies is placed on subjects. The transformation of the Letter from a work of political science into a propaganda tract is complete. Five false propositions concerning the relations between king and people said to be upheld by seditious preachers are listed and refuted, the conclusion reached being that when 'a King is restrained from the lawful use of his power . . . what can follow but a subversion of Government anarchy and confusion'.

These five points and their refutation bring us to another notable feature of the Letter which greatly limited its potential as royalist propaganda. Though the points are attributed to 'seditious preachers' none of them is concerned primarily with religion, and they are refuted almost entirely in secular terms. Yet the covenanters, in spite of their resort to Buchanan, mainly justified their rebellion on religious grounds. The Letter thus makes no direct attempt to undermine the most powerful of the covenanters' arguments. The reason for this is simply that Lord Napier had followed Bodin in pushing religion out of the centre of political debate. But Napier was not, it seems, willing to take the further step of fully accepting Bodin's ideas on the relationship of religion and politics. Bodin had argued that though religious unity in a state was preferable, once such unity was lost a king should not resort to persecution to restore it. This was too radical for Lord Napier; and in any case it would hardly provide acceptable royalist propaganda in a conflict in which the king was as determined as the covenanters to impose religious unity by force. So in the Letter Lord Napier largely ignored religion. But this rendered the Letter almost useless as propaganda, irrelevant in the eyes of the king's enemies, inappropriate in the eyes of his supporters. In 1640 Britain had not suffered sufficiently from civil wars partly religious in origin to convince men that the Bodinian separation of religion from politics was necessary.

The Letter closes with appeals to the covenanters, to the nobility and the gentry on the one hand, and to the people on the other, to think of the consequences of what they are doing. The nobility are warned that in using the people against the king they are stirring up a force that they cannot control. 'If their first act be against Kingly power, their next will be against you'. The people will cut the throats of the nobles or destroy their power. The threat was a traditional one which could be found in Bodin as well as in other sources.[1] Similarly, the Letter warned the people that the aristocracy, having overthrown the king, would seek to rule over them like tyrants; and there was a danger that power would fall into the hands of a few, and finally a single tyrant might emerge, 'one who of necessity must, and for reason of state will Tyrannize over you'.

Quite how commonplace these warnings at the end of the Letter to nobles and people not to trust each other were can be seen by looking at the works of William Drummond of Hawthornden the poet, who composed papers full of foreboding which in some respects are not dissimilar from those of Lord Napier. Thus in 1639 Drummond warned that it was dangerous to arm 'the Rascality and mad Multitude', for such 'Peasants, Clowns, Farmers, base People' might overthrow the nobles and gentry and seize their possessions. It was better to submit to the king than face civil war which might lead to tyranny. 'During these Miseries, of which the Troublers of the state shall make their Profit, there will arise (perhaps) one who will name himself Protector of the Liberty of the Kingdom'.[2] The influence of Bodin is discernible in Drummond's papers. He urges the necessity of obedience to the 'Power Sovereign' of princes if confusion and anarchy are to be avoided.[3] He shares the cynicism of Bodin and the Letter about the character and wisdom of princes 'living in the Sensuality of Courts'.[4] A speech on toleration which Drummond puts into the mouth of a councillor of James V argues that religious uniformity is the ideal, but that if diversity exists toleration is more expedient than persecution.[5] Here Drummond accepts fully an

1   Bodin, *Six bookes*, 711.
2   W. Drummond of Hawthornden, *Works* (Edinburgh, 1711), 179, 181; T. I. Rae, 'The political attitudes of William Drummond of Hawthornden', in G. W. S. Barrow (ed.), *The Scottish tradition. Essays in honour of Ronald Gordon Cant* (Edinburgh, 1974), 146.
3   Drummond, *Works*, 163–73.
4   Ibid., 180.
5   R. H. MacDonald (ed.), *William Drummond of Hawthornden. Poems and prose* (Edinburgh, 1976), 174–8, 199. The speech is in Drummond's *History of Scotland* (London, 1655), which was written as an answer to Buchanan's *History*. See T. I. Rae, 'The historical writing of Drummond of Hawthornden', *ante*, liv (1975), 38–42. Since the above was written an article by I. M. Smart has appeared pointing out that Drummond's ideas on toleration are similar to Bodin's, 'Monarchy and toleration in Drummond of Hawthornden's works', *Scotia. American-Canadian Journal of Scottish Studies*, iv (1980), 48.

argument from Bodin that Lord Napier had ignored, but in general 'Bodinian' features appear in Drummond in the wider context of traditional ideas of the order of the universe and the nature of obligation. They result from the gradual absorption of some of Bodin's ideas into European thought rather than from the direct influence of his work and conscious adoption of his ideas. There is no sign of Bodin in Drummond's library, though he would have found many of his arguments in Adam Blackwood's refutation of George Buchanan, the *Apologia* (1581).[1]

Bodin's ideas appear in Drummond as just one element in the rather diffuse political writings of a man who wished no part in politics but who felt forced into writing when the stability of the world around him collapsed and revolution threatened, though he doubted the wisdom of even this very limited involvement in politics; 'Wise Men keep their Thoughts locked up in the Cabinet of their Breasts, and suffer the Faults of Time patiently; Fools rail, cry out, but amend nothing.'[2] In the Letter, on the other hand, Bodin's main ideas and his approach to the study of politics have been taken over wholesale; the great majority of it is pure Bodin. The similarities are so great that there can be no doubt that Lord Napier had a copy of the *Six bookes*— or at least very detailed notes on it—open before him as he wrote. Napier may have used the 1606 English edition of the *Six bookes*, but as there are no direct quotations from it in spite of much similarity of wording it is perhaps more likely that he studied one of the French or Latin editions (like most English writers who cite or quote Bodin)[3] and made his own translations of relevant passages.

As to when the Letter was written, Mark Napier's suggestion that it was composed about Christmas 1640 is probably correct. At that time all the Plotters—Montrose, Napier, Keir and Blackhall—held a series of meetings in Montrose's lodgings in Edinburgh and in Napier's adjacent home, Merchiston Castle, to discuss the political situation and decide how to act. But far from being the credo of the Plotters the Letter was a draft manifesto, put forward by Lord Napier in the form of a letter by Montrose, which was discussed but then rejected by the other Plotters and laid aside as too extreme to be expedient.

The arguments that the Letter on Sovereign Power (1) was not written by Montrose, (2) does not represent his political philosophy, and (3) takes most of its ideas and historical information directly from Bodin, must obviously lead to a reassessment of its significance. Had it not been, in the past, so closely identified with Montrose it is doubtful that it would have emerged from obscurity; certainly it would not have attracted so much comment and praise.

---

1   R. H. MacDonald (ed.), *The library of Drummond of Hawthornden* (Edinburgh, 1971), 172.

2   Drummond, *Works*, 132.   3   Bodin, *Six bookes*, A65.

However, the severing of the Letter from Montrose's own ideas does not mean that it should revert to its former obscurity. Nor does the fact that its ideas are not original necessarily condemn it to oblivion; after all, the vast majority of works on political theory consist mainly of restatements of old ideas, yet many remain of great interest to the historian through the context in which old ideas are reasserted and adapted to new circumstances. It is of considerable interest that Lord Napier should have concluded in 1640 that Scotland was facing the same threat of anarchy that had hung over Bodin's France, and have decided that salvation lay in accepting Bodin's doctrine of sovereignty and his largely secular theory of political obligation. And it is equally of interest that the other Plotters showed so little enthusiasm for such ideas.

Finally, it is known that it was a Scot, John Maxwell, who was the first in Britain's mid-seventeenth century revolutions to place Bodin's concept of sovereignty at the centre of royalist theory in a published work. Now it emerges that another Scot, Lord Napier, had anticipated Maxwell by several years (though, of course, only in an unpublished paper). That it should be Scots who thus took the lead in applying Bodin's work to Britain's problems in this period should come as no surprise. As Scotland was the first part of Britain to revolt against Charles I it was Scots who were the first to need both justifications for resistance to legitimate kings, and arguments denying that such rebellion could ever be justified. When, a few years later, the English found themselves travelling the same road through resistance to civil war one reaction was to turn to Scotland for parallels, precedents, and theories. Many in England at first looked to Scotland for inspiration in political ideas and in religious and constitutional reforms—and for military aid.[1] 1644 saw the peak of Scottish influence—and ambitions—in England, with a large Scottish army intervening to help parliament against the king, and the year was marked by the publication in England of the two major treatises by Scots political theorists. In royalist Oxford John Maxwell's *Sacro-sancta* was printed, only to be promptly countered by the appearance of Rutherford's *Lex rex* in parliamentarian London, both works being, as already noted, founded on the thought of Jean Bodin. But one of the most interesting Scottish works on political theory produced in these years had no influence whatever either in England or Scotland. The Letter on Sovereign Power proves Lord Napier to have been a good Bodinian, but equally its fate proves him a singularly ineffective propagandist, unable to win support even from his own friends.

---

1   See D. Stevenson, 'Professor Trevor-Roper and The Scottish revolution', *History Today*, February 1980, 39–40.

VII

THE KING'S SCOTTISH REVENUES AND
THE COVENANTERS, 1625-1651

The King's Revenues

The ordinary revenue of the kings of Scotland in the early seventeenth century was drawn from a wide variety of sources. The comptroller received the revenues known as 'property' – fixed revenues and rents from Crown lands, payments from royal burghs, customs duties and the impost of wines. Out of these he met the expenses of the royal household. The treasurer was responsible for meeting nearly all other official and royal expenses out of the 'casualty', which included feudal casualties (irregular payments such as wards and reliefs), escheats, compositions and other profits of justice. The collector general and the treasurer of the new augmentations received various revenues from former church property. Administration of these revenues was simplified in 1610 when the earl of Dunbar, already treasurer, was appointed in addition comptroller, collector general and treasurer of the new augmentations, thus bringing responsibility for all branches of the ordinary revenue into the hands of one man, though he continued usually to be referred to simply as the treasurer. This amalgamation of offices became permanent, though the four offices all continued to exist in name until 1707, and separate accounting for the different branches of revenue continued until 1636.[1]

The treasurer was assisted in his work by the treasurer depute. Originally the depute had been the treasurer's servant, appointed by him, but he quickly became an important official in his own right, appointed by the king by 1614. This rise in importance was probably connected with the fact that after the union of the Crowns of 1603 the treasurer was often absent at court in England, leaving his depute to act for him in Scotland. This in turn left the depute with little time to attend to the routine intromissions with the revenues which had formerly been his main functions, and it therefore became usual for the king to appoint two or three receivers to deal with the actual collection of the revenues.[2]

On the accession of Charles I in 1625 Scotland had no permanent exchequer,

---

[1] A. L. Murray, 'Notes on the Treasury Administration', in C. T. McInnes (ed.), *Accounts of the Treasury of Scotland*, 1566–74, XII (Edinburgh, 1970), xii–xv.

[2] A. L. Murray, 'The Scottish Treasury, 1667–1708', *Scottish Historical Review*, XLV (1966), 92, 98.

The Historical Journal, XVII, I (1974), pp. 17–41. © Cambridge University Press

though there had been experiments with such a body in the late sixteenth century. Instead, temporary commissions of exchequer were appointed each year to meet for a short period to audit accounts. In the absence of a permanent exchequer the privy council exercised general supervision over the king's revenues, acting in the later years of James VI through a sub-committee, the commissioners of rents.[3]

By 1625 the ordinary revenues of the Scottish crown thus administered were inadequate to meet even routine demands upon them – the payment of fees and pensions, the costs of the royal household and the expense of administering the country. In 1628-9 ordinary royal revenues totalled just over £196,500 Scots, less than £16,500 sterling.[4] This was a tiny sum compared with the English ordinary revenue (which averaged about £620,000 sterling in 1631-5),[5] and far less even than the Irish ordinary revenue (about £40,000 sterling in 1625).[6] Indeed the Scottish ordinary revenue was far less than the income of the king's richest English and Irish subjects. The duke of Buckingham, for example, had a much higher income in the mid-1620s, and Lord Wentworth, the earl of Cork and the earl of Newcastle all had incomes of £20,000 sterling per annum or more in the late 1630s.[7]

Of course Scotland was a much smaller, poorer and less populous country than England, but even when allowance is made for this the poverty of the Scottish crown is remarkable. This poverty was the result of the previous weakness of the Crown, royal extravagance and, above all, inflation which continuously ate into the real value of fixed revenues such as crown rents. Partial compensation for this was provided by the customs duties and impost of wines; the yield of these revenues rose steadily with increasing trade and rising prices, until by 1628-9 they alone made up more than two-thirds of the total ordinary revenue. The union of the crowns also eased the situation by removing some of the burdens on the revenues; there was no longer a resident royal court to be supported.

Nonetheless, by the time of Charles I the ordinary revenues could not meet the demands made of them. This was clearly demonstrated by an estimate of some of the payments due from them annually, made in 1634 by commissioners who had been investigating the state of the exchequer. Payments due included:

[3] Ibid. p. 91.

[4] W. Purves, *The Revenue of the Scottish Crown*, D. M. Rose (ed.) (Edinburgh, 1897), pp. xliv–xlv. The Scots £ was worth 1s. 8d. sterling. All sums cited below are in £ Scots unless otherwise stated. The merk was worth 13s. 4d. Scots.

[5] G. E. Aylmer, *The King's Servants* (London, 1961), p. 64.

[6] H. F. Kearney, *Strafford in Ireland* (Manchester, 1959), pp. 33, 169.

[7] J. F. Cooper, 'The Fortune of Thomas Wentworth, Earl of Strafford', *Economic History Review*, 2nd series, XI (1958-9), 245-6; C. V. Wedgwood, *Thomas Wentworth* (London, 1961), p. 233; T. Ranger, 'Strafford in Ireland', *Crisis in Europe*, T. Ashton (ed.) (London, 1965), p. 275n.; C. H. Firth (ed.), *The Life of William Cavendish Duke of Newcastle* (London, n.d.), p. 77.

Pensions	£186,500
Fees and allowances to officials	£44,500
Household expenses and fees	£25,500
Interest on debts (of over £922,000)	£78,500
Total	£335,000 [8]

Thus expenditure (or rather payments due but not necessarily made) for these items alone greatly exceeded ordinary revenue, while debts approached £1,000,000. The burden of pensions illustrates the justice of the complaint made some years later by Lord Wentworth (later earl of Strafford) that the Scottish revenues were 'drunk and supped up to private ends'.[9]

Since it was impossible for the Crown to remain solvent on its ordinary revenues it had become increasingly dependent on extraordinary ones, on taxes granted by parliament or the convention of estates. Such taxes, payable by tenants in chief and feuars of Crown lands, had increased greatly in frequency and scale since the late sixteenth century. By 1621 they had come to be granted for several years at a time, and thus came to be payable annually. In 1617 the rate of the land tax was fixed at 30/- annually on each poundland of old extent (a traditional valuation), and this remained the rate up to the beginning of the troubles in 1637, being renewed in 1625, 1630 and 1633. In addition a new tax was imposed for the first time in 1621, a yearly payment of 5 per cent of annual rents (interest payments). This too became a regular tax, being reimposed in 1625 and 1630 at the same rate, and at 6¼ per cent in 1633. In the latter year a third tax was introduced, the 'two of ten'. It had been decided to reduce interest rates throughout the country from 10 per cent to 8 per cent but for the first three years the king alone was to benefit from this, for the 2 per cent no longer payable as interest was to be collected as a tax. Collecion of these taxes granted by the estates was left to specially appointed collectors, who accounted in the exchequer. Thus the earl of Mar acted as collector of the taxes granted in 1621, the earl of Kinnoull as collector of the 1630 taxes.[10]

At 30/- per poundland the land tax was estimated to bring in about £100,000 Scots annually (the tax roll for 1633 gives the total as £115,465) and the tax on annual rents about twice as much when levied at 5 per cent,[11] though collection, especially of the latter, was often difficult and inefficient. Thus, in theory at least, the burden of taxation on the country in 1621-33 was about £300,000 a year, after which it must have risen considerably with the increase in the tax on annual rents and the introduction of the 'two of ten'. Even when allowance

[8] Purves, *Revenues*, pp. xlv-xlvi; Scottish Record Office (S.R.O.), E.4/5, Exchequer Act Book 1634-9, fos. 21r-21v.

[9] Wedgwood, *Thomas Wentworth*, p. 251.

[10] G. Donaldson, *Scotland : James V to James VII* (Edinburgh and London, 1965), p. 302; R. S. Rait, *The Parliaments of Scotland* (Glasgow, 1924), pp. 492-4; *The Acts of Parliaments of Scotland* (APS) (12 vols., Edinburgh, 1814-75), v, 13-20, 39-40, 167-74, 209-16.

[11] Rait, *Parliaments of Scotland*, p. 494; Purves, *Revenues*, pp. 183-200.

is made for Scotland's poverty this burden does not seem extortionate. When added to the ordinary revenue the total theoretically available to the king was still only about £42,000 sterling before 1633, and collection of the taxes was often very inefficient. They provided enough to keep the regime solvent, but only just.

The conclusion that Scotland was a comparatively lightly taxed country was not one that many contemporary Scots would have accepted, for most of them stuck firmly to the old belief that the king should live and rule off his ordinary revenue. Extraordinary taxes should be imposed only on extraordinary occasions, and regular taxation was an abuse. They could not (or would not) see that the increasing inadequacy of the ordinary revenues made it impossible even for an absentee king, his court supported at English expense, to subsist on them. The taxes on annual rents were especially unpopular. In 1633 it was said that 'many evills are introduced, as are obvious to everie one' by the 'two of ten', and it was claimed that when the tax on annual rents had been introduced in 1621 it had been promised that it would not be reimposed. The need to value annual rents to assess what tax was payable was held to be particularly obnoxious; 'it is such an inquisition in men's estates, as is not practised in any other nation in Christiandome, and makes our nation contemptible by the discoverie made thereby of the povertie thereof, and gives occasion to the distresse of innumerable persons of good respect'.[12]

The Earl of Traquair and Attempts to Improve the Revenues

Charles had not been long on the throne before he began to consider ways of making the administration of his Scottish revenues more efficient and of increasing their yield. In 1626 he set up a permanent exchequer with the archbishop of St Andrews as its president,[13] though 'this praelate was the first and last president that ever the Exchequer of Scotland had', for when the archbishop was appointed chancellor in 1635 he was not replaced; in his place the treasurer or his depute presided in the exchequer.[14]

Also in 1626 the king ordered the treasurer depute to draw up each year a report on the state of the revenues and bring this to him personally.[15] Whether or not this was done, there was little improvement in the state of the king's finances in the early years of his reign. The administration was much divided, weakened by intrigue as rival factions competed for the favour of the new king, who had neither the experience nor the judgement of men to know what to

[12] J. Row, *The History of the Kirk of Scotland* (Wodrow Society, 1842), pp. 365–6, 380–1.

[13] *Register of the Privy Council of Scotland (RPCS)*, *1625–7* (2nd series, 8 vols., Edinburgh, 1899–1908), pp. 265–7.

[14] J. Balfour, *Historical Works* (4 vols., Edinburgh, 1824–5), II, 134; S.R.O., E.4/5, fos. 42v–43r, 52r.

[15] *The Earl of Stirling's Register of Royal Letters*, C. Rogers (ed.) (2 vols., Edinburgh, 1885), I, 93–4.

believe when conflicting reports reached him from Scotland. But with the rise of Sir John Stewart, Lord Traquair, there are signs of a stronger hand than before controlling financial affairs. In 1630, as the result of much intrigue, he won appointment as joint treasurer depute with Lord Napier (who had held the office alone since 1622), and in the following year Napier was forced to resign, leaving Traquair as sole depute. In 1633 Traquair was created an earl and in 1636 he was promoted to the office of treasurer.[16] Traquair seems to have been personally responsible for a sustained attempt to promote efficiency, push through reforms and generally advance the king's interests in financial matters.

The ineptitude of the administration in the early years of the reign can be seen in the disposal of tacks (leases) of the customs and of the impost of wines; these revenues were usually leased out for periods of several years to tacksmen who undertook collection, paying a fixed annual sum for the privilege, the leasing being done at a public roup or auction held by the exchequer. In November 1628 a tack of the customs (including additional customs worth £3,600 per annum) was set for fifteen years to a group of merchants for £54,000 per annum. Not only was such a long tack unwise in a period of inflation, but the customs had previously brought in more (£55,400 per annum) even without the additional customs. Though £54,000 was considered reasonable for 1628–9, when trade was interrupted by war, it was much less than the tack could have been set for in later years. Therefore in November 1634, on the advice of Traquair, the fifteen year tack was declared void (on the ground that tacks for longer than five years were illegal).[17] The following year a new tack for five years was set to William Dick of Braid (the richest Edinburgh merchant of the day) for £60,000 per annum.[18] There were allegations that Traquair had acted high-handedly, accepting Dick's offer privately without holding a public roup or even consulting his fellow commissioners of exchequer,[19] a charge which his known dislike of red tape and traditional methods makes plausible.

The impost of wines, the largest single source of ordinary revenue, was also disposed of irresponsibly, this time by the king himself. Charles made an outright gift of it for sixteen years from 1 August 1631 to the marquis of Hamilton, to repay sums he owed Hamilton in connexion with the latter's unsuccessful

---

[16] *Register of the Great Seal of Scotland* (11 vols., Edinburgh, 1882–1914), *1620–33*, no. 1659; *1634–51*, no. 503; *Stirling's Register*, II, 472, 497, 523–4; Historical Manuscripts Commission (H.M.C.) 8: *9th Report* (3 vols., London, 1883–4), II, 244. For some of the intrigues of the early years of Charles' reign, see *Memoirs of Archibald, Lord Napier : written by himself* (Edinburgh, 1793), passim.

[17] S.R.O., E.4/5, fos. 25v–29r.

[18] S.R.O., E.4/5, fos. 29r, 36v–39v, 110v–114v. Dick also paid a ' grassum ' or entry fee of 20,000 merks.

[19] *Stirling's Register*, II, 825; John Imrie, ' The " Impeachment " of John Stewart, Earl of Traquair ', paper read to the Fifth Scottish Historical Conference, Glasgow, 1970. I am most grateful to Mr Imrie for permission to use material from this paper, cited below as Imrie, Impeachment.

military expedition to Germany. The impost was already set in tack to William Dick for £74,666:13:4 per annum (over a third of ordinary revenue) and he was now to pay this to Hamilton instead of to the exchequer.[20] The only person who seems to have represented the folly of this to the king was Traquair, who ' suggested to the King, that [the impost of wines] were the readiest and surest Moneys that the King had, and that the Treasury would signifie little without them '.[21] Knowledge of the gift to Hamilton had helped to persuade Lord Napier to resign as treasurer depute, as he thought it ' would rander the service difficult '.[22] But instead of making the work of his great rival Traquair impossible, the gift helped to establish the latter's reputation as a loyal servant whose advice carried weight with the king, for he persuaded Charles that it would greatly damage his finances, and Hamilton agreed to surrender it.

The king's huge debts to Hamilton remained, however, and were partly responsible for the increased taxes imposed when parliament met in 1633. Hamilton was appointed collector general of all three taxes (30/- per poundland and $6\frac{1}{4}$ per cent of annual rents for six years, and the ' two of ten ' for three years). Out of these he was first to repay himself £480,000 owed to him by the king and about £240,000 of other royal debts. For the rest of what he collected he was to account to the treasurer.[23] Thus much of these taxes was to be devoted to paying off the king's debts. In the long term this was no doubt wise, but in the event collection was disrupted by the troubles in 1637, and nearly all that had been paid by that time must have gone to the king's creditors. This meant that the taxes which brought him so much unpopularity yielded little or no immediate benefit, giving him no help in strengthening his regime.

The king's main hope of increasing his ordinary revenues substantially lay in his act of revocation and the legislation which accompanied it, introduced in 1625 and ratified by parliament in 1633. The king stood to benefit financially in several ways. Feuars of former kirk lands were to hold their lands directly from the king and pay their feu duties to him instead of to the lords of erection (the laymen now holding these lands), though compensation was to be paid by the Crown to the lords. The king was given power to revoke gifts of offices and pensions, though again compensation was promised. In the settlement of the teinds (tithes) the king was to receive an annuity of 6 per cent of their value. Finally, the king took power to cancel alterations in tenures by which lands were held from him if these changes were to his disadvantage. Most land had originally been held by ' ward and relief ', in return for military service and ' casualties ' or occasional payments. But in many cases previous monarchs had agreed to change such tenures to ' taxed ward ', whereby the casualties were

---

[20] APS, v, 61–2.

[21] G. Burnet, The Memoires of the Lives and Actions of James and William Dukes of Hamilton (London, 1677), pp. 25–6.

[22] Memoirs of Archibald, Lord Napier, p. 95.

[23] RPCS, 1633–5, pp. 305–15; Stirling's Register, II, 499–500.

commuted for a fixed annual money payment which seldom represented their full value. In other cases 'ward and relief' had been changed to 'blench' tenure, whereby the land was held in return for a nominal annual payment. The king was now to be able to restore these to the original 'ward and relief'.[24]

In May 1634 the king appointed a commission anent the exchequer to consider abuses in the royal finances and their administration and unnecessary burdens on the revenues. It was to make recommendations as to how faults might be remedied and the king's rents raised.[25] The commission reported in October. Most of the ways of increasing revenues which it suggested were based on the act of revocation. The king could seize without compensation the feu duties of those of the lords of erection who had not signified their submission to the act, take over other feu duties of kirklands, cancel offices and pensions, and alter tenures. Some specific instances of how economies could be achieved by reform were listed: the king had no need for two solicitors; macers and escheators of exchequer were not necessary; the three receivers of the king's revenues were superfluous as they duplicated work that should be done by the treasurer and his depute; the expenditure of the king's wardrobe needed investigation.[26]

Charles gave orders that the recommendations of the report should be implemented in full,[27] but in fact he did not exercise all the powers he claimed under the revocation, and by no means all of the other recommendations were carried out. To have seized the feu duties of lords of erection who had not submitted would have been folly, uniting the country against the king, so he could only gain feu duties of kirk lands by paying compensation. As he was already deeply in debt such capital expenditure was only possible in a few instances. Similarly the need to pay compensation hindered the abolition of pensions and unnecessary offices and fees. Some offices, like those of the receivers, were suppressed,[28] but other ones deemed unnecessary remained; a new escheator and a new macer of exchequer were appointed in 1635 and 1636 respectively.[29] However, the king probably did benefit considerably from his right to restore tenures to ward and relief. An act of 1633 gave the exchequer power to decide all causes and actions concerning the king's property,[30] and acting through the exchequer Traquair did much to improve the financial position of the Crown – he claimed to have increased the king's rents by a third.[31] In December 1636 Charles thanked Traquair for his great care and industry in improving the customs and Crown rents without grievance to the people.[32] In fact his Scots subjects were very much aggrieved by Traquair's activities. At the first opportunity (June 1640) the covenanters were to pass an act ruling that the exchequer had only

[24] *RPCS, 1625-7*, pp. xix–ccii; *APS*, v, 23–8, 31–9, 189–207.
[25] *Stirling's Register*, II, 735–6.   [26] S.R.O., E.4/5, fos. 21v–23r.
[27] S.R.O., E.4/5, fos. 23r, 24r–24v; *Stirling's Register*, II, 794–5.
[28] Imrie, Impeachment.
[29] S.R.O., E.4/5, fos. 8ov, 162r–162v.   [30] *APS*, v, 35.
[31] Imrie, Impeachment.   [32] H.M.C. 8: *9th Report*, II, 247.

power to judge matters concerning the king's rents and casualties, and that it could not judge the validity of infeftments, which only the court of session could do.[33] It was said that: ' This acte was made to curbe Traquaire, then Lord Thesaurer, quho had assumed to himselue a boundlesse libertie of medling and disposing wpone mens estaites, quher he or his follouers and supports could alledge the King to pretend the werey least intresse, to grate praeiudice and wtter undoing of the subiects.' [34]

As the king's letter of thanks cited above suggests, Traquair was also success-ful in further increasing the revenue from the customs and impost. In spite of strong opposition from the burghs an extra rate of 2½ per cent was added to many duties, though the customs on salmon and plaiding, ' the cheiff commodi-ties exportit from this to forane cuntries ' were left unchanged.[35] The effect of the new augmentation of the impost of wines was seen in a new tack. William Dick and two other merchants agreed to pay £102,000 per annum for the tack (formerly set at £74,666 : 13 : 4 per annum) for five years from November 1637.[36] However, the troubles began before the king could begin to benefit from the new augmentations and in 1641 they were cancelled by parliament on the grounds that parliamentary approval was needed for such a change.[37] Since the 1612 book of rates according to which the rest of the customs and impost were collected had never been ratified by parliament this excuse was hardly convincing.

Traquair's activities as treasurer depute and treasurer made him one of the most unpopular men in Scotland. Even within the administration he was dis-liked and resented for his bullying manner and insistence on reform. By sup-pressing unnecessary offices, cutting through red tape and formality, changing traditional ways of doing things (as when he simplified the accounting system), and not consulting officials concerned before acting, he trod on many toes and offended many vested interests. Certainly all the changes he insisted on made for greater efficiency and were in the king's interests; he was an effective and ruthless treasurer, and much increased the king's revenues.[38] Yet in the long run he undoubtedly did his master far more harm than good. He showed no tact, no sign of understanding that he should try to win support for his reforms from those affected by them, no realization that the advantages of an increase in revenue might be outweighed by the bitter resentment it caused throughout the country. Partly no doubt this was the result of his zeal and impatience with those who could not understand his policies and how necessary it was to increase crown revenues. But he also seems to have enjoyed creating fear and uncer-

[33] *APS*, v, 285, 605.

[34] Balfour, *Historical Works*, ii, 377.

[35] S.R.O., E.4/5, fos. 170r–172v, 180v–181r; L. B. Taylor (ed.), *Aberdeen Council Letters, 1634–44* (London, 1950), ii, 55, 64.

[36] S.R.O., E.4/5, fos. 239r–243r, 245r–246r.

[37] *APS*, v, 431–2.   [38] Imrie, Impeachment.

tainty around him by boasting of his powers and exaggerating his influence over the king. Vague threats as to what would happen to those who opposed him, and dark hints as to what he and the king would do next, flattered his sense of his own importance. As treasurer he was virtually the king's chief minister, for though the chancellor (the archishop of St Andrews) had precedence over him, he was old and out of sympathy with royal policies – and in any case he was said to be terrified of Traquair.[39] None of the other officers of state or councillors were willing to stand up to Traquair; it was said that he ' now guides our Scotts affairs with the most absolute sovereigntie that any subject among us this fourtie yeares did kyth' and that he would enforce obedience with ' horrible fynes '.[40] Yet in reality he had little of the king's confidence outside financial matters, and indeed himself disliked the religious innovations which were central to Charles' policies in Scotland. Increases in taxation were bound to be unpopular, but Traquair's methods, his arrogance and impatience, made discontent much worse than it need have been. It may be that Traquair saw himself as the exponent of ' thorough ' in Scotland, the counterpart of Strafford in Ireland. If so, he flattered himself, but there are interesting parallels between the careers of the two men in the 1630s. Like Strafford, Traquair worked to raise the revenues of the crown and to promote efficiency and centralisation in government. Like Strafford, he tended to use his official position to indulge his defects of personality, his arrogance, his love of power and of bullying those who did not fully support him. Both men could be ruthless when necessary. Both seemed in their prime highly successful in making their master obeyed and in increasing his financial resources, yet both by the very methods by which they achieved this success contributed greatly to the disasters which destroyed the king and their lives' work. But whatever the similarities Strafford was by far the abler and more far sighted of the two, with an ideal of order and good government under a strong monarchy. There is little sign of anything of the sort behind Traquair; he had some love of order and efficiency but he seems to have given little thought to the implications of the king's policies. Certainly he never seems to have realized that royal domination and reform of the kirk was central to royal policy. The difference between the two men is perhaps summed up by their conduct after the troubles began. Strafford remained loyal to his master until death. Traquair from the start began to trim, to try to protect his own interests by retaining the favour of the king while winning that of his opponents.

How important was discontent at increased taxation and at the increased exactions of the exchequer in bringing about rebellion against the king in and after 1637? That such discontent was widespread is certain, but it is impossible to judge it in isolation. No doubt less would have been heard in the way of complaints at the increased financial demands of the Crown if the

39 R. Baillie, *Letters and Journals* (2 vols., Bannatyne Club, 1841–2), I, 7.
40 Balfour, *Historical Works*, II, 200; Baillie, *Letters and Journals*, I, 6,8,11.

king's other policies had been popular. And as with these other policies, it was probably as much fear of what the king might do as dislike of what he had already done which aroused opposition. Traquair's threats and hints created a tense atmosphere in which rumour thrived and uncertainty was widespread.

The Collapse of the Exchequer, 1637–41

The extent to which the weakness of the king's financial position contributed to the outbreak of revolt may be hard to assess; though certainly it was a minor issue compared with hatred of his religious policies. But, once revolt began, financial weakness undoubtedly contributed considerably to the hesitancy and irresolution of the regime's response to the covenanters' challenge. Decisive action would have required ready cash. The longer the crisis lasted the worse the situation became, for refusal to pay money due to the king quickly became widespread and the exchequer was powerless to enforce payment. The king's action in removing the exchequer (along with the privy council and court of session) from Edinburgh from November 1637 to March 1638 was intended to punish the burgh for supporting his opponents. Instead it hastened the decline of the exchequer; cut off from its records and wandering from Linlithgow to Dalkeith and then to Stirling,[41] it was completely ineffectual.

The financial plight of the regime became clear late in 1638 when the marquis of Hamilton was in Scotland as king's commissioner, trying to settle the troubles. He persuaded the earl of Mar to agree to surrender the governorship of Edinburgh Castle to the king for £2,000 sterling, but had to tell the king ' itt onlie restheth hou he shall be payed, for in your excheker heire ther is none, and lend no man uill, tho the securatie be neuer so good.' Mar prudently refused to accept an order on the exchequer for payment, preferring a guarantee of payment on the security of Hamilton's own estate. The archbishop of St Andrews insisted on similar security when he agreed to resign the chancellorship for £2,500 sterling. Hamilton himself got no payment for his work in Scotland for the king.[42]

Clearly, so far as Scotland was concerned, the king was virtually bankrupt, and when in the Bishops' Wars of 1639 and 1640 he tried to regain control of Scotland he had to rely entirely on English resources and the willingness of Scots royalists to use their own wealth to help him.

This being so, it is not surprising that the covenanters did not at first, when they took over the effective government of the country, attempt to uplift royal revenues to finance their cause and hinder the king's, preferring instead to raise their own taxes and loans.[43] The first major interference by the covenanters did

---

[41] S.R.O., E.4/5, fos. 238v, 245r, 246r, 257v, 258v.

[42] S. R. Gardiner (ed.), *Hamilton Papers* (Camden Society, 1880), p. 54; Burnet, *Hamilton*, pp. 64–5, 89; H.M.C. 21: *Hamilton* (London, 1887), i, 96.

[43] For which see D. Stevenson, ' The Financing of the Cause of the Covenants, 1638–51 ', *Scottish Historical Review*, LI (1972), 89–123.

not come until October 1639, after an attempt by the exchequer to set a tack of the customs had failed as no one appeared to bid.[44] The 'Tables' or committees through which the covenanters ruled therefore intervened and appointed William Dick collector general of both the customs and the impost of wines (his tack of the latter being cancelled) for two years from November 1639.[45] As collector general Dick was to account for all he collected instead of paying a fixed annual sum as tacksman, since in such troubled times no one was willing to commit himself in advance to fixed payments. Being a good covenanter, Dick paid what he collected to them, not to the exchequer. According to the royalist historian John Spalding the covenanters did not start uplifting rents of crown lands for their own use until mid-1640,[46] and this is consistent with other evidence. Thus the marquis of Argyll's commission from the committee of estates (the successor of the 'Tables') for uplifting the king's rents in Argyll is dated 17 September 1640, though it empowered him to intromit with all such rents due since 1637.[47]

With the treasurer, Traquair, denounced by the covenanters as one of the leading 'incendiaries' responsible for the troubles, and about half the commissioners of the exchequer (including four bishops) having fled, any pretence by the exchequer to be still administering the king's revenues collapsed. The frequency with which the exchequer met clearly demonstrates this breakdown. In 1635 and 1636, the last years before the troubles began the exchequer register records meetings on approximately 56 and 52 days respectively. In 1637, 1638 and 1639 the number of days on which meetings were held fell to 36, 29 and (up to 26 August 1639) 15.[48] From August 1639 until January 1642 no exchequer register survives, and probably none was kept for the exchequer minute book (which admittedly does not record all the meetings in previous years recorded in the register) notes only two meetings in 1640 and five in 1641, with none at all between 22 January 1640 and 8 September 1641.[49] At least one meeting did in fact take place in this period,[50] but clearly the exchequer was moribund and efforts by the king's servants to collect his revenues had virtually ceased.

Even where revenues were uplifted for use by the covenanters little was done to ensure that they were paid. Payment of the customs and impost was not enforced, even though Dick paid them what he collected. Thus when it was feared in January 1641 that the fact that the committee of estates had been meddling with the customs would be resented by the king and interfere with the treaty being negotiated with him, the committee could state that it had only acted after being continually petitioned for nine months by the collectors to help them in uplifting the customs and impost. The collectors had com-

[44] S.R.O., E.5/2, Exchequer Minute Book 1634-49, fos. 70r, 70v.
[45] S.R.O., PA.14/1, Register of the Committee for Common Burdens, fos. 256r-257r.
[46] J. Spalding, Memorialls of the Trubles (2 vols., Spalding Club, 1850-1), i, 301.
[47] S.R.O., PA.14/1, fos. 199r-199v.   [48] S.R.O., E.4/5, fos. 42v-294r.
[49] S.R.O., E.5/2, fos. 72v-80r.   [50] In July 1641, APS, v, 639-40.

28

plained that few or none would obey them, and that great numbers of ships had gone to or from Scotland without paying any customs. As some of the collectors' commissions had expired the committee had set the customs of Bo'ness, Glasgow, Dundee and Aberdeen. Elsewhere the committee had only tried to enforce payment. Many merchants argued that they should not pay customs to the king at a time when the king's English navy was capturing many of their ships and goods, William Dick was daily supplicating for action against those who would not pay,[51] and the committee of estates was the only effective authority in the country which could even attempt to enforce payment.

The exact total of royal revenues uplifted by the covenanters in 1639–41 is not certain. An account prepared in 1643 summarises the sums uplifted as follows:

From the customs and impost, by William Dick					£60,533: 12: 0
,,	,,	,,	,,	,,	by sub collectors	£11,666: 13: 4

Total from customs and impost	£72,200: 5: 4
From rents and other sources	£14,844: 13: 3

Total	£87,044: 18: 7 [52]

The committee for common burdens (established in 1641 to sort out the confused finances of the covenanters) confirmed that the total paid by Dick to the covenanters out of the customs and impost was £60,533: 12: 0, and guaranteed him repayment of any part of this sum that the exchequer would not allow him in his accounts.[53] But it is difficult to reconcile these estimates by the covenanters of royal revenues paid to them with exchequer accounts. Thus an account of Dick's intromissions with customs and impost in 1639–41, signed by the commissioners of treasury in December 1643, allows Dick £119,000 for payments made by him out of these revenues to the covenanters, and this is copied in the accounts of the receivers general.[54] This is nearly twice the estimate made by the covenanters, and directly contradicts a report that in January 1644 the exchequer refused to allow Dick even the £60,533: 12: 0 of the covenanters' estimate.[55] The most likely explanation for such discrepancies is that the £119,000 represents not only sums paid by Dick to the covenanters but also much other customs and impost revenue for which he was accountable but which the exchequer agreed to cancel as it had been impossible to collect because of the disturbed state of the country.

In any case, the total of royal revenue paid to the covenanters represents only a small proportion of the total arrears of royal revenue in the period; most of

---

[51] Edinburgh University Library, MS Dc.4.16, Transactions of the Committee of Estates, fos. 55v, 63v–64r. [52] S.R.O., PA.16/3/5/3, Army Papers, Accounts, p. 13.

[53] S.R.O., PA.14/1, fos. 157r, 221r, 256r–257r.

[54] S.R.O., E.73/9/1, Customs Accounts; S.R.O., E.27/1, Receivers General's Accounts, fo. 41r.

[55] S.R.O., PA.14/1, fos. 260v–262r.

the arrears represented payments due which were never made at all, to the covenanters or to the king's officials. Such non-payment had helped to ensure that the king's Scottish revenues were in no state to help him in the Bishops' Wars; and, moreover, the more money was withheld from the exchequer, the more there was available for the covenanters to collect through their own taxes and forced loans for use against the king.

The disorder into which the king's finances in Scotland had fallen since 1637 meant that when preparations for his visit to Scotland (to try to reach a settlement with the covenanters) began in mid-1641 there was little money available in the exchequer. On 7 June the privy council met and the councillors present agreed to borrow money on their personal surety for the king's use, but the committee of estates warned that any considerable sums of money required would have to be brought from England.[56] On 20 June the king sent the treasurer depute, Sir James Carmichael, to the privy council with a letter ordering it to raise whatever money was necessary for the royal visit. Carmichael told the council that ' the haill moneyis sent hame [from England] for advanceing of his majesteis service ' were not more than £1,600 sterling, ' quhilk wilbe litill moir then an earnest in so great ane Imployment '. The councillors therefore borrowed 100,000 marks from William Dick on their own surety.[57] Even in more settled times royal visits had strained the resources of the Scottish exchequer, and borrowing money from Dick to finance such visits had become almost traditional, 80,000 merks having been borrowed from him in 1617 and 250,000 merks in 1633. Unfortunately no accounts of the expenses of the king's visit in 1641, and how they were paid, seem to have survived, though it was said that the cost of the visit was 700,000 merks, excluding the cost of provisions for the household at Holyroodhouse which were sent from England.[58]

The Exchequer in the hands of the Covenanters, 1641–50

When the king left Scotland in November 1641 acts concerning his revenues to which he had given his assent had greatly weakened his control over them. He had accepted that all payments that had been made to the covenanters out of his revenues prior to 29 June 1641 should not be questioned.[59] He had agreed to acts cancelling the new augmentations of the customs and impost and limiting the powers of the exchequer. He had failed to reach agreement with parliament on a new treasurer but had accepted a commission of treasury as a compromise until the next parliament met. The five commissioners were the earl of Loudoun (chancellor), the marquis of Argyll, the earls of Glencairn

[56] Ibid. fo. 107r; National Library of Scotland, MS Wodrow, Folio LXXIII, fos. 101v–102r.
[57] Acts of the exchequer and parliament promised the councillors who had borrowed the money repayment out of the king's revenues as soon as possible, APS, v, 324, 639–40. The money was repaid to Dick (S.R.O., E.27/1, fo. 42r) though when is not clear.
[58] Purves, Revenues, p. xliv; RPCS, 1633–5, p. 309; Spalding, Memorialls, II, 95.
[59] APS, v, 416.

VII

30

and Lindsay (later Crawford-Lindsay) and Sir James Carmichael, whose position as treasurer depute was ratified.[60] Charles can have had little confidence
that such men would take much trouble to protect his interests, for though
Glencairn and Carmichael probably had some sympathy with him they were
willing to serve the covenanters, and the other three commissioners were leading opponents of the king. He was allowed to choose new commissioners of
exchequer without consulting parliament – perhaps an indication that a permanent exchequer was still regarded as an innovation and as not very important – and they consequently include a number of his supporters, such as the
earls of Roxburgh and Lanark and Sir James Galloway.[61] But the exchequer
was dominated by the commissioners of treasury and was soon to prove far
from obedient to the royal will. Adam Blair of Lochwood and William Lockhart of Carstairs were appointed by the king to be his receivers.[62] Whether it
was the king or the covenanters who took the initiative in making these appointments is not clear. It may be that the covenanters insisted on a return to the
traditional practice of appointing receivers, since the office had been abolished as
part of the unpopular exchequer reforms after 1634. But equally it may be that
the king himself, calculating that the new commissioners of treasury were
unlikely to prove efficient or loyal, decided to appoint receivers. Whatever the
reason for their appointment both Blair and Lockhart proved to be efficient
and hard working servants who carried on the routine work of collecting royal
revenues as best they could, with little help or encouragement, throughout all
the violent changes of the years 1641 to 1651.

The king's debts in Scotland had been greatly increased by the expense of
his visit in 1641, and he had optimistically granted pensions to most of the leading covenanters in the hope of buying their support, further increasing the
burdens on the exchequer. Thus Loudoun and Argyll were each granted
£12,000 per annum (which did not prevent them from joining the treasurer
depute in complaining at the king making so many gifts from his revenues
without the consent of the exchequer!).[63] Sir Archibald Johnston of Wariston
was given £2,400 per annum, Alexander Hamilton (general of the artillery)
£9,600 per annum, and the young earl of Rothes £10,000 per annum. Charles
made the kirk a grant of £6,000 per annum, to be devoted to pious uses and
other necessities as the general assembly thought fit.[64] These grants alone amounted to £52,000 per annum, a ruinous sum considering the state of the revenues.

The king had not been back in England long before he repented of his prodi-

[60] Ibid. v, 388, 428; *Register of the Great Seal of Scotland, 1634-51*, no. 970.

[61] S.R.O., E.4/6, Exchequer Act Book 1642-7, fos. 2r-3v.

[62] S.R.O., PS.1/109, Register of the Privy Seal, fos. 267v, 269r-269v; S.R.O., PS.1/110, fo.
161v; S.R.O., E.5/2, fo. 83r; S.R.O., E.4/6, fos. 10r-10v.

[63] R. K. Marshall, ' A Calendar of the Correspondence in the Hamilton Archives at Lennoxlove '
(Appendix to Edinburgh University Ph.D. Thesis, 1970), I, 229.

[64] *APS*, v, 497, 519, vi.i, 263-4, 271-2; S.R.O., PS.1/109, fos. 270r, 274v, 281r; S.R.O.,
PS.1/110, fos. 151v, 152r; S.R.O., PS.1/111, fos. 39r-40r.

gality, realising that it had not won him support. In December 1641 he wrote to the commissioners of exchequer that he had been informed that since the start of the commotions in Scotland he had granted gifts, pensions and precepts which amounted to a greater sum than his revenues could bear. He therefore ordered an inquiry into the condition of his exchequer, so that, having compared the state of his revenues with the burdens on them, he could decide what action to take. To help in this inquiry all gifts or precepts granted by the king were to be exhibited before the exchequer within three months or be cancelled. Some of the gifts had been assigned to be paid out of specific revenues, especially out of the customs and impost, and the king now annulled all such assignments as he had been told that they would be a hindrance in setting tacks of the customs and impost, which were the most considerable parts of his income.[65]

Yet in the event the king continued to make gifts prejudicial to his revenues (in spite of the complaints of his advisers)[66] in attempts to buy the loyalty of prominent Scots, and the new commissioners of exchequer soon showed that they had little intention of obeying the king's orders or serving his interests. They granted a tack of the customs and impost to Sir William Dick (knighted by the king in 1641) from November 1641 for five years at £134,666:13:4 per annum (impost £80,666:13:4, customs £54,000), though John Carmichael (son of the treasurer depute) complained that he had bid 5,000 merks per annum more than this; it would seem that Dick was favoured as the better covenanter and a man to whom the covenanters still owed great sums.[67] Nothing seems to have been done about the king's order for an inquiry into the state of the exchequer. In April and August 1642 he repeated his orders, adding that no payments whatsoever were to be made from his revenues until he had been informed of their present condition.[68] Both letters were ignored. The only one of the king's instructions that was acted upon (even when it inconvenienced covenanters) was the cancelling of assignments for payment of gifts and pensions. Thus in 1644 the committee of estates with the army in England complained that the exchequer, having found that the king 'by granting promiscuously to multitudes of persons how so ever affected, gifts of pensions and assigning of localities in them wes like to dilapidat his wholl revenues in that kingdome did without exception discharge all localities in any pension', thus defrauding the general of the artillery of his pension, payment of which had been promised out of the impost of wines.[69]

The exchequer's lack of obedience to the king was also seen in the matter of Sir James Galloway, the master of requests and himself a commissioner of

---

[65] S.R.O., E.4/6, fos. 4r–5r.
[66] E.g. Marshall, 'Calendar', I, 237, 246, 253.
[67] S.R.O., E.4/6, fos. 18r–25v, 210r–216v.
[68] Ibid. fos. 70v, 100v–101r.
[69] S.R.O., PA.11/2, Register of the Committee of Estates (Army), fos. 76r–77r; *A Collection of State Papers of John Thurloe*, T. Birch (ed.) (7 vols., London, 1742), I, 36–7; *APS*, v, 519.

exchequer. The exchequer had accepted many of the gifts of fees and pensions made by the king, but not Galloway's in spite of letters from the king in May and July 1642, to the former of which the king had added in his own hand ' I command that this servant of myne be payed '.[70] Galloway's case was exceptional in that he angered the covenanters by claiming (with the support of the king) to be joint secretary of state with the earl of Lanark. However, even royalists who tried to avoid upsetting the covenanters found it virtually impossible to get their pensions and fees paid by the exchequer after 1641. The king's orders in their favour were ignored. But there was no indiscriminate plundering of the king's revenues by the covenanters for their own use. The fact was that legitimate claims on the exchequer were far greater than the revenues could bear, especially as the disturbed state of the country made efficient collection impossible. In these circumstances it was hardly surprising that the covenanters should have given themselves preference, and that when there was not enough money to pay their own fees and pensions in full they should have ignored the equally legitimate demands of royalists.

From 1642 until Charles II's arrival in Scotland in 1650 the covenanting regimes were scrupulous in keeping distinct the king's ordinary revenues on the one hand and the money they raised by taxes, borrowings and fines on the other. The former were (with a few minor exceptions) used, as formerly, to pay pensions granted by the king, the expenses of the household, and the fees and expenses of traditional officials and courts. All the new officials and bodies created by the covenanting regime on the other hand were paid from the latter. Thus Archibald Primrose was paid as clerk of the privy council by the treasurer or receivers out of the royal revenues, and as clerk of the committee of estates by the commissary general out of parliamentary loans and taxes. Similarly Patrick Brown (a clerk of exchequer) received payments for organising postal services and the carrying of dispatches from both sources, for his services to the privy council and exchequer on the one hand, and to parliament and the committees of estates on the other. Early in 1643 the committee for common burdens suggested that the clerk of the commissioners for conserving the peace (Archibald Primrose again) should be paid by the exchequer. But this was only suggested as the burdens on the revenues which the committee controlled were already great, and the exchequer declined to make any such payment to Primrose.[71] No further attempt was made to confuse the uses to which the two types of revenue were devoted except that the Engagers used a small sum from the exchequer to help raise an army in 1648.

In 1642 and 1643 the exchequer register records that the commissioners of exchequer met on about 69 and 49 days respectively – as or more frequently than before the troubles. But this revival was not sustained. In 1644 and 1645

[70] S.R.O., E.4/6, fos. 75r–76v.
[71] S.R.O., PA.14/2, Proceedings of the Scots Commissioners for Conserving the Articles of the Treaty, 1642–3, pp. 36, 44; S.R.O., PA.14/1, fo. 206v.

meetings were held on only 19 and 12 days respectively as civil war in the north and plague in the south disrupted administration. Partial recovery followed in the relatively settled years of 1646 and 1647, with 30 and at least 35 days of meeting, but in 1648 meetings fell to about 15 (though the figures for 1647 have to be taken partly, and those for 1648 wholly, from the less reliable minute books as no exchequer register survives). This fall is associated with the bitter disputes between the moderate 'Engagers' and the extreme covenanting 'kirk party', culminating in the seizure of power by the kirk party after the Engagers' invasion of England had been defeated.[72]

In the continued confusion of these years little attempt was made to improve collection of the king's revenues. To the covenanters they were of minor importance, and it is possible that they calculated that it might prove dangerous to improve revenues which, though for the present under their own control, might one day be in the hands of the king.

The commission of treasury granted in 1641 expired when the Scottish parliament next met in June 1644. Commissioners who were being sent to negotiate with the king were therefore instructed to ask him to appoint the earl of Crawford-Lindsay treasurer; but parliament then proceeded to appoint him to the office without awaiting the king's reply. It also nominated new commissioners of exchequer, though the 1641 act giving parliament the right to advise the king in choosing officials and the power to reject his appointees had not originally been regarded as extending to the exchequer. In any case, in its appointments of a treasurer and commissioners of exchequer parliament was now turning the act upside down; instead of parliament accepting or rejecting appointments made by the king, it was asking the king to accept appointments it had made.[73] The king refused to ratify the appointments but this did not deter the new officials from acting as if he had. The position was not regularised until Charles joined the Scottish army in England in 1646; he at once became virtually a prisoner of the covenanters and agreed to ratify the 1644 appointments.[74] He tried to assert his authority by also nominating additional commissioners of exchequer, apparently in an attempt to win the support of the marquis of Argyll by giving his supporters a majority on the exchequer. But parliament refused to accept the changes, opposition being organised by the duke of Hamilton whose faction stood to lose control of the exchequer had the additions been approved.[75]

---

[72] S.R.O., E.4/6, fos. 1r–347v; S.R.O., E.5/2, fos. 146v–163r.

[73] *APS*, vi.i, 129, 192–3, 235–6, 354–5; Balfour, *Historical Works*, iii, 221; *S.R.O.*, E.4/6, fos. 2r–3v.

[74] The 1644 commission of exchequer was renewed several times and remained in force until the fall of the engagers in 1648, *APS*, vi.i, 303–5, 433, 460, 563, 633, 780.

[75] *The Diplomatic Correspondence of Jean de Montereul . . .* , J. G. Fotheringham (ed.) (2 vols., Scottish History Society, 1898–9), ii, 30–1, 51, 82. The cost of maintaining the king while he was with the Scots army was at first met by the commissary general out of the covenanters' revenues. Between May and September 1646 he paid out £4,314 sterling. Arrangements were then made for the exchequer to support the king, and in Sept.–Dec. it provided at least £2,623 sterling for this

34

The weakness of the king's position proved beneficial to Sir William Dick. His five year tack of the customs and impost (at £134,666:13:4 per annum) ended in November 1646. It had not been a profitable venture, for the civil wars in England and Scotland had much disrupted trade and collection of the duties. He estimated his losses under the tack at £184,666:13:4, and appealed for compensation under a clause in the tack which promised recompense to tacksmen who suffered losses through plague, war or invasion. Charles agreed to cancel £96,600 of the tack duties.[76]

It is not clear whether Dick bid for a new tack of the customs and impost. On the first two days assigned for the roup by the exchequer no bidders appeared, but on the third day a group of five prominent merchants were given a tack at £149,333:6:8 per annum. What had induced them to bid more than had ever been given before for such a tack at a time when the political situation was confused, plague, war and rebellion threatened and trade showed little sign of recovery from earlier disasters is hard to explain, though it may have been that the bidders were encouraged by the fact that Dick had received compensation for his losses on the previous tack to bid more than they expected to have to pay.[77]

After the defeat of the Engagers in the autumn of 1648 the committee of estates of the new kirk party regime set up a subcommittee on the condition of the exchequer and forbade anyone to intromit with the king's revenues, as most of the officials concerned had supported the engagement.[78] But there is little sign that these officials had made much use of the king's revenues to help the Engagers. The treasurer did use £24,000 (perhaps all he had at his disposal) for helping to raise a regiment and bring forces from Ireland,[79] but this was exceptional.

The minutes of the subcommittee on the condition of the exchequer show that (at first at least) it mainly concerned itself with the customs and impost, though it called for the rolls and all other records of the exchequer, and ordered the exchequer clerks and the receivers to appear before it and account for their actions.[80] The question of the customs and impost centred on the conditions

purpose, *Papers relating to the army of the Solemn League and Covenant*, C. S. Terry (ed.) (2 vols., Scottish History Society, 1917), II, 519, 549, 608; S.R.O., E.28/40/2, 3, 5, 11, Treasury Vouchers.

[76] S.R.O., E.73/10/5, Customs Accounts; S.R.O., E.73/11/11, Customs Accounts; S.R.O., E.26/8, Treasury Accounts.

[77] S.R.O., E.4/6, fos. 279v, 281r–281v, 284v–291r.

[78] S.R.O., PA.11/7, Register of the Committee of Estates, fos. 43v–44v; S.R.O., PA.7/5/38, Supplementary Parliamentary Papers.

[79] S.R.O., E.27/8, Receivers General's Accounts, fo. 27r. By contrast the duke of Hamilton and his brother the earl of Lanark spent about £264,000 Scots (£22,000 sterling) borrowed on their own security in raising the army of the engagement to try to help the king; H. C. Foxcroft, ' An Early Rescension of Burnet's Memoirs of the Dukes of Hamilton ', *English Historical Review*, xxiv (1909), 529–30.

[80] S.R.O., E.5/3, Minutes of Committee on the Condition of the Exchequer, fo. 2r.

of the tack granted in November 1646, especially the clauses concerning compensation to tacksmen for losses caused by war or plague, and allowing the tacksmen, if they were being caused such losses, to renounce their tack and instead act as collectors general, accounting to the exchequer for what they had collected instead of paying fixed tack duties. At some time, presumably after 30 August 1648 when the commissioners of the exchequer had last met,[81] the tacksmen had intimated their intention of renouncing their tack, and had taken instruments thereupon before the treasurer depute; was this in itself sufficient to release them from their tack? The subcommittee at first was inclind to insist that they pay the tack duties, but eventually accepted that declaring their intention of renouncing the tack was all that was needed to free them from it. The former tacksmen wished to be allowed to continue as collectors of the customs and impost, but the subcommittee refused to allow this; some of them had supported the engagement, and collection was less profitable and more trouble to the exchequer than a tack. Therefore the committee of estates was recommended to authorise a new roup of the customs and impost. This the committee did, entrusting the roup to the same subcommittee. Bidding (on 1 November) was between Sir William Dick, who opened with an offer of 180,000 merks per annum, and John Majoribanks who offered 190,000 merks per annum. Eventually Dick won the tack for himself and four others with a bid of 224,000 merks ($£149,333:6:8$) per annum for five years – exactly the same amount as the previous tack. The four men who joined Dick in the tack included two of the tacksmen of 1646–8 who were evidently considered less guilty of accession to the engagement than the others.[82]

The subcommittee for regulating the exchequer decided that the money paid in advance by the tacksmen, £80,000, should be distributed as follows:

to the collector of the kirk	£12,000
to the earl of Loudoun	£12,000
to the marquis of Argyll	£24,000
to Sir Archibald Johnston of Wariston	£12,000
to James Stewart, provost of Edinburgh	£17,433:12:0
to the earl of Lothian	£12,000 [83]

These payments all represented arrears of fees and pensions due to men who had suffered for their opposition to the engagement, though they do rather suggest a distribution of spoils among the victors (especially as four of those to be paid were members of the subcommittee).

Whether the subcommittee of the committee of estates continued to sit and direct exchequer affairs after it had settled the tack of the customs and imposts is

[81] S.R.O., E.5/2, fo. 163r.

[82] S.R.O., E.5/3, fos. 3v–5r; S.R.O., PA.11/7, fos. 52v–53v, 41r; APS, vi.ii, 314–5.

[83] S.R.O., E.5/3, fo. 5v. How these sums, totalling £89,433:12:0 were to be paid out of £80,000 was not explained.

36

not clear, but there was evidently no authority dealing with such matters by February 1649, for parliament then authorized the chancellor to pass suspensions in matters concerning the exchequer 'untill the exchequer be settled or some course takin thairwith'. The earl of Crawford-Lindsay was deposed as treasurer and Sir James Carmichael as treasurer depute in February and March respectively for having supported the engagement, though the receivers were allowed to keep their places. Sir Daniel Carmichael, son of Sir James but a follower of the chancellor, the earl of Loudoun, was appointed treasurer depute, and the treasury was put in commission, the commissioners including Argyll and Loudoun who had served in the same capacity in 1641–4.[84]

New commissioners for the exchequer were also appointed, on 16 March; eighteen commissioners plus all the officers of state. Whereas previously nearly all commissioners of exchequer had been nobles, or lairds who were officers of state or lords of session, the new commissioners (excluding the officers of state) consisted of five nobles, eight lairds (none of whom were lords of session), and five burgesses. Having been left to the king to appoint in 1641, and been appointed by parliament but limited in personnel to the type of men who had formally been appointed in 1644, the commission of exchequer now in 1649 became virtually a committee of parliament containing representatives of all three estates.[85] It was much more clearly subordinate to parliament than before, and only nominally obedient to the king, with little power or influence.

Charles II in Scotland, 1650–1

The importance of the exchequer revived briefly in 1650 when agreement was reached with Charles II that he should come to Scotland. On 23 May Parliament appointed a committee to consider accommodating and entertaining the king, and a week later another committee was set up to call for an account of the king's rents. That it was necessary to appoint a special committee to do this suggests that the commissioners of exchequer, the obvious persons to turn to for such an account, were not supervising the king's revenues very efficiently.[86] In its report, dated 17 June 1650, the committee made four proposals to help supply money for the king. First, that the commissioners of exchequer should be forbidden to authorize any further payments of pensions without warrant of parliament, and that the royal revenue should be used solely to pay for the upkeep of the king and his household. Secondly, that precepts for payments from the king's revenues granted since the beginning of 1650 and not already paid should not be paid without parliament's permission. Thirdly, that parliament should appoint some persons to try all pensions payable by the

---

[84] *APS*, vi.ii, 174–6, 204, 271–3, 274, 321; Balfour, *Historical Works*, iii, 389.

[85] *APS*, vi.ii, 321–2.

[86] Ibid. vi.ii, 567, 569, 570, 572, 573, 574. Unfortunately there are no surviving exchequer registers or minute books for the period 6 April 1649 to the Cromwellian conquest except for a fragment of a register, 7 Feb.–29 Mar. 1650, S.R.O., E.4/7.

exchequer, why they had been granted, and which of them should (in whole or part) be cancelled. Finally, the committee suggested that all gifts or dispositions of Crown lands since 1603 should be considered, together with how they could be restored to the Crown.[87]

The last two of these proposals were for long term reforms, and were impossible to implement at a time of crisis with an English invasion threatening, but they are interesting in that they recall some of the proposals made by the commissioners investigating the state of the exchequer in 1634. The committee also made an estimate of the total ordinary royal revenue, £211,331:5:0 per annum.[88] This report was read and accepted by parliament on 3 July, and a 'Commission anent the setiling of his Majesties rents' was set up. It was probably this commission (now referred to as the committee of accounts) whose membership was altered two days later and to which parliament recommended the king to 'give an Commission in the vsual way to them ... for calling in the accomptis of his Majesties rents since the last fitted accompts ... and to prosecute the 4 articles befor agreid on be parliament and to try and impruve the kings rents to his best advantage.' Again one would have thought that this was a job for the exchequer, four new commissioners of which were appointed to join those nominated in 1649.[89]

In spite of all this activity little progress seems to have been made at improving the king's revenues, and parliament had to raise special taxes for the king's use; these consisted of 80,000 merks to be advanced by the burghs and a total of three and a half months' maintenance – the monthly maintenance had been the covenanters' main tax since 1645.

Parliament also concerned itself with the organization of the king's household. On 27 June 1650 a committee was ordered to purge it of unsuitable officers and servants, who were to be replaced by the marquis of Argyll in his capacity as hereditary great master household. On 5 July Michael Elphinstone and Sir George Melvill were appointed jointly to the office of under master household, serving alternately.[90] John Dickson of Busbie, clerk of exchequer and dictator of the rolls, served the king as argentier; as the chief financial official of the household, it was his duty to receive all money necessary for the king's use from the receivers and supply provisions for the household. When in Scotland in 1641 Charles I had appointed James Durhame of Pitkerro clerk of exchequer, dictator of the rolls and argentier, but he had been deposed in 1649 for having supported the engagement and replaced by Busbie, whose gift was ratified by Charles II in April 1651.[91]

Supervision of the household in general was entrusted to a committee known

---

[87] Calendar of State Papers, Domestic, 1650 (London, 1876), p. 207.

[88] State Papers of John Thurloe, I, 153.

[89] APS, VI.ii, 600, 604.

[90] Ibid. VI.ii, 593, 605; Stirling's Register, I, 345.

[91] APS, VI.i, 419, 666; S.R.O., PA.11/8, fos. 39v–40v; S.R.O., PS.1/116, fo. 189r.

as the board of the green cloth. This name was an importation from England, where the board of that name was 'in direct charge of finance and organisation' of the household below stairs. Such boards had been appointed in Scotland before for royal visits; thus there are references to assessors and a clerk of the green cloth in 1617, and to the green cloth in 1633,[92] though it is uncertain whether such a board existed in 1641. The board which sat in 1650–1 was probably appointed by the commissioners of exchequer. Those who attended meetings of the board between 9 July 1650 and 7 July 1651 (for which period its minute book survives) were the three masters household and the argentier, the treasurer depute and the two receivers, John Rawsone (an exchequer clerk like the argentier), Sir Michael Balfour of Denmylne, and Sir Robert Drummond of Medhope. Adam Keltie (another exchequer clerk) acted as clerk to the board.[93]

In the confusion of the times, with the king frequently moving, provisions scarce, and uncertainty and fear ubiquitous the day to day running of the household can have been no easy task. A list of pay for servants in the household below stairs on 22 August 1650 shows its strength as about sixty-eight servants and a few servants' servants; a small number compared with the about 305 servants and 195 servants' servants of the English household below stairs in the 1630s, but surprisingly large in the circumstances, with money so short and the king so little regarded by the real rulers of the country.[94] After the battle of Dunbar (3 September) the diets of servants and the number of dishes served at the king's and other tables had to be reduced, and on 20 September it was recorded that 'the greene cloth for reasones knawn to them selffs have redactit the number of servands in under offices and their allowance'; the reason was obvious – plain necessity.[95]

It is possible that the king's lack of money was due to more than just the shortages inevitable in such a period of crisis; the regime which ruled in his name distrusted his intentions and may well have decided that to keep him short of money would increase his dependence on it. This would explain the anger which it is said to have displayed when the burgh of Aberdeen made the king a present of money.[96] At the restoration Charles II refused to continue Sir Daniel Carmichael in office as treasurer depute since Carmichael had refused to give him money he asked for in 1650[97]; the king believed the refusal had been a matter of policy.

At the end of December 1650 parliament again urged the commissioners of treasury to improve the king's rents, but with most of the country in English hands there was little that could be done. In March 1651 another committee was

---

[92] Aylmer, *The King's Servants*, p. 30; S.R.O., E.34/50/5, Papers relating to James VI's visit to Scotland; *RPCS, 1616–19*, p. 387; *RPCS, 1633–5*, p. 108.

[93] S.R.O., E.31/19, Minute Book of the Board of the Green Cloth; S.R.O., E.27/1, fos. 21v, 25v.

[94] S.R.O., E.31/19, fos. 16v–17v; Aylmer, *The King's Servants*, pp. 472–3.

[95] S.R.O., E.31/19, fos. 21r–21v, 24r.

[96] [F. Eglesfield], *Monarchy Revived* (London, 1661), p. 89.

[97] G. Mackenzie, *Memoirs of the Affairs of Scotland* (Edinburgh, 1812), p. 9.

set up to consider the accounts of the commissioners of treasury and the affairs of the king's house, but again without result, though the marquis of Argyll complained bitterly (as master household and one of the commissioners of treasury) that he had often represented to parliament the condition of the king's house through lack of money.[98] An extra month's maintenance was imposed for the king's use and all food for his household was freed from paying excise, but as little of the maintenance could be collected and payment of the excise had largely broken down anyway this was little real help. In June the king agreed to the accounts of his revenues being inspected by a parliamentary committee, as the accounts were 'now of lang tyme lyin over onfitted and endit thir many yeiris by past'; parliament insisted on such an investigation (especially into the accounts of the taxes granted by parliament to the king) before it would make any further grants to support him; once he had agreed another month's maintenance was voted for him.[99] A new receiver had to be appointed, John Campbell, formerly commissary of the Scottish army in Ireland,[100] as Sir William Lockhart had died,[101] but before he could take up his duties or the committee investigating the king's accounts could report, the Cromwellian conquest was completed.

How much the household received and spent in 1650-1 is not clear; of the parliamentary taxes imposed to support it only a small proportion was ever collected by the receivers – £46,971:3:4 out of £429,312:12:7 imposed.[102] From this and the ordinary royal revenues the receivers paid £76,020:5:4 to the argentier,[103] but as other household fees and expenses were paid directly by the receivers and not through the argentier it is impossible to assess the total devoted to the household.

The Aftermath

In spite of years spent after the restoration in trying to sort out the confused accounts of royal revenues during the civil wars none of the treasurers' accounts for 1636-51 were ever completely audited. But those of the receivers, Sir William Lockhart and his heirs and Adam Blair, were finally audited and closed in 1681.[104] There is no sign that previously the accounts of receivers had ever been audited separately from the accounts of the treasurers, but in this case it was found easier to audit the accounts of receivers who had remained in office for ten years than those of the various treasurers and commissioners of treasury

---

[98] *APS*, vi.ii, 631, 644, 650.
[99] Ibid. vi.ii, 656, 657-8, 684, 685-6.
[100] S.R.O., PS.1/116, fo. 183v.
[101] He was 'bedfast not able to sturr out of his dwellinghous in Perth' on 30 April 1651, S.R.O., E.31/19, fo. 38r.
[102] S.R.O., E.27/1, fos. 11v, 43v-46r.
[103] Ibid. fos. 22r, 45r.
[104] Ibid. passim.

40

of the period. The total 'charge' of the receivers' accounts (all the sums they were accountable for) was about £2,845,197:10:3 Scots. Of this at least £1,382,342:14:4 had not been received by the time of the Cromwellian conquest – though the accounts were not audited until 1681 they show the state of affairs at the time of the conquest, for the receivers took no part in efforts to collect what then rested unpaid. Some of these 'rests' (money due but not paid) were collected by the English conquerors, and some after the restoration, when the earl of Crawford-Lindsay (re-appointed treasurer) was authorised to collect all rests of ordinary revenue preceding 1660 and repay himself debts owed to him by the Crown out of what he collected. Separate arrangements were made for collecting the rests of extraordinary revenues,[105] but very little of the vast sums of arrears, ordinary or extraordinary, were ever paid.

Conclusion

The story of Charles I's Scottish revenues in the early years of his reign conforms to a common pattern. Traditional ordinary revenues were rendered inadequate by past weakness, inflation and extravagance, and comparatively little could be done to increase them except by improving efficiency of collection. To compensate for the decline in ordinary revenues, extraordinary taxation had to be imposed, arousing the opposition of subjects who insisted that the king should live on the ordinary revenues; they refused to recognize that this was no longer possible since their real objection was to any increase in taxation by a regime unpopular for other reasons. In spite of this, attempts to increase revenue had some initial success, but in the end (partly through the personal failings of Traquair) they did the king more harm than good.

When the troubles began in 1637 the Scottish revenues were still too weak to be a significant asset to the king in his struggle with the covenanters, and in any case collection and administration of the revenues soon collapsed. The covenanters were slow to take advantage of this situation by appropriating the king's revenues for their own use; such action might have roused more opposition than it was worth, and have lent strength to the king's claim that they were in open rebellion against him, greedily stealing his revenues. Moreover, on the whole it was easier for the covenanters to raise money by their own taxes and loans than to rely on the inefficiently collected and unproductive royal revenues. However, in 1639–41, when the exchequer virtually ceased to exist, the covenanters did organize the collection of substantial sums of the king's revenues, using them to help finance resistance to him.

On the whole the covenanters tended in finance as in other spheres not to take over and develop for their own use the organs of the old royal administration, but to leave them to continue to carry out routine functions (with little power or independence) and instead set up a parallel structure of new bodies

105 *APS*, VII. 326–7, 433.

and officials to rule the country and carry out new functions. Thus, after 1641 the exchequer, now dominated by the covenanters, remained in control of the traditional ordinary Crown revenues, applying them only (with very minor exceptions) to traditional uses, while a completely separate financial administration dealt with the covenanters' own taxes.

The lack of interest of the covenanters in the exchequer's work and the disturbed state of the country made any return by the exchequer to normal working and any improvement in efficiency in collecting its revenues impossible. By 1650, years of decay, the 1648-9 purges and interference by parliamentary committees had so weakened the exchequer that it was unable to play any effective part in the preparations for the arrival of Charles II. This had to be left largely to parliamentary committees, just as the financing of his stay in Scotland was largely dependent on parliamentary taxes. The only sign of sustained exchequer activity is the fact that its officials dominated the board of the green cloth. Any revival of the exchequer that might have followed from the increasing power of Charles II in 1650-1 was prevented by the completion of English conquest. The settling of royal finances on a firm foundation therefore had to await the restoration settlement of the 1660s.

VIII

The financing of the cause of the Covenants, 1638-51

THE BISHOPS' WARS, 1638-41

When agitation began in Scotland in 1637 against the policies of Charles I the small expense involved in sending messengers round the country with orders and exhortations, in drawing up protestations and instructions, could easily be borne by the leaders of the opposition. But once it became clear that the agitation would have to be prolonged and intensified if it were to succeed the cost had to be spread more widely. In February 1638, when the national covenant was being drafted, the earl of Rothes suggested at a meeting of nobles that a contribution should be raised by the shires and that the nobles should agree on a stent [assessment] for themselves while the lairds drew up one for each shire 'not according to their lands but to their abilities, without pressing any'. It was later agreed that collectors should be appointed in each shire to gather one dollar for every 1,000 merks of income of those willing to contribute.[1] This voluntary contribution was to be handed in to John Smith, a leading Edinburgh merchant, who thus became the covenanters' first treasurer. The stent of thirty-four noble covenanters required them to pay a total of about £1,787 Scots. It was stressed that no one was to be forced to pay, and that no one was to give more than his stent.[2] The motive for this limitation was probably to keep the amount collected so small that enemies would not be able to claim with any credibility that it was raised to finance armed opposition to the king.

Not until January 1639 did the covenanters begin preparing to raise money on the scale required to support an army. A letter was then sent to the shires by the Tables (the covenanters' committees which now formed the *de facto* government of the country), ordering the levying of forces and the assessment of the rents of each parish so that the burden of supporting these forces could be distributed equally.[3] As these valuations would take some time to complete,

---

1   The dollar was worth about 4 merks, R[egister of the] P[rivy] C[ouncil of Scotland], *1638–1643*, 240. One merk equalled 13s. 4d. Scots; £1 equalled 1s. 8d. sterling. All figures below are £ Scots unless otherwise stated.

2   J. Leslie, Earl of Rothes, *A Relation of Proceedings concerning the Affairs of the Kirk of Scotland* (Bannatyne Club, 1830), 71–72, 80–81, 127.

3   J. Spalding, *Memorialls of the Trubles* (Spalding Club, 1850–1), i, 132; *Cal. State Papers Domestic, 1638–1639*, 406–10.

200,000 merks were to be borrowed from William Dick of Braid, the richest Edinburgh merchant.[1] Many smaller sums were also borrowed and all available silver was sent to Edinburgh for coining.[2] The mint was taken over and its master undertook to coin all gold and silver supplied to him by the covenanters. Between June 1639 and April 1641 about £293,650 was coined under this agreement.[3] Loans, coining of silver work, the raising of men at the expense of their parishes and the supplying of arms and provisions on credit (voluntary or otherwise) financed the First Bishops' War. Few of the valuations ordered in January 1639 were completed until the following year and because of this no attempt was yet made to impose a tax throughout the country.

In January 1640 what was later described as a convention of estates met and issued new orders for preparing valuations. While these orders were being carried out a bond was circulated for subscription. This explained that the well-affected nobles, gentlemen, burgesses and others had spent great sums of money, and raised more on their credit, in the late troubles and that this was too great a burden for them to bear alone. Equity demanded that they be reimbursed and, as the benefits of the reformation of religion affected all equally, all ought to pay the expense of achieving it proportionally according to their means. Therefore subscribers bound themselves to pay their part of the common charges by Whitsunday 1640 (or whenever else was appointed). Nobles, lairds and heritors in each presbytery were to choose four or more landed men or others of good fame to take trial by parishes of the annual income of landholders. In royal burghs valuation was entrusted to the magistrates.[4] This bond caused consternation among royalists, for they thought its wording ambiguous and it obliged subscribers to pay sums which were nowhere defined (whence it became known as the 'blind band'). They feared that it was designed to trick them into undertaking to pay sums which would turn out to be ruinous, although it was later admitted that these fears had been groundless.[5]

Shortly after the first bond a second one was circulated, similar in terms but fixing at a tenth the proportion of yearly rent which was

1   R. Baillie, *Letters and Journals* (Bannatyne Club, 1841–2), i, 192; *Extracts from the Records of Edinburgh, 1626–1641* [*Edin. Recs.*], ed. M. Wood (Edinburgh, 1936), 214.
2   S[cottish] R[ecord] O[ffice], GD. 38/1/176, Dalguise Muniments; R. Chambers, *History of the Rebellions in Scotland* (Edinburgh, 1828), i, 312–13; A. Johnston, *Diary, 1639* (S[cottish] H[istory] S[ociety], 1911), 56–7.
3   D. Stevenson, 'The Covenanters and the Scottish Mint, 1639–41', *British Numismatic Journal*, xli (1972)—forthcoming.
4   A[cts of the] P[arliaments of] S[cotland], v, 280; Spalding, *Memorialls*, i, 248–9.
5   Spalding, *Memorialls*, i, 249–52; J. Gordon, *History of Scots Affairs* (Spalding Club, 1841), iii, 93–8; *Extracts from the Council Register of the Burgh of Aberdeen, 1625–1642* [*Abdn. Reg.*], ed. J. Stuart (Scot. Burgh Rec. Soc., 1871), 202–3.

to be paid. Its purpose was probably to allay fears caused by the first bond, and it also reflected a growing need for money; whereas the tax to be raised was originally intended to pay the debts of the 1639 war, money was now urgently needed to finance the new war which was obviously approaching. The date of payment was therefore brought forward to 1 April. This second bond proved to be as badly drafted as the first, and after complaints of its vagueness the Tables had to agree to the insertion of a clause making it clear that payment was to be for the year 1639 only. Some had offered to pay their tenth at once instead of signing such bonds promising payment, but they were ordered to sign lest they should seem to show 'an ill example'.[1]

Very little of the tenth was in fact paid by 1 April; few even of the valuations were completed. Orders for payment and for the sending to Edinburgh of valuations and signed bonds were therefore renewed on 17 April, and—as the tenth would not be sufficient to pay for the upkeep of the forces—each officer and soldier sent out by the shires and burghs was to be given forty days entertainment in food and money to take with him to the army.[2] A month later the Tables (now becoming known as the committee of estates) appointed a commissary general, Alexander Gibson, younger, of Durie, son of a lord of session; and at the same time or shortly after he was appointed collector general. He was to supervise and control the collection and distribution of money and provisions for the armies of the covenant. William Thomson and John Denholm acted as his deputies with the main army that was soon to enter England, with Archibald Sydserf as his deputy within Scotland. It was these deputies (all Edinburgh merchants) who carried out the day-to-day routine work; while Durie later explained that 'I did never actually intromet with any thing my self bot be my Deputes who have compted', he appointed them and was responsible for their actions.[3]

When parliament met in June 1640 an act for the common relief ratified the earlier orders for valuations and payment of the tenth, and promised repayment of those who had lent money or goods for the public use. Those who had signed the bonds but had not paid the tenth were to incur all lawful diligence, and those who refused to sign were to be treated as anti-covenanters, which meant that their whole estates could be seized for public use. As well as renewing orders for payment of the tenth, parliament imposed a loan of a

1   Gordon, *History*, iii, 96; *Abdn. Reg., 1625–1642*, 200, 203–7; L. B. Taylor, *Aberdeen Council Letters* (London, 1950), ii, 169.
2   SRO, GD. 32/1/17, Elibank Papers.
3   *APS*, v, 281, 286; vi, pt. i, 205–7; SRO, PA. 6/8, Warrants of Parliament, 27 Nov. 1644. In 1639 James Murray had acted as commissary for the country, SRO, PA. 15/1, Accounts of James Murray, 1639–40.

twentieth, assessed on the same basis as the tenth, to be paid by
1 July.[1]

The tenth, or the tenth penny as it became better known, was the
first national tax imposed by the covenanters. In the circumstances—
a time of war and urgent need for money—it might have been
easiest to raise a tax either by old and well-established methods or
by some rough and ready means suited to an emergency. Instead the
covenanters had devised a tax which included many innovations
based mainly on the desire to make it more equitable than previous
taxes. The main respects in which the tenth penny was original
were in using the presbytery as the unit for collection outside the
burghs, in being an attempt to tax all kinds of income, in taxing
landholders other than tenants-in-chief, and in being based on an
entirely new valuation of both shires and burghs.

The first of these was the least significant and was simply a
matter of expediency. Many of the shires were too large, the shire
committees of war (the covenanters' instruments of local government) were not yet fully established and had no organisation at the
parish level, whereas the existing system of presbyteries and kirk
sessions provided recognised units of convenient size. Previously
all taxation outside the burghs had been based on land and (since
1621) on annualrents, i.e. interest on loans often secured on land.[2]
But the tenth penny was supposed to be paid on all forms of income,
including 'all land trade [trade outside the royal burghs], shipping,
salmond fishing and other yearly commodity whatsoevir wherby
proffet did aryse'[3] and 'the rentis of byeris and selleris of victuall,
and utheris handleris and traffekeris without brughe'.[4] Trade outside the burghs was in fact a very insignificant part of total shire
valuations and was probably often omitted in this and later valuations, but the innovation was nonetheless important in principle.
The land tax (as opposed to the tax on annualrents) had been payable only by those who held their lands directly of the king, though
they could claim repayment of part of the tax from their vassals[5];
on the other hand, the tenth penny was payable by all heritors and
liferenters, that is by all who had possession of their lands for a
lifetime or longer.[6]

It had been these extensions of the basis of taxation that had made
a new valuation necessary before the tenth penny could be uplifted—
together with the fact that the 'old extent' according to which previous taxes had been paid was very much out of date. An entirely
new valuation of the country would have been a major undertaking

1   *APS*, v, 280–2.
2   R. S. Rait, *The Parliaments of Scotland* (Glasgow, 1924), 494.
3   *APS*, v, 281.   4   Spalding, *Memorialls*, i, 250–1.
5   G. Donaldson, *Scotland: James V to James VII* (Edinburgh, 1965), 352–3;
APS, v, 13.   6   Spalding, *Memorialls*, i, 250–1.

at the best of times; that it should have been embarked upon in time of civil war was remarkable. In 1633 attempts to value annual-rents had been denounced as 'an inquisition in men's estates, as is not practised in any other nation in Christiandome, and makes our nation contemptible by the discoverie made thereby of the povertie thereof',[1] while in England suggestions for a national valuation were dismissed as impractical or as an undesirable interference in private affairs.[2]

As far as the burghs were concerned, the valuations for payment of the tenth penny differed in two ways from those used for earlier taxes. Traditionally the burghs had paid one sixth of national taxes. But in 1639, instead of paying such a pre-arranged proportion, the burghs paid in proportion to the new valuations. When the valuations were completed the burghs' proportion was found to amount to about one twelfth of the total.[3] Perhaps as the result of the jealousy of the nobles and lairds at thus seeing the burghs paying only half their previous proportion, the covenanters reverted in all their later direct taxes to the procedure of assigning in advance one sixth of taxes to the burghs. Similarly, the burghs had normally apportioned the one sixth among individual burghs according to a stent roll agreed in 1612, but the 1639 valuation changed these proportions. Thus Edinburgh paid 28·75% and Aberdeen 8% of the total under the 1612 stent roll,[4] but about 34·1% and 14·5% respectively in 1639.[5] In later taxes the covenanters returned to the 1612 stent roll (revised in 1649), just as they reverted to assigning one sixth of taxes to the burghs.

When parliament rose on 11 June 1640 it entrusted a committee of estates with power to borrow money, draw up accounts of the public burdens and raise money to pay them.[6] This committee was soon collecting money in a variety of ways. Order was again given to bring in all silver work to be coined.[7] The revenues of bishoprics and of opponents of the covenant were already being devoted to public uses, and this was now done more systematically. Uplifting of the king's revenues by the covenanters now began.[8] The activities of a local committee in raising money by uplifting the rents and goods of non-covenanters, ordering the plundering of active opposers of the covenant, gathering the tenth and twentieth pennies, borrowing money and so on, under the stimulus of repeated orders and exhortations from the committee of estates, are well illustrated by

1   J. Row, *History of the Kirk of Scotland* (Wodrow Society, 1842), 366.
2   W. Kennedy, *English Taxation, 1640–1749* (London, 1913), 39, 42.
3   SRO, PA. 16/3/5/3, Army Papers, Accounts, p. 1.
4   T. C. Smout, *Scottish Trade on the Eve of Union* (Edinburgh, 1963), 282–3.
5   B[ritish] M[useum], Add. MS 33262, Book of Valuations, 1639, fos. 63–65.
6   *APS*, v, 283.   7   H. Guthry, *Memoirs* (Glasgow, 1747), 73.
8   Spalding, *Memorialls*, 301–2.

the minute book of the committee of war of Kirkcudbright. In August the committee of estates decided that the rents and estates of anti-covenanters should continue to be uplifted even if they became covenanters to avoid this, for it was considered unjust that those who had avoided earlier contributions by opposing the covenant should be able to recover their estates by a politic conformity.[1]

In spite of all efforts the shortage of ready money continued. The sum of £100,000 was borrowed from Edinburgh for the army, since the tenth penny 'came bot slowlie in: the valuation of men's estates drew to a great length, let be the payment: from England there was no expectation of monies till we went to fetch them: we called in the plait, and put it to the queinze house [cunzie house or mint]; we craved voluntarie offerings; whereby some prettie soums also wes gotten. Bot what was all this to twenty thousand merks a-day, which our armie required?' The commissary general was not even able to assemble two weeks' provisions for the army.[2] But once the army had entered England and occupied Newcastle the financial outlook improved. On 30 September, in their private instructions to their commissioners for the treaty at Ripon, the committee of estates told them to insist that England pay them £40,000 sterling a month for upkeep of their army.[3] In the end the Scots did not get nearly so much; the maximum the English would agree to pay them was £850 sterling a day or £26,350 sterling in a thirty-one day month, and the Scots accepted this on 16 October.[4]

Meanwhile in Scotland efforts to collect money continued.[5] In January 1641 the royal burghs agreed to lend 150,000 guilders (at £1 Scots per guilder) to pay for ammunition bought in Holland for the covenanters by the Scottish factors at Campvere. In fact only £97,167 15s. seems to have been advanced by burghs and by Edinburgh merchants, of which part must have been diverted to other uses as only £67,619 10s. ever reached the Netherlands.[6] But the main financial hopes of the Scots still centred on England and the peace treaty being negotiated in London, for the covenanters claimed that, since Scotland had been put to great expense to guard against invasion by English armies, England should pay these expenses as well as paying the Scottish army in England.

On 7 January 1641 the parliament of England agreed to pay the

1   *Minute Book kept by the War Committee of the Covenanters in the Stewartry of Kirkcudbright* (Kirkcudbright, 1855), 15, 19–28.
2   Baillie, *Letters*, i, 255–6.
3   Edinburgh University Library, MS Dc.4.16, Transactions of the Committee of Estates, fo. 9.
4   J. Rushworth, *Historical Collections* (London, 1659–1701), ii, pt. ii, 1295–6.
5   *Minute Book*, 76–78, 94–95, 98–104, 153–4.
6   *APS*, v, 708; vi, pt. i, 171–4; Spalding, *Memorialls*, i, 355; T. Cuningham, *Journal* (SHS, 1928), 54.

Scots £4,000 sterling towards the cost of refitting Scottish ships which had been captured during the Bishops' Wars.[1] Encouraged by this the Scottish commissioners moved on to request compensation for the cost of the wars. This demand was, as one of the Scots present put it, 'our great fear, and our enemies equall hope'.[2] The Scots put the cost of the 1639 war at just under £102,000 sterling. Similar items for 1640 (up to the time the Scottish army entered England), and losses caused by the capture of Scottish ships and subsequent interruption of trade, brought the total the Scots asked for up to £515,000 sterling. In addition the Scots declared themselves willing to pay some rather vague items totalling £271,000 sterling.[3]

The English commissioners at first opposed this demand and tried to get consideration of it delayed until all other articles of the treaty were agreed. The Scots refused this; wisely, for it would have eventually put them in a position of holding up agreement solely through their demands for money, a situation out of which their enemies would have been able to make much capital. However, the English gave way in the end and on 22 January the house of commons resolved to grant a friendly assistance to the Scots. Later they fixed the amount of this aid, which soon became better known as the 'brotherly assistance', at £300,000 sterling. The Scots accepted this. It was then decided that £80,000 sterling should be paid before the Scottish army withdrew from England and disbanded, with £110,000 sterling (half of the remainder) payable at midsummer 1642 and the rest at midsummer 1643, although originally the Scots had hoped for completion of payment before their army disbanded.[4]

THE COMMITTEE FOR COMMON BURDENS, 1641–3

On 25 August 1641 the Scottish army withdrew from England. The £80,000 sterling brotherly assistance had been paid, as had £266,050 sterling (£3,192,600 Scots) in daily allowance for the 313 days between 16 October 1640 and 25 August 1641.[5] The payments from

---

1   APS, v, 338.   2   Baillie, Letters, i, 289.
3   Z. Grey, An Impartial Examination . . . of Mr Daniel Neale's History of the Puritans (London, 1736–9), ii, Appendix, 112–20; N[ational] L[ibrary of] S[cotland], Wodrow MS Folio vol. lxxiii, fos. 50v–51v; NLS, Adv. MS 33.4.6, Treaties at Newcastle and London. The figures given in these three versions of the account differ in detail.
4   Baillie, Letters, i, 289; S. R. Gardiner, History of England (London, 1883–4), ix, 261–2, 272; Journals of the House of Commons [CJ], ii, 71, 78, 181, 182, 187.
5   SRO, PA. 16/3/5/3, p. 3. This in fact gives the total allowance received as only £3,054,900 as an error puts an item for 15 days' arrears at £15,300 instead of £153,000.

96

England and the subsequent disbanding of the army greatly reduced the urgency of the need to raise money in Scotland, but there remained the need to draw up accounts of what money had been raised and what was owed to or by the public as a result of the wars. The committee of estates recommended parliament to see to this, but progress was slow; in October a committee was appointed to hear the accounts of the commissary general, but in the event they were not properly audited for another three years.[1] Parliament had little time to deal with financial matters in any detail; it therefore repeated promises that all money owed by the public would be repaid and established a committee for regulating the common burdens of the kingdom with wide powers to settle the financial confusion of the previous three years.[2]

The committee first met in November 1641[3] and was soon busy ordering the bringing in of accounts and drawing up of lists of public debts and the rests (i.e. the part of the taxes not yet paid, or paid but not yet accounted for). It set up a subcommittee to borrow money to pay for current necessities, and on 7 December Sir William Dick of Braid and Sir John Smith (both recently knighted by the king as part of his attempt to win the support of prominent covenanters) each agreed to lend £10,000 sterling. This was to be repaid with interest out of the brotherly assistance due at midsummer 1642, and each of them was commissioned to receive half the £110,000 sterling then due on behalf of the public.[4]

The committee's register makes it clear that in spite of the repeated orders of the previous years few accounts of local collectors had been audited, and in many cases collectors had not even been appointed; thus on 7 March 1642 it was necessary to grant commissions for the collection of the rents of twelve bishoprics for 1639 and 1640. On the same day a proclamation related that a great part of the tenth penny and bishops' rents were as yet unaccounted for and summoned all who had intromitted with public money to make account by 1 June. The response was discouraging, and in August order was given to put over fifty collectors and local commissaries to the horn.[5]

Though the committee for common burdens had been established primarily to audit the accounts and settle the debts of the Bishops' Wars, early in 1642 it became involved jointly with the privy council in financing the levy and transport of a new Scottish army of 10,000 men to Ireland, to be paid by the English parliament

1 APS, v, 371–2, 628, 634, 691; vi, pt. i, 205–7; SRO, PA. 6/8, 27 Nov. 1644.
2 APS, v, 391–8, 708.
3 SRO, PA. 14/1, Register of the Committee for Common Burdens, fo. 2.
4 SRO, PA. 14/1, fos. 2–2v, 8–9v, 10v–12v, 15, 16v–17v, 18v–19, 25–26, 28–29v.
5 SRO, PA. 14/1, fos. 50–53v, 54v–56, 94, 136v–137v.

once it arrived there.[1] In March the committee, on the recommendation of the privy council, authorised the borrowing of £14,000 sterling for this purpose.[2] The English paid in advance £30,000 sterling of the brotherly assistance due at midsummer 1642 on condition that it be used to hasten the levy and transport of the army to Ireland. Though this was not the purpose for which the brotherly assistance had been intended, a joint meeting of the privy council and the committee for common burdens on 28 March agreed to it.[3] Payment of the rest of the brotherly assistance was not so prompt; the only two further payments received totalled £40,000 sterling.[4] These payments, together with the £80,000 sterling received in 1641, amounted to £150,000 sterling, exactly half of what England had promised. But the Scots did not press for payment, for civil war had begun in England and the Scots tacitly accepted that in these circumstances the English parliament should delay the remaining brotherly assistance. The civil war also led to the English parliament failing to pay the Scottish army in Ireland, and in August 1642 the Scottish privy council agreed to provide for that army until England was able to resume doing so.[5]

The failure of England to pay the army in Ireland and half the brotherly assistance meant that there was no longer any hope that the committee for common burdens would be able to pay off all public debts; in December 1642 it had to borrow more money even to pay the interest on such debts.[6] Two months later it was decided to raise a 'voluntary contribution' to pay the army in Ireland, with public surety for repayment (when England sent money for that army) guaranteed by the privy council, the conservators of the peace and the committee for common burdens. On 1 March 1643 the amount to be borrowed was set at £20,000 sterling or more if it was offered by 1 May (later extended to 1 July).[7] The privy council ordered such councillors as were in Edinburgh to write to sheriffs to convene the barons to lend money, but there is no evidence of any compulsion to lend, and few of the shires sent contributions. The money that was lent was ordered to be given in to William Thomson or John Jossie.[8] Jossie's receipts may be summarised as follows:

1   *APS*, vi, pt. i, 190–1.
2   *RPC, 1638–1643*, 218, 232–3; SRO, PA. 14/1, fos. 71–71v.
3   SRO, PA. 14/1, fos. 39–40, 69–71.
4   *RPC, 1638–1643*, 327; SRO, PA. 16/3/5/3, p. 4. The £4,000 sterling promised for the outrig of captured ships was also paid.
5   *RPC, 1638–1643*, 315.
6   SRO, PA. 14/1, fo. 158.
7   *RPC, 1638–1643*, 400, 403, 406, 407–9, 425–6; SRO, PA. 14/2, Proceedings of the Commissioners for Conserving the Articles of the Treaty, 37–39, 60–61.
8   *RPC, 1638–1643*, 407–9, 421, 639–41.

Paid by councillors, conservators and
members of the committee for com-
mon burdens   £107,000
Paid by the sheriffdoms of Fife, Mid
and East Lothian and Linlithgow   £20,533 6s. 8d.
Paid by the burgh of Edinburgh   £36,900

                                    _____

                    Total   £164,433 6s. 8d. Scots.[1]

Whether or not this was all that was raised by the voluntary contribution (and more may well have been accounted for by Thomson)
even the target figure of £20,000 sterling was totally inadequate for
the needs of the army in Ireland—it would have provided only about
two weeks' pay. The need to raise a much greater sum for the army
was one of the motives which led the privy council, the conservators
of the peace and the committee for common burdens to summon a
convention of estates to meet on 3 June 1643.[2] However, by far the
most important reason for the summons was the need to discuss
Scottish intervention in the English civil war, and the needs of the
army in Ireland provided a convenient excuse for holding a convention.

The committee for common burdens continued to sit during and
after the convention, but it fast declined in importance. It met less
frequently and confined itself entirely to trying to gather the taxes
and pay the debts of the Bishops' Wars, but with little success.[3]
Accounts were drawn up (probably late in 1643) of what money
had been gathered, what remained to be gathered, and what public
debts amounted to for 1639–41. The valuations for the tenth penny
had never been finally completed, but the amount of tenth due from
income which remained unvalued was probably small.

The following is a summary of the tenth penny accounts:[4]

	Total payable according to valuations completed	Paid and accounted for	Not accounted for	Percentage of total accounted for
Presbyteries	£431,967 6 8	£356,911 16 8	£75,055 10 0	c. 82·6
Burghs	£39,731 19 0	£38,561 6 8	£1,170 12 4	c. 97
Total	£471,699 5 8	£395,473 3 4	£76,225 2 4	c. 83·8

1   *RPC, 1544–1660*, 83–92; H. Hazlett, 'The Financing of the British Armies
in Ireland, 1641–9', *Irish Historical Studies*, i (1938–9), 39, gives the total as about
£336,000 Scots, a figure he appears to have reached by adding the charge and the
discharge sides of the accounts together!
2   *RPC, 1638–1643*, 426–7.
3   SRO, PA. 14/1, fos. 245v–246; SRO, PA. 16/1/65–67.
4   SRO, PA. 16/3/5/3, p. 1.

That nearly 84 per cent of the tenth penny had been paid and accounted for—and probably more paid but not yet accounted for—indicates that the covenanters had been fairly successful in collecting the tax, even though this figure was not achieved until nearly five years after the tax had been imposed.

A later (though also undated) account shows that of the £75,055 10s. not received from presbyteries £41,388 1s. 4d. was cancelled or suspended in compensation for losses and repayment of public debts due to those who should have paid, that letters of horning had been issued to enforce payment of £17,407 13s. 5d., and that £16,259 15s. 3d. still had not been accounted for by local collectors.[1] The twentieth penny should have brought in about £235,000, but in fact only about half of this, £116,425 5s. 4d., had been paid by late 1643. Since, unlike the tenth, it was a loan which would have to be repaid, collection had probably stopped once a settlement with the king had been reached in 1641. Including interest, the total due for repayment at Martinmas 1643 was £149,024 5s. 4d.[2]

Of the 1639–40 revenues of the bishoprics, £134,269 8s. had been accounted for to the covenanters, though much of this had been used to pay ministers' stipends and other fees.[3] Royal revenues uplifted totalled £87,044 18s. 7d., most of which came from the customs and the impost on wines. The sum of £108,895 9s. 8d. in rents of non-covenanters and fines paid by them was accounted for, but much of this was used to pay stipends and other fees. Voluntary contributions sent by burghs, parishes and presbyteries had raised £49,342 19s. 4d.[4]

The total known public debt of the kingdom in 1643 was put at £1,635,468 2s. 4d., made up of twentieth penny, other loans of money, provisions and silver work which were to be repaid, and interest on such items. But this was only what was due according to accounts which had been completed and audited[5]; much more was probably due on accounts which were still incomplete. Sir William Dick was by far the biggest creditor, for £474,126 19s. 7d.[6] As to the £150,000 sterling brotherly assistance that had been paid, there seems little doubt that (except for the £30,000 sterling used for the army sent to Ireland) it was employed, as intended, for paying the arrears of the army and public debts and losses. But no account was published of how it had been spent, nor was it even

1   SRO, PA. 16/3/4/1.   2   SRO, PA. 16/3/5/3, p. 2.
3   SRO, PA. 16/3/5/3, pp. 6–7, 10.
4   SRO, PA. 16/3/5/3, pp. 13, 15–20. According to this account and the committee for common burdens (SRO, PA. 14/1, fos. 256–7) Sir William Dick paid out £60,533 12s. of customs and impost on the orders of the covenanters. But his customs accounts (SRO, E. 73/9/1) and the accounts of the king's receivers general (SRO, E. 27/1, fo. 41) put the figure at £119,000.
5   SRO, PA. 16/3/5/2, pp. 1–3.   6   SRO, PA. 14/1, fo. 253v.

made clear that only half the promised total of brotherly assistance
had actually been paid, and this gave rise to suspicions that the
leading covenanters were using it to enrich themselves.[1]

THE ARMY IN ENGLAND AND MONTROSE'S RISING, 1643-6

By 20 July 1643 the convention of estates had decided to raise a
forced loan of £800,000 Scots for the army in Ireland. One sixth
was to be paid by the royal burghs, and a committee was set up to
apportion the rest among the shires. The roll drawn up by the committee was approved on 15 August and an act was passed which
added 100,000 merks to the loan (to cover the costs of collecting it)
and a tax of £120,000 (to be gathered in the same way as the loan)
to pay forces which were being levied in Scotland to guard against
any attempted rebellion.[2] The valuations made for the tenth penny
were not regarded as suitable for use now and orders were given for
compiling new ones. Commissioners were appointed in each shire
to convene on 3 October with the heritors, liferenters, tacksmen and
wadsetters and to choose some persons to be adjoined to the commissioners. Thus reinforced, the commissioners were to use all legal
ways to find the true worth of each man's rents, distinguishing constant land rent from casual rent.[3] It has been argued that by 'casual
rent' was meant 'the casualties or occasional payments included in
the conditions of tenure',[4] but this was not so. In 1645 profits arising
from coal and salt were called casual rents, and in 1649 they were
defined as 'salt, coal, salmond-fishing, and other fishings in pro-
pertie whereby there is yeerly benefit'.[5] This in itself does not invalidate the conclusion that the loan and tax 'was levied solely
upon land and upon burdens on land' (which included annualrents),[6]
since profits from coal, salt and fishing were regarded as part of
landed property, but there are other reasons for doubting the conclusion. The act is rather vague and never explicitly mentions the
taxation of income arising, for example, from trade outside the
royal burghs (as the 1640 act for the tenth penny had done) but
such trade seems to be included in the stipulation that loan and tax
should be paid on rents 'as weill of lands and teinds as of any uther
thing wherby yeirlie proffeit and commoditie aryseth'.[7] Moreover

---

1   Spalding, *Memorialls*, ii, 229-30; Guthry, *Memoirs*, 105.
2   *APS*, vi, pt. i, 18-19, 26-36.
3   See 'Minutes of the committee for loan monies and taxations of the shire of
Aberdeen', ed. J. Stuart, *Spalding Club Misc.*, iii, 143-50.
4   Rait, *Parliaments*, 497.   5   *APS*, vi, pt. i, 447-8, 524, 535.
6   Rait, *Parliaments*, 497.
7   *APS*, vi, pt. i, 30.

when a new valuation was being organised in 1649 it was laid down that it should be based on either the 1639 or the 1643 valuation; it is unlikely that this alternative would have been given unless these two valuations had been made on the same basis, and the 1639 valuations had certainly included (or at least had been meant to include) other than landed property. However, in 1643 as in 1639 trade outside the burghs was difficult to value and was so insignificant that it was probably largely ignored.

Subcollectors were to be appointed in the shires to collect the loan and tax and deliver it to the collector general. In the burghs (which paid their sixth of the the total proportionally according to the 1612 tax roll)[1] the provosts and bailies were to act as collectors, sending what they collected to the shire collector. In imposing a lump sum to be paid by each shire rather than (as with the tenth penny) a rate to be paid on the total valuation of the shire, the loan and tax conformed to contemporary English practice, but provision was made for adjusting the proportions paid by each shire if it was found after valuation and payment that some shires had paid at a higher rate than others. Sir Adam Hepburne of Humbie was appointed collector general of the loan and tax.[2] He drew up a list of what was due from each shire and the burghs in it, with declarations to be signed by the subcollector of each shire to the effect that he undertook to account for the loan and tax of his shire and burghs by 15 March 1644.[3] But only about half the subcollectors actually signed these declarations, and few if any accounted for their activities until long after March 1644.

As with the tenth penny, the date assigned for payment of the loan and tax was hopelessly optimistic, yet even that date was too far distant to supply what was needed. On 18 August the convention ordered the borrowing of £40,000 for equipping the forces being raised, to be repaid out of the tax,[4] and on 31 August the committee of estates ordered the borrowing of further sums for these forces; the members of the committee present agreed to set a good example by lending 39,000 merks among them. The committee also urged English commissioners with whom it was negotiating to pay the remainder of the brotherly assistance due at midsummer 1642; and though it agreed to a delay in paying the £110,000 sterling due at midsummer 1643 it demanded that interest be paid on this sum. As for the army in Ireland, £60,000 sterling was asked for it forthwith.[5]

Yet while still due such great sums from England for the Bishops'

1   For amounts payable by each burgh see SRO, PA. 8/2, The Charge of the Loan and Tax, fos. 2–3.   2   *APS*, vi, pt. i, 40–41.
3   SRO, PA. 8/2.   4   *APS*, vi, pt. i, 44.
5   SRO, PA. 11/1, Register of the Committee of Estates, fos. 6–7, 8v.

Wars and for the army in Ireland, the convention involved Scotland
in the English civil war, agreeing on 29 August 1643 to send an
army to England. In return the English parliament promised
£30,000 sterling monthly towards the army's pay, and Scotland
was to be given further satisfaction for her 'paines, chairges and
hazard' by way of brotherly assistance when peace was restored.
The cost of levying, arming and clothing the army and bringing
it to England was also to be borne by Scotland and repaid by England once the war was over. England was to pay £100,000 sterling
of the monthly allowance in advance, and Scotland was to help in
raising this sum by pledging her security, jointly with that of England,
for repayment of a total of £200,000 sterling which was to be borrowed. In September another treaty added £1,000 sterling to the
monthly allowance, two-thirds of the pay of a Scottish garrison
which was to be placed in Berwick.[1] Humbie, already collector
general, was appointed commissary general and treasurer of all
the Scottish armies.[2]

The problem of how to find money for levying and transporting
this new army was solved at the expense of the army in Ireland.
Indeed, many leading covenanters had probably from the first seen
the loan and tax as a source of money for military intervention in
England, and had used the needs of the army in Ireland as a pretext. In November the privy council and committee of estates
ordered that the loan and tax was to be used by the shire committees
of war to pay the soldiers their levy and transport money. It was
admitted that this was not the purpose for which the loan had been
imposed, but it was claimed to be justified by necessity. Some of the
committees of war interpreted this as giving them permission to pay
out of the loan the levy and transport money of auxiliary forces
that were being raised, as well as those of the army for England, and
fresh instructions had to be issued forbidding this. In March 1644
the committee of estates disclosed that most of the loan had been
spent on the army levied for England,[3] so the army in Ireland benefited little if at all.

Collection was slow of that part of the loan and tax which was not
to be retained in the shires for levy and transport money. In December
1644 the committee of estates complained that the shires were
retaining money for more men than they had been told to levy,
whereas most had not in fact levied even so many as ordered.[4]
In March 1645 Humbie's accounts of the loan and tax showed that
of £991,959 6s. 8d. imposed[5] only £242,970 19s. 4d. had been paid

1   *APS*, vi, pt. i, 48–49, 153–4, 155; SRO, PA. 11/1, fos. 17v–19v.
2   SRO, PA. 11/1, fos. 7v, 66v–68.
3   SRO, PA. 11/1, fos. 68–70v, 124–124v, 150.
4   SRO, PA. 11/3, fos. 137–137v.   5   *APS*, vi, pt. i, 35–36, 306–7.

and accounted for. Of this, £44,359 8s. 4d. had been spent on fees during collection and £51,759 4s. 4d. on levy and transport money; £121,904 2s. 4d. had been used to pay those who had previously advanced money and provisions for the army in Ireland, and the rest had been spent on forces raised in Scotland. Much of the £748,988 7s. 5d. which the collectors had not accounted for had probably been legitimately used for levy and transport money, but how much was thus used, how much paid but not accounted for, and how much remained unpaid could not be known until all the collectors had been brought to account.[1] This was a slow process and even in 1649 £416,833 of the loan and tax remained unaccounted for.[2]

The plan to raise a loan of £200,000 sterling on the joint security of England and Scotland soon ran into difficulties. The committee of estates commissioned Thomas Cuningham, factor at Campvere, and John Johnston, a Scottish merchant in London, to be joint treasurers of the loan with those appointed by the English parliament. 'According to the Commission wee used some endeavours at London, but finding no appearance of successe answerable to the expectation of both kingdomes it was thought fitte to forbeare and desist for a while.' In May 1644 the committee of estates appointed Cuningham to be agent for Scotland in the Netherlands and commissioned him to try to borrow the money there jointly with an English agent, 'but finding oure selves disappointed on all hands . . . wee resolved not to prostitute the reputation of both parliaments to any further hazard there'. The idea seems to have been abandoned. But Thomas Cuningham did manage to get some help in the Netherlands in 1644 for the Scottish army in England. He made an agreement with two Dutch merchants, Adrian and Cornelius Lampsins of Middelburg and Flushing, whereby they guaranteed payment for supplies which Cuningham obtained on credit for use of the army. He bought £185,185 Scots worth of arms and ammunition on bills of credit guaranteed by the Lampsins and due for payment by July 1648, and a further £75,700 worth on his own credit and that of the parliaments.[3]

Meanwhile the convention of estates, despairing of the loan and tax, had decided on 4 January 1644 to raise money for the armies in England and Ireland by imposing an excise.[4] The English parliament had done this the previous year, though only under 'extreme financial pressure', as excise duties had previously been regarded in England as foreign oppressions from which she was happily

1   SRO, PA. 16/3/2/5.
2   SRO, PA. 7/6/158/1, Supplementary Parliamentary Papers.
3   SRO, PA. 11/1, fos. 79–80, 219v–221v; Cuningham, *Journal*, 69–71, 82–85, 93–97.
4   *APS*, vi, pt. i, 61.

free.[1] The idea of an excise was no more popular in Scotland, and when news of the proposal spread there were riots in Edinburgh and threats to tear to pieces Lord Balmerino who was said to have been the first to suggest it. To quell the disturbances it was agreed to refer the idea to a better-attended meeting of the convention on 25 January. By that time the efforts of leading covenanters had been successful in reconciling the people to an excise[2] and when the convention repeated its conviction that an excise was the best way to raise money for the armies there were no further disturbances,[3] though the burghs continued to oppose it. The council of Burntisland, for example, wrote to its commissioner in the convention forbidding him to assent to an excise.[4] The act imposing the excise was passed on the last day of January 1644: 'Thus is this miserabill countrie overburdenit with uncouth taxationis . . . quilk this land wes unhabill to beir'.[5] Excise duties were to be paid on beer, ale, wine, tobacco, slaughtered cattle, sheep, goats and pigs, on various kinds of cloth, on exported coal, and on all imported manufactured goods. Thus the excise duties, though mainly payable on Scottish products used in Scotland, were also imposed on some imports and exports. Some of the new duties were the covenanters' equivalent of the king's customs and impost revenues, though given the name of excise to emphasise that the two were entirely separate. The new duties were to last from 10 February 1644 for as long as necessary, but not for more than a year.[6] The committee of estates appointed a sub-committee to supervise the collecting of the excise and issued instructions as to how it was to be paid, nominating James Stewart treasurer of the excise. By this time the first month of the excise had passed uncollected and it was therefore cancelled and payment ordered to begin on 10 March. But there was still no adequate machinery for collection, and in July parliament ordered that the excise be taken up for a year from 1 August 1644.[7] Even after this it is unlikely that the excise was collected with anything that could be called efficiency even by contemporary standards. Difficulty in getting men to serve as local collectors and surveyors had already led to their fees being raised.[8] In October Burntisland reported that no one in the burgh would act as collector, whereupon the bailies and council were ordered to collect the excise.[9] In December

1   Kennedy, *English Taxation*, 51–55.
2   Guthry, *Memoirs*, 144–5; Spalding, *Memorialls*, ii, 313; *APS*, vi, pt. i, 72.
3   *APS*, vi, pt. i, 73–74.
4   SRO, B. 9/12/8, Burntisland Council Minutes, fos. 11, 11v.
5   Spalding, *Memorialls*, ii, 313–14.
6   *APS*, vi, pt. i, 75–77.
7   SRO, PA. 11/1, fos. 121, 128v–133v, 150v–151, 158–158v, 173–173v; SRO, PA. 11/3, fos. 10v, 18, 19v–20; *APS*, vi, pt. i, 142, 158, 237–45; J. Balfour, *Historical Works* (Edinburgh, 1824–5), iii, 217, 218.
8   SRO, PA. 11/1, fo. 222v.   9   SRO, B. 9/12/8, fos. 33, 36.

Robert Farquhar, provost of Aberdeen, was forcibly appointed
collector of excise for the north of Scotland, a position he had already
refused, with the threat 'ye may mak no excuse for rejecting of this
imployment . . . if ye sould refuse we wilbe forced . . . to mak use of
that power gevin to us by the parliament for chargeing of you be
horneing to accept'.[1] But with Montrose and his supporters triumphant in the north little excise can have been collected there.

At about the same time as the convention imposed the excise it
reverted to the practice of 1639–40 of ordering private loans on
promise of repayment from the excise when it was collected or from
money from England. The committee of estates and the committees
of war were given the task of collecting money in this way[2] and
'blind' bonds obliged subscribers to lend 'ane certain amount of
money, equivilent to his estait', as a royalist put it with some
exaggeration.[3] This proved a far more successful, though far more
arbitrary, way of raising money than the 1643 loan and tax. Between 8 March and 26 July 1644, 366 individuals lent a total of
£562,733 6s. 8d. Scots.[4] Yet large as this sum was by Scottish standards, it would, for example, pay the Scottish army in England
(which the English parliament was proving incapable of supporting)
for only five or six weeks, and it had been raised only by what
amounted to seizing whatever money could be found, with many
threats and much issuing of letters of horning, poinding and ap-
prising.[5]

The need for money was ever increasing. In April 1644 new forces
had to be raised to counter Huntly's rising in the north and Montrose's incursion in the south. The committee of estates that accompanied the forces sent to the north sat in Aberdeen and enforced
subscription of the new blind bond and the lending of money under
threat of plundering refusers: 'nather covenanter nor noncovenanter,
minister, nor country men, wes spairit',[6] testified a royalist, sur-
prised at such impartiality. With the renewal of civil war in Scotland
the raising of money by fining 'malignants', or non-covenanters,
and uplifting their rents began again. As early as November 1643
order had been given to uplift the rents and goods of the marquis of
Hamilton and the earls of Roxburgh, Kinnoul, Morton and Carnwath, and in January 1644 all rents of non-covenanters were confiscated; but most such malignants soon submitted and the amount
of money raised at this time by such means was small. The convention in May 1644 set up a special committee to borrow money and

1   NLS, Gordon-Cumming of Altyre Papers, Box 66, no. 447.
2   APS, vi, pt. i, 75, 81.   3   Spalding, Memorialls, ii, 316–17.
4   SRO, PA. 11/1, fos. 250–60. The total should perhaps be a little higher as a
few entries may have been lost through trimming of the pages.
5   E.g. SRO, PA. 11/1, fos. 163–4, 175v–177, 207–209v.
6   Spalding, Memorialls, ii, 373–4.

uplift malignants' rents and its commission was renewed several times by parliament, though it was decided that those who had already lent money should not be called on to lend a second time, and that all borrowing should cease on 1 August 1645.[1]

When on 26 July 1644 a new committee of estates was appointed it was given powers to oversee the collecting of the excise and to audit all public accounts. It was also given the powers formerly exercised by the committees for borrowing moneys and uplifting malignants' rents, but it immediately delegated these to a sub-committee.[2] Parliament reassembled in January 1645 and again set up a committee for borrowing money and malignants' rents, with additional power to scrutinise public accounts. Power to borrow money in the north was given to a committee sent to assist the forces proceeding against Montrose under Lieutenant-General Baillie. It was decided to raise money by selling the lands of those forfeited for rebellion at ten years' purchase in cash or, if they could not all be sold for cash, half the price was to be paid in cash at ten years' purchase and half in the cancelling of debts due by the public to the buyer at fifteen years' purchase. A new attempt was made to improve collection of the excise: in royal burghs the magistrates and council and elsewhere the elders and deacons of each parish were made responsible for seeing that the excise was paid; to encourage them in this they were to be allowed to retain ten per cent of what they collected, to pay expenses and for charitable purposes. Out of the rest of the excise various public debts were to be repaid.[3]

This act anent the excise marked the abandonment of hopes that the excise would be a major source of income for entertaining the armies, and a replacement for it was badly needed. This was provided on 27 February 1645 by assigning to each shire and burgh the entertainment of a proportion of the forces raised against Montrose. Thus 12,000 men were to be paid a total of £108,000 monthly.[4] The 'men' were in fact units used in apportioning this monthly maintenance among the shires and burghs rather than the actual strength of the forces. Humbie, reappointed as collector general, was to supervise collection, which was to be carried out locally in the same way that the loan and tax had been according to the 1643 valuations.

This monthly maintenance was to last from 1 March to 31 August 1645, and the valuers appointed in 1643 were ordered to prepare revised valuations which were to be used for the last three months of collection. Few of the revisions were completed in time, and the

1   SRO, PA. 11/1, fos. 61v–62; APS, vi, pt. i, 61, 93, 98, 100, 101, 115, 141; Balfour, Historical Works, iii, 218.
2   APS, vi, pt. i, 213; SRO, PA. 11/3, fo. 11.
3   APS, vi, pt. i, 288–90, 292–3, 297–8, 301–2, 329–31, 344–5, 360–1; Balfour, Historical Works, iii, 249–50.
4   APS, vi, pt. i, 351–4.

coal and salt masters of Scotland therefore had to petition for revaluation of their casual rents. These had been very high in 1643 as London had then been using Scottish coal to replace that of Newcastle, which was occupied by the royalists, whereas by 1645 profits had slumped since Newcastle had been captured in 1644 and its coal trade reopened, and because many Scots miners were serving in the various Scots armies.[1] Like the excise, the monthly maintenance was inspired by an English expedient, the 1643 weekly (later monthly) assessment, though the English did not lay down detailed rules for collection as the Scots did.[2] From March 1645 until the Cromwellian conquest the maintenance was to be the main tax in Scotland, imposed at irregular intervals at varying rates (though usually £108,000 monthly) for a few months at a time.

Within a few months of the imposition of the maintenance the government of the covenanters found itself being crushed between the mill stones of plague in the south and Montrose in the north. In May 1645 the committee of estates and the committee for money, accounts and burdens which had been appointed when parliament rose in March[3] fled from the plague in Edinburgh, first to Linlithgow and then further north.[4] Their commissions were renewed by parliaments at Stirling and Perth in July and August, and the excise was reimposed for another year from 1 August 1645. But with most of the country in the hands of rebels or the plague little maintenance or excise can have been collected. Even in areas still controlled by the covenanters many had suffered so much at the hands of the rebels— or in some cases at the hands of the covenanters' own forces—that they could pay no taxes; and many commissions had to be granted for taking trial of losses and burnt and wasted lands to see who should be exempted from payment.[5]

When the covenanters re-established their authority after the defeat of Montrose at Philiphaugh they soon turned to fining those who had supported the rebels or complied with them. The committee of estates laid down that delinquents who were deserving of death but were spared should be fined a sum equivalent to five years' rent or, if their fortunes lay in money or goods, that a third of them should be forfeited.[6] Once parliament met it drew up in an act of classes details of how all delinquents should be fined according to their degrees of guilt. Those in the first class who were not executed were to be fined four to six years' rent, those in the second class two

1   *APS*, vi, pt. i, 447–8, 535.
2   Kennedy, *English Taxation*, 39–40.
3   *APS*, vi, pt. i, 383–5.   4   SRO, PA. 11/4, fo. 90[v].
5   *APS*, vi, pt. i, 388, 433, 434, 447, 460, 469–70.
6   SRO, PA. 11/4, fos. 144v–145.

to four years' rent, and those in the third class half a year's to two years' rent.[1] To encourage prompt payment of the fines, some of them were assigned to be paid to various regiments and officers as part of their pay, and the delinquents were handed over to the officers to be kept by them till they paid.[2]

Apart from such fining, little was done to improve the financial situation, but it is hard to see what could have been done. The public debts were great, yet with the country exhausted by plague and rebellion money could not be raised to repay them. Large forces had to be kept on foot, but payment of the maintenance to support them was greatly in arrears. Not surprisingly Humbie begged to be allowed to resign, pointing out the impossibility of one man acting as treasurer to armies in England and Scotland and collector general, and pleading ill health. He complained that, in spite of all that he and his subordinates could do, 'little money comes in [and] muche is to be given out. Everie man heares and may 'reid the hudge soumes contenit in the act of mantenance and manie have their mouthes filled with mountaines of money rysing out of fynes. Bot few will sie [to] the comeing in ather of the mantenance or the fynes.' Many delayed paying taxes and managed to get exempted from them 'upon some pretended reasone or uther'. Faced with this bitter complaint from its chief financial officer parliament did nothing whatever except refuse to accept his resignation,[3] for it would have had much difficulty in finding anyone willing to replace him.

On 3 February 1646 parliament appointed a new committee for money and process, with wide powers to govern the uplifting of money. It was to act as a committee for excise, and to try and to fine delinquents according to the act of classes, and sell or lease forfeited lands and goods. Its powers of borrowing were limited, though the previous order that all borrowing was to cease on 1 August 1645 was ignored. Not more than half a man's yearly rent was to be borrowed. Those whose free rent was less than 500 merks per annum were to be free from borrowing, as were those who had lent previously and had not been repaid, as well as those to whom the public owed considerable sums and those employed in the armies. Borrowing was to have an element of fining in it, for the behaviour and loyalty of those summoned to lend were to be taken into consideration. The committee was given sole power to distribute public money, which was in the first instance to be used to pay the army. The committee was to sit in two parts, one for Scotland north of the Tay and the other for the south.[4]

1   APS, vi, pt. i, 503.
2   APS, vi, pt. i, 601; SRO, PA. 14/3, Register of the Committee for Moneys (South) 1646, 23.
3   APS, vi, pt. i, 588–9.   4   APS, vi, pt. i, 567–70.

The committee in the north sat at Dundee from 9 March to 4 June 1646, and at Aberdeen from 12 to 28 October. One of those who sat on it later confessed that he and his colleagues had 'proceeded to rigerously in these things committed to us; and sometimes since, I have had some desires to repent for that unwarranted zeal',[1] and this may serve as a judgment on the activities of both sections of the committee. But there was some excuse for their harshness in fining and borrowing; the need for money was great, and they were neither the first nor the last self-righteously to believe that the defeated should pay for a war. In April the committee painted a gloomy picture of the situation in the north, complaining that it was unable to provide money for the army; what they had been able to borrow was so little that it would barely cover 'incident charges' (the running expenses of the committee). The maintenance could provide little, for the country was exhausted by quartering and plundering. As for the excise, there were no collectors whatever in the north except in Dundee, and anyway none of the committee understood how it was meant to be collected.[2]

The work of the committee in the south was similar. Most of its time was spent in collecting maintenance,[3] but many suspensions of payment had to be granted to those whose lands had suffered from plague and war. It ordered about 300 individuals to lend sums between 200 and 9,000 merks, but how many actually paid is uncertain.[4]

Humbie's accounts of the first seventeen months' maintenance (1 March 1645 to 31 July 1646) as audited in November 1646 confirm the picture of financial confusion. A total of £1,836,000 should have been accounted for, but only £437,011 13s. 8d. had been, less than a quarter of the total. As with the rests of the loan and tax, however, much of the rests of the maintenance may have been raised and used locally to pay for quarterings and losses, though not accounted for centrally. As for borrowed moneys Humbie received only £28,966 13s. 4d. between 31 January 1645 and 26 November 1646. But between 9 January and 28 October 1646 as many as 151 individuals were fined a total of £901,818, and though £332,111 13s. 4d. had still not been paid in November fines were the most lucrative source of revenue in 1646.[5]

From the time it had first entered England in January 1644 the

---

1   PA. 14/4, Register of the Committee for Moneys (North) 1646; A. Jaffray, *Diary* (Aberdeen, 1856), 29.
2   SRO, PA. 14/4, 46–47.   3   SRO, PA. 14/3, 52–53.
4   SRO, PA. 14/3, 399–432. The committee in the north issued 162 orders to lend, SRO, PA. 14/4, 302–27.
5   *APS*, vi, pt. i, 617, 630–1; C. S. Terry, *Papers relating to the Army of the Solemn League and Covenant* (SHS, 1917), ii, 348–62, 405–15.

Scottish army had suffered through the failure of the English parliament to pay more than a small fraction of the £31,000 sterling monthly it had promised. As the English civil war drew to a close in 1646 and religious and political disagreements between the two countries grew, it became obvious that many in England had come to see their nominal ally as a potential enemy whom it would be dangerous to strengthen by paying. But in negotiating a settlement of their financial claims the covenanters held two trump cards; possession of the king, who had fled to their army in May 1646, and the fact that their army occupied the north of England.

After the king's flight and the surrender of the remaining royalist forces the house of commons resolved that it had no further use for the Scots. They were promised satisfaction for what was due to them in arrears under the 1643 treaty; £100,000 sterling would be paid when the army left England and the rest later, after agreement had been reached as to how much was owed to it.[1] But the Scots were determined not to abandon their trump cards until the English parliament had promised a definite sum as the total due to the army. Eventually, after months of detailed negotiation, the Scots agreed to accept, in full settlement of their army's claims, £400,000 sterling, of which half was to be paid before the army crossed the Border.[2] This was much less than they had originally hoped for, but more than the minimum they had been prepared to accept; the committee of estates with the army had put the lowest acceptable sum at £350,000 sterling.[3] Payment of half the agreed total was completed on 3 February 1647 and the army then withdrew to Scotland.[4]

THE YEARS 1646–8

When the Scottish parliament met in November 1646 the financial outlook was bleak. Much of the north had been devastated by civil war and invasion, and the whole country was exhausted by heavy taxation and quarterings. Collection of the monthly maintenance was greatly in arrears, the supply of borrowable money was running

1   H. W. Meikle (ed.), *Correspondence of the Scots Commissioners in London, 1644– 1646* (Roxburghe Club, 1917), 184; *CJ*, iv, 551.
2   Meikle, *Correspondence*, 208; *CJ*, iv, 659, 660. The most recent discussion of these negotiations, G. F. T. Jones, 'The payment of arrears to the army of the covenant', *Eng. Hist. Rev.*, lxxiii (1958), 459–65, is rendered seriously misleading by being based on the belief that the terms of the 1643 treaty under which the army was sent to England have not survived. In fact the treaty is available in several contemporary printings and has been reprinted many times (e.g. *APS*, vi, pt. i, 48–49, 152–5). Many of the demands dismissed by Jones as unjustified are closely based on the Scots' rights under the treaty.
3   SRO, PA. 14/3, fos. 47v–48v.
4   *CJ*, v, 36–39.

out, and though fines had brought in large sums these were a non-recurrent form of income. A committee was set up to sit during the session and continue the work of the committee of money and process appointed in February, and a variety of small temporary committees were set up with overlapping functions to scrutinise various accounts, to decide whether the excise should be renewed and to consider losses.[1]

By this time the only remaining enemies of the covenants still in arms in Scotland were the Irish and highland rebels in Argyll. It was therefore decided to economise by disbanding the army which had withdrawn from England and also part of the army in Scotland, retaining only 7,400 men in arms as a Scottish new model army. As well as most of the £200,000 sterling paid by the English, nearly £50,000 Scots from the maintenance and £14,666 13s. 4d. from fines were to be used to pay the arrears of those being disbanded. To pay the forces which were being retained, a further eight months' maintenance was imposed, though some shires and burghs were granted partial suspensions of payment as compensation for losses.[2] As the maintenance would not pay even the reduced forces, the excise (which had ended on 1 August 1646) was reintroduced from March 1647 until 1 January 1648. A committee was to manage collection, with Sir James Stewart as treasurer of excise as before, but it was not to distribute the excise without the assistance of six members of the committee of estates. The same reinforcement was necessary for accepting offers to farm the excise, which it had been decided would be more profitable and less trouble than direct collection.[3] The reluctant Humbie was at last allowed to retire and was replaced as commissary general by Sir John Wemyss of Bogie.[4] When the session of parliament ended in March 1647 control of inbringing and distributing money was absorbed into the powers of the committee of estates.[5]

It seemed for a time that some improvement in the financial situation could be expected. Only a small army remained to be supported, and large sums of money were still hoped for from England in brotherly assistance. But such hopes proved over-optimistic. Increasing political tension between the two countries made it unlikely that England would honour her debts. The north was largely free from rebels and Irish, but the areas they had devastated showed little sign of recovery and all sea-borne trade was rendered hazardous by the activities of pirate frigates from Ireland and Dunkirk. If the rebels were no longer a serious problem, their partner in Montrose's triumph of 1645, the plague, was still active. The burgh

1   *APS*, vi, pt. i, 624, 627–8, 632, 677, 679.
2   *APS*, vi, pt. i, 672–4, 684–91, 700–3, 713.
3   *APS*, vi, pt. i, 722, 727–9, 750; SRO, PA. 11/5, fos. 6, 41v, 131.
4   *APS*, vi, pt. i, 698, 725–6, 752–3.   5   *APS*, vi, pt. i, 766–8.

VIII

of St Andrews, for example, had to be freed from paying all maintenance from February to October 1647 because of plague, and
Perth and Glasgow were freed for shorter periods for the same reason.
Nor did promptness in paying taxes improve with more settled
conditions: in May 1647 Lieutenant-General David Leslie complained that the army had not been paid for two months, and threatened that instead of pursuing the rebels he would march south with
the army and quarter it on the southern shires until they paid their
maintenance.[1] However, though few of the army's arrears were
paid it remained in the north until the autumn, when it was distributed among the shires and burghs in winter quarters. On
8 September the committee voted that the army should be disbanded
on 20 October. It was found that even if the maintenance and excise
already imposed were paid in full there would still be £250,000
Scots due to the army in arrears of pay, and therefore extraordinary
maintenance equivalent to three months ordinary maintenance was
ordered to be paid by 10 October.[2] But on 15 October it was decided
to delay disbanding until parliament met in March 1648, and the
order for collecting the extraordinary maintenance was cancelled.
The army agreed to accept reduced rates of pay in the meantime and
the maintenance was re-imposed at two-thirds the former monthly
rate until 1 March 1648. The excise, due to end on 1 January 1648,
was renewed for another three months and, since the maintenance
and the excise were insufficient to pay the army even at reduced
rates of pay, the commissary general was ordered to distribute meal
stored in public magazines to the army. Later, in October, an additional half month's maintenance was ordered to be delivered for
the use of the army in Ireland.[3]

Once parliament had met it soon became clear that, far from
being disbanded, the army would be increased in strength, for
use by those who supported the Engagement (the treaty with the
king) against the growing power of the Independents in England,
who had already neglected to pay the third £100,000 sterling (due
in February 1648) for the former services of the Scots army in
England.[4] The maintenance therefore was renewed at the full rate
of £108,000 monthly (£98,509 3s. 4d., allowing for suspensions
and exemptions)[5] and the order for collecting half a month's
maintenance for the army in Ireland was renewed, with the pro-
viso that it was to be counted as a quarter of the maintenance for

1   SRO, PA. 11/5, fos. 19v, 122–122v.
2   SRO, PA. 11/5, fos. 89–90, 92v, 93v–95, 99v.
3   SRO, PA. 11/5, fos. 119–119v, 132–134v, 137, 157, 193.
4   CJ, v, 438.
5   APS, vi, pt. ii, 59–62; SRO, PA. 15/10, Accounts of Sir John Wemyss of Bogie,
1648.

the months of May and June 1648.[1] The excise was reimposed for
1 May 1648 to 1 May 1649[2] and a new committee of excise appointed.
John Jossie was made treasurer of the excise, in place of Sir James
Stewart who was hostile to the Engagement.[3] The excise on
wines was renewed for 1 November 1648 to 1 November 1649, and
a tack of this was granted to Sir William Dick at 100,000 merks
per annum, which he was to deduct from the money owed to him by
the public. It was admitted that this was more than the wine excise
had brought in previously and provision was made to compensate
him if the value of the tack proved less. The rest of the excise was
farmed out for a total of £183,126 16s. 8d. Scots for May 1648 to
May 1649.[4]

By May 1648 the raising of levies for the army of the Engagement
was well under way. The burgh of Edinburgh was exempted at its
own request in return for a payment of £40,000, and this and another
£24,000 which was borrowed were sent to the army in Ireland to
help to persuade it to come to Scotland to join in the projected
invasion of England.[5] There was much difficulty in collecting the
maintenance for the army, especially in the west where opposition
to the Engagement was strongest. Repeated orders for collection had
to be issued.[6]

THE YEARS 1648-51

When the extreme presbyterians emerged in control of the committee of estates and the country after a few weeks of confusion
following the defeat of the engagers in England in August 1648,
one of their first acts was to dismiss Bogie and John Jossie. They were
replaced as commissary general and treasurer of the excise by Sir
James Stewart, whose main qualifications for office were his previous
experience as treasurer of the excise and the fact that he had been
mainly responsible for financing the forces which rose to overthrow
the engagers. Stewart had advanced £201,822 Scots in money and
provisions for this purpose, and the easiest way of guaranteeing

1   *APS*, vi, pt. ii, 66.
2   *APS*, vi, pt. ii, 71 appears to impose the excise for a year from 1 Nov. 1648
but all the tacks of the excise granted are from May, SRO, PA. 14/5, Register of
the Commissioners of the Excise, 1648; SRO, GD. 103/2/3/9, Account of the
Excise, 1648–9.
3   *APS*, vi, pt. ii, 71, 91, 97, 109, 205–6; SRO, PA. 11/6, fos. 16v, 21v, 25v.
4   *APS*, vi, pt. ii, 63–65; SRO, PA. 14/5.
5   *APS*, vi, pt. ii, 66; SRO, PA. 11/6, fos. 5v, 6, 7v; *Edin. Recs., 1642–1655*, 147–
50. After the defeat of the engagers it was decided not to repay the £40,000 to the
lenders, ibid., 175–8, 222, 224–5. But in June 1651 the king and committee of
estates ruled that it should be repaid, ibid., 298–302; *APS*, vi, pt. ii, 634–5; SRO,
PA. 11/11, fo. 69.
6   SRO, PA. 11/6, fos. 26v, 28v, 61, 65v–66, 118v.

him repayment was to make him commissary general and stipulate that all the maintenance and excise should in the first instance be devoted to entertaining the army and paying the debts due to him. A new committee of excise was also appointed.[1]

Two weeks after parliament met on 4 January 1649 it set up a committee for common burdens and money, with the usual powers of such committees to calculate public debts, examine accounts and consider the best way of raising money. It was also ordered to investigate losses caused to opposers of the Engagement either by the 'common enemy', the engagers, or by the forces raised to oppose the engagers.[2] To compensate for the losses and expenses of those who had opposed the Engagement in the western shires and burghs it was declared that all maintenance for 1 March to 31 October 1648 due from the well-affected in the west and not yet paid by them need not be paid. The total maintenance for the period was not to be reduced, for those who had supported the Engagement were to pay what the well-affected were excused from paying. This seems an extremely inequitable arrangement, for former engagers in shires which had mainly supported the Engagement would have very little extra maintenance to pay, while the relatively few engagers in the western shires would have to pay many times their usual maintenance. Of maintenance thus collected from former engagers, that for March to July 1648 was to be distributed among the anti-engagers according to their losses and sufferings, while that for August to October was to be paid to the commissary general as usual. All, engagers and anti-engagers alike, were to pay maintenance for November 1648 to January 1649.[3]

The 1649 act of classes, which excluded the engagers from public life, did not, like its predecessor of 1646, provide for fining these delinquents, since the treaty under which the engagers had disbanded their forces guaranteed that they would not be punished in person or property. But the extra maintenance imposed on the engagers was a not entirely honest expedient, designed to fine them in effect while claiming to be observing the treaty.[4] For the future, the maintenance was to be paid for February 1649 at two thirds of the full rate, and for March to May at the full rate plus one fifth.[5] The extra fifth was to be used to help to pay the debts due to Sir James Stewart by the public, and these totalled £379,543 9s. 2d.[6]

---

1   SRO, PA. 11/7, fos. 3–3v, 18v–19, 48, 124v–126; APS, vi, pt. ii, 126–7, 205–6, 520–1; SRO, PA, 15/10.
2   APS, vi, pt. ii, 141–2.   3   APS, vi, pt. ii, 153–4.
4   APS, vi, pt. ii, 143–7. In 1662 order was given to repay to engagers the extra maintenance which they had had to pay, APS, vii, 387–8.
5   APS, vi, pt. ii, 154–5, 219–20, 238–40.
6   £201,822 advanced to help defeat the engagers, the rest already owing to him at that time, SRO, PA. 11/7, fos. 124v–126. For Stewart's account see SRO, PA. 15/11.

At the suggestion of the committee for common burdens and money some of the rates of excise were increased. This additional excise was to last for three years, that on wines from 7 March 1649 and the rest from 1 May. Shortly after this the old excise on wines was re-imposed for five years from 1 November 1651 and the additional excise on wines for five years from 7 March 1652; this was to be used entirely for satisfying part of the public debts due to the mar-quis of Argyll and Sir William Dick, who were granted a tack of it.[1] It was also suggested that money should be raised by borrow-ing from those 'who by the public service have acquired great estates and fortunes'[2]; this probably meant simply the leading engagers. General borrowing of money was ordered to continue under the restrictions imposed in February 1646, though those who had lent previously only in order to support the Engagement were to be ordered to lend a second time. Persons to whom the government owed money who supplied names of those eligible to be fined or borrowed from were to be given half the money thus raised.[3] According to one (admittedly hostile) account at this time, 'Argyle's creatures, commanded by him, had their espials at public inns, private lodg-ings, stables, and where-ever strangers did alight at their coming to Edinburgh', so that immediately their arrival was reported they could be summoned to lend money.[4]

When parliament rose in March 1649 the committee of estates was given power to impose any further maintenance or excise that might be necessary,[5] and a new committee for money and accounts was appointed to supervise distribution and collection of all public money. Payments of incident charges were to be made from the excise; all other revenue was to be devoted to the army and to granting subsistence allowances to those who had been utterly ruined through opposing the Engagement. The appointment of this committee was renewed (with some changes in its title) in May and August 1649 and in May and December 1650, and similar committees were set up in December 1650 and January and June 1651.[6] The expedient that had sometimes been tried in the past of giving the powers of a committee for money to the committee of estates was thus abandoned, as was that of having a separate com-mittee of excise.

Since the last general valuation had been made in 1643, rebellion, invasion and civil war had led to many changes in land values and

1   APS, vi, pt. ii, 217, 237, 332–3.   2   APS, vi, pt. ii, 217.
3   APS, vi, pt. ii, 237–8, 281, 709–10.
4   R. Chambers, History of the Rebellions in Scotland, ii, 319, quoting NLS, Adv. MS 34.1.9, Memoirs of Father Hay, ii, 378–9.
5   APS, vi, pt. ii, 291–2.
6   Ibid., vi, pt. ii, 294–6, 379, 541, 563, 623, 631, 681, 685; SRO, PA. 10/10, fo. 20v.

individuals' rents. All attempts to allow for this had been piecemeal; commissions for trying the losses and waste lands of various shires and individuals, and orders for revaluing a few shires. These had produced a confusion of reports and estimates of losses occasioned at different times by various causes. Therefore in June 1649 parliament decided on á general revaluation of the whole country. Illogically, though the rents of all the individuals in each shire were to be revalued it was laid down that the total valuation of the shire should be not less than the total valuation of 1639 or 1643, whichever had been the highest. This meant that whatever losses had been suffered by a shire, an individual could have his valuation reduced only if other valuations in the shire were raised. In many shires, especially in the north, rents must have fallen sharply and the 'rents' given in the 1649 valuations therefore must often be fictitious, artificially altered to give as high a total as the 1639 or 1643 valuation.[1]

Without waiting for the new valuations, the proportions of the total monthly maintenance payable by each shire were altered. When the tax and loan had been imposed in 1643 it had been promised that if, when valuations were completed, it was found that the loan and tax imposed represented rates of taxation on the total valuation of the shire which differed from shire to shire, then the proportions would be altered. But this had never been done, and when the monthly maintenance had been introduced in 1645 it had been divided between the shires in exactly the same proportions as the tax and loan. Yet the 1643 valuations had already shown that this division was unjust, as the following table shows:

MONTHLY MAINTENANCE PAYABLE BY SELECTED SHIRES
1645–9 and 1649–51

	1643 valuation (some with later alterations)*	Maintenance payable at full rate of £108,000 in 1645–9†	Fraction of yearly rent payable monthly in 1645–9	Maintenance payable at full rate of £108,000 in 1649–51*	Fraction of yearly rent payable monthly in 1649–51
Sheriffdom	£ Scots	£ Scots		£ Scots	
Ayr	291,000	6,066	1/48	5,196	1/56
Renfrew	77,000	2,205	1/44	1,732	1/56
Lanark	196,240	5,382	1/37	3,504	1/56
Aberdeen	313,000	6,543	1/48	5,588	1/56
Fife	475,000	6,642	1/71	8,493	1/56
Linlithgow	110,720	1,746	1/63	1,967	1/56
Edinburgh	301,980	4,167	1/71	5,392	1/56

* APS, vi, pt. ii, 501–2. † APS, vi, pt. i, 352.

1 APS, vi, pt. ii, 389–90, 409, 414, 495, 522–3.

Thus, taking an extreme contrast, when maintenance was being raised at £108,000 per month the part paid monthly by Fife represented about 1/71 of the total yearly rent of the shire, whereas Lanark had to pay monthly about 1/37 of her total yearly rent. The reason that this injustice had not been put right was that the shires (mainly in the east) that benefited from these injustices were better represented in parliament, especially among the nobles, than those that suffered. Now, in 1649, the western shires were in a stronger position in parliament than before, for it was they who had taken the leading part in the overthrow of the engagers, and many of the nobles of the east were excluded from parliament for having joined the Engagement. The shires which were paying more than their fair share of the maintenance therefore had an act passed on 27 July by which, until the new valuations were ready, maintenance should be imposed on the shires proportionately according to the 1643 valuations (or in some cases later revisions of them.)[1] Each shire would now pay monthly 1/56 of its annual valuation.

The introduction of these new proportions for paying the maintenance led to a bitter dispute in parliament. Nearly half those present refused to accept the change, and rose and left the house. It was nearly two weeks before they agreed to return.[2] The maintenance had already been renewed for June at the old proportions, and was now renewed for July to October at the new ones; and orders previously given for quartering the forces among the shires and burghs in proportion as they paid maintenance were altered to take account of the changes.[3] The burghs also at this time altered their stent roll, which fixed the proportion paid by each burgh of the total maintenance and other taxes imposed on them. This was done by a convention at Queensferry on 3 July 1649. The main change was that the proportion of the total payable by Edinburgh was increased from 28.75 to 36%. Edinburgh's commissioners denounced this as unjust and declared that the way the new roll had been agreed was illegal, but without success.[4] The session was now drawing to a close, but before it ended parliament was shaken by a further violent storm caused by a financial measure. As has been mentioned, in 1644 Adrian and Cornelius Lampsins, two Dutch merchants, had guaranteed payment in July 1648 for arms bought on credit for use of the Scottish army in England by Thomas Cuningham. In July 1647 the committee of estates had promised to pay this and some debts due to Cuningham, and had later ordered the raising of a loan of £60,000 to pay him,[5] but nothing seems to have come

1   APS, vi, pt. ii, 501–2.   2   Baillie, Letters, iii, 98.
3   APS, vi, pt. ii, 383, 388–9, 414, 447–8, 506–8, 518–19, 528–31.
4   APS, vi, pt. ii, 491–2; Baillie, Letters, iii, 98; Smout, Scottish Trade on the Eve of Union, 282–4.   5   APS, vi, pt. ii, 537, 541.

of this. In seeking repayment for the Lampsins, Cuningham was for a long time hindered by their insistence that their identity be kept secret, as they feared punishment for breaking the Dutch edict of neutrality in the English civil war, issued in 1642.[1] Thus when Cuningham pressed for payment in his own name early in 1648 the engagers would not help him since he had refused to buy arms in Holland for the army of the engagement. The Lampsins therefore had in June to pay the £185,185 Scots due for the arms bought in 1644, still acting through Cuningham to conceal their identity. They also lent some other money to him, and as security for what was owed to them he gave them a bond on the public faith of Scotland for 200,000 guilders and three assignments previously granted for debts due to him totalling £139,702 4s.[2] Now, in August 1649, parliament decided to repay some of the money due to the Lampsins by adding £13,200 monthly to the maintenance for a year, starting on 1 August 1649 and giving a total of £158,400. The act imposing this extra maintenance also ordered a reduction in interest rates from 8 to 6 per cent per annum—evidently intended to compensate for the extra maintenance.[3] But this seems to have been a pretext rather than the real reason for reducing interest rates, for many nobles and commissioners of shires were deeply in debt. The burgh commissioners, on the other hand, being the representatives of the main lenders of money, furiously opposed the reduction and walked out of parliament, leaving the other two estates to pass the act in their absence and to end the session without them.[4]

In September the committee of estates appointed Gideon Morris, the Lampsins' agent in Scotland, to uplift the extra maintenance, half of which was to be paid in November 1649 and half in May 1650. Presumably with the consent of the Lampsins it was declared that anyone who would advance £120,000 to them would be given the right to uplift the whole £158,400 extra maintenance. For payment of the rest of the money due to them the Lampsins were given assignments to be paid out of money due from England.[5]

The new valuations were all to be given in by 1 November 1649; as could have been predicted from past experience they were not, and new orders were issued to report them by 15 January. Shires that failed to do so would have to pay 50% more maintenance from 1 November till they did. Until then collection of the maintenance was to continue to be according to the new proportions agreed in

1   Cuningham, *Journal*, 154–7, 178; SRO, PA. 11/5, fo. 88.
2   Cuningham, *Journal*, 162–4, 166–74.
3   *APS*, vi, pt. ii, 537, 540.
4   Balfour, *Historical Works*, iii, 422–3; Baillie, *Letters*, iii, 98–99.
5   Cuningham, *Journal*, 204–18; SRO, PA. 11/9, fo. 48.

parliament.[1] In May 1650 parliament set up a committee to consider the valuations, but nothing was done to alter the proportion of maintenance payable by each shire, and successive acts which reimposed it from 1 November 1649 to 1 August 1651 were all apparently based on the June 1649 proportions.[2] The reason for this was simple; no new proportioning could take place until all valuations were completed. Some probably never were, and most of those given in were unacceptable in that, in spite of the warning that 'no respect shall be had to any valuation to be reported that shall be under the totall of the former valuation', many shires did report lower valuations.[3] Of twenty-five shire valuations of 1649–50 only seven have totals higher than those of previous valuations, usually only slightly higher. The other eighteen are all lower than before, often dramatically so. Inverness reported that the total former valuations of rents were far higher than were being paid in 1649; Ayr's total was down from £291,000 to £196,840 15s.[4] The absurdity of the rule that total valuations must not be lower than previously was thus exposed. In the face of the disobedience of so many shires the scheme for new valuations was tacitly abandoned.

The position of Sir James Stewart as commissary general and treasurer of the excise was made increasingly awkward by his disapproval of the negotiations with Charles II. Therefore in February 1650 he offered to resign. But while those who wished to reach an agreement with the king would have been glad to see this extreme presbyterian removed from office, it would be hard to replace him in a time of financial confusion; he was persuaded to continue as commissary general though he was relieved of the burden of acting as treasurer of excise. No individual was willing to take his place, so Sir John Smith and Sir John Wauchope of Niddrie were appointed joint treasurers.[5] After parliament met in May Stewart seems to have refused to serve as commissary general any longer, for the commissaries depute, John Denholm and Giles Wright, were appointed to collect the maintenance for June.[6] On 8 August 1650 the committee of estates appointed John Campbell joint commissary general with John Denholm[7] but there is no evidence that they ever took office; there seems to have been no commissary general during the period of confusion that followed the English invasion and the battle of Dunbar (3 September 1650). When the committee of estates established itself at Perth after the

1 SRO, PA. 11/8, fos. 184–184v; SRO, PA. 11/9, fo. 6.
2 APS, vi, pt. ii, 560, 568, 569, 571, 578, 582, 605, 630.
3 SRO, E. 901/1, Valuation Rolls, 1649; APS, vi, pt. ii, 523.
4 SRO, E. 901/1; APS, vi, pt. ii, 501.
5 SRO, PA. 12/5, Warrants of Committee of Estates, Minutes 28 Feb., 1 Mar. 1650; J. Nicoll, A Diary of Public Transactions (Bannatyne Club, 1836), 5.
6 APS, vi, pt. ii, 570, 571, 574, 581.   7 SRO, PA. 12/5, Minutes.

battle, it proceeded (on 15 October) to elect as its new commissary general Sir Alexander Brodie of that Ilk.[1] But he apparently fled rather than accept office and John Denholm was elected in his place; Brodie was ordered to return but did not do so. Denholm also refused the position and there was no commissary general until parliament elected Sir John Smith, already joint treasurer of the excise, on 3 December 1650.[2]

In June 1650 Charles II's arrival in Scotland increased the financial difficulties of the regime. The burghs agreed to advance 80,000 merks for the king's household and for raising some troops of horse as a royal lifeguard, but seven hours of debate were required to secure this agreement.[3] As the 80,000 merks were for the king's use they were not accounted for by the commissary general but by the royal receivers general. The Scottish commissioners who had negotiated with the king in Holland had had power to borrow up to £300,000 Scots to pay their own expenses and those of the king. They had in fact borrowed £330,000, £60,000 of it from the Scottish factors at Campvere (who had needed to be persuaded to lend 'by promises and threatinings'). To help to repay this, the commissioners were given power to uplift £108,000 Scots in the same way as the maintenance was raised, and to do so by 1 August—in effect an extra month's maintenance.[4]

All further borrowing of money had been forbidden in March 1650,[5] but in July the committee of estates decided that it was necessary to raise a voluntary contribution to finance defence against England, and it was later decided that members of the committee should travel through the country to raise loans from the well-affected.[6] But after the defeat at Dunbar and the subsequent flight of the Scottish government north of the Forth, whatever order had been up to then retained in public finance quickly vanished. With most of the lowlands in the hands of the English and confusion and disunity elsewhere, little was brought in by the excise and maintenance. The excise was continued till 1 May 1652 and the maintenance till 1 August 1651,[7] but by that time regular taxation had been largely replaced by arbitrary requisitioning of all money and

1   SRO, PA. 7/24, State and Parliamentary Papers, fos. 36, 232; Balfour, *Historical Works*, iv, 124.
2   SRO, PA. 7/24, fo. 40; *APS*, vi, pt. ii, 614.
3   Balfour, *Historical Works*, iv, 61–2; *APS*, vi, pt. ii, 593, 600, 601.
4   *APS*, vi, pt. ii, 560, 604–5; Cuningham, *Journal*, 228, 231; SRO, PA. 7/7/125, Supplementary Parliamentary Papers. Of this extra maintenance £14,578 19s. 11d. remained uncollected in 1661, *APS*, vii, 292–4. In March and July 1651 two more months' extra maintenance were imposed for the king's use, *APS*, vi, pt. ii, 657–8, 684.
5   *APS*, vi, pt. ii, 561; Balfour, *Historical Works*, iv, 5.
6   SRO, PA. 12/5, minutes 16 July, 16 Aug.
7   *APS*, vi, pt. ii, 630.

provisions that could be found. In January 1651 all the shires between the Forth and the Spey were said to have advanced meal and
money since Dunbar which exceeded their maintenance for some
months to come, as well as having been under great burdens of
quarterings; the shires north of the Spey were therefore ordered to
demonstrate their willingness to bear equal burdens by forthwith
paying all their maintenance for October 1650 to March 1651 and,
later, to May 1651.[1]

In May the committee of money and some of the committee of
estates adjoined to it decided that the best way of raising more
money was by another voluntary contribution.[2] Parliament approved the idea, but just how 'voluntary' the loan was to be is
indicated by the fact that the names of those that refused to lend
were to be reported to parliament or the committee of estates.[3] In
the few months before the Cromwellian conquest £50,056 14s. 8d.
was collected.[4]

By May 1651 the main financial object of the regime was simply
to gather by whatever means were available enough provisions to
maintain an army to face the English. On 17 May 1651 the king
ordered the seizing of whatever meal could be found (security being
given for eventual repayment) as the provisions at Stirling would not
feed the army which was being gathered there for more than six
days; and shortly after this further orders were issued for searching
for meal. In June and July lists of the amounts of cattle, sheep and
cheese to be supplied to the army by various shires were drawn up.
Members of the committee of estates were ordered to pay 200,000
merks for buying meal, but only £3,133 6s. 8d. of this was ever
paid.[5]

In these last few months of independence the attempt to resist the
English with the resources of Scotland north of the Forth alone
caused the shires and burghs of the north-east greater sufferings and
losses, whether from taxation, quarterings, levies, or seizures of anything likely to be of use to the army, than they had had to bear since
the ravages of Montrose in 1644–5. It was estimated that between
June 1650 and June 1651 taxes, levies, quarterings and other
exactions cost Fife and Kinross alone £1,597,238[6]—far more than
the monthly maintenance of the whole country for a year would have
brought in.

1   SRO, PA. 11/10, fos. 12v–13, 88v–89.
2   SRO, PA. 12/7, Minutes 9, 13 May 1651; SRO, PA. 7/24, fo. 121.
3   *APS*, vi, pt. ii, 667, 675.
4   SRO, PA. 12/8, 12 Oct. 1660. See also SRO, PA. 16/5, Book of Receipts of
Foot Regiments, 1651, and SRO, PA. 16/6, Vouchers of Account of the Voluntary
Loan, 1651.
5   SRO, PA. 11/11, fos. 40, 53v, 76v, 84–85v, 94v, 100v, 101; SRO, PA. 12/8,
23 Oct. 1660, pp. 6–7.   6   Balfour, *Historical Works*, iv, 337–43.

It is impossible to give even an approximate estimate of the material cost to Scotland of the wars of 1639–51. Certainly the amounts of money raised yearly by the covenanters were far greater than had ever been raised before in Scotland. From 1639 to 1651, with brief respites in 1642–3 and 1647, public debts and the need for money had grown ever greater. Confident in their belief that the English parliament would eventually pay all or most of their debts, the covenanters had involved themselves in wars in Ireland and England that their resources could not sustain. The Scots expected England to pay for all the campaigns which they fought from the first Bishops' War in 1639 until 1648—and no doubt if the Scots had been successful in their invasions of England in 1648 and 1651 they would have expected the English to have paid for these too. Financially their reliance on promises of money from England was folly. By the time that the Scots agreed to send an army to England in 1643 the English parliament had already shown itself incapable of fulfilling its previous promises to pay the Scottish army in Ireland and the brotherly assistance agreed on in 1641. Clearly, greed for English gold was not a major factor in deciding the Scots to intervene in the English civil war, and their gullibility in accepting repeated though often vague English promises to pay them indicated how willing they were to intervene in England for religious and political reasons.

The main taxes imposed by the covenanters—the tenth penny, the 1643 loan and tax, the excise and the monthly maintenance— all showed originality and a desire to spread the burden of taxation more widely than before. Many of the innovations made in this period were retained or reintroduced after the Restoration, an indication of how much more efficient and equitable they were than traditional methods of taxation. Thus the excise continued after 1660, and the use of valued rents as a basis for imposition of taxes became established after 1665; the 'cess', a direct descendant of the monthly maintenance, was introduced.[1] However, as excise and a monthly assessment or maintenance had both been borrowed by the covenanters from England, and were the main taxes imposed during the Cromwellian occupation, their use in Scotland after 1660 was as much the result of the example of England as of that of the covenanters.

No matter how carefully planned the main taxes of the covenanters were, the need for money as emergency monotonously followed emergency led to frequent resort to less scrupulous methods: forced and voluntary loans and borrowings of whatever money and provisions were needed or could be found, and fines. The total

---

1   Rait, *Parliaments*, 499–500.

public debt of the covenanters by 1651 must have been many million pounds Scots. Much of this could have been repaid if England
had honoured her debts to Scotland, £150,000 sterling brotherly
assistance, £200,000 sterling due to the former army in England,
and pay and supplies due to the Scottish army in Ireland between
1642 and 1648, which probably amounted to nearly £1,000,000
sterling. But the English satisfied themselves that the Scottish
invasion of England in 1648 was a good reason for not making any
further payments.

IX

THE COVENANTERS AND THE COURT OF SESSION, 1637–1650

THE timing of the outbreak of " the troubles " in Scotland in 1637 was partly determined by the times when the Court of Session sat. In this period its terms were from the beginning of November to the end of March (with a vacation over Christmas) and from the beginning of June until the end of July. In July 1637, therefore, Edinburgh was crowded with men of all estates, from all parts of the country, who had business before the court. The king's advisers decided that the new liturgy or prayer book which Charles I was determined to impose on the country should first be used in Edinburgh before the court rose, " to the end that the Lords of the Session, and others who had any Law-businesse, might see the successe of it before the rising of the Session . . . and that so upon their returne to their severall Countries they might report the receiving of this Book at Edinburgh." [1]   The privy council and the bishops thus confidently assumed that the prayer book would be received peacefully. How unwarranted this confidence was became apparent on Sunday, July 23, when they, together with many of the lords of Session, joined the congregation in St. Giles for the first service based on the new liturgy, for violent riots began as soon as it was used.[2] Therefore when the Session rose on July 29 [3] the news that the dispersing crowds spread round the country was very different from that intended.

By the time the court was next due to meet, in November, the king was far from wishing crowds in Edinburgh to witness the success of his policies. On the contrary he was trying unsuccessfully to get the people who had flocked to the capital to petition and supplicate against the liturgy to return to their homes. So they should not have the excuse that they were attending on the privy council and the Session the king ordered the removal of these courts, first to Linlithgow for one session, then to Dundee.

---

[1] [W. Balcanquhal], *A Large Declaration concerning the Late Tumults in Scotland* (London 1639), 22.

[2] J. Gordon, *History of Scots Affairs* (Spalding Club 1841), i, 7.

[3] Scottish Record Office [SRO], Court of Session: Books of Sederunt, Vol. v, 1626–49, fo. 113r.

Reproduced by kind permission of W. Green, the Scottish Law Publisher. David Stevenson, 'The Covenanters and the Court of Session, 1637–1650', *Juridical Review* (1972), pp. 227–247

A proclamation to this effect was issued on October 17 [4] " for feare of present danger, if this great concourse of people should not some way be diverted and divided." [5]   This move proved a serious miscalculation.   The proclamation was followed by rioting and so infuriated the burgh council of Edinburgh, previously loyal to the king, that it now joined the supplicants.   The effect of removing the privy council and Session was simply to make it appear that the king had abandoned his capital to his enemies.

Moreover the moving of the Session was very unpopular with the judges, lawyers and others directly concerned, as it was well known "that the Session could sitte no wher commodiously but in Edinburgh." [6]   When the treasurer, the Earl of Traquair, and other privy councillors tried to arrange for the Session to sit in Linlithgow Palace on November 1, 1637, they found the palace in disrepair, the lords of Session unwilling to leave Edinburgh "and all the subjects grieved to see Edinburgh deserted for the common cause." [7]   The provost and baillies also proved obstructive, declaring "that they ware not ebill, aither to furnishe Intertainment or ludginge for the sessioneres, quherupone they returned to this towne [Edinburgh], so for the present there is no sessione at all." [8]   The attempt to have the Session sit at Linlithgow was therefore abandoned, "to the hyndering of justice." [9]

Having failed at Linlithgow, it was decided to try Stirling; a proclamation of December 7 ordered the Session to meet there on February 6, 1638, the king having given permission for this apparently at the request of the lords of Session themselves. [10]   On February 4 the privy council confirmed that the Session would sit, "least anie opinion be interteanned of a further delay, whereby our lieges might anie way suffer by want of that judicatorie." [11]   The Session duly sat in Stirling from February 6 to March 22, 1638; "Ye may gess gif the town of edinburgh wes angrie or not " a

4 *Register of the Privy Council of Scotland* [*RPCS*] *1635–7*, ed. P. H. Brown (London 1905), 537, 538; Gordon, *History*, i, 20; Sir Thomas Hope of Craighall, *A Diary of the Public Correspondence . . . 1633–1645* (Bannatyne Club 1843), 66.

5 [Balcanquhal], *Large Declaration*, 32.

6 Gordon, *History*, i, 21.

7 R. Baillie, *Letters and Journals* (Bannatyne Club 1841–2), i, 43.

8 SRO, GD.112/39/700, Breadalbane Muniments, Nov. 10, 1637, Archibald Campbell of Glencarradale to Sir Colin Campbell.

9 J. Spalding, *Memorialls of the Trubles in Scotland and in England* (Spalding Club (1850–1), i, 81.

10 *RPCS., 1635–7*, 547; Baillie, *Letters and Journals*, i, 43.

11 *RPCS., 1638–43*, ed. P. H. Brown (London 1906), 2–3.

contemporary remarked dryly.[12]   But Edinburgh had the last laugh, for though the court sat " in all this tyme not a caus disputit, nor ether subiectis or advocattis to plead," for " the Advocates of any note would not goe thither." [13]   It was reported that since " nether persewar nor defendar appere " the lords of Session were " in deliberatioun how to represent to his Majestie the desolatioun of the countrey," [14] but nothing came of such deliberations.   Eventually on March 22 the court " resolved to ryse this day " for Easter " and furder, it is not necessare that they should return heir this sessioune, seeing there ar only few days of sitting, and that there ar no actiouns whatsomevir to be decydit, there being no people to attend craving justice." [15]   The supplicants (now becoming known as the covenanters) had successfully carried out a boycott of the Session until it returned to Edinburgh.

The privy council, weak, divided and always unwilling to risk telling the king the truth, suggested to him that the difficulties of the Session were due to the lack of the registers, the records of the court, at Stirling, probably hoping that he would agree that the court should therefore return to Edinburgh.   Instead the king ordered the transport of the registers to Stirling.[16]   Before the Session was next due to meet, however, he was persuaded to change his mind by the Marquis of Hamilton, whom he sent to Scotland as his commissioner to settle the troubles.   Hamilton urged him to recall the privy council and the Session to Edinburgh " which he conceived would be very acceptable to Our Councellors, Judges, to all Advocates, and all dependents upon the Law, to all Our subjects which had businesse depending in any of these Courts, but most of all to the Citie of Edinburgh, which complained much of their being impoverished by absence of these Courts."   Their restoration, Hamilton hoped, would lead Edinburgh to revert to loyalty to the king.[17]

Charles accepted Hamilton's arguments, and on June 30 the privy council issued a proclamation which was a tacit admission of the complete failure of the policy of removing the courts from the

---

[12] *The Chronicle of Perth; A Register of Remarkable Occurrences* (Maitland Club 1831), 36; SRO, Books of Sederunt, v, fos. 114v–116r.

[13] Hope, *Diary*, 70; Baillie, *Letters and Journals*, i, 49.

[14] SRO, GD.45/1/35, Dalhousie Muniments, Feb. 24, 1638, note of proceedings.

[15] *The Acts of Sederunt of the Lords of Council and Session, from the 15th of January 1553, to the 11th of July 1790* (Edinburgh 1790), 50.

[16] *RPCS., 1638–43*, 16–17.

[17] [Balcanquhal], *Large Declaration*, 90–91.

capital. An effort was made to save the king's face by relating that the king had originally moved the courts to places where his subjects " might convenientlie repaire for administration of justice " but that he had learnt that the lords of Session " ar not there fitlie and sufficientlie provydit with all and everie thing necessar " for the administration of justice. Therefore " out of his tender and fatherlie care for the good of his people " he had agreed to allow them to meet in Edinburgh, the Session sitting there on July 3.[18]

This proclamation, according to Hamilton, " gaife greatt satisfaction to all good men, and troubled extremly manie disaffected." [19]   Others interpreted reactions differently; " This great benefite, not being looked for, not being sought nor thought upon by any at that tyme, was receaved bot with small acknowledgement "—especially as the proclamation explained it not as a concession but as done to prevent inconvenience to the lords of Session.[20]   Moreover the covenanters were suspicious of the king's motives in returning the Session to Edinburgh. The court contained some of their most determined opponents. The Chancellor, John Spottiswood, Archbishop of St. Andrews, had the right to preside in the Session, and the President of the court was his son, Sir Robert Spottiswood of Dunipace, " knowne to be a very ill instrument betuixt the King and his subjects." Closely associated with them was Sir John Hay of Barro, Clerk-Register and an ordinary lord of Session. The covenanters feared—or claimed to fear—that these men would show partiality in cases concerning them; royalists asserted that this was just a pretext to stir up resentment at the king's concession.[21] The covenanters' " Tables " or committees resolved to issue a declinator against them, declining to accept them as judges. They informed Hamilton of this, and though they were " assured the Chanceller had no mynd to come to the Sessione " they insisted on a declinator against the President and the Clerk-Register unless they were removed from the Session, accusing them of bribery and other crimes. Hamilton answered that to remove them would be to punish them without trial, and that only the Session itself could accept or repel declinators. He persuaded the covenanters to delay action, and to consider abandoning

18 *RPCS.*, *1638–43*, 30.
19 S. R. Gardiner (ed.), *Hamilton Papers* (Camden Society 1880), 21.
20 Baillie, *Letters and Journals*, i, 90.
21 [Balcanquhal], *Large Declaration*, 93, 95.

a general declinator in favour of separate ones by individual covenanters who had cases before the court.[22]

While the covenanters were still debating the matter Hamilton appeared before the Session when it first met on July 3. He reiterated to the Session that the king had recalled it to Edinburgh to prevent inconvenience. He urged speedy dispatch of justice, requiring " them to be very carefull and circumspect, that in these troublesome times no Order nor Decree might passe from them, which might be prejudiciall to Our Crown or service." The judges thanked the king for his favour and ordered that Hamilton's message be registered in the books of sederunt.[23] Content with the reaction of the judges, Hamilton wrote to the king " I find they may be of exsiding greatte yuse to your Majestie, which heath cased me apply myself with all the industre I can to gaine them." [24]

Hamilton was also able to draw satisfaction from the fact that no declinator was made by the covenanters, for they proved very divided over the expediency of one. The matter was " hotly and vehemently disput againe whither it sould be or not " on July 3 " yet with great present heat and fear of division, it was caryed." [25] On July 6 the covenanters resolved on a double attack on the President and the Clerk-Register. Firstly, they would demand proceedings against them before Hamilton (as king's commissioner) for their crimes committed as officials of the crown. Secondly, they would be proceeded against before the Justice-General for sedition, for sowing discord between the king and his subjects. Once Hamilton had agreed to this—or even if he did not—a declinator would be presented. A committee for the declinator met under the presidency of the Earl of Montrose, and Alexander Gibson of Durie (son of one of the ordinary lords of Session) drew up a bill against the two judges. But in the end the covenanting nobles agreed, under pressure from moderates like the Earl of Southesk and Lord Lorne, to abandon the declinator if Hamilton refused to agree to it. Hamilton duly asked them not to proceed in such an

---

22 *Ibid.*, 93–94; J. Leslie, Earl of Rothes, *A Relation of Proceedings concerning the Affairs of the Kirk of Scotland* (Bannatyne Club 1830), 171–172; Baillie, *Letters and Journals*, i, 93–94; Gordon, *History*, i. 74.

23 *Loc. cit.*; [Balcanquhal], *Large Declaration*, 95; Rothes, *Relation*, 172–173; Hope, *Diary*, 74; J. Balfour, *Historical Works* (Edinburgh 1824–25), ii, 274–275; SRO, Books of Sederunt, v, fo. 116r.

24 Gardiner, *Hamilton Papers*, 21.

25 A. Johnston of Wariston, *Diary . . . 1632–9* (Scottish History Society 1911), 359.

important matter until he returned from a visit to England to consult the king, and this was agreed.[26]

Since the question of the declinator was causing such divisions among them the covenanters were probably glad of the excuse to abandon it. The Session sat from July 3 to 31, and the President and the Clerk-Register attended regularly without any protest being made. But, though a few cases were decided, little was done " in respect of this troublous tyme." [27]

Hamilton's belief that he had won the support of the Court of Session for the king was soon put to the test. In September 1638 orders were given for the signing of the " king's covenant," a document prepared by Hamilton in the hope that it would prove a successful rival to the national covenant of the king's enemies. All subjects were to sign the new covenant, officers of state, privy councillors and lords of Session giving a lead. Most of the lords of Session were out of Edinburgh at the time, but Hamilton wrote ordering them to be present when the Session reassembled at the beginning of November to sign the king's covenant. Many replied that they would do so most willingly.[28]

Events did not go so smoothly as Hamilton had hoped, however. On October 29 Sir Thomas Hope of Craighall, the King's Advocate, announced that the king's covenant, as he interpreted it, made episcopacy and the innovations introduced into the kirk by the king and his father illegal [29]—an interpretation exactly opposite to that intended by Hamilton. Furthermore the covenanters bitterly opposed the new covenant, and when the lords of Session attended kirk on the morning of November 1 they were treated to a sermon by Henry Rollock denouncing signature of the king's covenant as unlawful.[30]

Hamilton must therefore have been somewhat apprehensive when later that day he went to the Court of Session to procure the signatures of the judges, though many of them had renewed their promises to sign. Thirteen of the fifteen ordinary lords were present (Sir James Learmonth of Balcomie and Sir George Auchin-

---

26 Rothes, *Relation*, 176–178; Gordon, *History*, i, 74–75; Johnston of Wariston also drafted a bill against the two judges, *Diary*, 361.

27 SRO, Books of Sederunt, v, fos. 116r–118r; Sir Alexander Gibson of Durie, *The Decisions of the Lords of Council and Session . . . From July 1621, to July 1642* (Edinburgh 1690), 857–862; Spalding, *Memorialls*, i, 91.

28 Gardiner, *Hamilton Papers*, 40.

29 Hope, *Diary*, 78.

30 [Balcanquhal], *Large Declaration*, 193.

leck of Balmanno being absent through illness) and one extra-ordinary lord, the Earl of Traquair.[31] Of the ordinary lords all but four signed, but though one covenanter wrote in disgust that Hamilton " got al thair subscriptions . . . without once reading it over " [32] the implication that Hamilton had little difficulty is false, for he spent several hours in argument with the judges.

Hamilton's task would probably have been much easier if he had not thought it necessary to declare that signature did not entail condemnation of innovations in the kirk (as the King's Advocate had claimed). Some of the lords had evidently only agreed to sign in the belief that this interpretation was a possible one. After making this statement Hamilton delivered to the lords a letter from the king ordering them to sign—or rather a letter Hamilton himself had written on one of the blank sheets signed by the king and given to him to use as convenient. Most of the lords desired a delay; Hamilton afterwards told the king that this was because they had been frightened by the bitterness of preachers against the king's covenant and because " the people of this toune so threatned and terrified thes Lords," but the dispute over interpretation was prob-ably more important than such fears; Hamilton should have been able to have foreseen such a dispute and was therefore reluctant to expose his error by admitting its importance. He refused to allow any delay, and eventually nine of the ordinary lords signed after three hours of argument. Sir Alexander Gibson of Durie, Sir John Scot of Scotstarvet, Sir John Hope of Craighall (son of the King's Advocate) and Sir George Erskine of Innerteil refused, though they stated that in doing so they did not act from any disloyalty or dis-obedience to authority " but meerly from the sollicitude we have to walk warrantably upon a matter of such importance." They could not accept Hamilton's interpretation of the king's covenant, and they claimed that interpretation should, as an ecclesiastical matter, be left to the general assembly which the king had summoned to meet later in November in Glasgow. Two days later the four judges put this in writing and signed and took instruments on it in the presence of Hamilton. He then took instruments that he accepted their declaration only as a supplication, and did not thereby imply any approbation of it.[33]

[31] SRO, Books of Sederunt, v, fo. 118r.   [32] Johnston of Wariston, *Diary*, 396–397.
[33] Sir John Scot of Scotstarvet, " Trew Relation of the Principall Affaires concerning the State," *Scottish Historical Review*, xiv (1916–17), 62–64. The original declaration of the four judges is to be found at National Library of Scotland, MS. Adv. 31.2.1,

Hamilton claimed to be content that nine of the ordinary lords had signed. He dismissed Innerteil as "ane ould doting fooll," Craighall as "a bigot puritanicall fellow," and claimed that Durie and Scotstarvet acted not out of conscience but "knouing ther oun guiltines in corruptiouns" feared that the covenanters would institute proceedings against them if they signed. The judges who had signed, the majority, would now feel obliged to support the king in any case before the Session, Hamilton told the king.[34] But in spite of this attempt to put a brave face on events, the fact that nearly a third of the ordinary lords who had been asked to sign had refused, and that others had only signed after long argument, was a major setback for Hamilton. And the judges who had signed " durst hardly walk the Streets " of Edinburgh. When they left the Tolbooth after signing they were abused by the townspeople and feared violence.[35]

It soon became clear that Hamilton's " victory " in the Session meant little. Though it was rumoured that the Session intended to forbid the presbytery of Edinburgh to proceed with its process against the bishops before the general assembly nothing came of this.[36] The assembly deposed the bishops, excommunicating some of them, and abolished the innovations in religion complained of by the covenanters. But the king refused to ratify the acts of the assembly, and this brought the Court of Session again into the dispute between king and covenanters. On December 21, 1638, the Earl of Traquair appeared before the Session and produced a letter from the king. This instructed the court not to grant any letters of horning or other execution of the acts of the assembly. The court asked for a delay to consider the letter, and Traquair (more accommodating than Hamilton) agreed. This delay gave the covenanting nobles time to hear of the letter, and they solicited the Session to refuse to obey it. " And trulie it was lyk to haive turned to a fearfull bussines," with the Session having to choose directly which side to obey, the distant king, or the covenanters who now controlled the country. But on December 22 Traquair offered the judges an easy way out; he let them know he was willing to " haine

Collections by Robert Mylne, fo. 30. Balfour, *Historical Works*, ii, 294–295; Gardiner, *Hamilton Papers*, 52; [Balcanquhal], *Large Declaration*, 193; G. Burnet, *The Memoires of the . . . Dukes of Hamilton* (London 1677), 89. See Hope, *Diary*, 90, for a different version (by Innerpeffer, an ordinary lord) of what Hamilton said as to interpretation of the king's covenant.
34 Gardiner, *Hamilton Papers*, 52–53.
35 *Ibid.*, 52; Burnet, *Memoires*, 89.   36 Johnston of Wariston, *Diary*, 397.

upe " [hold back, conceal?] the king's letter, making no use of it.[37] He may have done this because he believed the court would publicly declare in favour of the covenanters if he forced a decision on it; more likely, as on other occasions, he simply acted to avoid trouble, even though this meant betraying his master's interests.

However, the Session was still troubled by the problem of whether to help to execute the acts of the assembly when it met on January 8, 1639, after the Christmas vacation. Most of the judges were resolved not to acknowledge the assembly. They rejected all petitions and signatures in which the deposed bishops were called " late ministers " of their former parishes or " pretended bishops." But the four lords who had refused the king's covenant passed such petitions [38] and letters of horning were authorised by them against those of the bishops who had been excommunicated. Such execution of the assembly's acts was, however, further delayed by the flight of James Gordon, the Keeper of the Signet, to England with his seal rather than obey the covenanters.[39]

By now war between the king and the covenanters was virtually inevitable; both sides were arming openly. The staunchest royalists on the Session soon found it necessary to flee. Traquair last sat on March 2, the Clerk-Register last on March 16, the President last on March 22, Durie taking over as Vice-President the following day.[40] The same day, March 23, the remaining judges " wer requyrit be the nobilitie to subscryve the [national] Covenant." [41] On March 26 the court sent out 270 musketeers and 166 pikemen to a muster organised by the covenanters; " ane number of the auld advocattis and wryters " also attended. The contingent was led by the four ordinary lords who had refused to sign the king's covenant.[42] Clearly the Session was now firmly under the control of the covenanters. This was confirmed on March 30; since the Keeper of the Signet had fled with his seal a writer to the signet, George Hadden, was authorised by the Session to sign and mark all documents which should have passed the signet. This was to have the same authority as the seal normally had, and the arrangement

37 Hope, *Diary*, 83; SRO, GD. 112/39/751, Breadalbane Muniments, Dec. 29, 1638, Archibald Campbell of Glencarradale to Sir Colin Campbell.
38 Burnet, *Memoires*, 115.
39 Spalding, *Memorialls*, i, 125.
40 SRO, Books of Sederunt, v, fos. 122r, 123r–124r; J. A. Inglis, " Sir John Hay, the ' Incendiary,' " *Scottish Historical Review*, xv (1917-18), 141–142; Hope, *Diary*, 87.
41 *Loc. cit.*
42 *Ibid.*, 88.

remained in force until James Gordon returned with the signet in October.[43]

Connected with the virtual submission of the Session to the covenanters, the *de facto* government of the country, was the attempt of the court to take a political initiative to dissuade the king from going ahead with his plans to invade the country. On March 27 the court sent Sir John Hamilton of Orbiston, an ordinary lord and Justice-Clerk, to the king to acquaint him with the true state of affairs in Scotland and deprecate his wrath.[44] The letter which Orbiston took to the king from the Session was couched in flattering terms: " your majestie under God may solely allay the terrours of the menacing stormes and without the sunshine of your gratious and calme countenance the Land and inhabitants thereof will quickly become miserable." But underlying this was hard fact and sound advice. Most of the country, the king was told, was pleased by the acts of the general assembly. High hopes had been turned to sorrow by Charles' refusal to accept them. The king's advisers who " adde oyle and fewell to the fyre " by claiming that most Scots opposed the assembly were bad counsellors and patriots. Violent remedies were often worse than the disease, the king was reminded. Orbiston was instructed to stress to the king these points, showing him that those who opposed him acted out of conscience. In other countries resort to arms in matters of conscience had not been successful " and that bloodie warres have ever bein to harden the spirits of men to opposition in matters of conscience, and to increase their number." If the king invaded with an English army Scotsmen would see it as a national war, and even non-covenanters would fight to defend their country's liberties.[45]

Such sound advice had no effect on the king, who was now moving towards the borders to join his army. Invasion seemed imminent, and a group of lords of Session and moderate privy councillors decided to make a final attempt to avert such a catastrophe by going and making a personal appeal to the king. Organisation of such a mission began on April 2, and on April 11 ten councillors and nine lords of Session (including all four refusers

---

[43] SRO, Books of Sederunt, v, fos. 124r–v; Spalding, *Memorialls*, i, 125, 234–235; *The Acts of Parliaments of Scotland* [*APS*], v (Edinburgh 1870), 267–268.

[44] Hope, *Diary*, 89.

[45] Scot of Scotstarvet, " Trew Relation," *SHR.*, xiv, 64–66; A. Peterkin (ed.), *Records of the Kirk of Scotland* (Edinburgh 1838), 211–212.

of the king's covenant) held a joint meeting of the two courts. They resolved to proceed in a body to the king to explain the true state of Scotland. They would act unanimously before the king "and falling doun at his royall feete deprecat his Majesteis wrath aganis his subjects," seeking only "his Majesteis honnour and saifetie of this kingdome." [46]

The following day most of the councillors and lords of Session met in Durie's house with leading covenanters, whose opinion of their plan had been sought. The Earl of Rothes and Lord Loudoun for the covenanters stated that they did not think the mission expedient. The fact that the council and the Session had signed the king's covenant showed they were not all favourers of the covenanting cause; how then could they act unanimously? Sir Thomas Hope, King's Advocate and a councillor, replied that differences of opinion were not the point; it was the imminent peril to kirk and kingdom that had led to their resolution. They intended only to supplicate and mediate. Innerpeffer added that they had agreed to act together, evading giving individual opinions if the king asked for them. He tried to explain away the signature of the king's covenant by lords of Session, while Fodderance denied that the court had refused execution against excommunicate bishops; it had only delayed, and had written to the king to ask what to do. [47]

However, in the face of such opposition from the covenanters the council and Session abandoned their journey to the king. A month later the courts again met jointly and revived the plan; the Marquis of Hamilton was now in the Firth of Forth with a royalist fleet, and representatives were sent to consult with him. Probably as a result of these talks they resolved to go to the king as previously intended. But again the mission collapsed when the covenanters refused all their requests to go to the king [48]; no doubt the covenanters feared that the king would take such a mission from Scotland as a sign of weakness on their part.

In the event invasion was averted without the help of the Session; neither side was yet ready to fight, so a peace treaty was signed in June 1639, a treaty which merely delayed war until the following year. Because of the threat of war the Session had not met in June, but once the treaty was concluded the king gave orders

---

[46] Hope, *Diary*, 89–90; *RPCS., 1638–43*, 116–117.
[47] Hope, *Diary*, 90–92.   [48] *RPCS., 1638–43*, 117–118, 119.

that it should sit on July 9. Durie was again elected Vice-President as neither the Chancellor nor the President appeared.[49] The Clerk-Register was also absent; such royalists still feared for their safety and did not dare venture back to Edinburgh. As in February and March 1638 when the Session had sat at Stirling, it now found that there was no business for it to attend to, as the result of a boycott by the covenanters who claimed to be too busy settling their private affairs (neglected while they had been raising forces to defend religion) to attend the court.[50] On July 13 the court sent Sir James Carmichael, an ordinary lord since March and the Treasurer-Depute, to the king to tell him that the Session was sitting "and that nane of the subiectis repairit thairto; and cravit his Majestie's plesur if thai sould sitt or ryse." Perhaps as a result of Traquair's advice that the king should give no reply Charles ignored the message from the Session, and consequently it sat until the end of its term on July 31.[51] After that, as the books of sederunt record, " The sessioune stoppit by the trubles of the countrey and sessiones of the Parliament qlks endit upoune the 17 of Nov. 1641." [52] This, noted a royalist contemporary, was " to the gryte greif of the trew creditour, and plesour of the debitor vnwilling to pay his debt. Thus is this land so grevouslie abuseit." [53]

The Session next sat in January 1642. By that time great changes had been made in the position of the court, for after the covenanters' invasion of England in 1640 and the king's difficulties with his English subjects he had been forced virtually to surrender power in Scotland to the covenanters. They were not short of ideas on reforming the Session. When the lords of the articles (the parliamentary committee which prepared Acts for presentation to the full parliament) met in the autumn of 1639 they approved an Act anent the election of the President of the Session, though its terms are not known. The theories of the covenanters on church-state relations led to an Act for suppressing the distinction between temporal and spiritual lords of Session on the grounds that clergy

[49] *Ibid.*, 119–120; *Acts of Sederunt*, 50; Hope, *Diary*, 100–101.
[50] *A True Representation of the Proceedings of the Kingdome of Scotland since the Late Pacification . . .* (1640), part i, 30–40.
[51] SRO, Books of Sederunt, v, fos. 124v–125v; Hope, *Diary*, 101; Gardiner, *Hamilton Papers*, 96.
[52] SRO, Books of Sederunt, v, fo. 125v. As no cases had been heard in July 1639 Durie, *Decisions*, 887, dated the interruption of the Session from March when noting " Long cessation for near three years, because of the Troubles."
[53] Spalding, *Memorialls*, i, 234.

should not sit in a civil court; the distinction had already become meaningless in practice and was now to be removed in principle as well. Another Act abolished the Christmas or Yule vacation since it was regarded as perpetuating superstition. An attempt was made to remedy an abuse by laying down that the court should hear cases in strict rotation, to prevent favouritism leading some to obtain justice more speedily than others.[54]

None of these Acts were passed by the full parliament in 1639, but when it met in June 1640, at last completely free from royal control, many of them were revived. Spiritual lords were suppressed; all in future were to be temporal. The Yule vacation was abolished as tending to keep in memory the superstitious observation of days and as interrupting the course of justice. To compensate for the lost vacation the court was in future to rise at the end of February instead of the end of March.[55]

These Acts were accepted by the king the following year, and on September 16, 1641, he was forced to agree that in future he would nominate all officers of state, privy councillors and lords of Session with the advice and approbation of parliament. Those appointed would hold office *ad vitam vel culpam*.[56] This represented a major defeat for the king, who lost his freedom in appointing the most important officials in the country. So far as the Session was concerned the Act also marked the final failure of his attempts in the early years of his reign to change the tenure of the judges from *ad vitam* to *ad beneplacitum*.[57]

Appointment in accordance with the Act followed on November 13. Replacements were named for the judges most detested by the covenanters, and the other judges were reappointed under the new terms. Eleven of the ordinary lords were retained. Sir Robert Spottiswood (former President), Sir John Hay of Barro (former Clerk-Register), Sir William Elphinstone (former Justice-General) and Patrick Nisbet of Eastbank (knighted by Hamilton in 1638 shortly after signing the king's covenant)[58] were replaced by Sir John Leslie of Newton, Sir Thomas Hope of Kerse (soon to be

---

[54] *APS.*, v, 605, 606, 611, 612, 614.
[55] *Ibid.*, v, 266, 297.
[56] *Ibid.*, v, 354–355.
[57] P. G. B. McNeill, "The Independence of the Scottish Judiciary," *Juridical Review* (1958), 135–144.
[58] [G. Brunton and D. Haig], *An Historical Account of the Senators of the College of Justice* (Edinburgh 1849), 295.

Justice-General; son of Craighall, the King's Advocate),[59] Sir Adam Hepburn of Humbie and Sir Archibald Johnston of Wariston; all well known covenanters. As for the extraordinary lords, concern for the impartial administration of justice and the independence of the court might have suggested that they should be abolished. Their main task had always been to protect the king's interests in the court; " they be but as spies over the rest to mark their doings and inform the king of it " an English visitor had reported in 1629.[60] But far from wanting an independent court the covenanters wished to replace the king's influence with their own. Therefore two of the former extraordinary lords (the Marques of Argyll and Lord Angus) were retained, while the former Bishop of Ross and the Earl of Traquair were replaced by covenanting nobles, Lords Balmerino and Lindsay.[61]

Parliament ordered the reconstituted Court of Session to assemble on January 4, 1642, when the new Chancellor, the Earl of Loudoun, would take the oaths of the judges. This was duly done.[62] To prevent delays the court passed an act of sederunt anent wakenings which ruled that the normal processes for reopening actions which had been before the court when its sittings were interrupted would not be necessary.[63] The court was now almost ready to get down to the task of clearing the backlog of cases which had piled up in the last three years. But who was to preside? King and parliament had appointed lords of Session but no President. This was evidently the result of a tacit agreement that election of a President should be left to the court itself. At least this is what happened; on January 14 Sir Andrew Fletcher of Innerpeffer was elected by the court " conform to the power gevin unto thame be the right and priviledge due be the lawes and consuetude of this realme." The President was not to be a permanent official, but was to act only for one term and the first day of the next, when a new election would be held.[64] This procedure was followed regularly until 1650.

The terms of the court were held regularly for the next two years, but in August 1643 the covenanters agreed to help the

---

[59] *Registrum Magni Sigilli Regum Scotorum: The Register of the Great Seal of Scotland 1634–51* (Edinburgh 1897), nos. 1032, 1037.
[60] C. Lowther, *Our Journall into Scotland* (Edinburgh 1894), 34.
[61] *APS.*, v, 389; [Brunton and Haig], *An Historical Account*, xix–xx.
[62] *APS.*, v, 391, 429; SRO, Books of Sederunt, v, fos. 126r–128r; Hope, *Diary*, 157.
[63] *Acts of Sederunt*, 50–51.
[64] *Ibid.*, 51.

English parliament against the king by a military treaty and the solemn league and covenant, thus launching Scotland into a series of new wars. This soon had effects on the Session. The judges, advocates, clerks and writers of the college of justice signed the new covenant on November 14.[65] On December 21, the committee of estates, through which the covenanters were ruling the country, decided that the Session should rise for a time, so that men could go about their duties in raising an army without the distraction of attending cases before the court.[66] The following day a joint meeting (held at the request of the Session) of the committee, the Session and the privy council agreed that the court should rise until January 16, 1644, since otherwise many would not go about putting out forces and raising taxes as ordered.[67]

On January 16 the committee of estates ordered a further delay in the sitting of the Session until February 1. Again a joint meeting confirmed this, so the court rose on January 17.[68] The court managed to sit throughout February 1644 [69] but its history in the following years is largely a story of continued interruptions. In June and July 1644 parliament was sitting, and traditionally the Session could not sit at the same time. Though it was not certain when parliament would rise it cancelled the whole term of the Session on June 12 so people would not gather in Edinburgh in the hope that the court might sit. In any case, it was decided, the troubles of the kingdom made the sitting of the Session inconvenient.[70] In October the privy council cancelled part of the Session's next term; it was not to meet until January 8, 1645, because of the condition of affairs and " the necessarie attendance and service of manie of his Majesties good subjects in the armeis now leveyed for the defence of religion and saifetie of the kingdom so as they cannot goodlie attend their civill processes in law." [71] Covenanting armies were by this time fighting in England and Ireland as well as against the royalist rising of Montrose in the north.

The Session met on January 8, 1645, only to rise the next day on the orders of parliament, which cancelled the whole term, again to prevent people fruitlessly attending in the hope that parliament

[65] Hope, *Diary*, 198; SRO, Books of Sederunt, v, fos. 146v–147v.
[66] SRO, PA.11/1, Register of the Committee of Estates, 1643–44; fos. 101r–101v.
[67] *Ibid.*, fo. 102r; Hope, *Diary*, 200; SRO, Books of Sederunt, v, fo. 149v.
[68] SRO, PA.11/1, fo. 110v; *APS.*, VI, i, 64; Hope, *Diary*, 202; SRO, Books of Sederunt, fo. 150r.
[69] *Ibid.*, fos. 150r–153v.
[70] *APS.*, VI, i, 102–103.   [71] *RPCS., 1544–1660* (Edinburgh 1908), 27–28.

might be prorogued and that the court would therefore sit. An additional reason for cancellation was "in respecte of the plague." [72] An epidemic was widespread in the Lowlands, and people from infected areas might have introduced the disease to Edinburgh if they came to attend to business before the Session. In May 1645 the privy council confirmed that the Session would meet in June.[73] But by June plague had reached the capital, the covenanting régime had fled from it, and no attempt was made to hold the Session. Plague and the sitting of parliament again prevented the court meeting in November 1645 to February 1646.[74]

At last in June and July 1646 a complete term of the court was held, the first for three years—which necessitated another Act anent wakenings such as had been passed in 1642.[75] Death had produced three vacancies among the ordinary lords since 1641, and the other judges now submitted the names of three staunch covenanters to the king as replacements. These the king accepted—as he was now the prisoner of the Scots army in England he had no choice—and parliament ratified the appointments in November 1646.[76] But of course the fact that parliament was then sitting meant that the Session could not meet for the November 1646 to February 1647 term.[77] Normal sittings were resumed for the next two terms (June–July 1647, November 1647–February 1648), though in June it was ruled that no actions would be heard concerning people from parts of the country where plague was raging.[78]

After the Session rose in February 1648 the books of sederunt have the now familiar note "Sessione Interrupted be the trubles of the Countrie." [79] The "engagers," the royalists and moderate covenanters who wished to intervene again in England, this time to help the king, raised an army and invaded England. On their defeat by Cromwell at Preston the more extreme covenanters, the "kirk party," seized power in Scotland. This new régime was determined to exclude from public office all those who had supported the engagement, and it carried out the most thorough purge of the Session since the troubles had begun. Eight new ordinary lords and one new extraordinary lord were appointed by parliament

---

[72] Balfour, *Historical Works*, iii, 248; *APS.*, VI, i, 287; Hope, *Diary*, 211; SRO, Books of Sederunt, v, fos. 153v–155r.
[73] *RPCS., 1544–1660*, 44. [74] SRO, Books of Sederunt, v, fo. 155r.
[75] *Ibid.*, fos. 155r–159v; *RPCS., 1544–1660*, 49–50; *Acts of Sederunt*, 54.
[76] *Ibid.*, 54–55; [Brunton and Haig], *An Historical Account*, xx; *APS.*, VI, i, 615.
[77] SRO, Books of Sederunt, v, fo. 159v.
[78] *Ibid.*, fos. 159v–175r. [79] *Ibid.*, fo. 175r.

(without consent of the king) to replace those purged.[80]   And when the Session next met, in June 1649, all three clerks of Session had to be replaced, one having become an ordinary lord, the other two having been purged.[81]

One of the main causes of the interruption of the sittings of the Session had been the fact that it could not sit when parliament was meeting.   This had caused little difficulty before the troubles since the Scottish parliament had met rarely, and only for a few days (or weeks at most) at a time.   Now, under the covenanters parliament was in session for several months each year, paralysing the Session. In May 1649 parliament at last got round to doing something about this, by ruling that in June and July the Session should sit in the mornings, parliament in the afternoons.[82]   Thus the Session sat uninterruptedly in these months, and in November 1649 to February 1650 parliament was not sitting so the court could meet as normal.

In this last term it became clear that the victory of the kirk party in Scotland had not only meant a change in the personnel of the court of Session.   Though fanatical and intolerant the régime showed far more interest in reform than the earlier covenanting régime, especially moral, social and legal reform.   Such a new spirit was seen in such measures as a new poor law, in a commission to investigate the grievances of the people, in the revival of justices of the peace to provide better local justice.   In March 1649 a commission was set up to revise the laws, so that there might be " a constant certane and knowne modell and frame of Law according to equitie and Justice established be publict authoritie and published to all his Maiesties Leidges." [83]   It was this new reforming zeal that now led the Session to start to act against endemic abuses which had come to be seen as normal practice, and which had thrived unhindered for many years.   For example, it had long been common (though illegal) for advocates to buy a party's interest in an action, which they would then prosecute with more zeal and skill than they had for their original client.[84]   In December 1649, for the first time in many years, an advocate was punished for this. John Maxwell was fined, imprisoned and deprived of his right to plead before the court, his gown being torn and pulled over his shoulders as a public mark of his disgrace.[85]

[80] [Brunton and Haig], *An Historical Account*, xx; *APS.*, VI, ii, 283.
[81] SRO, Books of Sederunt, v, fos. 178v–185r.
[82] *APS.*, VI, ii, 376, 386, 387.   [83] *Ibid.*, VI, ii, 299–300.
[84] *E.g.* Lowther, *Our Journall into Scotland*, 32.   [85] *Acts of Sederunt*, 60–62.

IX

In January and February 1650 it was the turn of false witnesses to suffer. The Session ordered at least five to have their ears nailed to the Tron for an hour, one to have his tongue bored with a hot iron. All had their moveable goods escheated to the crown.[86] As one contemporary recorded "Much falset and scheitting at this tyme wes daylie detectit by the Lordis of Sessioun; for the quhilk thair wes daylie hanging, skurging, nailling of luggis, and binding of pepill to the Trone, and booring of tounges; so that it was ane fatall yeir for fals notaris and witnessis." He added that fornication and adultery were more common at this than at any other time,[87] but with these failings as with false witnesses the truth probably was not that these crimes were more frequent than before but that they were sought out and punished with greater zeal than previously.

The Session at this time also examined its own workings, reforming them in various details and arranging for the refurbishing of the rooms in which it sat and the keeping of the streets clean in the area,[88] so that the court might sit in greater dignity. However, the kirk party's reforms of the Court of Session were, like its other reforms, cut short abruptly before they had time to have much effect. The June-July 1650 Session was first delayed and then cancelled[89] as English invasion was imminent. In September Edinburgh was abandoned and the following year the Cromwellian conquest of the Lowlands was completed; the Session did not meet again until the restoration of the monarchy in 1660.

It has often been said that one of the popular features of the English régime in Scotland in the 1650s was the provision of cheap, impartial and speedy justice by the commissioners for the administration of justice who first sat in May 1652, replacing the Session.[90] There is some truth in this, but it has been exaggerated and has led to the uncritical heaping of abuse on the Court of Session (with very little evidence cited) to provide an extreme contrast with the new, efficient justice.[91] It is certainly true that there had been

[86] Ibid., 68–70; J. Nicoll, A Diary of Public Transactions and other Occurences (Bannatyne Club 1836), 1–2; J. Lamont, The Diary of Mr. John Lamont of Newton (Maitland Club 1830), 16. [87] Nicoll, Diary, 3–4.
[88] Acts of Sederunt, 57–59, 62–67; SRO, Books of Sederunt, v, fos. 191v–192r.
[89] APS., VI, ii, 568, 570, 591.
[90] A. R. G. McMillan, "The Judicial System of the Commonwealth of Scotland," Juridical Review, xlix (1937), 235–236; Nicoll, Diary, 93, 96.
[91] McMillan, op. cit., 234–235. The origin of much that has been written in this strain is A. Mackay, Memoir of Sir James Dalrymple First Viscount Stair (Edinburgh 1873), 58–62 (cited by e.g. McMillan, op. cit., 234n., and H. R. Trevor Roper, "Scotland

abuse in the old Session, but the fact that English justice was popular should not be taken to mean that the Session had been " hopelessly corrupt," " thoroughly unpopular " [92] or " hated." [93] Very likely English justice was popular largely because it was established after two years in which no supreme civil court had sat in Scotland.   And of course for thirteen years before that, since 1637, the sittings of the Session had been constantly interrupted for reasons beyond the Session's control.   It was not the fault of the Session that this had led to the build-up of a long backlog of cases by 1652.   It is naïve to take the fact that there were thousands of cases depending before the commissioners of justice in 1655 as an indication of the high quality of their justice [94]; it was the only justice available, and any justice was better than none.   Probably it was more impartial than the Session's had been, but this was not the basic reason for its popularity.

To conclude, the history of the Court of Session in 1637–50 is one of irregular and interrupted sittings caused by war, plague and the sitting of parliament, by " the troubles."   They were years " when the Voice of Law could not be heard for the Noise of Arms." [95]   1638–41 had seen a struggle for control of the Session between king and covenanters, ending in victory for the latter. This had not led to any major reform of the Session (except as regards the election of the president), but in 1649–50 interesting first signs of reform emerge, only to be cut off by English conquest. Through lack of contemporary comment the impartiality and efficiency of the court in this period are hard to judge.   No doubt

and the Puritan Revolution," *Religion, the Reformation and Social Change* (London 1967), 421n.).   Yet to support his claim that the Session was very unpopular Mackay (58n.) gives only two references, both from the late sixteenth century.   Mackay takes these references (and his attitude to the Session) from M. Laing, *The History of Scotland* (3rd ed, Edinburgh 1819), iii. 493–497, 585–586.   Mackay assumes that these citations are equally applicable to the early seventeenth century; Laing does the same but at least sees the gap in his evidence, trying to cover it by stating weakly that there is " no evidence that the court recovered its purity . . . before it was reformed by the covenanters," and by half-hearted and vague reference to the charges of corruption brought against Spottiswood and Hay in 1638 (iii, 586).   This is hardly convincing.   As to the popularity of English justice, Mackay (62n.) can only cite Nicoll, *Diary*, 104—" thair justice exceidit the Scottis in mony thinges as wes reportit " (Mackay wrongly quotes the last word as " reputed ").   This comment (made in December 1652) has often been called into service (*e.g.* McMillan, *op. cit.*, 236; Trevor Roper, *op. cit.*, 422) but has had far too much weight placed on it; it hardly proves convincingly the popularity of commonwealth justice in general, and indeed Nicoll's last phrase shows that it is only hearsay evidence.

[92] McMillan, *op. cit.*, 234.
[93] Trevor Roper, *op. cit.*, 421.
[94] McMillan, *op. cit.*, 236.
[95] W. Forbes, *A Journal of the Session . . . From February 1705, till November 1713* (Edinburgh 1714), xvi.

246   THE COVENANTERS AND THE COURT OF SESSION, 1637–1650

they left much to be desired, but it seems probable that the main criticism of the court should not be of the quality of its justice, but of its lack of quantity. And this was something over which the Session itself had no control.

Sederunts of the Court of Session, 1637–50, and Presidents of the Court, 1642–50

(SRO, Court of Session: Books of Sederunt, vol. v)

June 1–July 29, 1637

Feb. 6–Mar. 22, 1638
    (at Stirling: no cases
    heard)

July 3–31, 1638

Nov. 1–Dec. 22, 1638,
    Jan. 8–Mar. 30, 1639
    July 9–31, 1639 (no
    cases heard)

Jan. 4–Feb. 26, 1642	Sir Andrew Fletcher of Innerpeffer
June 1–July 30, 1642	Sir Alexander Gibson of Durie
Nov. 1, 1642–Feb. 28, 1643	Sir George Haliburton of Fodderance
June 1–July 28, 1643	Sir James Learmonth of Balcomie
Nov. 1–Dec. 23, 1643, Jan. 16–17, Feb. 1–29, 1644	Sir Alexander Gibson of Durie
Jan. 8–9, 1645	Sir Andrew Fletcher of Innerpeffer
June 2–July 31, 1646	Sir Andrew Fletcher of Innerpeffer
June 1–July 31, 1647	Sir James Learmonth of Balcomie
Nov. 2, 1647–Feb. 24, 1648	Sir Andrew Fletcher of Innerpeffer
June 1–July 28, 1649	Sir Archibald Johnston of Wariston
Nov. 1, 1649–Feb. 28, 1650	Sir John Hope of Craighall

All the Presidents were elected on the first day of their sessions, except that Innerpeffer was first elected on January 14, 1642. This list of Presidents corrects that in G. C. H. Paton (ed.), *An Introduc-*

tion to Scottish Legal History (Stair Society 1958), 460, in two respects.   Firstly, Sir George Erskine of Innerteil, though named first in the Act of Parliament of November 13, 1641, was never President as the *Introduction* asserts.   Secondly, that list omits Innerpeffer's re-election on June 2, 1646.

X

THE ENGLISH AND THE PUBLIC RECORDS OF SCOTLAND,
1650-1660

On 3 September 1650 Cromwell routed the Scottish army which represented the uneasy alliance of King Charles II and the Covenanters at Dunbar. As a result of this defeat the Scots abandoned Edinburgh a few days later to the English invaders, but the garrison of the castle refused to surrender and in the castle were stored the Registers (as the public records of Scotland were then usually called), and the Records of the Kirk since the Reformation, along with much other private and public property which had been sent there for safe-keeping. Earlier in the year there had been serious doubts as to whether the castle was well enough supplied to withstand siege; at the beginning of June the General, the earl of Leven, had protested in parliament that he should not be held responsible if the castle was lost to the enemy as it was not adequately supplied, and Sir Archibald Johnston of Wariston, the Clerk Register, had made a similar protest that he should not be blamed if the Registers in the castle were captured.[1] In the event the castle held out for over three months after Dunbar, not agreeing articles of surrender with the English until 18 December 1650. One of the articles then agreed provided that all the Registers and private papers in the castle would be handed back to the Scots, who would be allowed to transport them to Stirling or Fife (which, with the rest of the north of Scotland, were still held for the king).[2]

The Scottish parliament ordered Wariston, as the Clerk Register, to go to Edinburgh to arrange the safe transport of the Registers by sea or land to Stirling castle or some other burgh north of the Forth:[3] his wife, Helen Hay, was already in Edinburgh 'taking care of the Records'[4] and he joined her there at the end of December 1650 after receiving a safe conduct from Cromwell.[5] Wariston, an extreme and fanatical presbyterian, had taken a leading part in

[1] *Acts of the Parliaments of Scotland* (hereafter *APS*), VI, ii, 595, 597.
[2] J. Balfour, *Historical Works* (Edinburgh, 1824-5), iv, 230; *APS*, i, 25.
[3] *The Writings and Speeches of Oliver Cromwell*, ed. W. C. Abbott (Harvard, 1937-47), ii, 377; Scottish Record Office (SRO), Portfolio of Papers Regarding the Records of Scotland, Bundle Correspondence anent the Registers, Oliver Cromwell and the Lord Register, 1650, 1651 (hereafter cited as SRO, Correspondence anent the Registers), letter to Wariston, 25 Dec. 1650; *APS*, VI, ii, 626-7.
[4] *Mercurius Politicus*, No. 30 (26 December 1650-2 January 1651), 493; *APS*, VI, ii, 618.
[5] *The Writings and Speeches of Oliver Cromwell*, ii, 377; *Mercurius Politicus*, No. 31 (2-9 January 1651), 513.

inspiring Scottish resistance to the English before Dunbar, but he was probably now glad of an excuse to leave the Scottish held north, for since Dunbar (a defeat for which many regarded him as largely responsible) power had increasingly passed into the hands of moderate presbyterians and royalists who hated and distrusted him.

Once in Edinburgh Wariston wrote to the Commission of the General Assembly (meeting at Perth) asking what he should do with the Records of the Kirk—he had been ordered to send the Registers to Stirling but personally thought that all records would be safer in Dumbarton Castle or on the Bass Rock.[1] In reply the Commission simply ordered the bringing of the Kirk Records north of the Forth, leaving decision as to where they were to be deposited until after that had been done.[2] A sub-committee appointed by the king and Committee of Estates on 3 January 1651 decided that the Registers should first be sent by sea to Burntisland: the Clerk Register and the clerks under him who were responsible for the various types of record were to pay the transport costs, for which they would later be reimbursed. The final destination of the Registers, it was now decided, should be Dunnottar castle, not Stirling.[3] Later in January arrangements were made for carrying the Registers (after they had reached Burntisland) by sea to Stonehaven and thence in carts to the castle, and a sum of money which the burgh of Aberdeen had been ordered to pay instead of furnishing a levy of horsemen for the army was assigned to repaying the clerks for the cost of transport.[4] The Commission of the General Assembly on the other hand decided that the Records of the Kirk should be sent to the Bass Rock—its owner, John Hepburne of Wauchton, was a member of the Commission and agreed to receive and keep them.[5]

Cromwell signed a safe conduct allowing Wariston to carry the Registers to Fife on 13 January.[6] Some of them had evidently arrived in Burntisland by 17 January[7] but bringing them from Edinburgh was not completed until late February or early March.[8] Once at Burntisland they were put on board a ship for carriage to Stonehaven, being entrusted to John Moore who was instructed to hand them over to the Earl Marischal, the owner of Dunnottar castle.[9] Unfortunately almost as soon as the ship was clear of Burntisland harbour it was captured by an English frigate and taken as a prize to Leith. The Scots indignantly demanded that the ship be freed, claiming that the Registers were still protected by Cromwell's safe-conduct but the English argued that once the Scots had taken the Registers into their own quarters at Burntisland

[1] National Library of Scotland, Wodrow MS Folio XXV, ii, no. 92.
[2] *The Records of the Commissions of the General Assemblies of the Church of Scotland,* edd. A. F. Mitchell and J. Christie (Scottish History Society, 1892-1909, hereafter cited as *Recs. Coms. Gen. Ass.*), iii, 192-3.
[3] *Diary of Sir Archibald Johnston of Wariston, 1650-1654,* ed. D. Hay-Fleming (SHS, 1919), 317; SRO, PA.7/24, Parliamentary and State Papers, 1581-1651, fos. 67, 71, 72, 75v.
[4] *Wariston Diary 1650-4,* 317-8; SRO, Correspondence anent the Registers, *c.*20 Jan. 1651, Committee of Estates to Committee of War of Mearns.
[5] *Recs. Coms. Gen. Ass.,* iii, 265.
[6] Balfour, *Historical Works,* iv, 266-7.
[7] *Wariston Diary 1650-4,* 317-8.
[8] *ibid.,* 318.
[9] SRO, Correspondence anent the Registers, 18 Feb. 1651, Archibald Primrose to Earl Marischal.

the safe conduct had expired, and that as the Scots had then sent them to sea again on a new voyage they were a legitimate prize: in any case the ship carrying them was not covered by the safe conduct, and nor were the large amounts of plate and other valuables which were found hidden beneath the Registers in the ship.[1]

The king and parliament ordered Wariston to return to Edinburgh to try to persuade the English to part with the Registers a second time.[2] He was suspected of having been too friendly with Cromwell when he had previously been in Edinburgh, and of having since his return tried to persuade magistrates and others in Culross, Burntisland and Stirling to desert the cause of Charles II, but was sent back to Edinburgh in spite of this since he seemed to be the person most likely to succeed in getting the Registers restored—and it may also have been felt that it was safer to have him out of the way in Edinburgh than intriguing and conspiring north of the Forth. As for Wariston himself, he was living in fear of being arrested or even of being murdered by the Scottish soldiers, so great was popular hatred of him, and he saw the recapture of the Registers by the English as an act of providence, or at least as an event made use of by God to preserve his life by providing him with an opportunity to return to the comparative safety of Edinburgh.[3] He set off with his wife rejoicing, reaching Edinburgh on 29 March,[4] and was soon involved with her in negotiations with Cromwell and other English officers.[5]

Cromwell was eventually persuaded that his safe conduct had still protected the Registers when they left Burntisland, and on 12 April gave a pass to one of Wariston's servants to go to Fife and bring to Edinburgh the clerks responsible for the Registers under Wariston, but he insisted that a new safe conduct that he now granted for transporting the Registers should be valid only for one month. Wariston asked for the removal of this time limit (without success), arguing that it would be impossible to get the Registers to safety within a month: they had been unloaded from the ship at Leith and stored in an English magazine there, and they had been 'broken up', presumably to ensure that more plate and valuables had not been concealed among them. To sort them out, reload the ship and sail to Fife would take more than a month. Further complications which arose in the following days included a leak in the ship (and it was 'not weell knowen whear it is') and a fire in a haystack which almost set fire to the magazine.[6]

In spite of all this Wariston seems to have got the Registers on board ship and the ship ready to sail by the beginning of May,[7] and had received orders to bring the Registers to Stirling castle.[8] But he was now torn between his desire to get the Registers out of English hands and knowledge that once he succeeded

1 *Mercurius Politicus*, No. 42 (20-27 March 1651), 678, 681; SRO, Correspondence anent the Registers, 18 March 1650, Lambert to Governor of Burntisland.
2 *ibid.*, papers dated 20 and 21 March 1651; *APS*, VI, ii, 647.
3 Balfour, *Historical Works*, iv, 249-50; *Wariston Diary, 1650-4*, 32, 34, 37-8.
4 *Mercurius Politicus*, No. 44 (3-10 April 1650-1), 704, 708, 711, 718.
5 *Wariston Diary, 1650-4*, 34, 36, 37-8.
6 *ibid.*, 39, 43; *The Writings and Speeches of Oliver Cromwell*, ii, 404; *APS*, VI, ii, 888.
7 *Wariston Diary 1650-4*, 45.
8 *ibid.*, 42; SRO, PA.7/24, fo. 109v.

in doing this he would no longer have an excuse for staying in Edinburgh. If he accompanied the Registers to Stirling he feared he would be arrested, while if he remained in Edinburgh after the Registers had left he would probably be declared a traitor for remaining with the enemy.[1] However, he was temporarily relieved of this dilemma on 5 May: one Archibald Hamilton had been executed in Stirling by the Scots as a traitor for sending intelligence to the English, but Cromwell furiously claimed that Hamilton had been a commissioned officer in his army and should have been treated as a prisoner of war. He refused to allow the removal of the Registers until he had been given satisfaction for Hamilton's death.[2] Wariston argued at length that Hamilton had been a spy, and that in any case his death had nothing to do with the Registers but was being used as an excuse for detaining Registers which Cromwell admitted the Scots had a right to. Meanwhile the crew of the ship began to desert for lack of pay and its captain was tried (though evidently not punished) by an English council of war for saying (while drunk) what he thought of the English.[3] Wariston continued arguing with Cromwell, though still thanking God for, through the Registers, giving him an excuse to stay in Edinburgh, thus providing 'a shelter for me in this storme from many snares and daungers'.[4]

At the end of May Cromwell agreed to let the Registers go and the ship sailed with them on 5 June to Alloa: Wariston stayed in Edinburgh until he was assured that it was safe for him to venture north of the Forth but sent his wife with the Registers.[5] He recommended that the Registers should not be kept in Stirling, but should be taken to the Bass—the Records of the Kirk had been carried there from Burntisland in April[6]—but the king and Committee of Estates not unnaturally decided against risking another voyage in the Firth of Forth for the Registers, and they were placed in Stirling castle.[7]

Two months after the arrival of the Registers English forces were besieging Stirling castle, the king and Scottish army having invaded England. In the negotiations for surrender of the castle which soon began the English refused to agree to the Scots keeping the Registers, and the Scots were forced to give way on this and other points. Some of the highlanders in the garrison mutinied, saying 'they would fight for their king but not for their country's geer', but when the castle was surrendered they showed enough interest in such gear to ransack all the goods placed in the castle for safe-keeping before they marched out. The Registers were broken open and some of them taken away by the soldiers,

---

[1] *Wariston Diary 1650-4*, 45.
[2] *ibid.*, 47; *Mercurius Politicus*, No. 49 (8-15 May 1651), 797-8.
[3] Historical Manuscripts Commission (HMC) 72: *Laing,* i, 260-4; *Wariston Diary 1650-4*, 48, 51; SRO, Correspondence anent the Registers, 6, 7, 12 and 19 May Wariston to Loudoun, 9 May Committee of Estates to Wariston; SPO, PA.7/24, fos. 120, 122v.
[4] *Wariston Diary 1650-4*, 56, 58.
[5] *ibid.*, 60, 62, 63; *APS*, VI, ii, 683, 686; *Mercurius Politicus*, No. 53 (5-12 June 1651), 859, No. 54 (12-19 June 1651), 878.
[6] *Recs. Coms. Gen. Ass.*, iii, 404-5. One duplicate register of the General Assembly was on Wariston's advice sent to Dunnottar castle, and later entrusted to the earl of Balcarres; it was eventually destroyed in the fire which burnt down Westminster Palace in 1834 (*Booke of the Universall Kirk of Scotland*, ed. T. Thomson (Maitland Club, 1839-45), iii, pp. vi-xi).
[7] *Wariston Diary 1650-4*, 319-20.

they 'thinking it no trespass or wrong in such a case'.[1] In ad ition a few clerks took advantage of the confusion at the time of the surrender to make off with some of their Registers.

William Law, a clerk of the exchequer since 1646,[2] prevented some of the exchequer records falling into the hands of the English and, in the words of a letter of Charles II to the exchequer in 1664, 'while he lived, he was at great paines and charges in preserving from the violence of the late usurpers the publict registers, ancient and late, of our Exchequer . . . of Scotland: and that since his death by the faithful care of Mr. William Sharp, now husband to the executrix of the said William Law, they have beine so still preserved and now delivered in good condition to our Clerk of Exchequer'.[3] William Henderson writer to the signet, smuggled registers and warrants of parliament and the Committee of Estates for 1650-1 and other papers out of Stirling castle after it had been occupied by the English and kept them secretly in Edinburgh until 1660.[4] It was probably at this time that Andrew Martin 'absconded himself' with the registers and minute books of the privy seal for 1499 to 1650 and some exchequer records concerning taxation to the highlands 'where he preserved them from the Enemy with a great deal of Expenses and Fatigue, there being upwards of 100 large books'. These records were not re-united with the Registers until 1707.[5]

The rest of the Registers were seized by the English when they entered Stirling castle on 15 September 1651, and the Council of State in London ordered that they should be sent there (to be deposited in the Tower) on board the frigate *Speaker* (built in 1649 and carrying sixty-four guns) commanded by Major Bourne, and this was done.[6]

Wariston congratulated himself on having advised putting the Registers on the Bass instead of in Stirling, so that he could not be blamed for their capture,[7] but in fact Scottish resistance collapsed after the fall of Stirling—the army which had invaded England had been destroyed by Cromwell at Worcester on 3 September—and it was clearly only a matter of time until the Bass fell and the English came into possession of the Kirk Records. The Bass had been adequately garrisoned and supplied but its owner, John Hepburne of Wauchton, had unfortunately remained on the mainland and been captured by the English. Major General Richard Deane demanded that he should order the garrison on

[1] B. Whitlocke, *Memorials of the English Affairs* (Oxford, 1853), iii, 334-5; H. Cary, *Memorials of the Great Civil War* (London, 1842), ii, 329; C. H. Firth (ed.), *Scotland and the Commonwealth* (SHS, 1895), 3-4; *Wariston Diary 1650-4*, 118; J. M. Thomson, *The Public Records of Scotland* (Glasgow, 1922), 15.

[2] *APS*, VI, i, 850.

[3] SRO, E.8/14, Warrants of the Exchequer Register, 17 June 1664, cited in A. L. Murray, 'The Pre-Union Records of the Scottish Exchequer', *Journal of the Society of Archivists*, ii (1960-4), 93.

[4] SRO, PA.11/12, Register of the Committee of Estates, fo. 35v; SRO, PA.12/8, Warrants of the Committee of Estates, papers of 20 and 21 Sept. 1660.

[5] *APS*, xi, Appendix pp. 139-40.

[6] *APS*, VI, ii, 745-6; *APS*, i, 125; *Calendar of State Papers, Domestic* (hereafter *CSPD*), *1651*, 372, 373, 397-8; M. Oppenheim, *A History of the Administration of the Royal Navy* (London, 1896), 330-1.

[7] *Wariston Diary 1650-4*, 114.

the Bass to lay down its arms, threatening him with unpleasant consequences should he refuse. Wauchton agreed in the end but the garrison was reluctant to surrender. Negotiations over terms began late in February 1652, and one of the most important points at issue was the fate of the Kirk Records and some private property sent to the Bass for safety. The garrison demanded that the Records and other property should be returned to their owners, declaring on 2 March that they would rather die than betray their trust by surrendering the property in their keeping to the English.[1] Early in April however a compromise was agreed which, though it in effect handed over the Records of the Kirk to the English, went some way to salve the garrison's conscience. All the property sent to the Bass for safe-keeping was to be transported to Tantallon castle, and owners of such property who lived in shires or burghs which had accepted English proposals for a union of England and Scotland, or who would themselves accept such proposals, would then be allowed to come to Tantallon and claim their property.[2] As there was no possibility of the Kirk accepting the tender of union this amounted to a surrender of the Kirk Records, though Wauchton continued to plead with Deane to restore them: unless this was done Wauchton and the others who had agreed to the surrender of the Bass would 'be registrat to posteritie as betrayers of the Church of Scotland'.[3] Deane refused to listen and the Council of State ordered the Kirk Records to be packed in casks and sent to the Tower of London to be kept with the Registers of Scotland which were already there.[4]

When the Registers arrived in London from Stirling they were entrusted to the care of William Ryley, the Lancaster Herald, who had been appointed keeper of the records in the Tower under the Master of the Rolls.[5] They had reached the Tower by mid October 1651, for order was then given to pay Ryley for the expenses of carrying them to the Tower.[6] In December he was instructed to put the Registers in order so that they could be used;[7] it was intended to employ clerks to make extracts from them concerning relations between England and Scotland,[8] though there is no sign that this was in fact done.

The Registers had barely arrived in London when the sending back to Scotland of some of them began to be discussed. The first batch returned was very small; in December 1651 Ryley was ordered to search the Registers for all bills and bonds for money,[9] and the following month John Milwood (a clerk who had been helping in searching the Registers) was instructed to deliver the papers which had been found to Captain James Peacocke of the *Tiger* frigate who was about to sail for Scotland with money to pay the English forces there.[10] Probably many of the debts recorded in these records were due to the former

[1] SRO, RH.9/18/29, Hepburn Papers, Correspondence and Articles relating to the surrender of the Bass, 1652, nos. 1-6.
[2] *ibid.*, nos. 7-8.
[3] *ibid.*, no. 14.
[4] *APS*, VI, ii, 774.
[5] *APS*, i, 124; article on William Ryley in *Dictionary of National Biography*.
[6] *APS*, VI, ii, 746; *CSPD, 1651*, 480.
[7] *CSPD, 1651-2*, 47; *APS*, VI, ii, 747.
[8] *CSPD, 1651-2*, 5, 40; *APS*, i, 125.
[9] *CSPD, 1651-2*, 56, 90, 97; *APS*, i, 125-6.
[10] *CSPD, 1651-2*, 109, 119; *APS*, VI, ii, 747.

Scots government or to Scots who had refused to accept English rule, and the English regime hoped to collect them for its own use. The Scots not unnaturally demanded that all their Registers should be returned to Edinburgh. Thus when in April 1653 a committee of the Council of State discussed the proposed union of England and Scotland with Scottish deputies, one of the Scots demands was that the Registers be restored.[1] Probably as a result of this it was decided that all the Scots records in the Tower which concerned private property rights, securities and conveyancing of lands, and bonds and contracts should be sent back to Scotland. In addition the clerks in charge of the Registers which remained in the Tower were empowered to make extracts from them which were to be as valid in Scottish courts as extracts formerly made when the Registers were in Scotland. The Registers returned to Scotland were to be disposed of as the Commissioners for the Administration of Justice in Scotland thought fit:[2] they had replaced the Court of Session and it would be before them that most cases concerning property rights and contracts would be heard, and the absence of the relevant Registers concerning private rights must have made their work unnecessarily difficult.

By October 1653 the Registers to be returned to Scotland had been sorted out and placed in a separate room in the Tower. Orders were given to make an inventory of them and to pack them up ready to go to Scotland on the next man of war to sail there, and it was evidently intended that the rest of the Registers, those of public concernment, should be sent back later.[3] But while a few Registers may have been returned to Scotland in accordance with these orders the great majority were not, even after the orders for dispatching them were renewed in June 1654, though the existence of an English inventory dated 1654 of some Scottish private bonds for repayment of debts suggests that they may have been returned to Scotland in that year[4]—having presumably been overlooked when such bonds were sent there in January 1652. No reason was given for not carrying out the orders of 1653 and 1654 for returning the Registers concerning private rights, but it may have been that Cromwell held on to them as a bargaining counter for use in his negotiations with the various factions in Scotland. The Council of State again discussed the return of the Registers in April 1655, but evidently reached no conclusion[5] and nothing more was done until 1657 when, probably mainly due to the efforts of Wariston, the private rights Registers finally reached Scotland.

For several years after the English conquest Wariston refused to co-operate with the English regime, but in 1656 the marquis of Argyll urged him to accept a pension and employment from Cromwell.[6] He spent months wrestling with his conscience as to whether to accept or not. Religious scruples at first made him refuse, but they were eventually overcome by ambition, his desperate

---

[1] *CSPD, 1652-3*, 269; *APS*, VI, ii, 804.
[2] *CSPD, 1653-4*, 138, 139, 147, 171; *APS*, i, 127; *APS*, VI, ii, 750, 751.
[3] *CSPD, 1653-4*, 188, 194, 236; *APS*, VI, ii, 752.
[4] *CSPD, 1654*, 223, 225 (Public Record Office, SP.25/134); *APS*, VI, ii, 755.
[5] *CSPD, 1655*, 130, 136; *APS*, VI, ii, 756-7.
[6] *Diary of Sir Archibald Johnston of Wariston, 1655-1660*, ed. J. D. Ogilvie (SHS, 1940), 32, 33, 36, 45-6, 48.

X

need for money to support himself and his family, and concern for the fate of the Registers. Early in 1657 he accepted a pension and though Cromwell did not re-appoint him Clerk Register until 26 September 1657[1] he went to see the Registers in the Tower in March. 'It maid my heart seak to see them, especy-ally ane floore lying full of the papers lyk a great heape of dung . . .'.[2] It may be that this sad sight influenced his decision to accept employment, though his wife had urged him not to let his care for the Registers lead him to collaborate with Cromwell.[3]   Wariston petitioned the Council for the return of the Registers concerning private rights in accordance with the orders of September 1653, and on 23 July 1657 the Council agreed that they should be dispatched to Scotland. William Ryley, Wariston and others sorted out the relevant Registers and their dispatch by a ship provided by the Admiralty was ordered on 19 September.[4]   The Registers now carried to Scotland consisted of 1547 volumes:[5] they were delivered to Wariston at Leith on 12 November by Captain Michael Nutton of the frigate *Norwich*, after having met with extremely bad weather on their journey.[6]

It was decided in 1658 that all the Registers in the Tower concerning the revenue and exchequer of Scotland should be separated from the other records with a view of sending them to Edinburgh,[7] but before anything was done Cromwell died (September 1658) and no further action concerning the Registers was taken until after the restoration of Charles II in 1660.

It was then decided that all the Registers still in the Tower should be removed, and on 14 August 1660 William Ryley was ordered to deliver them all to Sir Archibald Primrose (who was appointed Clerk Register in January 1661). But this order was countermanded on 5 September[8] as the result of a suggestion made by the earl of Clarendon, the English Chancellor; would it not be wise to search the Registers before they were returned to the Scots, and remove from them any documents which the king had signed in 1650-1 in order to gain the support of the Scots against the English parliament? It was well known that the king had made concessions to the Scots to which he no longer intended to ad-here, but it would be none the less embarrassing if his opponents could produce the original documents with his signature on them. Primrose argued that such a search of the Registers could easily be made once they reached Scotland, but an immediate search was decided on and William Ryley, the antiquarians William Dugdale and Elias Ashmole and others were ordered to make a search.[9] However before they had begun their search William Ryley's son William found the documents required—the original of the concessions signed by

[1] *The Writings and Speeches of Oliver Cromwell*, iv, 633; T. Birch (ed.), *State Papers of John Thurloe* (London, 1742), vii, 537-8.
[2] *Wariston Diary, 1655-60*, 71.
[3] HMC 72; *Laing*, i, 305.
[4] *CSPD, 1657-8*, 37, 62, 88, 93, 99, 104; *APS*, i, 128-9; *APS*, VI, ii, 764; *Wariston Diary 1655-60*, 98.
[5] See the Appendix, *infra*, for details of the Registers returned to Scotland in 1658.
[6] *CSPD, 1657-8*, 182 (PRO, SP.18/157/137).
[7] *CSPD, 1658-9*, 19; *APS*, VI, ii, 766.
[8] *CSPD, 1660-1*, 370 (PRO, SP.29/21/162).
[9] G. Burnet, *History of My Own Times*, ed. O. Airy (Oxford, 1897-1900), i, 200-1; C. S. Josten, *Elias Ashmole* (Oxford, 1966), i, 133, ii, 792.

Charles II at Breda in 1650, and the copy of the National Covenant and the Solemn League and Covenant signed by him before he was allowed to land in Scotland. There was much argument among the king's Scots advisers as to what should be done with these documents. The more extreme royalists and haters of the covenants, led by the earl of Middleton, highly commended Ryley the younger for finding the copy of the covenants, and he was told that it would shortly be burnt by the common hangman! It is highly unlikely that there was ever any serious intention of having this done. Much as the king might hate the covenants he would hardly draw attention to the fact that he had signed them by having the copy he had signed publicly burnt—the whole point of removing it from the Registers had been to consign it to oblivion as soon as possible. Ryley found that by finding the papers he had earned the displeasure of the earl of Lauderdale (who was appointed Secretary of State for Scotland in January 1661) and other moderate royalists, and he later related that 'the Scotch men then in Towne intrusted for the sending of the Registers into Scotland, offered mee 2,000 lib. sterling, if I would haue delivered the paper (as they called it) into their possession'. It is not clear from the context if the paper concerned was the copy of the covenants signed by the king, the concessions signed at Breda, or both. While Ryley may have exaggerated the amount he was offered (he told the story when petitioning for payment for his faithful service to the crown), it is unlikely that he invented the whole incident. The Scots involved in offering the bribe may have included moderate royalists, perhaps even Primrose (whose reason for wanting the Registers moved to Scotland before being searched may have been to enable him to get possession of these papers) and Lauderdale. Presumably they hoped to use these documents to persuade the king to agree to a moderate, presbyterian settlement in Scotland.

However, Ryley refused the offered bribe and gave the copy of the covenants and the Breda concessions to Clarendon: they are now among the Clarendon Manuscripts in the Bodleian Library.[1] Apart from the removal of these two documents there was evidently no attempt made to censor the Registers to remove papers of the civil war period which might prove embarrassing to the king, but Ryley, acting on his own initiative, also abstracted from the Registers a document which he called 'that Originall memorable Recognition of the Kings Royall Grandfathers title to the Empire of great Brittane' which he presented to the king, and four volumes of the register of the parliament of Scotland for 1639-50. These four volumes Ryley had ready to hand as he had a few years before made an abstract of them, and he now gave them (on the king's orders) to Sir Edward Nicholas (the English Secretary of State) to be deposited in the state paper office. They remained among the state papers until 1826 when they were identified and sent back to Edinburgh.[2] Efforts were made to conceal the fact that any papers had been removed from the Registers,

[1] *CSPD, 1660-1*, 260 (PRO, SP.29/14/47, 48); *CSPD, 1668-9*, 135 (PRO, SP.29/251/149); D. Macray (ed.), *Calendar of Clarendon State Papers* (Oxford, 1869), ii, 66, 67 (Bodleian Library, Clarendon MS 40, fos. 80, 85); *APS*, v, pp. i-ii.
[2] *CSPD, 1656-7*, 115 (PRO, SP.25/136, 137), printed in Ayloffe, *Calendars*, 357-428. The abstract was made use of by John Rushworth in his *Historical Collections* . . . (8 vols., London, 1659-1701)—see vol. II, ii, 1041-2.

X

and these had some success; Gilbert Burnet, who knew that a search had been made, believed that nothing had been found.[1] Ryley was asked to give 'a noate that I knew not of any Registers stopt now from goeing into Scotland'.[2] The fact that their public records had been censored by Englishmen would doubtless have caused much indignation in Scotland if it had become generally known.

In November 1660, after the search of the Registers had been completed, Ryley was ordered to deliver them to John Young, who had been deputed by Primrose to receive them, and by 3 December they had been removed from the Tower to a warehouse packed in 107 hogsheads, twelve chests, five trunks and four barrels.[3] They were then put on board the frigate *Eagle* (twenty-two guns); built in 1654 she had originally been named the *Selby* after a parliamentary victory on the civil war, but this was changed at the Restoration.[4] The Registers were not the only cargo that the *Eagle's* captain, Major John Fletcher, was sent from the Tower, for he was also given charge of two important prisoners who were being sent to Scotland to be tried for treason, the marquis of Argyll and Sir John Swinton of that Ilk, who were taken by barge from the Tower to the *Eagle* during the night of 4-5 December.[5]

The *Eagle* sailed from Gravesend a few days later, but was forced by storms to anchor in the roads of Yarmouth as she was badly overloaded; presumably she had some other cargo on board apart from the 128 hogsheads, barrels and trunks of Registers and the two prisoners, for they do not seem to be an excessive cargo for a ship with a keel length of 85' 6" and a beam of 25' 6". The *Eagle's* mate, her pilot and a Captain George Grant who was on board (perhaps as part of the guard on Argyll and Swinton) all later swore that the *Eagle* had been in serious danger of sinking in the storm and would not have been able to continue had not some of the Registers been removed. John Young who had sailed with the Registers as Primrose's deputy refused to consent to any being removed but was over-ruled, it being argued that he had not sufficient know-ledge of seamanship to judge if the ship was overloaded.[6] On 13 December a Scottish merchant ship the *Elizabeth* of Burntisland, owned and captained by John Weymes, also anchored at Yarmouth, and Major Fletcher sent asking Weymes to take aboard the *Elizabeth* some of the hogsheads of Registers for carriage to Leith, but Weymes refused. Later, when Weymes had either gone ashore or was on his way to see Fletcher, men and boats arrived from the *Eagle* and began hoisting hogsheads aboard the *Elizabeth*, whose crew refused to help them. In all eighty-five hogsheads were thus transferred and Weymes accepted this *fait accompli*, arranging with Fletcher that the two ships should sail in convoy, the frigate firing a gun to indicate that she was ready to leave.

On the morning of Friday 14 December the *Elizabeth* weighed anchor after the *Eagle* had fired the signal gun and begun to set her sails, but though the

[1] Burnet, *History of My Own Times*, i 201.
[2] PRO, SP.29/14/47.
[3] *CSPD, 1650-1*, 370 (PRO, SP.29/21/162), 402, 419.
[4] Oppenheim, *A History of the Administration of the Royal Navy*, 334-5; J. R. Tanner (ed.), *A Descriptive Catalogue of the Naval Manuscripts in the Pepsian Library* (Navy Record Society, 1903), i, 260-1, 274.
[5] *Mercurius Publicus*, No. 49 (29 November-6 December, 1660), 792; *CSPD, 1660-1*, 406.
[6] *APS*, vii, 11, App. p. 3.

Elizabeth tacked to and fro for several hours waiting the frigate did not sail, so Weymes anchored again. The following morning the *Eagle* again fired the signal gun and again began to set her sails, but again did not sail when the *Elizabeth* was ready, so the *Elizabeth* sailed on her own. She was soon struck by a severe gale; a contemporary noted that at this time there were great storms 'by sea and by land, as hath not bene sene, nor knowin in the memory of man'.[1] By the morning of Sunday 16 December the *Elizabeth* was leaking badly and the leak, hidden under the hogsheads of Registers, could not be found. On Monday she met with a Newcastle ship which promised to stay by her, but there was no chance of transferring the Registers to her in the storm and the two ships soon lost contact. At about 3 a.m. on Tuesday 18 December in a dark and stormy night without moon or stars the crew of the *Elizabeth* abandoned their half-submerged ship, having been pumping continuously since 8 a.m. on Sunday, and the *Elizabeth* and the eighty-five hogsheads of Registers sank almost immediately. The crew reached the shore about eighteen miles away in the ship's boat.[2]

Alexander Irving of Drum, who had shipped several trunks and much household property aboard the *Elizabeth* in the care of one of his servants later claimed that the Newcastle ship had offered to take on board the *Elizabeth's* cargo but that Weymes had refused to allow such a transfer,[3] but as Drum held Weymes responsible for the loss of his goods and was claiming compensation from him his evidence is biased. Weymes seems to have done all that was possible to save his ship and its cargo and cannot be held responsible in any way for the loss of the Registers: he had not wanted them on board his ship in the first place, and indeed claimed that his ship could have been saved if the hogsheads of Registers had not prevented the crew from finding the leak. Perhaps he might have saved the ship and some of the Registers if he had thrown most of the hogsheads overboard to lighten the ship, but he can hardly be blamed for not taking such drastic action. He would have had a lot of explaining to do if he had arrived at Leith safely but announced that he had thrown most of his precious cargo overboard.

Major Fletcher's conduct is far more open to criticism. One of Weymes' reasons for at first refusing to take the Registers aboard the *Elizabeth* was that it was well known that the king had refused to allow the Registers to be taken to Scotland in a merchant ship, yet Fletcher had transferred most of them to such a ship at the first opportunity. Perhaps he would have stayed at Yarmouth and reported that another naval ship was needed to carry some of his cargo if he had not had the additional heavy responsibility of having two important prisoners on board whose presence was required in Scotland as soon as possible. The really inexplicable part of Fletcher's conduct is his refusal to sail in convoy with the *Elizabeth*, but even if he had done so he would probably have been able to do little or nothing to help the *Elizabeth* in the storm. Unfortunately his own account of the matter has not survived. The main blame

1 J. Nicoll, *A Diary of Public Transactions* (Bannatyne Club, 1836), 310.
2 *APS*, vii, 65-6, App. pp. 25, 26-7.
3 SRO, PA.7/9/1/18, Supplementary Parliamentary Papers.

X

for the loss of the Registers lies with the king and his advisers who sent so irreplaceable a cargo to sea in an overloaded frigate in mid winter.

The Eagle arrived safely in Leith on 20 December 1660 with Argyll, Swinton and the remaining Registers.[1] The Scottish parliament appointed a committee in January to investigate the loss of the Registers, and on its report parliament exonerated all concerned of any blame for the accident.[2] The Clerk Register wrote sadly that 'Haveing now tane some view of these few Records that were preserved in the frigot, there can be fund none of the ancient Records of the Crown, onlie some few Parliament books of King James the 6, neither any Records since the year 1637. There be lost 85 hogsheid, and I feare of more worth then all that is saiffe.'[3] This was an over gloomy estimate which suggests that Primrose had not examined the surviving Registers very closely; indeed historians have been hard put to it to think what records might have filled the eighty-five hogsheads which were lost. Thus Livingstone wrote 'having regard to the records still preserved for the period prior to the Civil War, and to the safe return, in 1657, of all those relating to private rights, it is difficult to believe that those remaining could have filled anything like that number of hogsheads. Had the prospect of an unusually safe and speedy transit suggested the conveyance on board the frigate of other less valuable and probably private property to Leith?'.[4] But it is certain that all the hogsheads contained Registers. William Ryley noted (as already mentioned) that the Registers packed for shipment in 1660 occupied 107 hogsheads, four barrels, twelve chests and five trunks. Moreover three years before he had certified to Wariston that the Registers he had received (in 1651) had been packed in 144 hogsheads, ten barrels, fifteen boxes and five trunks.[5] Thus the Registers dispatched to Scotland in 1660 were packed in thirty-seven hogsheads, six barrels and three boxes or chests less than the Registers which had left Scotland in 1651, the differences presumably being accounted for by the Registers returned to Scotland in 1657.

As no inventory was made before the Registers were dispatched on the Eagle it will never be known exactly what the contents of the lost hogsheads were, but some guesses can be made. They probably included most if not all of the Records of the Kirk captured in 1652, though there is no mention of their whereabouts after the order that they should be sent to the Tower. A few Kirk Records may have reached Leith in the Eagle or, more probably, not have been on the Bass Rock when it was captured, for some such records (including registers of the general assembly for 1638-42) are believed to have been burnt in 1701 and two volumes of the register of the general assembly (1590-1616) were destroyed when the palace of Westminster burnt down in 1834.[6] Most of the oldest records of the Scottish chancery are thought to have been burnt

---

[1] Nicoll, A Diary of Public Transactions, 309; CSPD, 1660-1, 419; SRO, PA.12/9, Warrants of the Committee of Estates, 20 Dec. 1660.

[2] APS, vii, 11, 65-6, App. p.2.

[3] O. Airy (ed.), The Lauderdale Papers (Camden Society, 1884-5), i, 64.

[4] M. Livingstone, Guide to the Public Records of Scotland (Edinburgh, 1905), xvi.

[5] Wariston Diary 1655-60, 98.

[6] Livingstone, Guide to the Public Records of Scotland, xvi-xvii; Booke of the Universall Kirk of Scotland, iii, pp. viiin, x-xi, App. p. xxxviii.

in 1544 or 1547,[1] and therefore cannot have been among those lost in 1660, but some chancery records for 1547-1650 may have been, together with some early charter rolls and various rolls or volumes of accounts.[2] The great majority of the eighty-five hogsheads which sank with the *Elizabeth* were probably filled with a large mass of loose papers; warrants and drafts of various registers and records, and miscellaneous state papers, many of which duplicated material in registers and records which have survived through having escaped capture by the English in 1651, having been returned in 1657, or having reached Leith on the *Eagle* in 1660. The records kept on board the *Eagle* alone are probably of more importance than those lost with the *Elizabeth,* though far less in bulk, as they evidently included most of the records of parliament, the privy council and the exchequer. Thus though the loss of the *Elizabeth* has undoubtedly deprived historians of Scotland before the middle of the seventeenth century of much irreplaceable and valuable material (though there are doubts as to the exact composition of this material), the loss could have been far worse and a surprising amount of records have survived. Indeed, this can be taken as a judgement on the whole history of the Registers of Scotland before the late eighteenth century: considering all the disasters by fire, water and neglect that have mutilated them over the centuries, it is astonishing how many remain intact.

---

[1] Livingstone, *Guide to the Public Records of Scotland*, xvi.
[2] *ibid.,* xv-xvi; *APS*, i, 26.

X

APPENDIX

The Registers returned to Scotland in 1658

Details of the Registers sent back to Edinburgh in 1658 are contained in two Inventories. One of these, retained in the Tower of London, was signed by Wariston, who acknowledged receipt of 1,609 volumes (PRO, SP.25/135), while the other, which accompanied the records back to Scotland, was signed by clerks of the Tower (SRO, An Inventory of some of the Registers of Scotland Remaining in the Tower of London). It is no credit to either Wariston or the English clerks that both Inventories give the total of volumes being sent to Scotland as 1,609, whereas in fact only 1,547 volumes were listed and returned; a mistake was made in totalling some of the volumes in the SRO copy of the Inventory and the error was repeated in the London copy.

The Inventories, summaries of which have been published in *APS*, i, 129-30 and Ayloffe (ed.), *Calendars of the Ancient Charters and of the Welch and Scotish rolls, now remaining in the Tower of London* . . . (London, 1774), 354-6, list the Registers under sixteen headings, and in most cases give the dates of the first and last entries in each volume. Not surprisingly (since the Registers had been sorted out by English clerks with little knowledge of the Scottish records) there is some confusion in the listing of the volumes, but with the help of the dates given for individual volumes in the inventories and in modern repertories and lists in the SRO most can be identified. Below a brief summary of each of the sixteen groups into which the Inventories divide the Registers is given in italics, followed by an identification (where possible) of the records comprised in the group and reference to the relevant pages of Livingstone, *Guide to the Public Records of Scotland.*

(1) *Contracts, 1560-1650. 486 volumes.* The Register of Deeds, First Series, begins in 1552 and covers 1560-1649 in 557 vols. (Livingstone, 92-6).

(2) *Decreet Books, 1492-1650. 505 volumes.* This is mainly Court of Session, Register of Acts and Decreets, which covers 1542-1650 in 558 vols. Other volumes of this Register are probably included in (7) below. In addition both (2) and (7) include some volumes of Acta Dominorum Concilii (1478-1532, 43 vols.) and Acta Dominorum Concilii et Sessionis (1532-1559, 29 vols.) (Livingstone, 81-2).

(3) *Lawborrows, 1591-1649. 26 volumes.* Court of Session, Register of Cautions in Lawborrows, covers 1603-1649 in 25 vols. (Livingstone, 88).

(4) *Register of Generall Seasings, 1617-1650. 65 volumes.* General Register of Sasines, First Series, covers 1617-1649 in 60 vols., RS.1/1-60. In addition the Inventories wrongly include a few volumes of Particular Registers of Sasines under this heading (e.g., RS.37/3 and RS.56/3) (Livingstone, 172).

(5) *Registers of Particular Seasings*, 1617-1650. 38 *volumes.* Volumes from Particular Registers of Sasines, RS.5-61. (Livingstone, 173-80).

(6) *Register of Suspensions with Acts of Caution and Consignation, 1574-1649. 90 volumes.* Court of Session, Register of Acts of Caution and Consignation in Bills of Suspension, now covers 1573-1650 in 85 vols. (Livingstone, 88).

(7) *Register of Acts,* 1478-1650. 57 *volumes.* See (2) above.

(8) *Register of Comprisings,* 1636-1647. 9 *volumes.* Eight of these can be identified: Diligence Records, Register of Apprisings 1636-1640, DI.1/2-4, 6-7, and Register of Apprisings and Adjucations 1641-1647, DI.14/1-3 (Livingstone, 151).

(9) *Minute Books.* 94 *volumes.* No details given in Inventories.

(10) *Valuations of Kirks.* 10 *volumes.* No details given in Inventories.

(11) *Registers of Hornings and Inhibitions, 1589-1630. 4 volumes.* These can be identified as Diligence Records, DI.1/29 (General Register of Hornings), DI.21/20 (Particular Register of Hornings and Inhibitions, Aberdeen), DI.25/1 (Ditto, Ayr) and DI.108/1 (Ditto, Wigtown) (Livingstone, 140-50). It seems that most of the General and Particular Registers of Hornings and Inhibitions either had somehow escaped capture by the English in 1651 or, if they had been brought to London, were not returned to Scotland until 1660.

(12) *Register of Lowsing of Arrestments, 1623-1638. 2 volumes.* Court of Session, Register of Cautions on the Loosings of Arrestments, vols. 2-3 (Livingstone, 88).

(13) *Protegalls. 6 volumes.* No details given in Inventories. The series of Notarial Protocol Books in SRO now has 89 vols. dating from before 1650, NP.1/1-77, 79, 81, 83B-84.

(14) *Old Decreets, Acts, Minutes and Protegalls.* 60 *volumes.* No details given in Inventories.

(15) *Register of Signatures,* 1541-1644. 45 *volumes.* Exchequer Records, Register of Signatures, covers 1561-1644 in 60 vols., E.2/1-59, 61.

(16) *Charter Books,* 1424-1628. 50 *volumes.* Chancery Records, Register of the Great Seal, covers 1424-1627 in 50 vols., C.1/2-51 (Livingstone, 152-4).

XI

Conventicles in the Kirk, 1619-37.
The Emergence of a Radical Party

Reactions to Innovation and Persecution in the Kirk

In the years after the triumph of the covenanters in 1638 the kirk in Scotland was troubled by bitter disputes concerning the legitimacy of conventicles or private prayer meetings. Most ministers considered such meetings incompatible with presbyterianism, while a radical minority supported the meetings. It is the purpose of this paper to provide a background to these disputes by tracing the history of private meetings in the preceding twenty years.

The disputes arose out of the varying answers given to the question of how the godly, those who saw themselves as upholding the true traditions of the kirk against James VI and Charles I, should react to persecution. What action should they take? And what should their attitude be to the kirk since it was (as they saw it) deformed by corruptions imposed by the monarchy?

There was general agreement over answers to the second question. Those who opposed royal religious policy continued to accept that the established kirk was basically a true kirk, even though corrupt. Samuel Rutherford (minister of Anwoth in Kirkcudbrightshire until banished to Aberdeen in 1637) summed up an extreme version of this attitude in startling phrases. He called the kirk "our harlot mother", "my whorish mother" and "that poor miserable harlot".[1] The kirk was his mother and thus he owed it loyalty. But it had fallen into prostitution and therefore he could not follow all its ways or obey it fully. His duty was to work to restore and reform it, neither abandoning it because of its sins nor condoning such sins.

So the kirk was a true kirk, but corrupt. What did this mean in practice? Those opposed to royal policy might be agreed on their basic attitude to it, but they differed widely over how this attitude should lead them to behave. How much obedience was to be given because it was a true kirk? How far was it to be resisted because it was corrupt? At the one extreme lay complete submission to the kirk's authority even though it was corrupt. The other extreme, of "separation" (as adopted by extreme English puritans), of disowning the established church completely and setting up a new one, was regarded as out of the question by all Scots ministers. But a few came near to separation in practice while in principle still continuing to accept the kirk as a true kirk. They refused to countenance its corrupt services, or to obey its corrupt hierarchy, but still regarded themselves as

---

[1] S. Rutherford, *Letters*, ed. A. A. Bonar (Edinburgh and London, 1894), 87, 103, 191, 204, 213, 216, 290.

members of it — an attitude analogous to that of New England puritans who in principle saw the church of England as a true church but in practice defied it and went their own ways.[2]

The great majority of Scots ministers and laymen who opposed the changes in church government and worship which were bringing the kirk into line with the church of England — "the creeping episcopalianism of the Stuarts" as it has been aptly called[3] — reached compromises somewhere between the two extremes of complete submission and virtual separation. Most verged on complete submission, albeit reluctantly, to the changes in the kirk rather than defy its authority. Here the government benefitted from the traditions and ideals of the reformed kirk in Scotland of disciplined and centralised church government. Men chose obedience even to corrupt practices rather than threaten the order and unity of the kirk — they had a horror of anarchy and schism. Many refused to practise innovations such as those introduced by the Five Articles of Perth of 1618 — but only so far as this was possible without direct defiance of authority. Thus many laymen stayed away from communion to avoid being ordered to kneel to receive the elements as one of the Five Articles directed. Some ministers connived at or secretly encouraged disobedience to the Articles, allowing communicants to accept the elements sitting. And, since on the whole the bishops were anxious to avoid trouble and were determined not to create martyrs, in many parts of the country a blind eye was turned to such fairly passive disobedience.

For a minority, however, a mere avoidance when possible of conformity to obnoxious practices was not enough. Some ministers felt the need to preach or otherwise testify openly against such corruptions, to denounce them publicly. A few such ministers were deprived of their livings; others by a judicious balance of defiance and partial recognition of the authority of the kirk managed to retain their livings while being recognised and revered as leaders of resistance to further changes in the kirk.

The opponents of royal authority saw themselves as conservatives, not revolutionaries. They wanted to restore the kirk to its pristine purity. But perhaps inevitably some of the staunchest opponents of the king began to go further. They still maintained — and indeed honestly believed — that they were merely asking for the restoration of former purity; in fact they were demanding more. These new demands arose in part naturally out of the circumstances of persecution, in part from the influence of English puritans. Firstly, they began to regard as corruptions in worship not only such recently introduced

2 E. S. Morgan, *Visible Saints. The History of a Puritan Idea* (Ithaca, 1965), 64-5.
3 H. R. Trevor-Roper, *Religion, the Reformation and Social Change* (London, 1967), 398.

ceremonies as those contained in the Five Articles, but other practices which had always been accepted in the kirk but which were disliked by many English puritans. Thus in opposing new ceremonies these radicals came to examine all details of their traditional worship, and rejected some of them which had previously been unquestioned. This, however, did not become evident until after the overthrow of episcopacy in 1638, and it is the second way in which the radicals diverged from the previous practice of the kirk that this paper is concerned with.

Suffering from persecution, unable to obtain pure and godly public worship, the radicals took to holding private meetings to pray, sing psalms and discuss the state of religion. Sometimes a minister was present, sometimes not. Those taking part maintained that such meetings were necessary and that holding them was compatible with recognising the kirk as a true kirk and with presbyterian principles. But such reassurances were unacceptable to the majority of those opposing royal policy. For the majority the only acceptable forms of worship were private prayer, family exercise or worship led by the head of the family, and public worship of congregations. Any sort of private meeting for worship they looked on with deep suspicion as at least potentially anarchic, a step on the road to separation recalling such sects as the Family of Love, Brownists and Anabaptists — all emotive names calculated to rouse horror as implying religious anarchy.

Moreover the question of private meetings brought up problems of the concept of a church and its membership. Should the church on earth, the "visible church", include all christians, or only the elect? Like other national churches, the kirk strove to be inclusive, to include virtually all inhabitants of Scotland. But separatists in England and elsewhere had tried to confine membership of their sects to the elect (so far as they could be identified). There was a fear that those holding private meetings in Scotland had such exclusive tendencies, that they looked upon themselves as better christians than their fellow men and would come in time to form a separate and exclusive church in Scotland. The radicals denied any such intentions, but in the event their beliefs and actions were to lead them nearer to such tendencies than they would admit. Just as the logic of events had driven some dissidents in the English church to adopt separatist and exclusive ideas, so a similar logic of persecution forced some Scots presbyterians some way down the same paths.

How far back the holding of private meetings by those opposed to James VI's religious policies goes is not clear, but their origin may date from the introduction of the Five Articles of Perth in 1618; it is only after this that they can be traced.

Conventicles in Edinburgh

In February 1619 John Mean, two other Edinburgh merchants and a reader were summoned before the court of high commission for not observing Christmas.[4] The following month a row broke out about kneeling to receive the elements at communion, the most hated of the Five Articles. There was bitter public criticism of burgh ministers, a leading part in this being taken by William Rig of Atherny, another merchant.[5] He was said to be "a great precision" who affected "a singularitye in his apperell, (which gave occasione to one who was none of the wysest to tell him, upon a tyme, that his relligion and his breeches wer both out of the fashione)".[5a] The matter was brought up in the kirk session. John Mean was an elder and outspokenly denounced kneeling; what else he said is not known, but it was enough to make one of the ministers present call him an anabaptist and a man disobedient to the king who refused to recognise the authority of the kirk.[6] "Anabaptist", needless to say, is here used loosely as a word of abuse for someone refusing to obey authority, and tells us little of Mean's beliefs.

At the Easter communion the next year, 1620, there was again trouble, and again Mean and Rig were involved, along with two booksellers and two skinners. They were charged with encouraging deprived and suspended ministers and receiving communion from them (without kneeling) instead of lawfully from their parish ministers. The king therefore ordered the exile of the six men to distant parts of the country, though in the end they were allowed to remain in Edinburgh — four on making some show of submission, Mean and Rig only through the leniency of the bishop.[7]

These six were regarded as the leaders of resistance in Edinburgh but they were not alone, for at this time the burgh's ministers were active in denouncing what the historian David Calderwood called "the private meetings of some good Christians in Edinburgh, who conveened to deplore the iniquite of the time". The ministers themselves had harsher words for the meetings, calling them privy conventicles of Brownists, Anabaptists, schismatics, separatists. One of the centres of such meetings was the house of Nicholas [sic] Balfour, the daughter of a former Edinburgh minister, and an English preacher called Hubert is mentioned as taking part in them.[8]

[4] D. Calderwood, *The History of the Kirk of Scotland*, ed. T. Thomson (7 vols., Wodrow Society, 1842-9), vii, 349.

[5] *Ibid.*, vii, 355-6.

[5a] J. Gordon *History of Scots Affairs* (3 vols., Spalding Club, 1841), iii, 239.

[6] Calderwood, *History*, vii, 357-9, 361, 362-4, 379.

[7] *Register of the Privy Council of Scotland* [*RPCS*], *1616-19*, ed. D. Masson (Edinburgh, 1894), 249-50, 264, 299, 328; Calderwood, *History*, vii, 434, 439-41, 447-8; D. Laing (ed.), *Original Letters Relating to the Ecclesiastical Affairs of Scotland, 1603-25* (2 vols., Bannatyne Club, 1851), ii, 624-6.

[8] Calderwood, *History*, vii, 449.

Almost certainly Mean and Rig also took part in such meetings by 1620; certainly they were doing so by 1624 when religious disputes in Edinburgh next came into the open through the actions of "a sort of mutinous people". Led by Rig (now a baillie of the burgh), "puffed up with a conceit of his own abilities" according to the archbishop of St Andrews, they publicly challenged the doctrine of Edinburgh ministers and demanded that Easter communion be celebrated in the old way. As a result Rig together with Mean, another merchant, a flesher, an apothecary and an advocate were summoned before the privy council on the king's orders. In their depositions the six burgesses explained their scruples over kneeling. The flesher was accused of separating from the kirk, but denied it or any such intention. The archbishop of St Andrews denounced John Mean as one of those who kept private conventicles and as having formerly kept a Brownist minister in his house (who had since gone to Ireland and died there). Mean only denied that the minister had taught in his house, thus it seems tacitly admitting that there had been such a minister and such meetings.[9]

The privy council decided that the six burgesses were guilty of setting a very bad example "caryeing with it verie probable appeiranceis of mutinie and shisme" worthy of rigorous punishment. Mean, incidentally, was described by the council as a poor man, Rig was a wealthy one.[10] The advocate, regarded as less guilty than the rest, was spared, but the other five were declared incapable of holding public office in kirk or burgh. In addition all five were banished from Edinburgh. Mean was sent to Elgin, Rig (the ringleader) was for a time held prisoner in Blackness Castle and then confined to his own house of Atherny in Fife. The king also imposed a very large fine on Rig, but this seems to have been cancelled after opposition from the privy council.[11]

The banishments were of fairly short duration. Mean was allowed home at the end of 1624 to look after his family during an outbreak of plague, and though he was sent back to Elgin as the Easter communion of 1625 approached he was probably allowed back to Edinburgh soon afterwards. Similarly Rig's confinement was lifted in September 1626. The bishops had some sympathy with the dissidents' point of view and had no stomach for harsh persecution.[12]

9 J. Spottiswoode, *The History of the Church of Scotland* (3 vols., Bannatyne Club and Spottiswoode Society, 1850-1), iii, 268-9; *RPCS., 1622-5*, ed. D. Masson (Edinburgh, 1896), 490; Calderwood, *History*, vii, 596-606; Laing, *Original Letters*, ii, 740-5, 828.
10 *RPCS, 1622-5*, 503-4.
11 *Ibid.*, 521-2, 524, 534, 538, 541; Calderwood, *History*, vii, 607, 609-10, 618-19; J. Row, *The History of the Kirk of Scotland* (Wodrow Society, 1842), 337; Laing, *Original Letters*, ii, 748-50, 752-5, 767, 775-6, 779-80.
12 *RPCS, 1622-5*, 597, 664, 666, 677-8, 690, 694, 700, 708-9; Calderwood, *History*, vii, 628, 632.

The sort of fears raised by the activities of the dissidents are shown in a proclamation against private meetings published on 10th June 1624. This related that some "affecting hypocriticallie the glorie of puritie and zeale above others" cast off obedience to the king and ministers, abstaining from worship "and in end, numbers of them have assembled themselfs in private houses in Edinburgh, and other places, to hear from intruding ministers, preachings, exhortations, prayers, and all sort of exercises fitting their unrulie fantasies". Moreover they did this in time of public worship in the kirks, and gave their seditious conventicles the name of congregations. This introduced corruption in church government, and previously "such pernicious seeds of separation, singularitie of blind or fained zeale, have brought furth damned sects of Anabaptists, Familie of Love, Brounists, Arminians, Illuminats, and many such pests, enemies to religion, authoritie, and peace, and occasioned the murther of millions of people, and infinite other disturbances". Such meetings were therefore forbidden, except for religious exercise in families, which might be joined by any visitor eating or lodging with the family, but by no other stranger.[13]

This outspoken proclamation was followed up in July when members of the privy council took oaths purging themselves of holding conventicles and then (on the king's orders) summoned the provost, baillies and council of Edinburgh to do the same. All did so, and promised to seek out and punish conventicles. But one of the councillors, John Fleming (who was related to John Mean by marriage), when asked to say whether he had attended conventicles asked the chancellor, Sir George Hay, to define a conventicle. Hay replied that "it is a private meeting of men and women to a private religious exercise in time of public sermon", and Fleming then swore that he had attended no conventicles.[14] This very narrow definition of a conventicle deprived the proclamation against them of much of its force, and it seems that in the years following private meetings at other times than public worship were held in Edinburgh virtually without hindrance. The king's intention of suppressing all such meetings had been thwarted by a council anxious to avoid trouble. John Mean and his friends probably continued their meetings though, now they were no longer persecuted, it is impossible to trace them in detail. Moreover now that he and others like him had been deprived of their elderships it was easier for the kirk to ignore their activities than before. The only time John Mean

---

[13] *RPCS, 1622-5*, vii, 612-13.
[14] *Ibid.*, vii, 620-1; Laing, *Original Letters*, ii, 758-9, 760, 761. John Fleming's brother Bartholomew married a sister of Mean's wife, R. Wodrow, *Select Biographies*, ed. W. K. Tweedie (2 vols., Wodrow Society, 1845-7), i, 150-1; C. B. B. Wilson (ed.), *Roll of Edinburgh Burgesses and Guild Brethren, 1406-1700* (Scottish Record Society, 1929), 184.

appears to have been in trouble again before 1637 was in 1635 when he was summoned before the presbytery for not attending public worship on a fast day, and he escaped without punishment.[15]

What significance are we to attach to the controversies surrounding John Mean, William Rig and their supporters in the 1620s? All too often the abuse directed at them by their enemies has been taken at its face value, and these years have been taken as marking the beginnings of congregationalism and the entry of sects to Scotland.[16] This is surely a mistake, for even though English puritan ideas may have influenced them these men were no separatists. They recognised the kirk as a true church, but tended to abstain from its worship through its corruptions and hold, so far as they could, pure worship of their own. William Rig declared that he detested all opinions of popular power over ministers "as smelling of that odious opinioun of the Browneistis", and protested he was free of such impious and scandalous beliefs.[17] The fact that Mean and Rig were elders until deprived of office, their later careers and, above all, their connections with other radicals show that they were definitely presbyterians wishing to reform a corrupt but true kirk, not separatists or sectaries. One may conclude, as their opponents did, that their activities in attending conventicles held the seeds of separation, but this is a very different matter from saying that they were separatists.

Turning now to some of John Mean's friends and relations, it becomes clear that, far from being an isolated separatist, he lies in the heart of a wide circle of radical opponents of royal religious policy; and these friends and relatives are staunch presbyterians even though they are prepared to encourage conventicles, private meetings.

Conventicles in the South-West and Ulster

John Mean was married to Barbara Hamilton, and it was later said that it was she who was responsible for starting one of the riots in Edinburgh kirks on 23rd July 1637 which sparked off "the troubles".[18] Their son John became minister of Anwoth.[19] Many of Barbara Hamilton's relations married ministers. In particular, one of her sisters married Robert Blair, and two of her nieces married John McLellan and John Livingstone.[20]

15 Row, *History*, 390.
16 H. Escott, *A History of Scottish Congregationalism* (Glasgow, 1960), 6-7; W. I. Hoy, "The Entry of Sects into Scotland", *Reformation and Revolution*, ed. D. Shaw (Edinburgh, 1967), 178-9.
17 *RPCS, 1622-5*, 524; Laing, *Original Letters*, ii, 748-50.
18 R. Wodrow, *Analecta, or Materials for a History of Remarkable Providences*, ed. M. Leishman (4 vols., Maitland Club 1842-3), i, 64.
19 H. Scott (ed.),*Fasti Ecclesiae Scoticanae* (9 vols., Edinburgh, 1915-50), ii, 386.
20 R. Blair, *Autobiography*, ed. T. McCrie (Wodrow Society, 1848), 117, 134; Wodrow, *Select Biographies*, i, 150-2.

Mention of these ministers takes us at once to Ulster and to the western Lowlands, the centre of opposition to the corruptions of the kirk, for it was in these areas that these ministers were most active. All three of them had close connections with other ministers in the south-west who were fast coming to be recognised as leaders of such opposition, David Dickson, minister of Irvine, and Samuel Rutherford, minister of Anwoth. As we shall see, both favoured the holding of private prayer meetings, and both had close connections with those holding them in Edinburgh. These men all won themselves widespread popular support in the south-west by their preaching. The two outbreaks of religious revivalism in Scotland in these years, the "Stewarton sickness" of 1625 and the Kirk of Shotts revival of 1630 were both inspired mainly by David Dickson and John Livingstone. [20a]

These radical ministers of the south-west were in many ways the heirs of Andrew Melville. To some of them — Dickson, Blair and Livingstone — Melville's teaching had been passed by his old friend and former Edinburgh minister, Robert Bruce (died 1631).[20b] The same three had also come under the influence of the "Melvillian" Robert Boyd, who had been principal of Glasgow University from 1615 to 1622. During Boyd's years as principal Blair had been a regent in the university, Dickson and Livingstone students.[20c] Yet it would have been an over-simplification simply to label the radical ministers of the 1620s and 1630s "Melvillians". Certainly they accepted Melville's ideas on church-state relations and on the need for a presbyterian church polity. But their holding of conventicles and their wish to purge the kirk of some of its traditional ceremonies seem to owe nothing to Melville. These were later developments arising as reactions to persecution.

Both Robert Blair and John Livingstone left autobiographies, and it is from these that we derive much of our information about the radicals in the kirk in the 1630s. Both, also, through their opposition to bishops and their dislike of ceremonies, failed to obtain parishes in Scotland and turned instead to the freer conditions in Ulster. It had only been a generation before that most of Ulster had been conquered from the native Irish and colonised by English and Scots settlers, most of the settlers in Antrim and Down being Scots. It was still in some ways a frontier area, where the power of central government, both civil and ecclesiastical, was weak. Moreover many of the Ulster bishops were Scots who had some sympathy with the opponents of the kirk in Scotland, and were prepared to make concessions to such as settled in Ulster, an area very short of ministers of

[20a] W. J. Couper, *Scottish Revivals* (Dundee, 1918), 26-39.
[20b] W. M. Campbell, *The Triumph of Presbyterianism* (Edinburgh, 1958), 11; D. C. MacNicol, *Robert Bruce* (Edinburgh, 1907, reprinted 1961), 158, 159, 178-9.
[20c] Campbell, *Triumph of Presbyterianism*, 24.

any sort. Therefore in the 1620s many who quarrelled with the Scots bishops found a safe refuge in Ulster when things got too hot for them in Scotland. Most prominent among them were Blair and Livingstone.

Blair became minister of Bangor in 1622, Livingstone minister of Killinchy in 1630. Together with other Scots ministers in the area they established what was a presbyterian system in all but name — elders and deacons were elected in parishes, making up virtual kirk sessions with the ministers, and all the ministers met monthly in Antrim to preach and pray to large congregations assembled there. Such meetings, said Livingstone, were "sometimes as profitable as either presbyteries or synods".[21]

Thus they remained loyal to a presbyterian system though they had left Scotland through their refusal to accept the authority of a corrupt kirk. They still regarded themselves as members of their native kirk though they defied it, just as New England puritans maintained they were still members of the church of England. When some English separatists came to Antrim the Scots ministers would have nothing to do with them.[22] Yet in spite of their loyalty to the kirk some of the Scots ministers in Ulster took advantage of their freedom to introduce practices abhorrent to many in Scotland and which perhaps revealed English puritan influences. Probably they omitted from their worship some points traditional in the kirk which they had come to think unjustified. Though Livingstone's statement that in Ireland he had "publict worship free of any inventions of men"[23] may only mean that he laid aside the Five Articles, one suspects that he and others also gave up the traditional practices which they were to emerge as opposing in and after 1639. And certainly Livingstone encouraged private prayer meetings, even when not driven to hold them by force of persecution. Thus sometimes crowds gathered on the Saturday before communion to hear a sermon, and spent the Saturday and Sunday nights "in severall companies, sometimes an minister being with them, sometimes themselves alone in conference and prayer"; "it is hard to judge whether there was more of the Lord's presence in the publick or private meetings".[24]

Livingstone and Blair also used Ulster as a base for forays into Scotland, preaching and praying at both public and private meetings, retreating back to Ulster before the bishops could take effective action against them. The complaints of the Scots bishops to the king about this led Charles to spur the Irish bishops into

[21] Wodrow, *Select Biographies*, i ,139-43; Blair, *Autobiography*, 68, 71; P. Adair, *A True Narrative of the Rise and Progress of the Presbyterian Church in Ireland*, ed. W. D. Killen (Belfast, 1866), 1-2, 16-17. For background see J. S. Reid, *The History of the Presbyterian Church in Ireland* (3 vols., Belfast, 1867).
[22] Blair, *Autobiography*, 83-4; Adair, *Narrative*, 27-8.
[23] Wodrow, *Select Biographies*, i, 142.
[24] *Ibid.*, i, 144.

action. In 1631 Livingstone and Blair were suspended, and finally deposed from their ministries in 1634-5.[25] During these years when persecution was coming to interfere with his activities in Ulster Livingstone had ' private meetings in severall places' in his parish, preaching every Sunday in his mother-in-law's house. He was often in Scotland, preaching and attending communions. Sometimes he visited Edinburgh "where there were frequent privat meetings of Christians."[26]

Similarly Robert Blair continued to preach in private in Ireland[27] and visited Scotland. Thus in 1635 he came to Edinburgh to get married a second time. There he attended "many private meetings . . . in private families, where some few eminent Christians convened, and spent the time mostly in prayer, with fastings and humiliation of soul". When possible a minister was present at such meetings "but often private Christians convened for prayer and conference" without one. And Blair's closest Edinburgh associates were William Rig of Atherny and his first wife's relations — and she of course had been the sister of John Mean's wife.[28]

By this time the private prayer meetings of opponents of royal policy in Scotland were widespread, regular and well organised. From 1633 or 1634 onwards radical ministers kept regular fasts on the first Sunday of each quarter, privately inviting sympathetic members of their congregations to meetings to lament the corruptions of the church and pray for remedy "by which course they prevail'd much upon the Commons".[29] This practice was strongly supported by Samuel Rutherford when "some of the worthiest ministry in this kingdom" recommended it to him.[30]

But though private meetings flourished the outlook seemed bleak. Persecution in Scotland seemed to be increasing and the activities of the Irish bishops in Ulster were destroying the safe refuge ministers had had there. Robert Blair therefore resolved on a drastic solution to their problems; "considering how precious a thing the public liberty of pure ordinances was" he decided to emigrate to New England, following the example of many English puritans. Early in 1634 he and others in Ulster who were willing to emigrate put their plan to John Livingstone, John McLellan (who was working in Ulster as a schoolmaster) and John Stewart, the provost of Ayr, all of whom agreed to take part in the emigration. Two men, Livingstone being one of them, were chosen to go to Massachusetts to consult the governor and council there and find a place to settle. They got no further than England, returning to Ulster after a series of delays and setbacks.[31] But the scheme

25 Wodrow, *Select Biographies*, i, 145-6, 147; Adair, *Narrative*, 33-40.
26 Wodrow, *Select Biographies*, i, 147-8, 152-3, 157.
27 *Ibid.*, i, 153.
28 Blair, *Autobiography*, 137.
29 H. Guthry, *Memoirs* (Glasgow, 1747), 9-10.
30 Rutherford, *Letters*, 92-3.
31 Blair, *Autobiography*, 104, 106-7; Wodrow, *Select Biographies*, i, 148-9.

was not abandoned. In July 1634 John Winthrop, the governor of Massachusetts, received letters from "a godly preacher, Mr Levinston a Scotchman in the north of Ireland, whereby he signified, that there were many good Christians in those parts resolved to come hither, if they might receive satisfaction concerning some questions and propositions which they sent over".[32] The questions probably concerned religion and the availability of land, and were evidently satisfactorily answered; in September it was agreed that the Scottish and Irish gentlemen who intended to settle in Massachusetts should have land on the Merrimac river.[33]

In January 1635 the would-be emigrants received further encouragement; they met John Winthrop junior in Antrim "by whom they were thoroughly informed of all things, and received great encouragement to proceed";[34] Blair found Winthrop "a man of excellent parts",[35] while Livingstone told him that he hoped to see him again "in that land where a great part of my heart is already". Livingstone also suggested that Winthrop visit John Stewart in Ayr, David Dickson, and one James Murray in Edinburgh, telling him that he could rely on them.[36] Winthrop is known to have visited Scotland after leaving Ulster[37] but nothing is known of his activities there — though it seems likely that he continued to urge "godly people", such as he had met in Ulster, to emigrate.

Encouraged by letters from Massachusetts "full of kind invitations and large promises of good accommodation" as well as by Winthrop's visit, Blair, Livingstone and their friends built a ship near Belfast and they and their families, with many of their supporters, set sail in the Autumn of 1636. But they met with bad weather which nearly sank their ship, and eventually they turned and fled back to Ireland before the storms which had been opposing them. Convinced that this indicated that God did not wish them to emigrate, they made no further attempt to leave.[38]

The readiness to go to New England was not confined to those who had actually made the attempt. Samuel Rutherford, now in banishment in Aberdeen, wrote to Blair, Livingstone and John Stewart sympathising with them over their venture's failure, saying that "If I saw a call for New England, I would follow it", for it was a place where one could "dwell among a people whose God is the Lord".[39]

32 J. K. Hosmer (ed.), *Winthrop's Journal: "History of New England"* (2 vols, New York, 1908), i, 127.
33 N. B. Shurtleff (ed.), *Records of the Governor and Company of the Massachusetts Bay in New England* (5 vols., Boston 1853-4), i, 129.
34 Hosmer, *Winthrop's Journal*, i, 164.
35 Blair, *Autobiography*, 105.
36 A. B. Forbes (ed.), *Winthrop Papers* (5 vols., Massachusetts Historical Society, 1929-47), iii, 187-8.
37 Hosmer, *Winthrop's Journal*, i, 164.
38 Blair, *Autobiography*, 108, 140-7; Wodrow, *Select Biographies*, i, 153-6.
39 Rutherford, *Letters*, 188, 191, 298, 301.

This willingness to emigrate to escape the authority of a corrupt kirk does not indicate that those involved were adopting separatist ideas. Like most English puritans in New England, they still recognised their mother church as a true one. But though this might be the theory, in practice by going to New England the ministers would have been abandoning a corrupt kirk and establishing a new one — or joining a new one by fitting in with English puritans already there. Thus far down the road to separation had some of the more radical opponents of royal policy in the kirk been driven by their willingness to cut themselves off from the worship of the kirk and by their readiness to defy its authority. From a practical point of view their actions were only really consistent with maintaining that the kirk was a true kirk while there was a real hope of reformation to purge it of its corruptions. As hope of reformation receded so did the possibility of returning to full membership of and obedience to the kirk. Those who had set themselves partially outside the kirk would eventually cut themselves off from it completely in practice, whatever connection they claimed to maintain in principle. Migration to New England was convenient in that it allowed one thus to separate in practice while denying that one was doing so in theory; the mere separation in distance from the mother church involved in the move solved the problem.

So one may argue that some of the radicals in the kirk had moved down the road towards separation — though without admitting or realising that they were doing so. But the fact is that they never reached the end of that road, in spite of the circumstances driving them that way. This is partly an indication of how strong loyalty to the kirk was, even among the strongest opponents of its corruption. It was the "harlot mother" and needed reformed, not abandoned. And it is significant that the three ministers who attempted to settle in New England were all men who had, because of their views, failed to obtain parishes in Scotland. Those of the radical ministers who had Scots parishes hung on to them grimly, even if at times this meant being less open in propagating their views than they would have liked, for the ministry within the mother kirk was a great trust and responsibility which they would not give up unless forced to. Rutherford only talked of going to New England after he had been banished from his parish and seemed to have little hope of ever being allowed to return to it.

If this loyalty to the national kirk was one element in keeping men from separation, its counterpart was the relative weakness of persecution. The king's instruments in imposing his policies, the bishops and the privy council, were less than whole hearted in crushing opposition. Partly through sympathy with some of the dissidents' attitudes, partly through a weak fear of stirring up trouble by repression, the authorities often ignored the activities of their opponents, only intervening when most blatantly defied.

Whatever the covenanters were later to say of the terrible perse-
cutions of the bishops, no regime which allowed men like Rutherford and Dickson to spread their ideas for years on end with
little hinderance can really be accused of brutal, unremitting
repression. One of the reasons that Scotland produced no
separatists was that men were not driven to such a last resort by
effective repression.

Lack of efficient persecution helped to prevent the appearance
of separatists, but it allowed the growth of organised and only
partly secret opposition to royal policies with, as we have seen,
private meetings or conventicles widespread at least in Edinburgh
and the south west. This opposition gathered increasing moderate
support among both laymen and ministers in the mid 1630s. The
king's conduct in the parliament of 1633, the new book of canons
of 1636, the news that a new liturgy was to be imposed, and wild
rumours of the king's further intentions each provided a spur to
mounting fear, frustration and determination to resist. Reformation,
which many had despaired of achieving, suddenly began to seem
a real possibility. And in organising the resistance to the king that
was to bring about this reformation the radical favourers of private
meetings whom we have been discussing took a leading part.

John Livingstone and Robert Blair found no refuge in Ulster
when their voyage to New England failed. Their arrest was ordered
and they fled to Scotland. Here they were helped and encouraged
by David Dickson at Irvine. Livingstone went to Edinburgh where
he stayed for some time "being at some private meetings every
day" so frequent had conventicles become, but he returned to
Irvine in March 1637 and spent the following months in the west
preaching in public and leading the worship in private meetings.
As persecution in Ireland increased many Scots settlers fled back
to Scotland and he ministered to them.[40] Blair too preached in
public and private in the west[41] though, still despairing of reform
in Scotland, he tried at one point to go to France as chaplain to a
Scots regiment, only changing his mind at the last minute. While
in Edinburgh over this business he stayed with John Mean and
Barbara Hamilton.[42]

The Radical Party: Triumph and Schism

Of the detailed planning of resistance we know little — in the
first few months of disorder it is hard to judge how much was
spontaneous and how much carefully planned; and one has a

---

[40] Wodrow, *Select Biographies*, i, 157-8, 161.
[41] Blair, *Autobiography*, 147-8, 150.
[42] *Ibid.*, 151-3. Little is known of Mean's activities after 1637, but as
late as 1649 John McLellan and Robert Blair stayed in his house,
Wodrow, *Select Biographies*, i, 331. In the same year Mean became
a member of the burgh council, M. Wood (ed.). *Extracts from the
Records of Edinburgh, 1642-55* (Edinburgh, 1938), 213.

strong suspicion that powerful laymen had a much more prominent part in the planning that was done than the surviving evidence indicates. But we do know enough about the organisation of the Edinburgh riots of 23rd July 1637 which sparked off the crisis to see that the radical conventicle holders played an important part. As already mentioned, Barbara Hamilton was reputed to have begun one of the riots. One of the meetings held to organise them took place in the house of Nicholas Balfour, who had been in trouble for holding conventicles in the 1620s. One of the two ministers at the meeting was David Dickson, the other being the more moderate Alexander Henderson.[43] The same two ministers were at the best documented of the meetings (on 6th July) held to plan the riots.[44]

The growth of the revolt need not be related here. In the early months Dickson and Henderson were outstanding among the ministers involved. Rutherford, Blair and Livingstone also played important parts. In 1638 the movement triumphed in the general assembly at Glasgow. Bishops and the court of high commission were abolished, along with the Five Articles, the book of canons and the new prayer book. Livingstone and McLellan became ministers of Stranraer and Kirkcudbright respectively in 1638, Blair minister of St Andrews in 1639. In the same year Rutherford became professor of divinity at St Andrews, and the following year Dickson took up the same office in Glasgow.

The victory of the covenanters did not bring unity in the kirk, however. For many of the radicals abolition of the Five Articles was not enough; some older practices in the worship of the kirk seemed to them illegal human inventions, and many denied even that they were traditional in the kirk. Moreover they wished to continue to hold private meetings, as they had been accustomed to in years past; they did not see this as any threat to presbyterian church government or discipline. But the great majority of covenanting ministers regarded any further changes in worship and the holding of private meetings with horror, even if they were supported by a disproportionately large number of the best-known ministers. They saw such ideas as the result of English puritan and Brownist influences, and were determined to eradicate them before they infected the newly achieved purity of the kirk. The radicals on the other hand saw these ideas not as an infection but as things necessary to complete the restoration of the purity of the kirk.

The ideas which the radicals tried to impose arose primarily out of the circumstances of persecution. In opposing the Five Articles it was a natural step to go on to question other ceremonies. Denied pure public worship, it was natural to resort to private meetings. Undoubtedly English puritan ideas in these

[43] Guthry, *Memoirs*, 23-4.
[44] J. M. Henderson (ed.), "An 'Advertistment' about the Service Book, 1637", *Scottish Historical Review*, xxiii (1925-6), 199-204.

matters had some influence on the radicals, but such influences are impossible to trace and were probably of relatively minor importance. The actions of the radicals mainly grew out of the mainstream of Scottish presbyterianism under the pressure of persecution. Those who opposed the radicals tried to deny this. They represented these ideas as introduced from England and Ireland, thus freeing the kirk of responsibility for spawning such dangerous alien innovations. Certainly a few English puritans did come to Scotland after revolt began in 1637. Certainly many of the Scots who fled from Ulster as persecution intensified proved supporters of the radicals when they arrived in Scotland. But, at least as regards prayer meetings, the evidence shows that they were widespread in Scotland in the 1630s; they were not innovations introduced after 1637 as those opposed to them maintained. In the great majority of cases it was not outsiders who persuaded people in Scotland to support private meetings and changes in worship, but ministers of the kirk.

Both Robert Baillie and Henry Guthry asserted that such ideas had been brought to Scotland by refugees from Ireland; neither mentioned that private meetings had long been known in Scotland, and had indeed perhaps been introduced from Scotland to Scots settlers in Ireland rather than *vice versa*. Guthry does admit that Rutherford, Blair and Dickson countenanced such ideas, but he puts his emphasis on refugees and English puritans as their source — he mentions a tailor called Thomas Livingstone and a surgeon called Cornall who came from England after the troubles began and were suspected of spreading Brownist ideas, but nothing is known of their activities.[45] Whatever the influence of such English puritan "missionaries" in spreading private meetings in Scotland, it was far outweighed by the influence of the radical Scots ministers.

The growth of what has in this paper been called a radical party in the kirk in the 1620s and 1630s, holding private meetings and advocating alterations in worship, was to have far reaching effects on the future development of the kirk, as a summary of these by way of conclusion will show.

After the covenanters triumphed in 1638 most ministers wished to suppress private meetings and innovations in worship.[46] But the radical minority, strongest among the leaders of the kirk, managed to resist this pressure. After a series of confrontations in the general assembly a compromise act of 1641, grudgingly and only implicitly, admitted the right to hold private meetings, disguised under the name of "mutual edification". Attention then turned to the innovations in worship demanded by the radicals.

[45] R. Baillie, *Letters and Journals*, ed. D. Laing (3 vols., Bannatyne Club 1841-2), i, 249; Guthry, *Memoirs*, 78.
[46] For these later developments see D. Stevenson, "The Radical Party in the Kirk, 1637-45", *Journal of Ecclesiastical History* (1974-forthcoming).

They got their own way in this matter in and after 1645 through the Westminster Standards. The majority of ministers reluctantly adopted the innovations, not to please the radicals but to bring religious unity with England nearer by satisfying English puritans.

The victory of the radicals was short lived, however. In 1650 the kirk turned increasingly towards the king and war with the English Independents; a minority, the protesters, refused to accept this and the kirk split into bitterly hostile factions, the protester minority and the resolutioner majority. Most of the radicals of the 1630s and 1640s (with the important exception of David Dickson) emerged as leaders of the protesters. In practice the protesters virtually separated from the resolutioner-dominated kirk, setting up their own kirk sessions and presbyteries in some areas, even holding their own general assembly. Of course they denied the charge of schism by claiming, as so many in similar situations had done before them in other lands, that they were the true kirk, the resolutioner majority a corrupt one. But the charges of the opponents of the radicals that their tendencies led towards Independency and separation seemed confirmed by events. In fact it was probably not such inherent tendencies in their ideas that led the radicals to split the kirk so much as new ideas and influences absorbed from England during the 1640s — though doubtless they absorbed these new influences all the more easily as they had something in common with their existing ideas. Much as the radicals might hate the English Independents in some ways, they recognised that they had something in common with them and were impressed by their success. It was such new influences — admittedly often unconscious — which led the radicals virtually to secede from the corrupt kirk of the majority in the 1650s, though in the 1620s and 1630s they had refused thus almost to abandon their "harlot mother".

To conclude and summarise, a minority of religious radicals in the 1620s and 1630s encouraged private meetings as a form of resistance to the bishops. Such meetings became widespread at least in the Western Lowlands and Edinburgh. After the fall of the bishops the radicals forced the majority of ministers, who were deeply suspicious of such meetings, to countenance them and various innovations in worship. This success helped to restore unity in the kirk, but this was soon destroyed by the resolutioner-protester split. The protesters were led by former radicals. Thus there is continuity between the holders of prayer meetings under persecution, their supporters in the 1640s, and the protesters. And through the protesters there is continuity with the conventicles of the 1660s to the 1680s under renewed persecution and with the prayer societies of the eighteenth century. Thus the origins of the protester movement and of the conventicles of the later covenanters lie much deeper in the history of the kirk than is often realised.

XII

The Radical Party in the Kirk, 1637–45

In the Scottish General Assembly of 1638 the Covenanters, openly defying Charles I, reformed the kirk to remove what they saw as its corruptions. Bishops and the Court of High Commission were abolished. The Five Articles of Perth (regulating certain points of worship), the 1636 Book of Canons and the hated Prayer Book of 1637 were all condemned.

These reforms were enough to satisfy the great majority of ministers; they wished to restore the kirk to what they believed were its pristine purity of government and its traditional forms of worship. But a radical minority, strong among the leaders of resistance to the king, wished to go further. In resisting new ceremonies like the Five Articles they had come to question other, older practices in the kirk's worship, finding no warrant for them in scripture. These they wished to abolish, claiming (unhistorically) that they, too, were later corruptions and not traditional in the kirk. As well as advocating such changes in worship, the radicals supported the holding of private prayer meetings or conventicles. These had become widespread (at least in Edinburgh and the Western Lowlands) in the previous twenty years; the more radical opponents of the religious policies of James VI and Charles I had taken to such meetings since they regarded the worship of the kirk as corrupt. They now wished to continue to hold them, seeing nothing in them incompatible with presbyterian church government.[1]

The majority of ministers however detested the changes in worship proposed by the radicals, and were deeply suspicious of their private meetings. They saw both as being the result of English puritan influences, as tainted by Brownists who separated from the Church of England to form their own churches. It is true that the radicals were to some extent influenced by English puritans, though this influence is difficult to trace or assess accurately, but essentially their policies had arisen naturally as reactions to persecution. Their opponents, however, charged them with trying to impoverish the traditional worship of the kirk, depriving it of time-honoured and well-loved practices, and with posing a serious threat to presbyterian government and discipline by private meetings which would lead to disunity and schism. For most ministers the only legitimate forms of worship were private prayer by individuals, family exercise or worship, and the public worship of congregations. Private meetings had

[1] See D. Stevenson, 'Conventicles and the Kirk, 1619–37. The Emergence of a Radical Party', *Records of the Scottish Church History Society* (forthcoming).

Journal of Ecclesiastical History, Vol. XXV, No. 2, April 1974. © Cambridge University Press

no place in the kirk and must be suppressed. The radicals denied that there was any danger from their meetings; they had remained loyal to their mother-kirk when it was corrupt, not separating from it but working to reform it.

Disputes over these issues led to bitter quarrels within the kirk for several years, and had important long-term effects. Yet the controversies are very little known,[1] partly because attempts were made to keep them secret and thus preserve an appearance of unity in the kirk. This was done to avoid encouraging its enemies and so as not to undermine the argument that Presbyterianism provided a strong, united and disciplined Church and should therefore be adopted in England.

The best known of the radical ministers who supported private meetings were Samuel Rutherford (minister of Anwoth, transferred to the chair of divinity at St. Andrews in 1639) and David Dickson (Irvine Professor of divinity at Glasgow 1640). With the exception of the more moderate Alexander Henderson (Leuchars) these were, perhaps, the best known ministers of the day, both being revered for their learning and their long histories of opposition to the bishops. Closely associated with them were Robert Blair (St. Andrews, 1639), John Livingstone (Stranraer, 1638), James Hamilton (Dumfries, 1638) and John McLellan (Kirkcudbright, 1638). Blair, Livingstone and McLellan were related by marriage, and all four had spent several years in Ulster—McLellan as a schoolmaster, the others as ministers of parishes settled by Scots colonists. As a result of their activities and those of other Ulster Scots who returned to Scotland at this time, the opponents of the radicals claimed that their ideas had been introduced to Scotland from Ireland.[2]

During the purging of the Church of its corruptions in 1637–9 the holding of private meetings by radical ministers and laymen continued and, indeed, spread, partly as a result of English and Ulster influences but primarily as an extension of the holding of conventicles in Scotland in earlier years; now that persecution had been removed the practice spread. Some may for a time have had doubts as to the wisdom of continuing to encourage private meetings now that the kirk was reformed; John Livingstone chose rather to hold daily public prayers in his kirk,

---

[1] Most attention has been paid to these controversies by writers on the history of worship in the kirk, especially G. W. Sprott, *The Worship of the Church of Scotland during the Covenanting Period 1638–61*, Edinburgh 1893. See also G. W. Sprott, *The Worship and Offices of the Church of Scotland*, Edinburgh 1882, 18–20; G. W. Sprott, *The Book of Common Order of the Church of Scotland*, Edinburgh 1901, xvii–xxi, xxviii–xxxi, lx–lxiii; W. McMillan, *The Worship of the Scottish Reformed Church, 1550–1638*, London 1931; W. D. Maxwell, *A History of Worship in the Church of Scotland*, Oxford 1955, 88–91, 98, 106–8. Writers on sects and congregationalism have also noted these events, though hardly their real significance: H. Escott, *A History of Scottish Congregationalism*, Glasgow 1960, 7–8; W. I. Hoy, 'The Entry of Sects into Scotland', in *Reformation and Revolution*, ed. D. Shaw, Edinburgh 1967, 178; G. L. S. Thompson, 'The Origins of Congregationalism in Scotland', Edinburgh University Ph.D. thesis, 1932, 40–61.

[2] R. Baillie, *Letters and Journals*, Bannatyne Club 1841–2, i. 249; H. Guthry, *Memoirs*, Glasgow 1747, 78.

than to allow parishioners to attend his family exercise as they had asked.[1] On the other hand, when, in 1639, the parishioners of Kilmacolm complained to Samuel Rutherford of 'a dead ministry' in their parish, he replied 'I recommend to you conference and prayer at private meetings', citing scriptural references in support of this advice[2]—thus encouraging them to go behind their minister's back. But though to his more conservative colleagues some of Rutherford's actions might seem to come close to encouraging Brownism, he stated firmly 'As for separation from worship for some errors of a church, the independency of single congregations, and other tenets of Brownists, they are contrary to God's Word'.[3] Private meetings should be attended in addition to public worship, not instead of it.

Public controversy over private meetings was sparked off by the case of Alexander Leckie of that Ilk, a Stirlingshire laird. He had been an elder in the parish of Gargunnock, where the lands of Leckie lay, in 1625–31,[4] but had then settled in Ulster, where he became a prominent opponent of the bishops of Ireland. In 1639 his arrest had been ordered and he had fled to Scotland, where he immediately became a thorn in the side of Henry Guthry (Stirling). He established 'privy exercises' or prayer meetings in Stirling in spite of Guthry's opposition.[5] Guthry saw this as a threat to the authority of the kirk and referred the matter to his kirk session in July 1639. It was represented to the session that some of their congregation, seduced by strangers from England and Ireland, 'convein thameselffes, confusedlie out of diverse families, about bed tyme in some privat house, and thair for ane great pairt of the night, employ thameselffes in ane publick exercise of religione, praying successivelie, singing psalmes, exponing scripture, discussing questiones of divinitie . . . by whiche vncowth and confused meitings, the commone people ar drawin to vilifie and sett at naught the exercise of Gods worship in privat and particular families apairt; yea some of thame to lightlie and sett at naught the publick worship of God in the Congregatione, conceaving (as they ar taught by thir trafficking strangers) thir privat meitings as they call thame to be moir effectuall for turning soules to God then preaching it selffe'.

The session considered that if such meetings were allowed to spread they might in time introduce Brownism and so overturn the true worship of the kirk. The meetings were held to be a breach of the national covenant which bound its signatories to refrain from practising any innovation, for the meetings were 'never known nor practised among us' before February 1639. Such meetings were, therefore, banned and the matter was referred to the presbytery 'that they may consider seriouslie of the perrell

---

[1] R. Wodrow, *Select Biographies*, Wodrow Society 1845–7, i. 161–2.
[2] S. Rutherford, *Letters*, ed. A. A. Bonar, Edinburgh and London 1894, 561, 564.
[3] Ibid., 611.
[4] R. G. E. L[eckie], *Leckie of that Ilk*, Vancouver 1913, 93.
[5] P. Adair, *A True Narrative of the Rise and Progress of the Presbyterian Church in Ireland*, Belfast 1866, 61–2; Baillie, *Letters*, i. 249; Guthry, *Memoirs*, 78.

imminent to our kirk by thir seids of Brownisme, which Sathan is begune to sowe'.[1]

The ban on meetings proved ineffective; the session, therefore, asked Guthry to write to David Dickson and Alexander Henderson (recognised as the leaders of the covenanting ministers of the West and East Lowlands respectively) informing them of the situation. Meanwhile, order was given for the warding of five ringleaders of private meetings.[2]

On the same day (12 August 1639) as this action in Stirling the General Assembly met in Edinburgh, and David Dickson was elected moderator. Guthry was a member and by his 'verie loud complaints'[3] soon stirred up fears among many of Brownist influences at work in the country. In this he was supported by Alexander Henderson, Andrew Ramsay (Greyfriars, Edinburgh) and the historian David Calderwood; Calderwood, during exile in Holland, had seen the activities of separatists there and had returned with a deep hatred of anything that hinted at Brownism.[4] It was proposed that an act should be passed against private meetings, but Dickson, Blair and Rutherford opposed this and the matter was referred to a privy conference attended by seven radicals—the other four being Livingstone, McLellan, George Dick (Glenluce) and James Hamilton—and seven of their opponents. Both parties wished to avoid a public quarrel; the triumph of the Covenanters was not yet complete and the main business of the Assembly was to persuade the king's commissioner to ratify the acts of the 1638 Assembly. They were, therefore, anxious to emphasise their strength and unity, for nothing could have given their enemies more encouragement than the news that the kirk was deeply divided and infected by Brownist influences. After much argument in the conference, in which Henderson 'vented himself, at manie occasions, passionatelie, opposit to all these conceits', agreement was reached. Leckie gave in a conciliatory paper explaining his beliefs and 'was found to differ from us in nothing considerable'.[5] Robert Baillie (Kilwinning) was commissioned to draft an act to settle the issue. This renewed former acts encouraging family exercise, but also made provision for limiting it to prevent it developing into general prayer meetings; because the meeting of people from many families when the Church had full liberty and pure worship might prove hurtful—especially if held at night or in time of public worship—they were to be banned, for fear of abuses such as preaching and expounding of scripture by men who were not ministers. However, this should 'no wayes hinder privat persouns to mak use of ther christian libertie and fellowship for mutuall edificatioun when tuo or thrie meets by occasioun'; 'Such a part of the comunioun of saints we did evir allow, only we intend seriously to opose all scandalous novell-

---

[1] A. Macdonald and J. Dennistoun (eds.), 'Extracts from the Register of the Kirk Session of Stirling', *Maitland Miscellany*, Maitland Club 1834, I. ii. 475–6.

[2] Ibid., 476–7.

[3] Baillie, *Letters*, i. 249.

[4] Guthry, *Memoirs*, 78–9.

[5] Ibid., 79–80; Baillie, *Letters*, i. 250.

THE RADICAL PARTY IN THE KIRK, 1637-45

ties, and to give way to no inovation at all' until authorised by the Assembly.[1] Thus Baillie strove to limit strictly private meetings, but not to ban them entirely.

In the end, however, it was decided that even such a compromise act might prove too controversial, and therefore 'to leave off making of ane act, leist our adversaries should triumph in our so hastie disputations, if not divisions'.[2] But, though no public act was made, a private agreement was reached in the conference and signed by Henderson and Dickson. This was, according to Guthry, that whatever had been the effects of private meetings in time of corruption, now that peace and purity had been restored they must be disallowed as tending to hinder family exercise and public worship. Thus it would seem that instead of having a public act passed severely limiting meetings, the radicals preferred a private agreement condemning them completely, but framed in such general terms that they could pretend that it did not apply to their prayer meetings. However, Guthry's account of the agreement may well exaggerate the extent of the concessions made by the radicals.[3]

The Assembly did pass two acts relating to the dispute. One laid down that no innovations which might disturb the peace of the kirk were to be introduced unless approved by the General Assembly.[4] To those who did not know of the controversy over private meetings the purpose of the act was obscure: 'This acte many thought misticall, and that it needed a glosse'.[5] In answer to the popularity of private meetings another act stressed the value of family exercise, which was to be held in every family both morning and evening.[6] This, it was hoped, would replace private meetings, and Henderson drew up a paper for publication explaining how family exercise should be conducted.[7]

Hopes that these acts and the secret agreement would restore unity in the kirk proved unfounded. As part of the settlement Guthry had undertaken to preach in favour of family exercise, Blair, Livingstone and McLellan 'against night-meetings, and other abuses quhilk were complained of'. But Blair 'in his sermon, did not so much cry downe these meetings as was expected; wherefore Mr Guttrie refused to preach at

[1] University of Edinburgh, New College Library [NCL], MS. MH.5/5, Baillie's Letters and Journals, i. fol. 256ʳ. The original foliation of this volume runs 1–255 then in error 226–40, corrected in pencil to 256–70. The corrected numbers are cited here.

[2] Baillie, *Letters*, i. 250.

[3] Guthry, *Memoirs*, 79–80. The paraphrase which Guthry gives of the paper agreed by Dickson and Henderson is the same in substance (and indeed largely the same in wording) as part of directions for private worship issued by the General Assembly of 1647: *Records of the Kirk of Scotland*, ed. A. Peterkin, Edinburgh 1843, 473. This throws serious doubts on the reliability of Guthry at this point.

[4] Baillie, *Letters*, i. 250; Peterkin, *Records*, 208.

[5] J. Gordon, *History of Scots Affairs, from MDCXXXVII to MDCXLI*, Spalding Club 1841, iii. 60.

[6] Peterkin, *Records*, 208–9.

[7] Baillie, *Letters*, i. 250. Henderson's paper may be that known from a version printed in 1641 (*Familie Exercise, or, The Service of God in Families*, Edinburgh 1641), though its bias against read prayers perhaps indicates that it is not.

all'.[1] Edinburgh citizens complained of Henderson's zeal against their private meetings,[2] and radicals continued to encourage them. They spread 'generally throughout the west' and elsewhere. In Edinburgh 'their way came to be so cried up, that such as favoured, or kept, those private meetings, were by the rigid sort esteemed the godly of the land'.[3]

When a committee appointed by the General Assembly to attend parliament met in Edinburgh in September 1639 Guthry renewed his complaints. The radicals, fearing condemnation in the next Assembly, proved ready to make concessions; all the ministers present 'agreed on a paper of caveats' by Alexander Henderson limiting private meetings.[4] Henderson's paper is in many ways an extension of Baillie's draft act. He did not condemn private meetings in principle but, instead, tried to limit them to ensure that they should not undermine presbyterian government by introducing separatist tendencies. Private meetings, the paper stated, are only detrimental to public worship if abused through corruption or weakness. Mutual prayer, conference, admonition and confession of faults are acceptable not only when people meet together for other purposes, but at meetings specially arranged. Yet care should be taken that nothing be done in private that might hinder the public worship of congregations. Only three or four should meet together. Meetings should not take place at night or in time of public worship, and they should not be regular. Those taking part should be of 'such qualitie that they need not to be ashamed to be found togider'. Meetings should not lead to any division between those who take part and the rest of their congregation. All should be avoided that might 'ather mak or fostir schisme in the kirk'. Any doubts concerning the order of the established kirk should be referred to the ministers and courts of the kirk 'that it may be seen that they seek edificatioun and no[t] to mak a rent or divisioun'. All this was to preserve unity and satisfy those 'as have no other ends bot edifie one another'; 'if any entir amongst us who intend any novatioun or disturbance they wold be dilligently marked and avoyded'.[5]

This paper, with its detailed limitations on meetings was a genuine attempt to reach a compromise settlement with those supporting private meetings, even though the limitations were so strict as to abolish large meetings and emasculate small ones. But the radicals, or at least the more extreme of them, seem to have made no attempt to honour the settlement. They took the fact that it accepted such meetings in principle as allowing them to continue their activities unabated.

Moreover, to the disputes over private meetings there were now added closely related disputes over certain practices in public worship which the radicals condemned. The most important of these were reading the

---

[1] Baillie, *Letters*, i. 250; Guthry, *Memoirs*, 80.

[2] Baillie, *Letters*, i. 250.

[3] Guthry, *Memoirs*, 80–1.

[4] Baillie, *Letters*, i. 250; National Library of Scotland [NLS], Wodrow MS. Quarto XXVI, fols. 72–107, Account of the General Assembly at Aberdeen, 1640, fol. 92[r].

[5] NCL, Baillie MS., i. fols. 256[r]–256[v].

creed (in baptism) and set prayers, bowing in the pulpit, and singing doxologies.[1] These might seem minor points but they were symptoms of wider controversies, of the distrust of all set forms and liturgies which had emerged among radicals through opposition to the 1637 Prayer Book and other changes in worship imposed by James VI and Charles I. Developments of federal or covenant theology, leading to 'a more inward-looking subjective preoccupation with penitence and personal assurance of election' than before, gave support to such attitudes. Worship must be freer, more spontaneous, more based on individual needs. Set forms were seen as empty and meaningless, hindering the individual's relationship with God.[2] Forms must be kept to a minimum, and must be justifiable from scripture.

The Book of Canons of 1636 had banned the use of extemporary prayer in public worship.[3] Previously both read and extemporary prayers had been common in the kirk (a practice approved by James VI),[4] but in reaction to Charles I's insistence on read prayers only some of his opponents went to the opposite extreme and claimed that only extemporary prayer was godly. Thus Rutherford believed 'Anent read prayers . . . I could never see precept, promise or practice for them, in God's word. Our church never allowed them, but men took them up at their own choice . . . it were good if they were out of the service of God'.[5] Rutherford and those who thought like him would even have abandoned the use in public worship of the Lord's Prayer. Many also gave up saying the creed and the confession of sins. But most ministers in Scotland hated such changes and resolutely opposed them.[6]

The misleadingly named custom of 'bowing in the pulpit' was that of the minister kneeling in private prayer in the pulpit for a few minutes before starting his part of the service, the earlier part having been taken by a reader. The practice seems to have been universal in Scotland, but radical ministers came to regard it as superstitious, and unwarranted by scripture. Rutherford concluded in January 1640 'Whatever hath been my practice before I examined this custom, I purpose now no more to confound worships'. His objections were that it was a 'human custom' and that it was incongruous for a minister to pray privately in a kirk while public service was being conducted. Those who thus 'pray in public in a private manner, and join not with the public service of the kirk' were 'more pharisaical than the other case is Brownish'[7]—an indication

---

[1] J. B. Torrance, 'Covenant or Contract: A Study of the Theological Background of Worship in Seventeenth-Century Scotland', *Journal of Scottish Theology*, xxiii (1970), 71–3.

[2] Gordon, *History*, iii. 250.

[3] W. Laud, *Works*, ed. J. Bliss and W. Scott, Oxford 1847–60, v. 597.

[4] G. Donaldson, *The Making of the Scottish Prayer Book of 1637*, Edinburgh 1954, 30.

[5] Rutherford, *Letters*, 611. In saying the kirk never allowed read prayers Rutherford does not mean that it never permitted them, but that it had never specifically approved their use.

[6] Donaldson, *Prayer Book*, 29–30; McMillan, *Worship*, 68–73.

[7] Rutherford, *Letters*, 578–9. The letter is rather obscure, but almost certainly refers to 'bowing'; McMillan, *Worship*, 161–2.

that he realised that his decision would lead to accusations of Brownism. Objections to bowing were really part of a wider issue; the radicals attacked all private or solitary prayer in churches, since such buildings were places for public worship alone.[1]

The third point of worship which caused controversy was the doxology, conclusion, or *gloria patri*. This was a short stanza sung at the end of a psalm, a pre-reformation practice continued by the reformers.[2] But now conclusions began to be attacked by radicals as no part of the text of the psalms and, therefore, an unwarranted ceremony. As with read prayers and bowing, most ministers were reluctant to abandon old habits.[3] Robert Baillie recorded a conference he had (c. 1640–2) with 'thrie or four yeomen of my flock who refused to sing the conclusioune'. He warned them of the dangers of straying from his orthodox teaching; 'I forwarne yow the rejecting of the conclusion is on of the first links of the whole chaine of Brunisme'. They would be drawn on to reject singing the psalms in metre 'and then to refuse our prayers, then our sacraments, then our preching, ye at last our church, our covenant and all'.[4]

The controversies over private meetings and points of worship became public in the General Assembly of 1640. Circumstances were very different from those of the previous year's Assembly. In 1639 the Assembly had met in Edinburgh, in the strongly covenanting south; in 1640 it met in Aberdeen, centre of the north-east, the area where conservative and royalist sympathies were strongest. In 1639 the covenanters were anxious to preserve unity to help to consolidate their victory; many nobles attended as elders to force through measures opposed by the king. In 1640 there was little fear of opposition within the Assembly and few nobles bothered to attend. The importance of this was that previously the nobles had used their authority to prevent public squabbles among the ministers; the lack of such restraints was now to be felt,[5] especially as the most conciliatory of the leading ministers, Henderson, was also absent.

The Assembly met in Aberdeen on 23 July. As in the previous year, it was Henry Guthry who brought up the matter of private meetings.[6] He had refused to preach at the opening of the Assembly, pleading illness and lack of time for preparation, and 'all these who had relation to the Irish business', the radicals, demanded his public censure. He was duly reproved, but did not let this (as had been intended) cow him; he still insisted on bringing up matters 'which some of us were afrayed so much

[1] Glasgow University Library [GUL], MS. Gen. 1209, Wodrow MSS., Biographical Collections, Life of Andrew Ramsay, p. 19.
[2] *The Scottish Metrical Psalter of A.D. 1635*, ed. N. Livingston, Glasgow 1864, facsimile 20.
[3] McMillan, *Worship*, 87–92; M. Patrick, *Four Centuries of Scottish Psalmody*, Oxford 1949, 54; Livingston, *Psalter*, 4, 35–6, 67.
[4] NCL, Baillie MS., ii. fols. 129ʳ–130ʳ; Livingston, *Psalter*, 36–7.
[5] Baillie, *Letters*, i. 252.
[6] For the 1640 Assembly, see ibid., i. 251–5; Gordon, *History*, iii. 221–3; Guthry, *Memoirs*, 81–2; NLS, Wodrow MS. Quarto XXVI, fols. 72–107.

as publicklie to name', working to gain the support of the conservative ministers of the north.[1]

It was ruled that all matters should be considered by a committee of bills or overtures before being debated by the full Assembly.[2] On Guthry's complaints about private meetings the committee advised that Henderson's paper of caveats, acceptable to all in the previous September, should be read to the Assembly as the basis of a settlement. But the Assembly refused to allow this, partly to avoid making the dispute public, partly because the opponents of the radicals were no longer content with such a compromise.[3] On 30 July Guthry tried to bring up the matter again, complaining that 'some bretheren are slandered as enymies of familie worschip, howbeit we presse it to our uttermost, but we desyre that the act wold restraine it according to the name, unto the exercise of them that are of one familie, and no further'. Thus defined family worship could no longer be an excuse for private meetings. This and a later demand by Guthry 'that familie excercise be exponed' met with procrastination,[4] but on 3 August he got his way. An act concerning family exercise was passed[5] and, though nothing was said in the act of limiting such worship to one family, the debate on it gave him a chance to air his grievances. He demanded 'that the familie excercise be rectified seing it has turned to great abuses, by frequent and nocturnall meitings', which were very scandalous in his presbytery. From depositions taken from those who had attended private meetings he showed that 'some base and unlearned persones' expounded scripture in turn; that so many people attended that men and women spent the night out of doors 'greaping one another filthilie'. Leckie was denounced 'for keeping his night meittings, called at that tyme the Familie of Love, because there wes foull pranks played at it amongst young men and young women'. During the day they met in houses in time of public worship. Thus Guthry 'uttered manie things verie odious if trew'.[6]

David Dickson denied their truth, accusing Guthry of slandering honest persons who met for religious exercise. When Guthry claimed that the representatives of the presbyteries of Stirling, Dunblane, Auchterarder and Perth supported him, George Dick accused him of subborning them. But Guthry had the majority of the Assembly on his side. He produced, and got Dickson to read out, the paper of caveats of September 1639 'quhereof some did condemne these conventicles, and some againe did open a doore unto them, quhilk all the assemblie in a schout did con-

[1] Baillie, *Letters*, i. 251–2.

[2] Peterkin, *Records*, 279.

[3] Baillie, *Letters*, i. 251–2.

[4] NLS, Wodrow MS. Quarto XXVI, fols. 76ᵛ, 82ᵛ.

[5] Ibid., fols. 91ᵛ–92ʳ.

[6] Baillie, *Letters*, i. 252; C. Rogers (ed.), *Historical Notices of St Anthony's Monastery, Leith, and Rehearsal of Events which Occured in the North of Scotland from 1635 to 1645*, Grampian Club 1877, 55.

demne' as inadequate to suppress private meetings.[1] Guthry then persuaded Dickson to agree that the paper of caveats was not signed,[2] the
implication being that it was not a valid agreement. He then triumphantly produced the paper condemning private meetings agreed on at the
conference during the 1639 Assembly, signed by Henderson and by
Dickson himself.[3] It was clearly seen that the radicals had ignored this
secret agreement, and in spite of their efforts to gain support[4] the Assembly
turned against them.

Andrew Ramsay, as moderator, helped to ensure that this remained
the case by asking if any knew of private meetings in other parts of the
country than those already mentioned. Naturally none of the radicals
wished to describe such meetings to a hostile Assembly, so the initiative
remained in the hands of their opponents. George Galloway (Glasserton)
'declared a number of uncouth passadges, reflecting on' Rutherford,
Livingstone and McLellan,[5] saying meetings were frequent in his presbytery. Such large numbers attended that they had 'preaching in all the
corners of the kirkyeard'. The meetings lasted so long that attenders
could not return home but lay all night in the kirkyard or fields. Sometimes they met in houses at night 'sometymes with light and sometymes
withought light quhilk is werie scandalous'. Other members then added
their accounts. Some spoke of meetings in Edinburgh to which none were
admitted except those who would 'swer to keip quyet'. James Simpson
(Bathgate) told 'manie scandalous things of that sort of people',[6] saying
such meetings were common around Linlithgow. He had put up with
them in his own parish until complaints were made; when he had then
tried to gain entry to such meetings those attending had refused him
admission.[7]

These stories stirred up the Assembly 'to a heat and confused dinn'.
All the members from the north, led by the earl of Seaforth sided with
Guthry, with shouts of 'Away with them, reforme them'. Ramsay as
moderator proved incapable of controlling the Assembly; the authority
of the covenanting nobles was sorely missed. In support of the radicals
William Rig of Atherny (who had been in trouble for holding conventicles in Edinburgh in the 1620s) brought up a question that lay at the
root of the problem. 'I have seine some good professors conveine after
sermone, and conferre upon that quhilk they had hard, and will ye condemne sik conferences?'. And might they not pray God to bless their
conference? The problem was: how could one condemn meetings which

---

[1] Baillie, *Letters*, i. 251–2; NLS, Wodrow MS. Quarto XXVI, fols. 92ᵛ–93ʳ.
[2] Ibid., fol. 93ʳ.
[3] Guthry, *Memoirs*, 81–2. The account in the Wodrow MSS. surprisingly makes no
mention of Guthry's production of the August 1639 paper, but Guthry's question about
signatures suggests that it came at this point.
[4] Guthry, *Memoirs*, 81.
[5] Baillie, *Letters*, i. 252.
[6] Loc. cit.
[7] NLS, Wodrow MS. Quarto XXVI, fols. 93ʳ–93ᵛ.

might undermine the kirk without banning all discussion of religion among sincere and Godly men?[1]

Andrew Ramsay answered that none condemned such meetings of two or three men together, quietly, without scandal, but that that was very different from large-scale meetings. This still left the awkward question of how exactly to distinguish between the two, though Ramsay did state that family exercise should consist of members of one household, plus any strangers who happened to be present, provided they had not come purposely to attend the worship. Andrew Cant (Newbattle) claimed, in reply, that such a definition condemned family exercise as authorised in the previous Assembly—an indication of how the radicals were using the lack of a definition of a 'family' to comprehend their private meetings under family exercise.[2]

Dickson then tried a new tack in defending private meetings; 'Breithren, I will tell yow a secreit: we have manie friends in England and other partes quho congratulate our reformatione, bot are not pleased with sundrie thinges in our kirk, especiallie in our discipline, and ordour; and now quhen we are labouring, for ane uniformitie in England, we sould be loath to give them offense as this course certainlie will, if ye condemne this [private] exercise'. Thus, the radicals used hopes of religious unity with England, and the consequent inexpediency of offending English puritans, as an argument to avoid condemnation of their practices by the Assembly. The move proved ill-judged. Seaforth spoke for the majority when he replied 'Mr David, If we can not have thair peace but at so dear rate, of changeing our discipline, and suffering sik misorder in our kirk, we will not buy it so deare, but rather comitte our selves into the hands of God and the sword'. Thinking that 'Mr David meaneth of the Brownistes, or sik other sectes in England, and Amsterdame', the Assembly ordered a reinforced committee of bills to draw up an act against such tendencies.[3]

The committee's proceedings began with further enquiries as to whether the abuses of meetings really were serious. 'Sundrie Breither testifie of the scandall of them, and other novationes too thair are brought in by the favourers of these meittinges'—these other innovations being the radicals' alterations in worship. Such ministers did not bow in the pulpit; they condemned the reading of any set prayer, calling the Lord's Prayer a threadbare prayer which it was unlawful to say. Their supporters, when attending kirk, remained in the kirkyard until after the confession of sins, if it was to be read. They refused to sing doxologies. Some 'Gentlemen of good qualitie' had complained that they were taught from the pulpit that it was a sin to use set prayers, and that this had led them to give up family exercise because they were incapable of extemporary prayer. Meetings were held in time of public worship, and those present

---

[1] Ibid., fol. 93ᵛ; Baillie, *Letters*, i. 252.
[2] NLS, Wodrow MS. Quarto XXVI, fols. 93ᵛ–94ʳ.
[3] Ibid., fol. 94ʳ; Sprott, *Worship of the Church of Scotland during the Covenanting Period*, 10.

led prayers and expounded scripture one after another, though ignorant and uneducated. Radical ministers were said to be bringing in a new way of preaching; just as set prayers were held to be sinful so were set sermons; all learning and study was cried down in favour of preaching 'extemporarie thoughtes, without methode, and without prooff of that quhilk they speake, out of or by the Scripture'. Rutherford tried to cite scripture in support of the radicals, but was abused for his pains and the committee appointed four or five ministers each to draft an act to deal with the situation.[1]

The drafts were read to the committee on 4 August. Dickson simply produced Henderson's paper of caveats limiting meetings, hoping to have it passed as an act, but it was rejected as the full Assembly had already shouted it down. Robert Baillie's act was similar, being based on the caveats, but was condemned by Guthry as leaving back doors open to private meetings. Guthry's own act was short and uncompromising. More than one family, or persons out of more than one, must not meet together for family exercise. His act stressed that the Assembly did not condemn set prayers, and that only ministers had authority to expound scripture to the people. Dickson protested that 'this act wold condemne all religious conference among neighbours', while others felt the act did not do enough to condemn innovations in worship. Baillie had a more general complaint; Guthry's act limited family exercise only, and the private meetings were not family exercise but a different kind of worship and, therefore, would not be affected by the act. Guthry refused to accept this obvious point.[2]

A fourth draft act was read but no agreement was reached.[3] By now the radicals were threatening to make a formal written protest if a strict act was passed against them; this was 'the thing that the devill was seeking, and would have been sweet pastyme to that town of Aberdeen, and our small favourers in the North, who was greedilie gazeing on the event of that broyle'.[4] A last attempt was made, therefore, to agree a settlement before returning the matter to the full Assembly. Andrew Ramsay and the authors of the draft acts met and thrashed out an act acceptable to all. This was based on Guthry's draft, with additions mainly suggested by Dickson. Family exercise was limited to one family, except that the minister of a parish might have others present, though he should be careful to avoid any 'abuses and inconveniences' arising from this. Guthry and his supporters had little objection to meetings at which ministers were present, believing that the real danger to the kirk lay in meetings without ministers. The act did not disallow set prayers, on the grounds that everyone had not the gift of extemporary or 'conceived' prayer and that conceived prayer was not fitting at all times. None but ministers

---

[1] Ibid., 11; Baillie, *Letters*, i. 252–3; NLS, Wodrow MS. Quarto XXVI, fols. 94^r–95^r.
[2] Ibid., fols. 95^r–95^v; Baillie, *Letters*, i. 253–4.
[3] NLS, Wodrow MS. Quarto XXVI, fols. 95^v–97^v.
[4] Baillie, *Letters*, i. 254.

and expectants were to expound scripture, and none were to practice any innovation in worship until it was approved by a General Assembly. This act was read to the Assembly and passed unanimously.[1]

The matter of private meetings and changes in worship now seemed settled. But dispute flared up again on 5 August. A bill was read in the name of the ministers of the south and west demanding that a committee be appointed to try the justice of the complaints about private meetings and punish the guilty. Such a trial, the radicals hoped, would prove the complaints to be exaggerated and would vindicate the holders of private meetings. But the great majority were infuriated by the suggestion, taking it as an attempt to overthrow the decisions of the Assembly. They demanded to know who was the author of the bill, and eventually John McLellan admitted that he was. The Assembly then hissed him and asked that he be censured, though Dickson and Cant stood up for him. Dickson said that it was strange that exception should be taken to a bill that simply asked that offences be punished. Leckie, that 'worthie and religious gentleman', averred that he had been condemned without being heard. The Assembly would not listen. Dickson was shouted down by cries of 'Away with it! Away with it!' (the bill) and 'No moe Bischopes, no moe Bischopes'. At this suggestion, that a few leading radicals were trying to gain power over the kirk as the bishops had done, Dickson and his colleagues wisely 'held thair peace'.[2]

Such a public trial of private meetings as McLellan suggested would 'have fyred our Church, more than any other brand that Satan at this tyme, in all his witt, could have invented'.[3] It would inevitably have divided the kirk even more deeply and given much publicity to such divisions.

The act passed in the Assembly on 4 August 1640 undoubtedly represented a partial defeat for the radicals. Some claimed that it would never have been passed had not the Assembly sat in Aberdeen 'a place disaffected to reformation' with an unusually high proportion of ministers from the conservative north.[4] But, though outvoted, the radicals could console themselves that they could evade the intentions of the act through the faults in its wording. It only restricted family worship, so they could claim that this did not include private meetings. It condemned innovations in worship, but the radicals asserted their practices were not innovations. And though the act had been passed in public in the Assembly, it was then kept secret to avoid giving publicity to the divisions in the kirk.[5]

---

[1] Loc. cit.; Sprott, *Worship of the Church*, 11; Guthry, *Memoirs*, 82; NLS, Wodrow MS. Quarto XXVI, fols. 96ᵛ–98ʳ.

[2] Ibid., fols. 104ᵛ–105ʳ; Baillie, *Letters*, i. 254-5.

[3] Baillie, op. cit., i. 255.

[4] Gordon, *History*, iii. 223.

[5] The commission set up by the Assembly to attend parliament ordered that the act should not be printed, a ruling confirmed by the 1643 Assembly: Scottish Record Office [SRO], CH.1/1/9, Acts and Proceedings of the General Assemblies, 1642–6, 1643 Assembly, 22; Baillie, *Letters*, ii. 91; Peterkin, *Records*, 360.

Thus the royalist minister, Robert Gordon (Rothiemay), could only give a garbled account of the act 'as neer as I can remember it, for it was industriously concealed'.[1] But this attempt at secrecy came too late; royalists had heard all about the divisions in the kirk and took heart from them.[2]

The radicals ignored their defeat in the 1640 Assembly. After it 'there was a continuall heart-burning betwixt' the supporters of Guthry and Leckie. Robert Baillie advised leading lay Covenanters to try to bring the parties together, but if they did try to intervene it was to no avail. In July 1641 on the eve of the next meeting of the General Assembly Leckie and his supporters gathered to denounce Guthry and to get the 1640 act repealed, while Guthry was equally determined to have the radicals censured. Andrew Ramsay did not help matters by preaching at the opening of the Assembly at St. Andrews on 20 July 'as if our Kirk was presentlie burning with schisme'. In reply, Dickson passionately vindicated religious people from unjust slanders. Furthermore, he urged the repentance of ministers who by 'conformitie, had brought latelie our Church to the brink of ruine'. Not surprisingly, this 'did highlie offend very many'.[3] Dickson was clearly hinting, and with some justification, that it had been the radicals who had led opposition to the bishops; thus they represented the true traditions of the kirk, not their more conservative opponents who had meekly obeyed the bishops. This was too near the bone to be palatable to the majority.

Time was given for tempers to cool, however, by the decision to move the Assembly to Edinburgh.[4] It did not reassemble there until 27 July, and the intervening week 'was spent in privie consultations for accommodating the feared differences'. These meetings took place in the earl of Loudoun's chamber. The earls of Argyll and Cassillis attended, together with leading ministers. The Edinburgh ministers demanded the banning of all private meetings, being 'chaffed at their people's carriage toward them', while the radicals wanted the 1640 act recalled or interpreted in their favour. As before, David Calderwood was one of their strongest opponents, claiming that for an act to permit even the smallest private meeting was in effect to approve all such meetings.[5] Several draft acts were rejected before one by Henderson met with general approval, though Calderwood 'started mightilie at it'. Dickson, Blair and others suspected of innovating purged themselves of any such intention. Questioned about omitting the doxology, bowing in the pulpit, and rejecting read prayers, they managed to give 'answer to satisfaction, that betwixt us and them there was no discrepancie at all'—though such satisfaction can only have been in the vaguest of terms. It was agreed that Henderson's act should

[1] Gordon, *History*, iii. 223.
[2] Ibid., iii. 222–3; J. Spalding, *Memorialls of the Trubles*, Spalding Club 1850–1, i. 312.
[3] Baillie, *Letters*, i. 358–60.
[4] Ibid., i. 360–1.
[5] Ibid., i. 362.

be presented to the Assembly, he and Argyll having been 'the happie instruments' of this concord.[1]

The extent to which news of private meetings had spread was indicated to the Assembly when a letter from some English ministers who favoured unity between the two countries was read. This complained of the opposition of Independents in England and asked for the Assembly's opinion of them 'because we sometimes hear from those of the aforesaid judgement, that some famous and eminent Brethren, even amongst your selves, doe somewhat encline unto an approbation of that way of government'.[2] Henderson explained that the Scots ministers thus rumoured to favour the Independents were Dickson and Cant. In fact, though they might have some things in common with the Independents, they were strongly committed to a presbyterian system and 'none in all the Assemblie were more against Independancie than these two'. The Assembly, therefore, unanimously rejected the charge that some in Scotland favoured Independency.[3] As a move towards unity it was suggested by Henderson that a catechism, confession of faith, directory of public worship and form of church government be drafted for acceptance by both countries.[4] The Assembly agreed and laid on him the preparing of preliminary drafts.[5]

Undoubtedly the main reason for the decision to prepare these documents was the hope of religious unity with England, a unity to be based on such definitive statements of the position of the kirk. But the decision was also influenced by the disputes within the kirk over private meetings and points of worship. One of the reasons why these disputes were so hard to settle was that there had never been clear rulings by the kirk on many of the points at issue. Varying interpretations of what were the true traditions of the kirk were, therefore, possible. Certainly the radicals had much to hope for from such documents, for the kirk would have to make some concessions to English puritans if unity was to be achieved, and it was likely to have to concede some of the changes demanded by the radicals.

On 1 August 1641 Robert Blair preached before the Assembly. To the surprise of many who thought of him as a radical, he spoke 'very gravelie for peace, and abstinence from all such meetings, as in former tymes had been very profitable, bot now were unexpedient, unlawfull, and schismaticall', thus showing his willingness to help to heal the divisions in the kirk,[6] perhaps under the influence of the news that the radicals' activities were thought of in England as favouring independency. The next day Henderson, as moderator, brought up the matter of private meetings in the Assembly, which immediately remitted it to a committee

---

[1] Ibid., i. 362–3.
[2] Peterkin, *Records*, 295.
[3] Baillie, *Letters*, i. 364.
[4] Peterkin, *Records*, 295–6.
[5] Ibid., 297; Baillie, *Letters*, i. 364, 365.
[6] Baillie, *Letters*, i. 367.

of the moderator and his assessors. The fact that an act had already been agreed on in the secret conference was not known to the Assembly; all the committe had to do was revise this act. It was then submitted to the Assembly and passed unanimously, though some thought it 'too generall and insufficient'.[1]

The criticism was just. Like previous acts dealing with the problem it represented a compromise and was only acceptable to both sides because of its vagueness. Entitled an 'Act against Impiety and Schism', it distinguished four types of religious exercise. To public worship, family worship, and private prayer by individuals it added the duty of 'mutuall edification, by instruction, admonition, exhorting one another to forward-nesse in Religion, and comforting one another in whatsoever distresse'. But this duty of mutual edification (mentioned by Robert Baillie in his draft act of 1639) was one which 'few know how to practise in the right manner'. The danger was that, on the one hand, it might lead to mocking by the ungodly and, on the other, to 'many errors and abuses, to which the godly through their weaknes may fall . . . such as are Error, Heresie, Schisme, Scandall, Self-conceit, and despising of others, pressing above the common calling of Christians, and usurping that which is proper to the Pastoral Vocation'. Therefore, though religion was to be 'universally practised in every Family, and by every person at all occasions', all were to beware that, under the name of religious exercise, they did not fall into abuses. Meetings breeding scandal and schism were to be avoided. Those who disobeyed the act were to be punished by presbyteries and synods.[2]

Thus, by Henderson's act of 1641 meetings leading to heresy, scandal and schism were banned, but 'mutual edification' was to be encouraged. But this mutual edification was nowhere precisely defined. Was it, for example, to take place only when people met together by chance, or could meetings be arranged specifically for this purpose? The act was silent. Nonetheless, it took much of the heat out of the controversy. It was a reasonable compromise, banning meetings subversive to the kirk without going to the ludicrous extreme of forbidding all religious discussion and conference among godly men. Yet, in effect, the act was a victory for the radicals, and allowed them to continue many private meetings with little further trouble. We hear little of private meetings in the years after the act, not because they had been suppressed but because, through the tenacity of the radicals, they were becoming widely accepted for the sake of peace in the kirk. Fearing the consequences of continued controversy—disunity in the kirk, encouraging its enemies and endangering plans for religious unity with England—the conservative majority had partly given way to the radicals. Dispute between the two groups did continue in the following years, but increasingly it was con-

[1] Ibid., i. 369.
[2] Spalding, *Trubles*, ii. 59; Peterkin, *Records*, 294. The Assembly also renewed the 1639 and 1640 acts against innovations: loc. cit.

cerned with the radicals' innovations in worship, not with their private meetings.

Mainly designed to damp down controversy within Scotland, the act was probably also intended to still the fears of English puritans that a presbyterian Church would forbid all prayer meetings. This, at least, was how Rutherford used the act in 1642. In a work addressed to the puritans he paraphrased the act as 'Our Assembly also commandeth godly conference at all occasionall meetings, or as Gods providence shall dispose' though only ministers had the right to preach. He also pointed out that the kirk did not insist on the use of set prayers, which were abhorrent to many puritans.[1]

In the 1641 Assembly, as in 1640, dispute broke out again briefly after the matter seemed settled. Leckie gave in a complaint against Guthry for slandering him. The complaint was referred to the moderator and his assessors, and they at length managed to reconcile Guthry and Leckie, each declaring in writing his good opinion of the other.[2]

In May 1642 Robert Baillie was still worried by the spread of Brownist ideas in Scotland (some of them brought back by the covenanters' own army when it had withdrawn from England in 1641)[3] and was writing a treatise against them,[4] but Henderson urged him not to have it published—'it would seem good yet once againe in the Generall Assemblie to trie the estate of our Kirks, and whether such a work be necessarie'.[5]

When the Assembly did next meet, at St. Andrews on 27 July 1642, the matter of innovations in worship was still a major issue, though that of private meetings had receded. As in 1641, the question was mainly dealt with by a committee of the moderator and his assessors. Cant 'did much extenuate' the innovations; Henderson and Robert Murray (Methven) 'fell sharplie on him'. Some tried to delay decision, hoping the Assembly would rise before action was agreed on. But the enemies of the radicals pressed the issue and presented a petition to the committee[6] urging the suppression of innovations, for ministers were coming to differ greatly in the forms of worship they practised and some congregations were deeply divided. Something must be done.[7] But what? Any attempt to restore unity might instead increase disunity. In the end the committee decided on an act explaining that of 1641. The new act was again prepared by Henderson. Innovations were defined as practising what had not formerly been done, or ceasing to use former practices without permission of the Assembly. This was specific enough, and (if observed)

---

[1] S. Rutherford, *A Peaceable and Temperate Plea for Pauls Presbyterie in Scotland*, London 1642, 325-6. For a paper of about this time arguing in favour of private meetings and against set prayers, see NLS, Wodrow MS. Quarto XXIX, fols. 53ᵛ-55ᵛ.

[2] Baillie, *Letters*, i. 371. This is the last known appearance of Leckie in these controversies; he died between October 1642 and June 1644: Leckie, *Leckie of that Ilk*, 96.

[3] Baillie, *Letters*, ii. 185-6.

[4] Ibid., ii. 27.

[5] Ibid., ii. 1.

[6] Ibid., ii. 46, 51.

[7] NCL, Baillie MS., i. fols. 366ᵛ-367ʳ.

would have solved the problem. But for this very reason it was not generally acceptable, and the committee timidly ruled that the act should not
be presented to the Assembly.[1]

Instead, less public action was taken. A letter signed by the moderator
was sent to the presbyteries most troubled by innovations in worship—
Glasgow, Hamilton, Lanark, Paisley, Dumbarton, Irvine, Ayr, Stranraer,
Kirkcudbright and Wigtown. The list is a striking indication of the extent
to which the radicals' activities were concentrated in the south-west.
Baillie prepared the letter to be sent,[2] but it was later substantially altered,
not being dispatched until 1 September.[3] The letter was sent semi-
officially, as from the moderator of the Assembly (Robert Douglas) and
those who had met with him. Taking heed of the 'dangerous and divisive
evill of novations within your bounds, both in pastors and people', they
urged that no innovators should be received into the ministry. 'God hath
recently and evin now delyvired us from the evills of arminianism poperie
and roman conformitie, and sall we be so farr blinfolded as to be draune
by the spirit of divisioun so suddenly into errors of another kynd'. England
and Ireland were looking to Scotland as a pattern for their reformations;
at such a time, with the great work of unity in hand, it would be disastrous
to allow in Scotland innovations which are 'a maine cause of divisiouns
and sects' in England. Innovations must be rooted out; ministers who
refuse to say the Lord's Prayer, sing the doxology or bow in the pulpit
'therby give occasioun of stumbling and divisioun to simple people' and
should be censured by their presbyteries.[4]

So, in the 1642 Assembly the matter of innovations was largely hushed
up, only being debated and condemned in the moderator's committee.
According to Baillie, if the subject had come before the full Assembly
the members from the north 'would have made ane violent act' against
innovations.[5] There was, however, discussion in the Assembly about
'Diverse practises of the brethren of Galloway' which 'wakened many of
us against their new way'; how closely their 'new way' was connected
with innovations in worship is not clear, but it certainly had something
to do with the dominance of the radicals in that area. The Assembly
repealed some acts of the synod of Galloway, including the deposition
of Gilbert Power (Stoneykirk).[6] Uchtred McDowall younger of Freugh
had accused Power of a wide variety of oppressions and moral failings,
and most of the heritors and elders of the parish seconded him. The
presbytery of Stranraer had, therefore, suspended Power in November
1641, and deposed him from his ministry in June 1642.[7] The motives of

---

[1] Ibid., fol. 367ʳ; Baillie, *Letters*, ii. 51; Sprott, *Worship in the Church*, 15.
[2] NCL, Baillie MS., i. fols. 367ʳ–367ᵛ.
[3] Baillie, *Letters*, ii. 51.
[4] NCL, Baillie MS., i. fols. 367ᵛ–368ʳ; Sprott, *Worship in the Church*, 16.
[5] Baillie, *Letters*, ii. 51.
[6] Ibid., ii. 51, 52–3; Peterkin, *Records*, 333.
[7] SRO, CH.2/341/1, Stranraer Presbytery Register, 1641–52, fols. 4ʳ–35ᵛ, 40ʳ–42ʳ.
The pages of the register have been bound and foliated in the wrong order. Only one

those involved in the matter are not clear, but it seems that this was a case of a conservative (and rather lax) minister who found it impossible to get his stipend paid by radical heritors. His attempts to raise the money due to him led to accusations of oppression and cruelty, accusations which the strongly radical synod and presbytery were willing to take at their face value to get rid of an uncongenial colleague.

This, at least, was how the General Assembly seems to have viewed the matter, for it ordered the restoration of Power to his parish.[1] But, when, in August 1642, James Bonar (Maybole) and other ministers gathered at Stoneykirk to restore Power, people gathered to resist, including Freugh's brother and members of families of heritors and elders. As soon as Bonar 'satt doun on his knees' in the pulpit, observing the practice of bowing in the pulpit, a riot broke out. The ministers were denounced as 'soul murtherers who had not the Spirit'. The true kirk had deposed Power, it was shouted; the false kirk was restoring him. When the ministers left the kirk and tried to hold a service in a field they were pelted with peats and Power's life was threatened by Andrew McDowall of Killaster, an elder. Those guilty of rioting were summoned before the Privy Council but they probably escaped with little punishment,[2] though at least the women involved seem to have done public penance for their conduct, on the orders of the presbytery of Stranraer.[3] Moreover, it was some time before those involved submitted to the Assembly's orders after the riot. The Stoneykirk elders gave in a new supplication against Power in April 1643,[4] and not until August 1644 did the presbytery register the Assembly's act restoring Power.[5] This whole episode—the Assembly repealing acts of the synod of Galloway and violent resistance to the carrying out of the Assembly's orders—illustrates how widespread support for radical policies within the kirk was in the south-west, and how determined the supporters of such policies were not to submit to the majority of the kirk.

The letter from the moderator of the Assembly to the presbyteries of the south-west had little effect, though in October 1642 the synod of Ayr and Glasgow inserted in its orders for visitations of kirks a stipulation that ministers and elders were to be asked whether they took care to stop innovations.[6] This stirred up six or seven radical ministers from Ayr presbytery and two or three from other areas to write in defence of innovations. But it was said that support for them was not increasing; 'the

---

minister in the presbytery supported Power—James Baird (Portpatrick), who was probably related to him, having married one Jean Power (*Fasti Ecclesiae Scoticanae*, ed. H. Scott, Edinburgh 1915–50, ii. 350). Freugh also accused Baird of various offences, but the charges were dismissed: SRO, CH.2/341/1, fols. 29ᵛ, 38ʳ–38ᵛ.

[1] Ibid., fols. 61ʳ–61ᵛ.

[2] Ibid., fols. 45ᵛ–46ʳ; *Register of the Privy Council of Scotland, 1638–43*, ed. D. Masson, Edinburgh 1906, 322–4, 556; *1544–1660*, Edinburgh 1908, 76; Baillie, *Letters*, ii. 53.

[3] SRO, CH.2/341/1, fols. 43ᵛ–44ʳ, 45ᵛ–46ʳ, 48ᵛ, 49ʳ.

[4] Ibid., fols. 48ᵛ–49ʳ, 50ʳ–50ᵛ.

[5] Ibid., fols. 61ʳ–61ᵛ.

[6] NCL, Baillie MS., i. fol. 371ʳ; Sprott, *Worship in the Church*, 17.

excesses of some of their followers, who have fallen to rigid Brounisme in whole, does much skarr good people from that way'.[1]

Yet tendencies which were feared to be Brownist were still widespread. When the commission of the kirk (a standing committee of the Assembly) met in November 1642 it heard complaints from the presbytery of Hamilton of one Alexander Taes, a Brownist and 'a great seducer in Clydesdale', and from the synod of Aberdeen of increasing Brownism in the north and the activities of Gilbert Gardin of Tillyfroskie, who was said to spread the absurdest tenets. The commission advised that no rash action be taken, to avoid 'offence to the good people of England that favoured these ways'[2]—another indication of how the radicals were protected by their enemies' fear of upsetting English puritans. Edinburgh presbytery, however, did take some action in answer to these reports; a 'Warning against Brownism' was read out by ministers from their pulpits. The activities of the Brownists were described as 'repugnant both to our covenant and to the practise of all reformed kirks'. People were to beware of Brownist propaganda and to denounce those who spread it: 'Seducers of that kind' were being harboured in Edinburgh. But the warning added 'that we speak nothing against . . . such as have beine in tymes of corruptioun . . . named puritanes'.[3]

The Edinburgh warning had been partly inspired by the doings of George Gardin, younger, of Tillyfroskie in Aberdeenshire. Gardin is interesting as being virtually the only person in Scotland at this time who can be called a Separatist with any certainty—on his own testimony and not just that of his enemies. He had apparently recently returned from Holland, where he had adopted anabaptist ideas; he is said to have forbidden the baptism of his infant child 'because at its age it was as yet unable to believe'. It was even said that his faith (or presumption) was so strong that he believed he could walk on water and had to be rescued from drowning when he attempted it. This information is from a somewhat suspect source, a Jesuit missionary in Scotland who was prone to believe in wild rumours,[4] but other sources confirm that he was a Separatist. In October 1642 a complaint was made to the synod of Aberdeen that Gardin and his family would not attend worship in their parish kirk; instead, he held his own worship in his house. Gardin admitted that this was true 'and forder declairit the religioun whiche he professit wes the onlie trew religioun'. Further questions received equally unacceptable answers and his excommunication was ordered.[5]

Gardin refused to submit, and about a year later he was arrested in Edinburgh 'for mainteining sum poyntes of Brunaisme', on the orders of

[1] Baillie, *Letters*, ii. 51, 54.
[2] Guthry, *Memoirs*, 123.
[3] Baillie, *Letters*, ii. 54; NCL, Baillie MS., i. fols. 368ᵛ–369ʳ.
[4] W. F. Leith, *Memoirs of Scottish Catholics during the XVIIth and XVIIIth Centuries*, London 1909, i. 252.
[5] Spalding, *Trubles*, ii. 203.

the presbytery of Edinburgh.[1] He was said to have worsted the burgh ministers in debate and when imprisoned in the tolbooth to have been 'eagerly listened to, and entertained crowds of visitors at his table'.[2] He remained in the tolbooth—'in the most disgraceful place among the whores, thieves, murderers and witches' according to another account— for about eighteen months. He was released early in 1645 on promising to confine himself to his father's house of Tillyfroskie, none having access to him without licence of the presbytery. This confinement for 'following the light of his own conscience' is said to have lasted for five years.[3] Gardin's case was unique, though he was said to have spread his ideas 'along the northern coast'. The Jesuit's suggestions that sectarian ideas were common in the north are doubtless greatly exaggerated, as are his accounts of great meetings of 'familists', or the family of love, in the south-west with 'iniquities and abominations, and extinction of the lights'.[4] This is an indication of the rumours to which the activities of the radicals gave rise, rather than a description of the actual state of affairs.

But what were seen by opponents as signs of Brownism did appear elsewhere in the north at this time. These were, in part at least, connected with the transportation of Andrew Cant to Aberdeen from Newbattle. His move had been ordered by the Assembly in 1640 but he did not settle in Aberdeen until 1642.[5] He quickly aroused the suspicions of his conservative colleagues. Soon after his arrival an Irishman called Othro Ferrendaill, or Ochtrie Fairindaill, a glover and perfumer, came to Aberdeen. Cant showed him favour and helped him to become a burgess 'be resone thair is none uther of that calling within the toun'. Not long afterwards Ferrendaill was accused of preaching at night in some houses in the burgh behind closed doors 'nocturnall doctrein, or Brounaisme, as wes said'.[6]

In October 1642 the synod of Aberdeen discussed Brownism, which was said to have appeared in the area lately. Ferrendaill and two other men, William Maxwell (a wheelwright) and Thomas Pait, were accused of practising it and preaching in houses at night, and others were suspected. Cant and John Oswald, another Aberdeen minister, were believed to sympathise with them. A committee set up to try the matter ordered Maxwell and Ferrendaill to prove their innocence by signing the Covenant, denying the tenets of Brownism and declaring the kirk to be the true church. This they were able to do in their kirks on a Sunday after sermon. But Cant allowed Ferrendaill to submit rather less publicly, on

[1] Ibid., ii. 271; Baillie, *Letters*, ii. 54.
[2] Leith, *Memoirs of Scottish Catholics*, i. 252–3.
[3] Ibid., i. 253; R. Pittilloh, *The Hammer of Persecution*, London 1659, 13; *History of the Baptists in Scotland*, ed. G. Yuille, Glasgow [1926], 25; SRO, PA.11/3, Register of the Committe of Estates, 1644–5, fols. 68ᵛ, 173ᵛ.
[4] Leith, *Memoirs of Scottish Catholics*, i. 252, 253, 261–2.
[5] Spalding, *Trubles*, i. 313, ii. 173; Baillie, *Letters*, i. 248.
[6] 'Aberdeen Burgess Register', ed. A. M. Munro, *Miscellany of the New Spalding Club*, ii. Aberdeen 1908, 387; Spalding, *Trubles*, ii. 187.

a Saturday. This failed to content the presbytery of Aberdeen; Cant was forced to apologise, his excuses being dismissed as frivolous. Ferrendaill was made to give the full satisfaction ordered; Maxwell refused and apparently fled from Aberdeen.[1]

Thus, Cant's sympathy for private meetings met with strong opposition in Aberdeen. But some of his innovations in worship proved more generally acceptable. He gave up saying the Lord's Prayer in favour of extemporary prayer, and was copied in this by the other Aberdeen ministers. He also introduced the practice of giving lectures expounding scripture on weekdays in the place of read evening prayers in the kirk;[2] such lectures were becoming increasingly popular among the radicals.[3]

In the south-west of the country, their place of origin, innovations in worship continued unchecked. The attempts of the synod of Ayr and Glasgow to interfere simply stirred up the innovators to action. Gabriel Maxwell (Dundonald) drew up a treatise arguing their case, and this received the support of John Nevay (Loudoun), Mathew Mowat (Kilmarnock), William Adair (Ayr), William Cockburn (Kirkmichael), George Hutcheson (Colmonell) and William Fullarton (St. Quivox). This paper was 'in a verie bitter and arrogant straine against the three nocent ceremonies, *Pater Noster*, *Gloria Patri*, and Kneeling in the pulpit'. The radicals were confident that they could prove the validity of their views, and declared their willingness to suffer persecution in support of them. While anxious to avoid public scandal, the synod resolved to take some action in the face of this defiance when it met in Spring 1643. The presbytery of Ayr was censured for not opposing innovations and complaints were made against ministers who spoke and wrote in favour of them. But, as a conciliatory gesture, the innovators were given a chance to state their case. They gave in Maxwell's paper and another by George Hutcheson, these papers having the support of seven ministers within the synod and twice as many from the synod of Galloway.

It is notable that the radical ministers in the synod of Ayr and Glasgow who now supported the innovations in worship were none of them men who had taken leading parts in the controversy over private meetings, and it soon became clear that they did not have the full support of the best known radical ministers. Leading ministers of the kirk, both radicals and their opponents, met in Edinburgh to consider the actions of the innovators in the synod; and all of them, including radicals like Dickson, Rutherford, Blair and George Gillespie (Greyfriars, Edinburgh), expressed their grief at the innovations. Among those who promised to write answers to the papers of the innovators were Blair and Rutherford. Dickson had already written such an answer and he persuaded William Adair to submit to the 'three nocent ceremonies'.[4] The General Assembly

[1] Ibid., ii. 203, 217, 226, 229, 241.
[2] Ibid., ii. 205, 226.
[3] McMillan, *Worship*, 131, 143, 145; Maxwell, *Worship*, 97–8, 106–7.
[4] Baillie, *Letters*, ii. 69–71.

in August saw the radicals still divided in this way. Livingstone and McLellan joined John Nevay in supporting innovations, while Rutherford and Dickson argued against them. But Rutherford and others did suggest that, for the sake of peace and unity with England, bowing and doxologies might be given up—not as illegal but as inexpedient. Thus some radicals seemed to be showing a new willingness to compromise; and though the conservative ministers made no attempt to take advantage of this new spirit, neither did they press for action against the innovators.[1]

What lay behind this new forbearance shown by both extremes? The answer lies in the wider political context of the time. The civil war in England was going badly for parliament, and the covenanting regime in Scotland felt that it could not stand by idly while the king overcame his enemies in England, for obviously he would then try to regain power in Scotland. The Covenanters were, therefore, moving towards military intervention in England on the side of parliament. Part of the price they demanded in payment for this was religious unity between the two countries on a presbyterian basis. The English parliament had indicated, or so it seemed to the Covenanters, its willingness to pay this price by setting up an assembly of divines, the Westminster Assembly, to advise it on a religious settlement, and the kirk had been invited to send commissioners to attend. When the General Assembly met in August 1643 it and the Scots parliament negotiated the Solemn League and Covenant and a military treaty with the English commissioners. In these circumstances radicals like Rutherford were ready to forbear pressing their demands for changes in worship for the sake of unity. To cause divisions in the kirk at such a critical time would encourage royalists in Scotland and limit the influence of the kirk in England. Moreover, as Rutherford's advice to lay aside bowing and doxologies as inexpedient suggests, he and other radicals probably calculated that any agreement for religious unity with England would involve abolition within the kirk of the practices they opposed, as these were hated by the English puritans. It was therefore both unnecessary and inexpedient to press innovations on the kirk for the time being as the kirk would soon be forced to accept them as the price of unity.

The reason for the docility of conservative ministers in the Assembly was also connected with the political situation. Many were suspected of royalist sympathies, and in the enthusiasm for intervening in England the tide of opinion was running strongly against them. Henry Guthry had already been shaken by the hostility aroused earlier in the year by his royalist inclinations,[2] and when he pointed out that though the English parliament had agreed to abolish episcopacy it had not said whether it would put presbyterianism or independency in its place he was shouted down by the Assembly as a rotten malignant.[3]

[1] Ibid., ii. 94–5.
[2] Ibid., ii. 69, 91.
[3] Guthry, Memoirs, 136–7.

The 1643 Assembly, therefore, took no immediate action over innovations. Instead, it revived the idea put forward by Henderson in 1641 of compiling a 'directory of worship' and other standards to define disputed points. Henderson had not proceeded with this task, feeling that for the kirk to define its worship too strictly in advance would hamper negotiations for unity with England.[1] The Assembly now ruled that a directory should be prepared. Until this was ready all dispute, verbal or written, about differing practices in worship in the kirk was banned on pain of censure. All were to strive for unity within the kirk so 'that all beginnings of Separation, all scandall and division, be by all means avoided'.[2] It was decided to send commissioners to the Westminster Assembly, the ministers chosen being Henderson, Douglas, Baillie and two radicals, Rutherford and Gillespie. Among their duties was to be the preparation with the Westminster Assembly of a Directory of Worship Confession of Faith, Catechism and form of church government for adoption in both countries.[3]

The kirk's commissioners to the Westminster Assembly travelled to London late in 1643. They have usually been assigned much of the blame for the failure of their efforts, this being attributed to their bitter hatred of toleration and independency, to their determination to impose an alien Scottish presbyterian system on England without taking any account of English preferences or needs, all this resulting from their narrow-minded bigotry. There is an element of truth in this, but it is much exaggerated; it is a caricature imposed by the propaganda of their enemies. Although determined to remain unshaken on what it regarded as essentials, the kirk was willing to make concessions in other matters. And though from the first the Independents were rightly seen as the kirk's most dangerous opponents, at least the more radical ministers could also see some virtue in them. In 1644 Rutherford called the Brownists and the Independents those 'who, of all that differ from us, come nearest to walkers with God'. He could state that in London 'The best of the people are of the Independent way' while recognising them as 'mighty opposites to presbyterial government'.[4] George Gillespie told the Westminster Assembly, referring to the Independents, 'You have here some dissenting brethren to whom I owe great respect . . . a word of love and affection. . . I wish they prove to be as unwilling to divide from us, as we have been unwilling to divide from them. I wish that instead of toleration, there may be a mutual endeavour for a happy accommodation'.[5] The kirk was strongly opposed to toleration, being naturally horrified by the idea of accepting more than one Church in a State, but it was willing to accept some measure of comprehension or accommodation, some latitude within

[1] Baillie, *Letters*, ii. 1.
[2] Ibid., ii. 94; Peterkin, *Records*, 349.
[3] Peterkin, *Records*, 359.
[4] Rutherford, *Letters*, 616, 618, 619.
[5] *Minutes of the Westminster Assembly of Divines*, ed. A. F. Mitchell and J. Struthers, Edinburgh 1874, 28.

the Church to allow for differing opinions. The Scots commissioners also declared their willingness to recognise the Church of England as a true church, like the kirk. They stated 'we are neither so ignorant nor so arrogant, as to ascribe to the Church of Scotland such absolute purity and perfection, as hath not need or canot admit of further Reformation'.[1]

Such statements of the kirk's willingness to compromise were reflected, to some extent at least, in action. The kirk accepted as binding on it the 'Westminster Standards' (Directory, Catechism, Confession and form of church government), standards drafted by an English Assembly. Of course the Scots commissioners to the Westminster Assembly, though not full members, had been very influential in it. It is, nonetheless, a very notable indication of the sincerity of the kirk's desire for unity and of its readiness to make sacrifices to attain it. The kirk was immensely proud of its national traditions, but it was ready to endanger some of them in the cause of unity.

The General Assembly met in January 1645 to consider the Directory of Worship agreed by the Westminster Assembly. Not all liked the changes it involved in worship. Baillie feared that there would be much opposition, and tried to persuade his fellow commissioners from Westminster to oppose the changes. But, though Henderson felt as he did they were won over by the other commissioners to support the changes. Moreover, many believed not only that the Directory should be adopted but that various practices not condemned by the Westminster Assembly but disliked by English puritans should be laid aside as inexpedient, to further the cause of unity. Baillie's fears, therefore, proved groundless; 'all did lovinglie condescend to the alterations I had so much opposed', he noted with surprise. The Assembly approved the Directory 'with great applause, and contentment of all', and accompanying legislation dealt with matters not fully explained in it. Many of the changes in the kirk's traditional worship which were now authorised had formerly been advocated by the radical ministers. Lectures expounding scripture were to be established. It was ruled 'That the Ministers bowing in the Pulpit, though a lawful custom in this Kirk, be hereafter laid aside'[2] for the sake of uniformity with England. No act was made against doxologies, perhaps as a result of the plea of the venerable David Calderwood: 'Moderator, I entreat that the Doxology be not laid aside, for I hope to sing it in Glory'; instead, it was decided to 'let desuetude abolish it' and it soon fell out of fashion.[3] Similarly, set prayers were not banned but equally they were not encouraged—the Directory of Worship merely suggests general themes for prayers—but in practice many ministers came to abandon them.

[1] [A. Henderson], *Reformation of Church-Government in Scotland, Cleered from some Mistakes and Prejudices, by the Commissioners of the Generall Assembly of the Church of Scotland, now at London*, London 1644, 15-16.
[2] Peterkin, *Records*, 422.
[3] Ibid., 418-19, 421-2; Baillie, *Letters*, ii. 123, 258-60; Sprott, *Worship of the Kirk*, 22-5; Livingston, *Psalter*, 67; G. Gillespie, *Notes of the Debates and Proceedings of the Assembly of Divines and other Commissioners at Westminster*, Edinburgh 1846, 108.

The radicals in the kirk had triumphed. A 1641 Act had given tacit allowance to their private meetings; the 1645 Assembly authorised or, at least, allowed many of the changes in worship they had advocated. In 1639–41 the majority of more conservative ministers had been deterred from outright condemnation of private meetings by the need to avoid offending English puritans and weakening the kirk. In 1645 such considerations again worked in favour of the radicals. Changes in worship which would never have been made to satisfy them alone were made to further the great cause of unity with England. And, with the royalist rising led by Montrose successful in the north, the need for unity, both within the kirk and with England, was so clear that those with reservations about the changes held their peace. Montrose might make play in his propaganda with the argument that the kirk was corrupted by Brownist and Independent influences,[1] but most within the kirk had decided that the policies of the radicals were consistent with a presbyterian system, as the radicals themselves had always maintained.

Controversy over the points at issue was not entirely stilled, however. In 1646 the laird of Haliburton accused James Guthry (Lauder), James Simpson (Sprouston) and their adherents of keeping 'Brownistical conventicles'. The General Assembly refused to consider the matter, referring it to the commission of the kirk, which found the conduct of the ministers not censurable. But Calderwood, that old enemy of private meetings, with four or five other ministers and two or three elders, recorded their dissent from this decision.[2]

Calderwood returned to the attack in 1647. He and his supporters came to the Assembly 'with resolution to make great dinne about privie meetings and novations, being persuaded. . . that our Church wes allready much pestered with schisme'. They soon found their mistake, 'for they have obtained, with the hearty consent of these men whom they counted greatest patrons of schisme, all the acts they pleased against that evill'.[3] An act forbade the importation of books and conversation with persons tainted with the errors of Independency and Separatism, which were said to be spreading like gangrene in England.[4] Directions of the Assembly, written by Robert Blair, for private worship, mutual edification and family exercise were issued. These repeated that none had authority to interpret scripture but ministers. Family exercise should not be led by any vagrant person, for 'persons tainted with errours or aiming at division' might in that way 'lead captive silly and unstable souls'. Strangers might not attend family exercise unless they were in the house for some other reason—for a meal, or to stay the night. Whatever might have been the

---

[1] Sprott, *Worship of the Church*, 26.
[2] Guthry, *Memoirs*, 221, 230; *The Records of the Commissioners of the General Assemblies of the Church of Scotland*, ed. A. F. Mitchell and J. Christie, Scottish History Society 1892–1909, i. 7–9, 16, 23–7, 29–30, 34, 39–44, 72–3, 107, 137–8, 142, 198, 226, 237, 239–40.
[3] Baillie, *Letters*, ii. 20.
[4] Peterkin, *Records*, 476.

effects of 'meetings of persons of divers Families in the times of corruption or trouble (in which cases many things are commendable, which otherwise are not tolerable)' they were now, in time of peace and purity, to be disapproved. But, though family exercise was strictly limited, the loophole for private meetings under another name, that of mutual edification, remained.[1] Thus, though the act evidently satisfied Calderwood, it simply repeated the substance of earlier acts, and the act against spreading Independent propaganda was acceptable to the radicals in that, as they had always claimed, they were no friends of Independency.

Already by 1647, however, the victory of the radicals was going sour. Largely through events in England, the hopes of the Covenanters for religious unity were being shattered, and differing reactions within the kirk to these events were to split it more than ever before and destroy the covenanting movement.

After the Covenanters' intervention in the English civil war dislike of the Scots and their attempt to dominate a religious and political settlement in England grew fast. This dislike was at first restrained by the necessity for Scots military help, but by the time the war ended in victory for parliament in 1646 tension between the nominal allies was great. The strongly Independent New Model Army had done much to win the war and resolutely opposed the type of religious settlement advocated by the Scots. To the Covenanters it seemed that they had been tricked. They had agreed to help the English parliament in return for a presbyterian settlement in England and now, having received their help, the English were refusing to carry out their side of the bargain.

Since the English parliament refused to promote religious unity between the two kingdoms some Covenanters turned to the king and the royalists, hoping to impose unity with their help. Such hope led to the agreement with the king known as the Engagement—and to the first great split in the covenanting movement, for many (including the commission of the kirk and the General Assembly) rightly refused to trust the king. The Engagers, nonetheless, managed to raise an army and invade England, but were defeated by Cromwell at Preston in August 1648. The more extreme Covenanters of the 'kirk party' (whose supporters among the ministers were led by the radical George Gillespie), who opposed the Engagers, then seized power in Scotland. In the following months the kirk purged itself of Engagers, and in doing so the radicals settled some old scores. Henry Guthry's deposition was thought to owe something to his opposition to the radicals in and after 1639,[2] and Andrew Ramsay seems to have believed that his dislike of the radicals' innovations in worship was connected with his deposition as an Engager.[3]

---

[1] Ibid., 472–4; Baillie, *Letters*, iii. 15.

[2] Gordon, *History*, iii. 222; Robert Mitchell, one of the ringleaders of the Stirling conventiclers in 1639, was abused as a 'false puritane knave' for having had a hand in the removal of Guthry, *Maitland Miscellany*, I. ii. 477, 484.

[3] GUL, MS. Gen. 1209, 19; Maxwell, *Worship*, 90–1. Conversely some radicals benefited from the fall of the Engagers; in 1648 the veteran holder of private meetings,

The attitude of the new regime in Scotland to the English parliament, now dominated by the Independents, was ambivalent. On the one hand, the Independents were recognised as having much in common with the kirk in all matters but church government, and their alliance against royalists was needed; on the other hand, Independency was seen as one of the most dangerous enemies of the kirk. The execution of Charles I soon broke the uneasy alliance of kirk party and Independents, for the action aroused horror throughout Scotland and greatly increased support for the royalists. The kirk party was not strong enough to stand alone against Independents on one side, royalists on the other, and in 1650 negotiated an agreement with Charles II. Once the new king reached Scotland, and Cromwell invaded the country, what the kirk party saw as primarily a religious war quickly turned into a national one. In order to satisfy the royalists and to resist the enemy effectively the kirk was increasingly driven to admit royalists to power in the army and the State, even though their promises to uphold the covenants were insincere—as indeed were the king's own. A minority in the kirk, strongest in the south-west, refused to agree to this. In October 1650 this party drew up the western remonstrance, denouncing the king and disowning his cause. The 'remonstrants' denied the authority of the State and withdrew from the commission of the kirk. Their party gained wider support in December, when resolutions by the commission accepted the admission of royalists to the army. The remonstrants and others protested at this. During the following months the kirk split into two bitterly hostile factions; the minority of 'protesters' (with perhaps one hundred ministers actively supporting them) and the majority of 'resolutioners'. In 1651 the pro-testers disowned the General Assembly and withdrew from it. In 1653 rival general assemblies of the two parties met; in some areas rival kirk sessions and presbyteries emerged.

In practice the protesters had virtually seceded from the kirk and set up their own Church. Of course they denied this, claiming that it was they who formed the true church; it was the resolutioners who had destroyed the unity of the kirk by their corruptions. Thus the kirk which had remained united since the Reformation, recognised as a true kirk even by those who opposed its policies at various times, split, in effect, into rival churches, each with its own structure, in the 1650s.

When one examines the protester ministers who led this schism one finds that they include nearly all those who can be identified as leaders of the radical party in the 1640s. Samuel Rutherford, Andrew Cant, James Guthry, John Livingstone, Gabriel Maxwell, Mathew Mowat, John Nevay, William Adair, James Simpson were all protesters.[1] Three

John Mean, was elected a member of the committee of estates for the first time and was appointed postmaster of Edinburgh: SRO, PA.11/7, Register of the Committee of Estates, 1648–9, fols. 11ᵛ, 79ᵛ–80ʳ, 122ᵛ. In 1649 he was elected to the burgh council for the first time: *Extracts from the Records of Edinburgh, 1642–55*, ed. M. Wood, Edinburgh 1938, 213.

[1] Scott, *Fasti*, ii. 99, iii. 8–9, 35, 105, 119–20, iv. 289–90, 318–19, vi. 37, vii. 419.

known radicals died before 1650 (George Gillespie, George Dick, John McLellan)[1] and the allegiance of several others is not clear. Only two radicals are known to have become resolutioners; Robert Blair, whose attachment to the radicals had been weak for many years, and David Dickson, the one major exception to the generalisation that leading radicals became protesters.[2]

It seems clear, therefore, that, though the protester–resolutioner split of the 1650s was caused by the disintegration of the covenanting movement in the face of political disunity and military defeat, its seeds lie much further back in the history of the kirk. Those who defied the resolutioner majority in the 1650s were those (or the heirs of those) radicals who had most openly defied the bishops in the 1620s and 1630s, and who in the 1640s had persuaded the majority of ministers to tolerate their private meetings and accept their innovations in worship. The split of the 1650s seemed to confirm what the enemies of the radicals had said all along; that they had separatist tendencies which might lead to schism. The radicals had denied this, but their actions appeared to have confirmed it.[3]

Yet, though the radicals did virtually separate from the corrupt majority of the kirk in the 1650s, this does not prove that their ideas had always tended towards separation. If their beliefs remained constant, why had they not separated from a corrupt kirk in the 1630s as they were to do in the 1650s? In the 1630s they had defied the bishops, abstaining from what they saw as corrupt practices and holding prayer meetings. But they had not attempted to set up a rival church structure claiming to be the true church, as the protesters were to do. The reason for this change in reaction seems to lie partly in the experience of the 1640s. The radicals had tasted success and the prospect of submitting again to the domination of the more conservative elements in the kirk was too bitter to bear. Moreover, though the radicals had bitterly opposed the views of the English Independents and sectaries on church government they had much in common with them in other matters; they admired and were influenced by their godliness—and by their success which seemed a sign of divine favour.

This is not to suggest that the protesters or their radical predecessors openly adopted Independent or sectarian ideas. They remained true to the ideal of a single Presbyterian Church in Scotland. But it was partly the influence, conscious or unconscious, of English puritan ideas and actions in the 1640s that led radicals to become protesters, and this was one of the reasons why they reacted in their quarrel with a corrupt kirk

[1] Ibid., ii. 348, 417.
[2] Ibid., i. 65, v. 232–3.
[3] Many of the few Scots who became Independents in the 1650s had been protesters, but none of the protesters who had been prominent among the radicals in the 1640s were among them: G. D. Henderson, 'Some Early Scottish Independents', *Religious Life in Seventeenth Century Scotland*, Cambridge 1937, 107–16; Hoy, 'The Entry of Sects into Scotland', in Shaw, *Reformation and Revolution*, 181–7.

by almost withdrawing from it and denying its authenticity to a greater degree than they had done in the 1630s.

It has been said that what killed Presbyterianism in England in the later seventeenth century was the gap between theory and practice. In theory it might form a National Church; in practice under persecution it was driven increasingly towards sectarian positions. Richard Baxter claimed that it was persecution that drove presbyterians into sectarianism, 'So that their Congregations were, through necessity, just of Independent and Separating Shape, and outward Practice, though not upon the same Principles'.[1] The same tendency can be seen in seventeenth-century Scotland, but the drift of the radicals towards conventicle-holding and sectarianism was slowed by the fact that a presbyterian system of church courts remained in the Established Church even in its times of 'corruption', and by the triumph of Presbyterianism after 1637. Nonetheless, the tendency remained. It was revived by the protesters in the 1650s, when they could not win over the majority in the kirk, and by the conventiclers under renewed persecution in 1660–88, though in general the 'tradition of a united church' was still strong and few would 'separate from the church of God'.[2] Such conventicles survived into the eighteenth century as prayer societies 'and may be said to have formed a sect within the church',[3] just as the private meetings of the 1630s had done.

The radicals and the protesters reacted to persecution in a manner which pointed the way to later seventeenth-century and eighteenth-century secessions. Support for such reactions came from developments in federal theology which justified moving apart or separating (especially in communion) from the corrupt masses.[4] Robert Baillie was justifiably worried by the great exclusive communions of the protesters: 'They will exclude such multitudes for one cause or another, that the end will be the setting up of a new refined congregation of their own adherents'.[5] Conventicle-holding and the justification of it had influenced the whole concept of the Church in the minds of those taking part. From the 'visible church', the Church inclusive of all believers in the community, including both saints and sinners, the elect and the reprobate, they moved towards trying to set up on earth an exclusive Church, approximating as far as possible to the 'invisible church', which contained only the elect.[6] Such a move followed logically from the holding of conventicles, from the godly meeting together, setting themselves apart from the rest of the community. For a time, after 1637, it had been possible to reconcile the different

[1] Quoted in W. M. Lamont, *Godly Rule: Politics and Religion 1603–60*, London 1969, 145.

[2] G. Donaldson, *Scotland: James V to James VII*, Edinburgh and London 1965, 366.

[3] G. D. Henderson, *The Claims of the Church of Scotland*, London 1951, 101. For the prayer societies see A. Fawcett, *The Cambuslang Revival*, London 1971, 55–74.

[4] Torrance, 'Covenant or Contract?', *Journal of Scottish Theology*, xxiii. 51–76, esp. 70.

[5] Quoted in G. B. Burnet, *The Holy Communion in the Reformed Church of Scotland*, Edinburgh and London 1960, 129.

[6] For the 'visible' and 'invisible' Churches, see E. S. Morgan, *Visible Saints: the History of a Puritan Idea*, Ithaca 1965.

THE RADICAL PARTY IN THE KIRK, 1637–45

concepts; in the euphoria of success, with Scotland seen as a covenanted nation specially favoured by God, it had seemed that the visible and the invisible churches might coincide (as Rutherford taught)[1]—Scotland was an elect nation. But with division and defeat in the later 1640s it became clear that the mass of the population was corrupt and unregenerate. The godly again saw the need to move apart from the corrupt majority in the kirk to keep themselves pure. Strict control of entry to communion was an indication (justified by federal theology)[2] of such disillusionment, an admission of failure to reform society as a whole[3] and a consequent turning inwards by the godly to preserve themselves untainted by the reprobate. Robert Baillie might state, in showing the errors of English sectaries, that 'Scripture makes the Church of God so long as it is upon earth to be a mixed multitude, of Elect and Reprobate, good and bad',[4] but the conclusion was one which his more radical colleagues would have increasingly questioned.

To conclude, it seems clear that the radicals of the 1620s, 1630s and 1640s are the direct ancestors of the protesters, though it was the experience of the 1640s that turned them into protesters. Moreover, the long history of private meeting or conventicle-holding within the kirk contributed much to the form of the later covenanting movement when persecution was renewed in the 1660s. The conventicles of the restoration period were not innovations, but, on the contrary, long established practices within the kirk.

[1] Torrance, 'Covenant or Contract?', 70.
[2] Ibid., 68.
[3] See Lamont, *Godly Rule*, 146–7.
[4] Quoted in A. R. Dallison, 'Contemporary Criticism of Millenarianism', in *Puritans, the Millennium and the Future of Israel: Puritan Eschatology 1600 to 1660*, ed. P. Toon, Cambridge and London 1970, 106.

XIII

The General Assembly and the Commission of the Kirk, 1638-51

Any discussion about the central government of the Kirk during the years that the covenanters ruled Scotland must take account of "management", the ways in which the dominant groups in the kirk won control of it, and then maintained this control. For throughout this period a large minority of ministers, and at times a majority, did not wholeheartedly support some of the main policies implemented by the general assembly and the commission of the kirk. How, then, was it that these bodies could impose such policies successfully? Basically, the answer is simple. History affords many examples of zealous, well organised minority groups controlling institutions (of church or state) successfully in the face of more moderate majorities which are unwilling or unable to unite and organise themselves effectively, since they consist largely of men anxious to avoid trouble, with no taste for controversy and no ambition to lead factions or parties. The covenanting kirk had, on many occasions, such a "silent majority" of men who, for good reasons or bad, refused to compete with the active minority groups, which were thus able to force their policies on the kirk.

The trump card held by the minority of ministers who demanded revolution in 1638, not just reform, was lay support. The more moderate ministers were over-awed by the strength of the support powerful laymen gave the more extreme covenanters. These laymen forced their way into presbyteries as elders, thus gaining a voice in the election of commissioners to the general assembly. It is clear that the Glasgow Assembly of 1638 was effectively packed by elders taking part in elections and themselves sitting in the assembly, supporting the minority of more extreme ministers. Threats of violence deterred some anti-covenanters from attending; others were excluded on the grounds that they had been cited to appear before the assembly for trial. As if this was not enough four to six gentlemen from each presbytery, and up to six burgesses from each burgh, were to accompany commissioners to the assembly as "assessors" to advise them how to vote.[1]

Elections to assemblies did not have to be organised so elaborately in later years; the covenanters were firmly in control of the country and their active opponents had been purged from the ministry. Moreover other, less blatant, ways of managing assemblies were tried and found to be effective.

[1] See D. Stevenson, *The Scottish Revolution: 1637-44, The Triumph of the Covenanters* (Newton Abbot, 1973), 105-8, 112-14, 120.

First of all, the more extreme ministers had sought a way of controlling the business put before the assembly. One way in which they achieved this was by holding semi-secret preparatory meetings before each assembly met. Thus just before the Glasgow Assembly " we held som privat meitings anent choysing the Moderator and the Clerk "; it was decided to get Alexander Henderson elected moderator, Archibald Johnston of Wariston clerk.[2] This was not all the meeting decided; according to Wariston the assembly " proceided publickly according to the treatise of proceidings in privat ".[3] What was to be done, and how, was decided on before the assembly even met.

Such private meetings of leading ministers and lay covenanters before general assemblies became regular events. In 1643 " some few of us meeting in Waristoun's chamber, advysed whom to have on committee for bills, reports, and on other things " — including on who should be moderator.[4] By 1648 Robert Baillie could write that " In all prior Assemblies, some few of us mett the night before the Assemblie in Warriston's chamber, with Argyle, the Chancellour, and some other of our wisest friends, to consider about the choising of the moderator, committees, and cheife points of the Assemblie "; this had not been done in 1648 since many of the leading lay covenanters had retired from Edinburgh to avoid being forced to accept the Engagement, the treaty with the king which the state supported but the kirk opposed.[5]

Decision on a moderator was obviously important in managing the assembly; but how could it be assured that the man agreed on would be elected? In 1638 the fact that Alexander Henderson was the covenanting leaders' choice was circulated to members of the assembly, and he was then elected from the leet unanimously (except for his own vote).[6] After 1638 the candidates put on the leet were chosen by the previous moderator; in 1639 this was called an " antient and laudable custom ", in 1641 the " old fashion ".[7] This allowed the previous moderator to so manipulate the leet that the person chosen at the preparative meeting was almost certain to be elected — by choosing as the other ministers on the leet men of little standing

[2] A. Johnston of Wariston, *Diary* . . . *1632-9*, ed. G. M. Paul (Scottish History Society, 1911), 400.

[3] *Ibid.*, 401.

[4] R. Baillie, *Letters and Journals*, ed. D. Laing (3 vols., Bannatyne Club, 1841-2), ii, 83.

[5] *Ibid.*, iii, 53. For meetings before assemblies preparing business for them prior to 1638 see, e.g., D. Calderwood, *The History of the Kirk of Scotland*, ed. T. Thomson (8 vols., Wodrow Society, 1842-9), iii, 385, vii, 94.

[6] Johnston, *Diary* . . . *1632-9*, 401; J. Gordon, *History of Scots Affairs*, eds. J. Robertson and G. Grub (3 vols., Spalding Club, 1840-1), i, 143-4.

[7] *Ibid.*, iii, 39; A. Peterkin (ed.), *Records of the Kirk of Scotland* (Edinburgh, 1838), 242; Baillie, *Letters*, i, 363.

or popularity. Most members of assemblies at first accepted this custom, but opposition to it soon appeared. Sometimes the assembly insisted on adding names to the leet, as in 1642, when the earl of Cassillis did so for "the keeping of the Assemblie's libertie ".[8] Again, when in 1643 the previous moderator leeted Henderson (as decided in advance) along with three ministers who had no chance of gaining many votes, the arrangement was nearly upset when members "who knew not the secreit" demanded additions to the leet.[9]

By 1647 organised opposition to the system of choosing a moderator was strong enough to get it altered. David Calderwood (revered as the historian of the kirk) and others failed by only a few votes to get their own candidate elected, and they pushed through an "Act concerning the choosing of the Moderator ".[10] Robert Baillie denounced the act as "a new ridiculous way of choiseing the Moderator " which "puts in the hand of base men to get one whom they please ".[11] By "base men " he evidently meant the ordinary members of the assembly!

The new system was, evidently, that the previous moderator would name two men to be on the leet, and the whole assembly then would agree on another three names. Baillie's opinion of the act had mellowed by the time it was first put into effect in 1648; he did complain that the system was "very longsome " but admitted that it was "a equall and satisfactory way ". He was probably reassured by the fact that the candidate elected was one of those named by the previous moderator in spite of the new act.[12] In 1649 Robert Douglas as previous moderator (in 1647; the 1648 moderator, George Gillespie, had died) leeted Andrew Cant "in earnest " and Mungo Law "for a fashion ", it being intended that Cant should be elected. But instead the assembly put Douglas himself on the leet and elected him.[13]

This was significant, for Douglas was a much more moderate man than Cant; the kirk party, which now controlled the kirk, had gone too far by trying to get Cant elected, and had failed. Usually this mistake was avoided; the "official " candidate for the moderatorship was a man carefully selected to ensure that he was someone who would win the votes of moderates while carrying out the plans of the more extreme covenanters. Most of the best known ministers in the kirk in the 1640s can be identified with what has been called the "radical party ", a

---

[8] *Ibid.*, ii, 45-6. See also Peterkin, *Records*, 242.
[9] Baillie, *Letters*, ii, 84.
[10] Peterkin, *Records*, 483.
[11] Baillie, *Letters*, iii, 20, 21.
[12] George Gillespie received over 150 votes, John Smith about 40, Robert Blair a few, Andrew Cant two, and David Dickson none. Baillie, *Letters*, iii, 52-3; Scottish Record Office [SRO], GD.40/II/67, Lothian Papers, Robert Moray to the Earl of Lothian, 13th July 1648.
[13] Baillie, *Letters*, iii, 91.

group of ministers who pressed for the holding of prayer meetings outside congregational worship and for other changes in traditional forms of worship which were (at first) unacceptable to most ministers. Men like Samuel Rutherford, David Dickson, Robert Blair, John Livingstone, James Guthrie, Andrew Cant, and George and Patrick Gillespie were all of this group.[14] But these radicals, though playing a leading part in the general assemblies (and especially in the private consultations preparing for assemblies) seldom moderated. In the fourteen assemblies of 1638-51 radicals moderated only four times. Two of these occasions were towards the end of the period, when the radical-dominated kirk party was briefly able to control the kirk. George Gillespie was elected in 1648 when reaction against the Engagement led to ministers looking with more favour than usual on the radicals, and in 1650 Andrew Cant (after failing to be elected the previous year) moderated. The two radicals who moderated before this were David Dickson in 1639 and Robert Blair in 1646. What is interesting about this is that these were the two most moderate of the ministers who can be identified as radicals; they were to be the only two radical leaders who, when the kirk was split by schism in 1650-51, joined the moderate resolutioners rather than the extremist protesters.[15]

Of the leading covenanting ministers who were not radicals Alexander Henderson and Robert Douglas were by far the best known. Both were active and sincere covenanters, but nonetheless men with some breadth of outlook and lack of fanaticism which won them the respect and trust of the more moderate ministers. It was therefore to them that the covenanters frequently looked for moderators. Henderson moderated three times (1638, 1641, 1643) before his death in 1646, Robert Douglas no fewer than five times (1642, 1645, 1647, 1649, 1651), while lesser known men of rather similar character presided in the other two assemblies of the period (Andrew Ramsay in 1640, James Bonar in 1644). Radical ministers might often dominate the private consultations which usually decided on the moderator, but they clearly realised that they would not themselves be usually acceptable as moderators either to more moderate ministers in the assembly or to most lay covenanters.

As well as deciding who should be moderator, the meetings before each assembly often decided, as some of the passages already quoted indicate, who should be on the most important committees which would sit during the assemblies — especially the committee for bills and overtures, and that for references and reports. As an act of 1640 laid down that no motion should normally come before the full assembly except through these

[14] See D. Stevenson, "The Radical Party in the Kirk, 1637-45", *Journal of Ecclesiastical History*, xxv (1974), 135-65.
[15] *Ibid.*, 162-3.

committees,[16] they effectively controlled what the assembly debated and what it did not — and this 1640 act was passed specifically to prevent Henry Guthry (minister of Stirling) making controversial charges in the full assembly against some radical ministers.[17]

With meetings before each assembly proving able to determine who should be moderator and who should sit on committees, the hold of those who dominated these meetings on the assemblies was strong. Yet the covenanters resorted also to an additional expedient; the privy conference of the moderator and his assessors. In this, during each assembly, the moderator and leading covenanters (laymen as well as ministers) exercised general oversight over the detailed work of the committees, and planned tactics as the assembly proceeded.

The need for such a privy conference was evidently decided on by the covenanters before the 1638 assembly, for once Henderson was elected moderator he, "professing his owne insufficiencie for so weightie a charge ", asked that assessors be nominated " to joyne with him in a privat conference for ordering of matters to be proponed in Assembly ". This led immediately to strong protests, led by David Dalgleish who said " I have seen Assemblies of old, and such pryme [presumably a misprint for ' pryvie '] conferences, according to my poore observation, hath wrought great prejudice to the Kirk; therefore, I would wish that all were done by a voluntar consent, and by the concurrance of the whole Assembly ".[18]

Dalgleish was right. "Privy conferences" under various names had become regular in general assemblies after 1577, as assessors were appointed to consult with the moderator about the business to be done " for the better expedition of matters ".[19] As early as 1580 " certain brether were offendit with the ordour of Assessours . . . as though some tyrannie or vsurpation might creip in therby, or libertie takin from the brether ". However, assessors continued to be appointed.[20] References to them disappear in the later 1590s (though they probably still existed), but in 1600-18 the privy conference developed into one of the main means whereby James VI dominated assemblies; it became the master of the assembly instead of its servant.[21] It was said,

---

[16] Peterkin, *Records,* 279.
[17] Baillie, *Letters,* i, 251.
[18] Peterkin, *Records,* 139.
[19] E.g., T. Thomson (ed.), *Booke of the Universall Kirk of Scotland* (3 vols., Bannatyne and Maitland Clubs, 1839-45), i, 382, ii, 403, 418, 427; Calderwood,. *History,* iii, 378, 398, 410, 443.
[20] Thomson, *Booke of the Universall Kirk,* ii, 449-50 and passim; Calderwood, *History,* iii, 463-4 and passim.
[21] Thomson, *Booke of the Universall Kirk,* iii, 979-80, 1024, 1046-7; Calderwood, *History,* vi, 3, 161, 606, 752, 757, vii, 223, 285, 317-18; J. Row, *The History of the Kirk of Scotland* (Wodrow Society, 1842), 275-6, 306, 314; Peterkin, *Records,* 139-40.

for example, of the 1610 assembly that its main acts were "set down *verbatim* in the privy conference" and "only read to be ratified in the Assembly" without debate.[22] The parallel with the way in which the Lords of the Articles had developed until they effectively controlled the Scottish parliament is close; in each institution the excuse for concentrating power in the hands of a few members was the same — it was efficient, and shortened meetings.

The historian John Row concluded that privy conferences "hes been the wrack of almost all our Assemblies continuallie";[23] yet the leading covenanters wished to revive them. The conferences were too useful a method of controlling assemblies to be rejected just because of their unfortunate associations. But David Dalgleish's protests won the support of the 1638 assembly, in spite of Henderson's argument that though conferences might have done harm in the past there was nothing wrong with them in principle. The assembly "altogidder reicted" them, passing "an Act of disallowing anie private conference with the Moderator".[24] But then, astonishingly, the assembly agreed instead to something that was much more dangerous to its liberty. It refused to allow a conference or to appoint moderator's assessors, but it agreed that he should be able informally to choose assessors himself, though they were to confine themselves to preparing business for the assembly and were not to take decisions.[25] This, hardly surprisingly, "some judged to differ little from the private conference and constant assessors".[26] In fact it was worse; the assembly had refused the chance itself to elect assessors, but had sanctioned unofficial ones over whom it could have no control. One source suggests that this was what Henderson had intended from the start;[27] though possible, this seems unlikely.

While the assembly as a whole contained many more ministers than elders (see appendix), and the composition of committees elected by it usually reflected this, the assessors Henderson chose for himself consisted of eleven elders and only four ministers.[28] Similarly the following year David Dickson chose nine elders and seven ministers, the assembly having again refused to appoint assessors but agreed that he might "crave their assistance in privat".[29] Thus men who remained essentially

[22] *Ibid.*, 25.
[23] Row, *History*, 275-6.
[24] Peterkin, *Records*, 46.
[25] Stevenson, *Scottish Revolution, 1637-44*, 120-1; Baillie, *Letters*, i, 137; Sir J. Balfour, *Historical Works* (4 vols., Edinburgh, 1824-5), iii, 302; Peterkin, *Records*, 139-40.
[26] Gordon, *History*, i, 159.
[27] *Ibid.*, i, 158-9.
[28] Baillie, *Letters*, i, 137.
[29] Peterkin, *Records*, 243-4.

laymen, though called elders, not only played a leading part in elections and themselves sat in assemblies, they also formed a majority on the privy conference; they were determined to keep control of the ministry, in order to keep their pretensions in check.[30] Whether laymen continued to form a majority on the unofficial privy conference after 1639 is not known, but they certainly continued to play a leading part in it — as in 1642 when the marquis of Argyll was especially active; " Our privie committee, before or after the Assemblie [met], he never missed ",[31] a comment which indicates how the preparatory meetings before an assembly could merge into the privy conference during it.

In 1641 Henderson (again moderator) formed the conference by sending privately for " those whom most he needed ",[32] and in 1642 the moderator's assessors " were secretlie advertised; for none were allowed publicklie ", which seems to indicate that suspicion of the conference was growing. In this assembly members of the main committees were chosen by the moderator and his assessors after the assembly had begun. Members who, it was feared, would prove troublesome (like Henry Guthry) — " these men from whom we expected most fasherie " — were put on a minor committee for considering the state of Orkney and Shetland to distract them from more contentious matters. The assembly duly agreed to the membership of the committees " as we had resolved ". The conference also considered a list of business to be submitted to the assembly, drafted by Wariston;[33] under the vigorous Wariston the clerkship of the assembly was developing into an office of great influence. By 1649 we hear that " The Committees were formed according to the custom by the Moderator and clerk in private ".[34]

In spite of the fact that the conference during the 1642 assembly evidently had had to be kept secret, in 1643 the assembly agreed to remit the most important business to it — while still leaving its status unofficial. English parliamentary commissioners had arrived to negotiate a civil and religious alliance with the covenanters. The moderator asked the judgement of " several brethren " in the assembly about how negotiations for a religious agreement should be carried out. Those he asked (as had no doubt been arranged in advance) advised that negotiations should be left to " himself and his assessors ", and this the assembly accepted. Thus it was the moderator and his assessors who drew up the solemn league and covenant. It was then produced before the full assembly, read twice, and an

---

[30] Stevenson, D., *Scottish Revolution, 1637-44*, 299-304.
[31] Baillie, *Letters*, ii, 47.
[32] *Ibid.*, i, 362, 364.
[33] *Ibid.*, ii, 46-7.
[34] *Ibid.*, iii, 91.

immediate vote on it demanded. One minister ventured to suggest "that before men were urged to vote about it, leisure might be given them for some few days to have their scruples removed". This was rejected, and an immediate vote taken without any debate at all.[35] The assembly seemed in danger of reverting to its state of 1610, ratifying without debate acts drafted in the privy conference.

The 1643 assembly, however, was unusual; it met in an emergency situation when quick decisions and a show of unanimity were necessary. Usually in this period there was at least some debate in the full assembly on important acts — though the progress of these debates was doubtless often carefully orchestrated by the moderator and his assessors.

The effectiveness of the usual management of assemblies by the privy conference and committees was emphasised in 1648 when the system was not fully used. "The want of these private preparatory meetings, which the Moderator's health permitted him not to attend, did make our Assemblie needlessly long, and very tedious" while "his unacquaintance with the affaires of the committee before they came to the face of the Assemblie, made the reports unrype and unadvysed" so that they often had to be referred back to the committee concerned.[36]

This confusion in the 1648 assembly underlines the fact that, of course, some organisation, some management, was necessary if general assemblies were to achieve anything. With no rules of procedure, no committees to select and prepare business, assemblies would have dragged on endlessly. Realisation of this obvious fact was doubtless one of the main reasons that most members of the assemblies accepted the existence of the unofficial preparatory meetings and privy conferences. Nonetheless the success of the covenanters' management of the assemblies is surprising. Important matters over which the majority (or even a vocal minority) of members disagreed with the covenanting leaders were not put before the assembly, were held back until circumstances seemed favourable to them, or were referred to the commission of the kirk. Or they might be debated but no vote taken. Robert Wodrow wrote (in 1709) that in this period those whom he calls "the honest ministers" "durst scarce lett things of any ticklish nature come to a vote, but caryed things by the force of reasoning and their influence in their charrangues in open Assembly".[37] This certainly well describes the conduct of the covenanting leaders over complaints made against radical ministers for holding prayer meetings and

---

[35] H. Guthry, *Memoirs* (2nd ed., Glasgow, 1747), 136-8; Baillie, *Letters,* ii, 85.
[36] *Ibid.,* iii, 53.
[37] R. Wodrow, *Early Letters,* ed. L. W. Sharp (Scottish History Society, 1937), 303.

introducing innovations in worship; so far as possible discussion of these matters was confined to the privy conference and other committees, since the full assemblies were opposed to the radicals.[38]

Most ministers might accept such management, but they often did so grudgingly and suspiciously, to avoid trouble and being persecuted as malignants. Many were over-awed by their social superiors, nobles and lairds, who sat as elders. It is significant that the fears of moderate ministers were most openly expressed in the 1640 assembly, for this " confused misorder of a Generall Assemblie " was partly attributed to the fact that not so many nobles as usual sat as elders; " some of our respected nobles " were needed to keep the ministers in order.[39] Others, undeterred by respect for social superiors or fears of persecution, held their tongues for fear of causing disunity. The covenanting kirk was continually in danger from outside, as one political emergency followed another, and many felt that this obliged them to refrain from raising contentious issues. This was especially so in the 1638 assembly, when most of the votes taken were virtually unanimous, so that the voting process " grew but tedious to the hearers " since once it was heard how the first member whose name was called had voted it was clear what the result was going to be. Not surprisingly some put " ane ill constructione " on this, suspecting (no doubt correctly) that it showed " palpable praeagreement " among members.[40] Long debates and votes showing disunity would merely serve to encourage the king, so many voted with the majority in favour of acts they had doubts about; but it always tended to be the mass of moderate ministers who were thus brought to compromise for the sake of unity, not the radicals or the lay interests represented by the elders.

The privy conference had its origins in practical necessity — the need to prepare business to be put to the assembly — but soon came to overshadow its parent body.

The same may be said of the commission of the kirk; it developed in a period of crisis to meet the kirk's need to have some permanent, central body at a time when political changes effecting religion were quick and unpredictable. But from being a temporary convenience it soon developed into a court dominating the whole kirk. It was also like the privy conference in that it had precedents which might have given warning of the ways in which it would develop. In the sixteenth century commissions had often been appointed by general assemblies to discuss (after the assembly was dissolved) with the state matters con-

[38] See Stevenson, " The Radical Party ", 139, 140, 142-52, 154.
[39] Baillie, *Letters,* ii, 252. For the 1640 assembly see Stevenson, " The Radical Party ", 142-8.
[40] Gordon, *History,* ii, 39.

cerning the kirk, presenting proposals to or urging policies on the king, his officials, the privy council, or parliament.[41] But in the 1590s James VI had taken over the commission of the kirk for his own purposes. Previously he had denounced such commissions, but after 1594 he had usually managed to get men sympathetic to him appointed to advise him on church affairs, with commissions wide enough to allow them to make decisions in matters effecting the kirk. Men of presbyterian outlook saw clearly (at least in retrospect) that the commissions of the kirk became one of the main instruments of royal power over the kirk. John Row said of the 1594 commission that " This wes the first evident and seen wrack of our Kirk, and it was the thing that the King aimed at, and would faine have been at long before ". It allowed the king to get his own way more easily in religious affairs, having only to persuade a few commissioners to support him instead of a whole assembly. The commission " was ratified and amplified in severall ensueing Assemblies; and albeit there were many heavie complaints and greevous given in aganis thir commissioners, yet the King gott them ay continued, whereby great distractions among the ministers, and much miserie ensued ".[42] David Calderwood agreed, saying of the 1597 commissioners that " They were the king's led horse, and usurped boldly the power of the General Assembly and government of the whole kirk ".[43]

However, in the end the commission did not prove an effective instrument of royal control of the kirk, through which the king could exercise the ecclesiastical jurisdiction which he claimed, since it tended to regard itself as bound by decisions of the general assembly and as answerable to it. " The king had not succeeded in turning the commissioners into another committee of the articles and the Assembly into a rubber stamp ", and therefore (so Maurice Lee has argued) turned to a full revival of episcopacy to control the kirk. After 1600 commissioners of the kirk were still appointed, and still proved useful to the king, but their importance declined.[44]

Nonetheless, commissions of the kirk had played a significant part in bringing the kirk under royal control, and it is therefore hardly surprising to find that when they were revived by the covenanters many ministers showed deep suspicion of them. Yet

[41] D. Shaw, *The General Assemblies of the Church of Scotland, 1560-1600. Their Origins and Development* (Edinburgh, 1964), 172-3.

[42] Row, *History*, 162-3.

[43] Calderwood, *History*, v, 644, quoted in M. Lee " James VI and the Revival of Episcopacy in Scotland: 1596-1600 ", *Church History*, xliii (1974), 57. See also *loc. cit.* 50-64 and W. L. Mathieson, *Politics and Religion* (2 vols., Glasgow, 1902), i, 274.

[44] Lee, " James VI and the Revival of Episcopacy ", 63-4; Thomson, *Booke of the Universall Kirk*, iii, 959-60, 971-2, 996, 1057-8; Calderwood, *History*, vi, 121-2, 164-5, 177, 754; Mathieson, *Politics and Religion*, i, 257, 309-10.

in the circumstances of 1638-51 some such body was undoubtedly necessary; on the one hand to deal with the external relations of the kirk, negotiating with the state (the committee of estates and parliament), with English commissioners and with the king; on the other hand to maintain internal communications and discipline within the kirk by keeping ministers informed of events, exhorting them how to react to them, and disciplining dissidents. But such a body was open to two main criticisms; first, that by maintaining close relations with the state it was interfering in civil affairs, and second, that it represented a transfer of power from the ordinary courts of the church to an extraordinary one which had no legitimate place in a presbyterian system of government. By the late 1640s it was clear that both fears were justified.

Perhaps because of such doubts the commission of the kirk was at first only gradually revived after 1638. The Glasgow Assembly appointed only a limited commission, in the form of " An Act appointing the commissioners to attend the Parliament ", to represent the desires of the assembly that acts of parliament be passed to add civil sanctions to religious ones to legitimise the changes made in the kirk.[45] Even such a limited commission roused doubts; Robert Baillie evidently thought it was incompatible with an act just passed forbidding ministers to exercise civil office or power.[46] Other powers which later assemblies were to give to the commission of the kirk were delegated in 1638 to separate commissions, such as those appointed to purge the kirk of anti-covenanting ministers,[47] while power to summon a general assembly in an emergency was granted to the presbytery of Edinburgh.[48]

In the 1639 assembly it was again proposed to nominate a commission to represent articles to parliament, but the earl of Traquair (the king's commissioner) refused to allow this. Charles I had specifically stated that " We will not allow of any Commissioners from the Assembly, nor no such Act as may give ground for the continuing of the Tables or Conventicles ".[49] But in the end Traquair weakly compromised; he agreed to a commission to attend parliament being granted to the presbytery of Edinburgh, on condition that it only met at its usual times.[50] In 1640 and 1641 the assembly reverted to appointing commissioners to attend parliament[51] without any further royal protests,

[45] Peterkin, *Records*, 47; Balfour, *Historical Works*, iii, 313-15.
[46] Baillie, *Letters*, i, 174-5.
[47] Peterkin, *Records*, 47, 181.
[48] *Ibid.*, 40.
[49] G. Burnet, *The Memoires of the Lives and Actions of James and William, Dukes of Hamilton* (London, 1677), 150.
[50] Peterkin, *Records*, 209, 265, 270; Stevenson, *Scottish Revolution, 1637-44*, 165.
[51] Peterkin, *Records*, 297; Baillie, *Letters*, i, 376-7.

but Charles I was right in regarding the appointing of commissioners to parliament as a pretext to establish a standing commission to provide central control of the religious side of the covenanting movement, as the unofficial " table " or meeting of ministers had done in 1637-8. The commissioners to attend parliament are thus frequently referred to simply as the commissioners of the general assembly or of the kirk.[52] And they did much more than just attend parliament. In February 1640 and December 1641 (and doubtless on other occasions) " the Commissioners of the Generall Assembly " sent supplications to the king.[53] In September 1639 they felt qualified to intervene in a serious dispute between moderate and radical ministers, and to work out a compromise settlement.[54]

Opponents of the commission of the kirk were thus right to see its origins in these commissions to attend parliament of 1638-41. James Gordon, minister of Rothiemay, wrote of the 1640 commission, " Thus was the foundatione laid of that extravagant churche judicatorye, which wantes all precedent in all antiquitie; which, in the following yeares, grew so troublesome to the state. . . . We will see this judicatory, which heer appeared but lycke a cloude of the bignesse of ones hands, in end, in the yeares following, covering the whole heavene. . . . The comissione of the Church I meane, which in following Assemblyes was lickd into a shape, midwyfed by politicians, and its power added to it by peece meale, in a surreptitiouse waye; not all at once, for that would have startled the creators of it of the ministrye, who did beginne to qwarell with its usurpatione too late ". The commission destroyed church, king, and country,[55] and " did engrosse almost all the power of the Generall Assemblye ".[56]

It was in 1642 that the commission finally emerged with the title that it was to keep until the end of the covenanting period, " The Commission for the Public Affairs of the Kirk "; there was no longer a parliament sitting or about to sit to make its former title plausible. Moderates in the assembly expressed fears that the new commission would encroach on the normal courts of the church, but such doubters were assured " that this commission was not to meddle with the affairs belonging to the ordinary judicatures; but only to correspond with the English

---

[52] E.g., National Library of Scotland, Wodrow MS Folio LXIV, nos. 30, 31 (overtures and articles presented to parliament in 1639); Wodrow MS Folio LXV, no. 3 (minutes of the commission of the kirk, August-November 1641); *The Acts of Parliament of Scotland*, ed. T. Thomson and C. Innes (12 vols., 1814-75), v, 263, 277, 279, 594, 595, 598, 645-6.
[53] *Calendar of State Papers, Domestic, 1639-40* (London, 1874), 472; Baillie, *Letters*, ii, 476-8.
[54] Stevenson, " The Radical Party in the Kirk ", 140.
[55] Gordon, *History*, ii, 165.
[56] *Ibid.*, iii, 221.

for promoting reformation there, and to continue no longer than that cause required ".[57] The commission granted by the assembly duly stressed that the main duties of the commissioners concerned negotiations with the English, but it also authorised them to determine any other matter committed to them, and gave them power " as any Commissions of Generall Assemblies have had, and have been in use of before ".[58] This was conveniently vague, and could be used to justify almost any action by the commission. No wonder Robert Baillie, after stating that the commission " which before was of small use, is lyke to become almost a constant judicatorie, and verie profitable ", commented that it was " of so high a straine, that to some it is terrible allreadie ".[59]

Such fears were justified. The commission was soon looking not only outwards through negotiations with the state, the English and the king,[60] it was also looking inwards at the condition of the church, and sending orders to other church courts. In January 1643 the commission issued a declaration denouncing the royalist inspired " Cross-Petition ", and sent orders to presbyteries that all ministers were to read the declaration from their puplits, together with a warning about the political situation.[61] This was, thought Baillie, " a verie good and necessar, bot a most peremptor and extraordinar course " which was " lyke to get punctuall obedience by all the ministers of the land ".[62] This was a little over optimistic; many moderate ministers not only disliked the contents of the declaration and warning, they questioned the right of the commission to order presbyteries to have them read. The presbytery of Stirling boldly wrote " We doubt if the generall assemblie meaned that this commission wherof 12 ministers with 3 ruling elders make a quorum should emit conclusions obligatorie to the whole church of Scotland, and urge the publication therof by the whole ministrie so peremptorlie ". This " seemeth to ws to come too neer the usurped power of the 12 pretended bishops ".[63] Bishops were not

---

[57] Guthry, *Memoirs*, 120-1.
[58] Peterkin, *Records*, 330-1; J. Spalding, *Memorialls of the Trubles*, ed. J. Stuart (2 vols., Spalding Club, 1850-1), ii, 173-4.
[59] Baillie, *Letters*, ii, 55.
[60] E.g., Stevenson, *Scottish Revolution, 1637-44*, 252, 258-60, 278-9; SRO, CH.8/110 (petition to the king, 1642); J. Rushworth, *Historical Collections* (8 vols., London, 1659-1701), III, ii, 406-10.
[61] Stevenson, *Scottish Revolution, 1637-44*, 260-1; Guthry, *Memoirs*, 125; *A Declaration against the Crosse Petition . . . By the Commissioners of the Generall Assembly* (Edinburgh, 1643); *A Necessary Warning to the Ministers of the Kirk of Scotland* (Edinburgh, 1643).
[62] Baillie, *Letters*, ii, 59-60.
[63] University of Edinburgh, New College Library, MS of Baillie's Letters and Journals, ii, ff. 140r-141v, 16th February 1643, Presbytery of Stirling to [Robert Douglas, moderator of the commission?]. Folios 141v-145r contain " Observations " on the letter.

the only form of tyranny that might trouble the kirk. However, in the end, the presbytery of Stirling "to our great joy . . . became better advysed" and obeyed the commission.[64]

The presbytery of Auchterarder resisted longer; the 1643 general assembly suspended one minister from it and rebuked several others for defying the commission and admitting "a great number of gentle men who were not ruling Elders" to the presbytery when the commission's orders were discussed. The presbytery was thus "made an example to all who would be turbulent".[65] Outside the church courts the royalist William Drummond of Hawthornden sarcastically denounced "the Great Commissioners of the General Assembly, Inquisitors of the Faith, and Men of unerring Spirit", "haughty by their Place and Arbitrary Power",[66] but his protests had no more effect than those of the presbyteries; the first major challenge to the growing power of the commission had been easily defeated, for most accepted the need for unity to preserve the kirk.

When a convention of estates met in June 1643 to consider intervention in the English civil war the commission presented it with outspoken remonstrances urging the need for intervention.[67] Some doubts were expressed from within the commission about whether such interference in civil affairs was justified, but the ubiquitous Wariston cited precedents persuading members that such remonstrances had once been customary.[68] Within a few months the commission appointed by the 1643 assembly was busy, on its orders, in imposing the solemn league and covenant on the kirk.[69] Many no doubt still suspected the power of the commission, but were terrorised into silence or accepted the need for strong central control in an emergency situation. Henry Guthry (who had been active in the presbytery of Stirling in opposing the commission, and had expressed doubts about the new alliance with the English) later wrote that at this time "this new-modelled commission of the general assembly (notwithstanding the fair professions made two years ago, when it was first established . . .) assumed a legislative power and enjoined obedience to their acts, *sub poena*; Yea, they became so tyrannical, that it may be admired how so much violence and

[64] Baillie, *Letters*, ii, 63, 76.
[65] SRO, CH.1/1/9, Acts and Proceedings of the General Assemblies, 1642-6, pp. 36-9, of account of 1643 assembly; Baillie, *Letters*, ii, 76, 86, 91-2. The claim in Spalding, *History*, ii, 228, that 14 presbyteries refused to read the declaration is evidently a wild exaggeration.
[66] W. Drummond, *Works* (Edinburgh, 1711), 194. This was probably one of bitter papers which Baillie refers to as having been circulated against the commission, Baillie, *Letters*, ii, 76.
[67] *The Remonstrance of the Commissioners of the General Assembly . . . June 1643* (Edinburgh, 1643); *Acts of Parliament of Scotland*, VI, i, 7, 9-11; Guthry, *Memoirs*, 132-3.
[68] Baillie, *Letters*, ii, 75; Stevenson, *Scottish Revolution 1637-44*, 278-9.
[69] *Ibid.*, 290; Peterkin, *Records*, 359-60; Guthry, *Memoirs*, 141.

cruelty (as already began to appear amongst them) could lodge in the breast of churchmen, who pretended to such piety, as did Mr Douglas, Dickson, Blair, Cant, and some others, who over-ruled the commission at their pleasure; there being nothing but the worst they could do, to be expected by any that should happen in the least to oppose them. This prevailed upon men to submit, for exchewing persecution ".[70] Few would have expressed hatred of the commission in such extreme terms, but many would have agreed with Guthry's basic arguments.

By 1644 the commission had assumed power to depose ministers who were not staunch enough covenanters.[71] Protests at this soon appeared. In 1647 David Calderwood tried to deprive the commission of such powers,[72] and won at least partial agree-ment from the general assembly; in future the commission was only to carry out depositions at quarterly meetings, at which more commissioners than usual were expected to be present.[73]

The following year more general opposition to the commis-sion emerged. The assembly agreed to revive a 1601 act whereby trial of the conduct of the commissioners was to be the first act of each assembly;[74] a supplication "for moderating, in some things, the power of the Commission of the Church " was circulated; and the Engagers were said to have resolved that if their army succeeded in England they would abolish the com-mission "as a judicatorie not yet established by law ". In the event of course the Engagers failed in England, and the next general assembly (1649) denounced the supplication as having " been ane overthrowing, in favour of the malignant partie, the power of the Kirk ".[75] Opposition to the commission was now taken to be proof of malignancy.

In these circumstances it is hardly surprising to find that the most sustained attack on the commission came from someone beyond its jurisdiction. In March 1649 William Spang, minister to the Scottish congregation at Campvere in Holland, wrote " Generally, the grit pouer quhilk the Commission of the Kirk exerceth displeaseth all: It is but a extraordinary meeting, and yet sits constantly and more ordinarily than any Synod; yea and without the knouledge of provincial Synods and Presbyteries, deposes ministers, injoyns, pro authotitate, what write they please to be read, inflicts censures on these who will not read them. If the Kirk of Scotland look not to this in tyme, we will

[70] *Ibid.*, 148.
[71] E.g., H. Scott (ed.), *Fasti Ecclesiae Scoticanae* (9 vols., Edinburgh, 1915-50), iv, 258; there was a precedent of 1597 for commissions of the kirk deposing ministers, Lee, " James VI and the Revival of Episcopacy ", 57.
[72] Baillie, *Letters,* iii, 21.
[73] Peterkin, *Records,* 477-8, 514-15, 549-50.
[74] *Ibid.,* 496.
[75] Baillie, *Letters,* iii, 65, 95.

lament it when we cannot mend it. They say four or fyve rule that meeting; and is not the liberty of the Kirk come to a fair market thereby. . . . For God's saik, look this course in tyme be stopped, else the Commission of the Kirk will swallow up all uther ecclesiastick judicatories; and such ministers who reside in and about Edinburgh, sall at last ingross all church pouer in their hands. I know ther is a peece of prudence herby used, to get the pouer in the hands of these who are good; but what assurance have we but they may change, or uthers, following this course, creeping into their places. . . . I wishe we used prudence, leist we open a door to tyrannie, whilst we think to shut out tyrants out of the Kirk ".[76]

The charges that the commission came to exercise great power over other church courts, and that the power of the commission was exercised by a few leading ministers were true. The minutes of the commission which survive (after 1646)[77] indicate that a large proportion of its time was devoted to sending instructions and advice on a great variety of matters to synods and presbyteries, and to investigating the conduct of both ministers and laymen, and punishing them; functions which many thought should rest mainly in the hands of lower courts. When it came to persecution the commission of the kirk's activities were on a much larger scale (and were much more effective) than those of the old court of high commission, which the covenanters had denounced as worse than the Spanish Inquisition.[78]

As to power within the commission, it does seem to be true that the same ministers and elders who usually dominated the general assembly also dominated the commission. In 1642 the assembly left it to the moderator and the clerk to "consider of a list of the fittest Persons" to be on the commission,[79] and this procedure was probably also followed in subsequent years. Membership of the commission could thus be decided in the privy conference. The minutes indicate that a fairly small group of ministers, appointed to sit on the commission year after year came to wield great powers; they were the experts, with great experience, the well known public figures, to whom other members deferred. Much business was referred to committees of the commission, and on these committees the same few names tended to recur again and again. Robert Douglas was not only moderator of the general assembly five times, he became virtually the constant moderator of the commission. His name occurs as moderator of the 1642-3 commission, and of that of

[76] Ibid., iii, 81-2.
[77] A. F. Mitchell and J. Christie (eds.), The Records of the Commissions of the General Assemblies [RCGA], (3 vols., Scottish History Society, 1892-1909).
[78] Stevenson, Scottish Revolution, 1637-44, 180.
[79] SRO, CH./1/1/9, account of 1642 assembly, p. 74.

1643-4 until he left to join the Scottish army in England (whereupon William Bennet took over).[80] In 1646-7 Robert Blair moderated at first but later William Bennet and Robert Douglas sat in his absence. In 1647-8 Douglas moderated, and in 1648-9 he took over from George Gillespie who fell ill soon after being appointed moderator. In 1649-50 and 1650-1 Douglas again moderated.[81] Like Douglas, most of the ministers who dominated the commission were men who had parishes in or relatively near Edinburgh, for not surprisingly these were the members who attended meetings most regularly. At least one meeting indeed consisted of ministers entirely from the synod of Lothian and Tweeddale who happened to be in Edinburgh for the synod when a meeting of the commission was called at short notice.[82]

For most of the covenanting period the commission of the kirk was the instrument of the more extreme covenanters for controlling the kirk between meetings of the general assembly. It by no means gave them absolute power; they always had to limit their ambitions to some extent in deference to the more moderate ministers, to elders, and to lay covenanters outside the church courts. Nonetheless, their management of the assembly and the commission gave them far greater influence in the kirk than numbers alone entitled them to. But eventually internal disputes among the leading covenanters altered this situation. In 1650-1 the more extreme and the more moderate leading ministers of the kirk party split on political issues, especially over attitudes to Charles II and the English Commonwealth. The more moderate men of the kirk party, like Robert Douglas and Robert Blair, began to favour making concessions to the king and his allies; these were bitterly opposed by the extremists. With the leading covenanting ministers divided among themselves the opinions of the mass of moderate ministers came to be heard increasingly — and the more extreme no longer had powerful lay support to counteract this. They tried to continue to " manage " the central courts of the kirk but failed, and their efforts at management roused increasing resentment, even from some who had formerly co-operated with them; it is rather strange to find Robert Baillie writing " I have oft regrated of late to see the Judicatories of the Church soe easily ledd to whatever some few of our busie men designed "[83] since in the past he himself had been not the least of these " busie men ".

First the extremists (now the remonstrant or protester party) lost control of the commission of the kirk; they withdrew from it when (still under Douglas's moderation) it rejected the

[80] SRO, CH.8/110; Guthry, *Memoirs,* 149.
[81] *RCGA.,* passim, especially i, 6-7, 10, 22, 304, ii, 7, 35, 302, iii, 7.
[82] *Ibid.,* i, 515.
[83] Baillie, *Letters,* iii, 115.

Western Remonstrance.[84] They then demanded that the members of the commission who opposed them be tried by the 1651 general assembly, and claimed that, as their opponents were to be tried by the assembly they could not sit in it. This was one of the management tricks that had been used in 1638 to exclude the bishops and their supporters from the Glasgow Assembly. Now, however, it failed to work; the extremists were isolated and their demands ignored. The assembly approved the work of the commission, whereupon the protesters withdrew from the assembly and refused to recognise its legitimacy.[85] Having failed to "manage" the more moderate majority in the kirk any longer, the extremists disowned it.

APPENDIX: MEMBERSHIPS AND ATTENDANCES

Complete membership rolls survive for the general assemblies of 1638 and for 1643-6, along with incomplete ones for 1639 and 1642.[86] In the complete rolls membership varies between 163 and 237, while the percentage of elders among members fluctuates from 31% to 43%, as Table 1[87] indicates:

Year	1638	1643	1644	1645	1646
Ministers	142 (60%)	137 (59%)	134 (62%)	128 (57%)	113 (69%)
Nobles	16 (7%)	17 (7%)	10 (5%)	22 (10%)	6 (4%)
Lairds	33 (14%)	44 (19%)	45 (21%)	35 (16%)	29 (18%)
Burgesses	46 (19%)	36 (15%)	27 (12%)	38 (17%)	15 (9%)
Total Elders	95 (40%)	97 (41%)	82 (38%)	95 (43%)	50 (31%)
Total	237	234	216	223	163

TABLE 1: Membership of the General Assembly, 1638, 1643-6

Analysis of the rolls for 1643-6 show that in these four years about 345 different ministers sat in the assembly (about a third of the total number of ministers). About 226 of them attended only one assembly, 88 attended two, 20 attended three and 11 attended all four.[88] Elders were less likely to attend assemblies regularly; of about 260 elders who sat in 1643-6 no fewer than 203 sat only once. Thus about 80% of the elders sat only once in four years, compared with about 65% of the ministers.

---

[84] *RCGA*, iii, 132; W. Stephen (ed.), *Register of the Consultations of the Ministers of Edinburgh* (2 vols., Scottish History Society, 1921-30), i, 300-1.
[85] Peterkin, *Records*, 626-7, 629, 630-2.
[86] *Ibid.*, 109-11, 237-8; SRO, CH.1/1/9.
[87] In Table 1 the figures for ministers include the few university commissioners — 2 (1%) in 1638 and 4 (2%) in the other four assemblies.
[88] These figures can only be approximate; in a few cases two ministers of the same name may have been treated as one, while a few who changed parishes and therefore sat in different assemblies for different presbyteries may have been counted twice.

Of the elders who had sat in the Glasgow Assembly of 1638 under one-third (about 30 out of 95) appear in any of the 1643-6 assemblies, compared with over half of the ministers who had been present in 1638 (at least 75 out of 142). This confirms the pattern that ministers were more likely to attend several assemblies than elders.

These figures do not at first sight appear to support charges that the general assemblies of this period were made up of much the same members, with just a few changed;[89] what gave this impression was the fact that year after year the most prominent men in the assemblies remained the same. Those who sat in all four assemblies in 1643-6 included David Dickson, David Calderwood and James Guthrie, while Robert Blair and Andrew Cant attended three of the four.[90]

Membership of the commission of the kirk (see Table 2) between 1642-3 and 1650-1 varied between 73 and 163, while the proportion of elders moved between 34% and 43%[91] — roughly the same proportions as in the general assembly.

	1642-3	1643-4	1644-5	1645-6	1646-7
Ministers	48 (66%)	53 (59%)	70 (57%)	105 (65%)	89 (63%)
Nobles	10 (14%)	16 (18%)	20 (16%)	23 (14%)	15 (11%)
Lairds	8 (11%)	13 (14%)	20 (16%)	20 (12%)	24 (17%)
Burgesses	7 (10%)	8 (9%)	13 (11%)	13 (8%)	14 (10%)
Total Elders	25 (34%)	37 (41%)	53 (43%)	56 (35%)	53 (37%)
Total	73	90	123	161	142

	1647-8	1648-9	1649-50	1650-1
Ministers	97 (62%)	100 (63%)	96 (59%)	90 (60%)
Nobles	19 (12%)	12 (8%)	11 (7%)	13 (9%)
Lairds	29 (19%)	30 (19%)	40 (25%)	30 (20%)
Burgesses	11 (7%)	17 (11%)	16 (10%)	18 (12%)
Total Elders	59 (38%)	59 (37%)	67 (41%)	61 (40%)
Total	156	159	163	151

TABLE 2: Membership of the Commission of the Kirk, 1642-51

A total of about 296 different ministers were appointed to sit on the nine commissions of 1642-51. Only five sat nine times (Robert Blair, Robert Douglas, David Dickson, Andrew Cant, Samuel Rutherford), nine sat eight times (including Robert

---

[89] Gordon, *History*, iii, 249.
[90] In 1643-6 Alexander Henderson, Robert Baillie, George Gillespie and Samuel Rutherford could not sit in the assembly regularly since they spent much of their time in England attending the Westminster Assembly.
[91] Membership of, and attendance at, the commissions of 1651-2 and 1652-3 have been omitted since by then the kirk was split by schism and the commission had lost most of its power.

Baillie, Patrick Gillespie and David Calderwood), and five sat seven times. As with the figures for membership of the assembly these figures do not fully bear out complaints that the commission consisted of exactly the same men year after year.[92] But, again as with the assembly, the commission was dominated by a relatively small number of ministers who sat regularly; of the 296 ministers appointed to the commission 190 were appointed only once, and thus had little chance to gain experience or reputation. Moreover though membership of the commission was large, regular attendance was not; as Table 3[93] shows the commission was in practice a fairly small body. Many members seldom if ever attended, while a few sat almost continuously. On average meetings of the commissions of 1646-7 to 1649-50 were attended by only one-fifth of members, those of the 1650-1 commission by less than one-sixth of members.

	1646-7	1647-8	1648-9	1649-50	1650-1
Ministers	22	25	21	24	20
Elders	7	6	8	7	4
Total	29	31	29	31	24

TABLE 3: Average number of Members present at meetings of the Commission of the Kirk, 1646-51

Analysis of attendances at the commission's meetings indicates that ministers were better attenders than elders. Table 4 shows, for each commission, the result of dividing the percentage of total membership of the commission constituted by each group within it, into the percentage of total attendances at meetings constituted by each group. A score of over one indicates that members of that group attended more frequently than the average member. Thus, for example, in 1646-7 ministers made up 63% of membership of the commission, but they accounted for 77% of attendances at meetings, so ministers score (on Table 4) 77 ÷ 63 = 1.2. Ministers consistently score over one, elders less than one. Among elders, the nobles emerge as the least frequent attenders.

	1646-7	1647-8	1648-9	1649-50	1650-1
Ministers	1.2	1.3	1.2	1.3	1.4
Nobles	.3	.2	.4	.6	.3
Lairds	.8	.5	.9	.6	.6
Burgesses	.6	.8	.5	.4	.4
Total Elders	.6	.5	.7	.5	.5

TABLE 4: Attendance at the Commission of the Kirk, 1646-51

If the lay covenanters were determined to retain ultimate control of the kirk (as has been argued in this paper and else-

[92] Guthry, *Memoirs*, 148, 177-8, 221, 281.
[93] Calculated from the sederunts in *RCGA*, passim.

where),[94] why did they show so little interest in trying (as elders) to dominate the commission of the kirk? Probably this was a sign of the confidence of the leading lay covenanters, of their belief that the ministers well realised that the covenanting reformation had only been possible through lay support, and that therefore they had to avoid alienating lay interests. Laymen did not need to attend church courts in strength as elders in order to make their influence felt. If this was the case, such confidence proved misplaced in 1648 when the commission defied the state by denouncing the Engagement. But when this happened the noble elders simply withdrew from the commission; at the last 84 meetings of the 1647-8 commission (13th March-12th May 1648) noble elders were present on only 13 occasions.[95] Instead of sitting more regularly to try to win over the commission they turned their backs on it, confident that they could successfully defy the commission and even the general assembly. Events proved that the Engagers were correct; it was defeat in England that destroyed them, not the opposition of the kirk, though the latter was certainly a serious nuisance to them.

[94] Stevenson, *Scottish Revolution, 1637-44.*
[95] *RCGA*, ii, 389-50. Even some of the elders who undoubtedly had a deep interest in the government of the kirk often failed to attend meetings of the commission regularly, since much of their time was taken up with affairs of state. Thus in 1646-51 the marquis of Argyll and Johnston of Wariston were each present at only 49 meetings of the commission out of a total of 559 recorded.

XIV

Deposition of Ministers in the Church of Scotland Under the Covenanters, 1638-1651

The period 1638-1651 saw the first major purges of the ministry of the reformed kirk in Scotland since the Reformation. These were the forerunners of the later great purges associated with the Restoration (of monarchy and episcopacy) in the 1660s and with the Revolution and re-establishment of presbyterianism in 1688-1690. Before 1638, for all the conflicts within the kirk and in its relations with the state, deposition of ministers had been rare. J. K. Hewison's estimate of 49 deprivations or depositions in 1560-1638 is probably too low, but is of the right order.[1] No detailed study of depositions under the covenanters has ever been made. Hewison calculated that 138 ministers were deprived in the whole of the period 1638-1660, but this figure is far too low.[2] More recent estimates (again covering 1638-1660) of about 200,[3] and of about 210[4] depositions come much nearer the truth, but they also are too low; there were more depositions than this even in 1638-1651. Considering the importance attached to the depositions after 1660 and after 1688 as indicating the acceptability to ministers of the religious changes then introduced and the extent of persecution, it is rather surprising that so little attention has been paid to the predecessors of these purges—though James Bulloch's two useful local studies of depositions do cover the whole of the seventeenth century.[5]

Too many records of the kirk's courts have been lost for a complete list of ministers deprived in 1638-1651 ever to be compiled, but enough material has survived to make a study of the matter profitable. By far the most important source of information on the subject is the *Fasti Ecclesiae Scoticanae*.[6] The *Fasti* is far from perfect; it omits a few depositions, and includes erroneously a few which never took place, but nonetheless it has provided the skeleton of this study—and a good deal of the flesh as well. Surviving records of the general assembly[7] and the commission for the public affairs of the kirk,[8] together with printed extracts from synod, presbytery and kirk session records[9] have been utilized, and the printed narrative

1. J. K. Hewison, *The Covenanters*, 2 vols. (Glasgow, 1913), 1:496.
2. Ibid.
3. G. Donaldson, *Scotland: James V to James VII* (Edinburgh and London, 1965), pp. 365-366.
4. A. L. Drummond and J. Bulloch, *The Scottish Church, 1688-1843* (Edinburgh, 1973), p. 5.
5. J. Bulloch, "Conformists and Nonconformists," *Transactions of the East Lothian Antiquarian and Field Naturalists Society* 8 (1960): 70-84; idem, "Ecclesiastical Intolerance in Seventeenth Century Berwickshire," *History of the Berwickshire Naturalists' Club* 36 (1962-64): 148-58.
6. H. Scott, ed., *Fasti Ecclesiae Scoticanae*, 8 vols. (Edinburgh, 1915-50).
7. A. Peterkin, ed., *Records of the Kirk of Scotland, containing the Acts and Proceedings of the General Assemblies* (Edinburgh, 1838); Scottish Record Office (hereafter SRO), CH. 1/1/9, Acts and Proceedings of the General Assemblies, 1642-1646.
8. A. F. Mitchell and J. Christie, eds., *The Records of the Commissioners of the General Assemblies of the Church of Scotland, 1646-1652* (hereafter RCGA), 3 vols. (Edinburgh, 1892-1909).
9. For these see P. Gouldesbrough, A. P. Kup and I. Lewis, eds., *Handlist of Scottish and Welsh Record Publications* (London, 1954).

Reprinted with permission from *Church History* 44 (September 1975), pp. 321-335

322

sources for the period have also proved rich sources of information.[10] Little use, however, has been made of manuscript records of synods, presbyteries and kirk sessions,[11] since most relevant information from these records has been incorporated in the *Fasti*. A detailed search of them might reveal a few depositions previously overlooked, but the amount of work involved would be disproportionate to the results. Reliance mainly on printed material has undoubtedly revealed the great majority of depositions of which any record survives, and there is no reason to suppose that the few other cases which may remain concealed in the manuscript records would alter the conclusions of this study in any way.[12]

Deprivation or deposition is defined as the removal by church courts of a minister from his parish and ministry. Alexander Henderson as moderator of the 1638 general assembly explained that whereas the Church of England made a distinction between deprivation (taking away the benefice), deposition (taking away the office) and degradation (taking away of ordination), in Scotland "deprivation and deposition we take to be ane, becaus, when he is depryved of his benefice, so of his office" and there was no formal degradation.[13]

The great majority of cases making up the figures cited below are ones of proved deposition, together with a few where deposition is very probable (about eleven cases). With some hesitation, a few other cases have been included which amount to concealed deposition. At least six ministers demitted, or resigned, under pressure in circumstances which strongly suggest that they would have been deposed had they not done so. Thus, for example, John Barron (Kemback: St. Andrews)[14] demitted in 1648 while under investigation (and already suspended from the ministry) for not preaching against the engagers,[15] and James Carmichael (Cleish: Dunfermline) demitted in 1649, "being sensible of his weakness for the ministrie."[16] In particularly grave cases, however, demission was not accepted; Christopher Knowles (Coldingham: Chirnside) was deposed for adultery and other faults in 1641 though he had offered to resign.[17] Another method of getting rid of a minister without actual deposition was for the church courts simply to declare his parish vacant. This was done in two instances in Haddington Presbytery on the grounds that the ministers concerned had never been lawfully admitted to the ministry. In 1639 the Synod of Lothian and Tweeddale declared that John Trotter (Dirleton) had never been properly admitted, and in 1641 Alexander

10. The most important of these being R. Baillie, *Letters and Journals*, ed., D. Laing, 3 vols. (Edinburgh, 1841-42); J. Balfour, *Historical Works*, ed., J. Haig, 4 vols. (Edinburgh, 1824-25); J. Gordon, *History of Scots Affairs*, ed. J. Robertson and G. Grub, 3 vols. (Aberdeen, 1841); H. Guthry, *Memoirs* (Glasgow, 1747); and J. Spalding, *Memorialls of the Trubles*, ed. J. Stuart, 2 vols. (Aberdeen, 1850-51).
11. See *Records of the Church of Scotland preserved in the Scottish Record Office and General Register Office* . . . (Glasgow, 1967).
12. Considerations of space prevent inclusion of a full list of the ministers deposed and of sources of information about them; instead a table showing the distribution of depositions has been appended to this article, and the main sources have been listed above.
13. Peterkin, *Records of the Kirk*, p. 160.
14. After the name of each minister, the names of his parish and of its presbytery are given in brackets; where only one name appears the name of the parish and the presbytery were the same.
15. Scott, *Fasti*, 5:206; [G. R. Kinloch, ed.], *Selections from the Minutes of the Synod of Fife* (Edinburgh, 1837), Appendix, p. 257; [G. R. Kinloch, ed.], *Selections from the Minutes of the Presbyteries of St. Andrews and Cupar* (Edinburgh, 1837), pp. 44-45; *RCGA*, 2:287-288.
16. Scott, *Fasti*, 5:61.
17. Ibid., 2:36-37; Bulloch, "Berwickshire," p. 150; Baillie, *Letters*, 1:165; Gordon, *History*, 2:143-145.

Trotter (Bara), who was perhaps John's brother, met with the same treatment.[18] In at least three other cases opponents of the covenant who had fled from their parishes had them declared vacant through their desertion; again. these have been counted as depositions.

Thus the figures for depositions include known depositions, very probable depositions, forcible demissions and parishes declared vacant. They do not, however, include the many cases where ministers simply disappeared without trace; it is true that some of these men probably were deposed, but most doubtless simply died or resigned. Therefore to have included them would have greatly exaggerated the extent of depositions, especially in areas where local church court records have been lost.[19] Furthermore, only depositions of parish ministers are included in this study. Thus the twelve bishops and two archbishops deposed in 1638 are not included, though John Guthrie, the former bishop of Moray, is included since in 1639 he was deposed from the ministry of Elgin, which he had held along with his bishopric.[20] Similarly depositions of university staff are excluded unless the individual concerned was also deprived of a parish ministry—like John Barron, forced to demit the principalship of St. Salvator's College, St. Andrews as well as the ministry of Kemback.[21]

Finally, before describing the course of depositions in these years, something must be said about their significance. James Bulloch has written that depositions offer a guide to the extent of persecution "so long as the reader does not regard one example . . . as tyranny and another as simple justice."[22] This is entirely justified insofar as it is a warning not to take depositions by one faction as persecution, those by another as justifiable. It is also valid as a warning against being taken in by the convenanters' tendency "to blacken the opposition to the ruling party."[23] But it is misleading if it be taken to imply that every deposition must be seen as resulting from factional persecution. Certainly charges of immorality were often added to charges of heresy, of opposing the covenanters or of royalist tendencies; but this does not mean that no charge of immorality was ever true. In many of the cases where the only charges against a minister were of immorality it seems likely that they were the true reason for deposition. The covenanters were not ashamed of deposing men for opposing them. They might add charges of immorality to others being made against their enemies, but there is no evidence that they proceeded against their factional enemies on charges of immorality alone, suppressing the real reasons for the deposition. Clear cases of deposition resulting solely from immortality can be found: William Wedderburn (Meldrum: Garioch) was deposed in 1642 for fornication, which (according to a royalist source) he confessed.[24] The most striking such case is that of Thomas Lamb (Kirkurd: Peebles). He had been deposed from Glen-

---

18. Scott, *Fasti*, 1:294, 359, 365; Bulloch, "Conformists and Nonconformists," p. 73.
19. Thus Bulloch, "Berwickshire," p. 151 refers to twelve ministers deposed in Berwickshire after the engagement. Of these, three were evidently deposed in 1652-1659 and are therefore outside the scope of the present study. But of the remaining nine I know of evidence for the deposition of only four; the other five just disappear. Two are known to have been suspended, but there is no evidence of their deposition; two more probably continued in the ministry until their deaths, while the fifth was probably never settled in his parish.
20. Scott, *Fasti*, 7:351; Peterkin, *Records of the Kirk*, pp. 27-28.
21. Scott, *Fasti*, 5:206, 7:411.
22. Bulloch, "Berwickshire," p. 148.
23. Ibid., p. 150.
24. Scott, *Fasti*, 6:173; Spalding, *Memorialls*, 2:136, 203, 260.

324

luce for opposition to royal religious policies in 1629, but was restored to the ministry by the covenanters ten years later. In 1641, while already suspended on a charge of killing a man, he murdered a farmer. For this he was deposed, and then executed by the civil authorities; that he had committed the crime on the Sabbath roused added indignation, but hardly makes it plausible to argue that it was really the strict sabbatarianism of the covenanters that led to his deposition![25]

How often immorality alone—fornication, adultery, drunkenness, swearing, gambling—led to deposition is impossible to calculate: in many cases we have no direct evidence of why depositions were carried out. From the information that is available a figure of ten or fifteen might be suggested. About the same number were probably deposed solely for "insufficiency"—failure to carry out the duties of of a minister adequately through weakness, laziness or (more commonly) sickness or old age. Insufficiency, like immorality, might be added to other charges to blacken the character of an enemy, but where it was the only charge it was in most cases probably the real reason for the deposition. Thus in 1643 the Synod of Argyll deposed James Mc'Kirdie (Kilmorie in Arran: Kintyre) as unfit through age to exercise spiritual functions, but allowed him to retain two thirds of his stipend.[26] In 1642 the Synod of Galloway deposed George Kincaid (Mochrum: Wigtown) when he was nearly eighty for insufficiency. The general assembly declared that this was unjust, and ordered his restoration on condition that he accept a helper or assistant[27]—a common expedient whereby an old minister could retain part of his stipend while a younger man carried out the work of the ministry. Harshness would not have been tempered with charity in such cases had those deposed really been opponents of the covenant. However, such cases of deposition for immorality or insufficiency were only a small proportion of the total; perhaps 10 per cent. The rest were depositions of those who opposed, or failed to support enthusiastically enough, the predominant faction in the kirk.

Depositions began as soon as the covenanters took over effective control of Scotland in 1638. In the autumn three ministers were deposed by presbyteries or synods, and one minister who fled was replaced. The general assembly held in Glasgow in December deposed about eleven more. Of these fifteen known depositions in 1638, eleven were in the five synods south of the River Forth (Glasgow and Ayr; Lothian and Tweeddale; Merse and Teviotdale; Dumfries; Galloway), and two more in Fife, just to the north.[28] Many more complaints against ministers were given in by presbyteries than the assembly had time to discuss. To deal with them, as Alexander Henderson put it, "it is expedient . . . to appoynt Commissions through the Kingdome, for discussing of complaints and Lybells given in against Ministers." He added that "if the Church were well established in her owne power and jurisdiction, there could be no neid of such Commissions" which were to decide cases "in such partes of the countrie where provinciall Assemblies cannot be had."[29] In fact many of the commissions were for areas where there was no difficulty holding provincial assemblies or synods; commissions were appointed to sit in Edinburgh, St. Andrews, Dundee, Forres, Chanonry, Irvine,

25. Scott, *Fasti*, 1:276-277, 2:348; Baillie, *Letters*, 1:367-368, 383.
26. Scott, *Fasti*, 4:62; D.C. MacTavish, ed., *Minutes of the Synod of Argyll, 1639-1661*, 2 vols. (Edinburgh, 1943-44), 1:80, 150.
27. Scott, *Fasti*, 2:370; SRO, CH. 1/1/9, 4 August 1642.
28. See Table on p. 335.
29. Peterkin, *Records of the Kirk*, p. 181.

Jedburgh and Kirkcudbright.[30] These commissions had the advantage that their members could be (and were) all convinced convenanters, who could depose their enemies much more expeditiously than the normal local courts of the church, which included all the ministers from the area. It was said that in the Dundee area there was "a considerable pairtye of the gentrye and ministrye disaffected to the Covenants," so that most of the members of the commission appointed to sit in Dundee were ministers and elders from Fife "who wer mor generallye zealotts."[31] Thus from the start the covenanters in establishing presbyterianism proved ready to turn to special centrally appointed commissions to interfere in what were normally the functions of local courts. The right of presbyteries to depose ministers was reaffirmed,[32] but clearly the covenanters suspected that many of them would not be zealous about deposing enemies of the regime.

Largely as a result of the work of the commissions appointed by the 1638 assembly, 1639 saw about fifty-two depositions; at least twenty-eight of these were the work of the commissions.[33] As in the previous year, the overwhelming majority of the 1639 depositions took place in the five southern synods—forty of them, with five more from Fife. In the Presbytery of Edinburgh alone nine ministers were deposed.

This geographical distribution of depositions might at first seem surprising; it is well known that the area in which ministers were most favorably inclined to the kings' religious policies was the Northeast, yet 1638-1639 saw very few depositions in that area. There are several explanations for this. First, the commissions were probably confined to trying ministers about whom complaints had been made to the general assembly by presbyteries. Naturally few such complaints would have come from presbyteries where ministers hostile to the covenanters predominated. Complaints, and therefore depositions, were concentrated where support for the covenant was strong enough for covenanters to predominate and complain against any of their colleagues who were not whole-hearted covenanters. Second, it was in the southern part of the country that the covenanting regime was most firmly established; it could enforce depositions and be confident that this would not lead to any public outcry in the locality concerned. By contrast the covenanters' hold on the North was still weak; it must often have been difficult to investigate whatever complaints were made against ministers, and in any case it would be impolitic to embark on large-scale purging of ministers when many of them had powerful local support. Of the commissions appointed in 1638 those which operated north of the River Tay (at Dundee, Forres and Chanonry) proved least active in deposing.

Whatever the reason, no purge of the ministers of the Northeast took place, and this was evidently acceptable to the 1639 general assembly; it approved all depositions made by the commissions without commenting on the lack of action in the North.[34] Towards some of those who had been purged the assembly showed itself ready to show some mercy; it was enacted that ministers who had been de-

30. Ibid., p. 47; Baillie, *Letters*, 1:170; Balfour, *Historical Works*, 2:308; Gordon, *History*, 2:152-153. For the commission for Edinburgh see *Calendar of State Papers, Domestic, 1638-1639*, ed. J. Bruce (London, 1871), p. 149.
31. Gordon, *History*, 2:95.
32. Peterkin, *Records of the Kirk*, p. 26.
33. Calculation of the exact number of depositions by the commissions is made impossible by the fact that the records often confusingly call the commissions ''synods.''
34. Peterkin, *Records of the Kirk*, p. 205.

posed only for using the new prayer book of 1637 (which had provoked the revolt against the king) or for refusing to accept the legality of the 1638 assembly,
and not for gross faults in doctrine or morals, might be restored to the ministry if
they repented.[35] In many such cases ministers were duly restored. Others who
had fled to the king in England, deserting their parishes, were allowed to return
to their parishes and continue their ministry—provided they came from areas
where sympathetic presbyteries were ready to turn a blind eye to their conduct.
Francis Thomson (Peterculter: Aberdeen)[36] and three ministers of the Presbytery of Ellon[37] thus quietly returned to their ministries. Such ministers had looked
to the king to secure their rights in his treaty with the covenanters at Berwick
in 1639, but he did nothing; "the King was weary of them; the whole Court did
hate them." All most got was a few pounds of charity,[38] and they were left to try
to make their own peace with the covenanters.

As might have been expected, when the covenanters tightened their hold on
the Northeast, some purging took place. In 1640 the general assembly sat in Aberdeen to demonstrate the covenanters' power in the largest center of resistance
to them. Of eleven depositions in 1640, eight were of ministers from the Synods of
Aberdeen and Moray, including all four carried out by the general assembly.
What is remarkable is not that this purge took place, but that it was so limited;
the covenanters, out of expediency, were ready to let many men whom they knew
at heart opposed them continue in the ministry in the North. It might have been
expected that the 1640 depositions were just the start of a gradual purge designed
to avoid stirring up too much trouble at once in areas where royalist sympathies
were strong, but the figures for depositions in the following years do not support
this interpretation. There were only five depositions in 1641, seven in 1642 and
three in 1643. Even these few were not concentrated in the North, and they include
several arising from immorality or insufficiency.

In the first six years of their rule (1638-1643) the covenanters are thus
known to have deposed about ninety-three ministers. This was a much more severe purge than the kirk had ever experienced before, involving over a tenth
of its ministers. Nonetheless, it was not so severe as one might have expected, especially since many of those deposed were later restored; at least twenty-two of
the ninety-three had been "reponed," or declared capable of exercising the ministry, by 1651, though not all of them actually returned to the ministry. The fact
that the purge was no greater is an indication both of the extent to which the
covenanters were ready (in some parts of the country) to accept the nominal support of ministers who clearly were not enthusiastic about the ecclesiastical
changes introduced in 1638, and of the extent to which such ministers were willing
to continue to serve in the kirk under the new regime rather than disown it, thus
leading to the danger of schism.

Some covenanters were convinced that purging had not gone far enough.
Samuel Rutherford, perhaps the best known minister of the day, wrote to a cor-
respondent in about 1644 that he hoped God would send him "a pastor according
to God's heart; and that's as rare as ever, for all our reformation."[39] Moderation

35. Ibid.
36. Scott, *Fasti*, 6:71.
37. T. Mair, ed., *Narratives and Extracts from the Records of the Presbytery of Ellon* (Aber-
    deen, 1898), pp. 140, 142-143; Guthry, *Memoirs*, pp. 77-78.
38. Baillie, *Letters*, 1:221.
39. S. Rutherford, *Letters*, ed. A. A. Bonar (Edinburgh and London, 1894), p. 616.

in limiting purging might be humane, and it helped to give an outward impression of more unity in the kirk than actually existed, but it made it difficult to bring about the spiritual and moral reform of the country that enthusiastic covenanters among the ministers wished for. Moreover hesitance in purging might avoid trouble in the short term, but in some ways it stored up trouble for the future; the later 1640s were to see the kirk split into factions bitterly opposed to each other, and the more extreme ministers would, perhaps, have had more chance of retaining control of the kirk had they been able to purge it more thoroughly in the early years of the troubles.

"At first they received all [ministers] that offered themselves; but afterwards they repented of this, and the violent men among them were ever pressing the purging the Kirk."[40] Sixty years later, historian Robert Wodrow saw lack of purging as having gravely weakened the covenanting movement.

The Church wanted [lacked] hands at that time to make a th[o]rough reformation in the ministry, and because they could doe noe better, the whole of the clergy that had served under Episcopacy wer lett sitt still in their charges throu many parts of the kingdom. All that took the Covenant wer suffered to continou, and except the Bishops and some feu others, all almost wer comprehended . . . . this corrupt part of the ministry was a dead weight in most of the judicatorys upon the honest party, and even in the Generall Assemblys them selves the honest ministers durst scarce lett things of any ticklish nature come to a vote, but caryed things by the force of reasoning and their influence in their charrangues in open Assembly.[41]

The difficulties and fears of the more extreme covenanters could hardly be put better.

The general assembly itself began to show some doubts about the wisdom of its own relative moderation when, after the 1639 act allowing the restoration of ministers deposed for the least serious faults if they repented, "the lately deposed episcopall ministers beganne to crowde so thicke at this wicket into ther owne pulpitts againe, by the assistance of ther parishoners, that the following Assemblyes this latitude was restrained."[42] In 1641 an act was passed whereby men deposed "for the publicke cause of the Reformation of this Kirk" were not to be restored until they had convinced both their presbytery and their synod of their repentance, and this had been reported to the general assembly.[43] Two years later, it was ruled that no minister could be restored by a court inferior to that which had deposed him[44] to prevent sympathetic local courts from restoring ministers deposed by higher courts. In 1645 restoring of ministers to the parish they had previously held was forbidden.[45]

In spite of doubts about the wisdom of restoring ministers too easily, however, the general assembly was in no mood to countenance any increase in the intensity of purging. In 1642 it ordered the restoration of Gilbert Power (Stoneykirk: Stranraer) and George Kincaid (Mochrum: Wigtown). Both had just been deposed by the zealous Synod of Galloway, Kincaid for insufficiency resulting from

40. G. Burnet, *History of My Own Times*, ed., O. Airy, 2 vols. (Oxford, 1897-1900), 1:58.
41. L. W. Sharpe ed., *Early Letters of Robert Wodrow, 1698-1709* (Edinburgh, 1937), p. 303.
42. Gordon, *History*, 3:54.
43. Peterkin, *Records of the Kirk*, p. 293.
44. Ibid., p. 349.
45. Ibid., p. 427. It was declared that the act would not apply to John Grahame (Auchterarder) and George Halyburton (Perth, second charge), who were both restored to their former parishes. Both men had powerful lay supporters; see Scott, *Fasti*, 4:234, 258; Guthry, *Memoirs*, pp. 181-182; SRO, CH. 1/1/9, 13 February 1645.

old age, Power evidently for the negative fault of lack of enthusiasm for the covenanting cause.[46]

The years between 1638 and 1640 had seen systematic deposition of ministers who were active opponents of the covenant, especially in the South. In 1641-1643 a few scattered depositions of anti-covenanters occurred; in 1644-1647 came the renewal of systematic depositions as new crises threatened the covenanters. Ministers who supported, failed to denounce, or unwillingly countenanced the leaders of the royalist risings of these years—the Marquis of Huntly in the Northeast, Alasdair Macdonald and other Highland royalists in the Northwest and, above all, the Marquis of Montrose. Of seven depositions in 1644, two (both in the Synod of Perth) were of ministers who had spoken or eaten with Montrose. Both these depositions (and at least one of the others in 1644) were carried out by the commission for the public affairs of the kirk. Set up by the general assembly to' provide a central court for the kirk between meetings of the assembly, the commission had grown fast in power and competence since its establishment in 1642; these were evidently the first depositions it carried out.

There was a minimum of ten depositions in 1645; five of them arose from ministers' conduct towards Montrose. Three of these were in the Synod of Glasgow and Ayr; as in 1638-1639 purging was most thorough and prompt where the covenanters were strong, not in areas where many ministers had royalist sympathies. Similarly, of the three depositions (out of a total of nine) in 1646 known to have resulted from contacts with the royalists, two were in the Synod of Glasgow and Ayr. Not until 1647 were the many ministers in the Northeast who had shown royalist sympathies dealt with. Apparently exasperated by the lack of action of the local kirk courts, the commission of the kirk came to Aberdeen in May. In thirteen days it deposed ten ministers (out of the twelve known depositions in 1647) from the Northeast; seven for associating with or supporting Huntly, one for associating with both Huntly and Montrose and two for supporting the Earl of Seaforth.[47]

Thus between 1644 and 1647 there were at least thirty-eight depositions. This second round of purging by the covenanters aroused little controversy, though Henry Guthry later denounced the deposition of learned and pious men on the evidence of sycophants at this time.[48] Montrose's Highland and Irish troops, many of them Catholics, were loathed even by many with royalists leanings. Many might sympathize with those deposed, knowing that often they had had no option but to compromise themselves by countenancing the rebels or face violence and plundering—four ministers were killed by the rebels in these years—but it was felt necessary to make an example of them.[49] Leniency was shown to some; Alexander Balnevis (Tibbermore: Perth) escaped deposition in spite of the fact that when accused in the presbytery of having shown Montrose hospitality (by giving him a drink of water), he is said to have told his accusers that "there was not one of them who, about the time of the battle, durst have refused to kiss, in the meanest

46. Scott, *Fasti*, 2:353, 370: Baillie, *Letters*, 2:51, 52-53; SRO, CH. 1/1/9, 4 August 1642; D. Stevenson, "The Radical Party in the Kirk, 1637-45," *Journal of Ecclesiastical History* 25 (1974): 152-153.
47. *RCGA*, 1:242-273.
48. Guthry, *Memoirs*, p. 205.
49. Scott, *Fasti*, 2:129; 5:258; 6:130, 445; A. Mitchell, ed., *MacFarlane's Geographical Collections*, 3 vols. (Edinburgh, 1906-08), 1:218.

XIV

manner, the Marquis, if he had commanded them to do so."[50] Though somewhat inelegantly put, the point was one with which many, fortunate enough not to have themselves come face to face with the royalist leaders, must have seen the force of. Most probably accepted the need for some purging after the royalist risings. By contrast, the new wave of depositions which began in 1648 arose from a major split in the kirk, and helped to widen that split. The Scottish parliament, supported by most of the nobility, made a treaty with Charles I, the engagement, promising to intervene in England on his behalf. The commission of the kirk and later the general assembly denounced the treaty as betraying the covenants and true religion, but many moderate ministers supported the engagement; while many more, as since the troubles began, tried to sit on the fence and avoid offending anyone. The extreme covenanters who opposed the engagement, becoming known as the kirk party, reacted by demanding thorough purging as essential to purify and unite the kirk.

The actions of the 1648 general assembly clearly presaged a new purge once the engagers were overthrown. An act forbade the readmitting of deposed ministers to parishes until the ends of the solemn league and covenant had been secured; they might still be declared capable of the ministry but were not to be actually restored at this dangerous time.[51] No minister deposed for malignancy (royalist or engager sympathies) was ever to be restored to a parish where a previous minister had been deposed for the same reason "and may be supposed to have put on the people a stamp and impression of Malignancie."[52] Most significant of all was an "Act for censuring Ministers for their silence, and not speaking to the corruptions of the time." By this act a minister might be deposed not only for supporting the engagement, but merely for failing to denounce it publicly;[53] this implied an attitude clearly stated in a declaration of the kirk published in 1645; "he that is not with us, is against us."[54] A neutral was an enemy. Politic compromisers sitting in the fence were as much of a danger to true religion as open opponents. A few opposed the act; Robert Baillie "wished, if men were modest, and otherwise offended not, that this fault might carrie no more but [than] ane rebuke,"[55] but the majority in the assembly was against him.

As in 1638 it was felt necessary, in order to make the purge effective, to appoint special commissions of visitation for areas where local courts could not be trusted. The Presbyteries of Dun and Chirnside had not denounced the engagement, so a commission "consisting of the most zealous brethren of Edinburgh, Lothian and Merse" was established to carry out a visitation. A similar visitation was directed to the Presbyteries of Dunblane and Stirling, which were thought slack in investigating malignancy among their ministers.[56] Other visitations were ordered for Ross, Sutherland, Caithness, Orkney and Shetland.[57]

At least one of these commissions was soon at work; in November two supporters of the engagement were deposed in each of the Presbyteries of Stirling and

50. M. Napier, ed., *Memorials of Montrose*, 2 vols. (Edinburgh, 1848-50), 2:313-314.
51. Peterkin, *Records of the Kirk*, p. 496.
52. Ibid., p. 517.
53. Ibid., pp. 509-510.
54. Ibid., p. 426.
55. Baillie, *Letters*, 3:58.
56. Ibid., 3:55.
57. Peterkin, *Records of the Kirk*, pp. 517, 518, 520.

330

Dunblane.[58] Altogether in 1648 about twenty ministers were deposed, at least half for being engagers.[59]

The purge of the engagers had begun as soon as their regime in Scotland had collapsed after military defeat in England, being replaced by a kirk party government. The new regime was strongly committed to thorough purging, in the state and army as well as in the kirk. God's favor, it was believed, could be secured only by limiting power and offices, civil and spiritual, to the godly minority. Previous failures had resulted from incurring God's wrath by accepting the help of unworthy men.

The main purge in accordance with this belief came in 1649. At least fifty-two ministers were deposed, many of them sincere supporters of the covenants who had believed the engagement to be the best means of implementing them. Such were the Edinburgh ministers William Colville (Tron Kirk) and Andrew Ramsay (Old Kirk),[60] both widely respected covenanters, but "the current of the tymes went so, that in respecte they wold not dance to the play of the leaders . . . they wer deposed."[61] The kirk party was purging not only open enemies and peace loving time servers, but also moderate covenanters. To some this helped make 1649-1650 "the best two years that Scotland saw" with "the ministry . . . notablie purified."[62] Others, many covenanters among them, were not convinced. William Spang, Scottish minister at Campvere in the Netherlands, protested at the deposing of ministers "who have proven your grit freinds ever before." "We meet with the dayly regrait that the antient ministers are contemned, and the insolency of young ones fostered, the very forrunners of Jerusalem's destruction." He warned that "these who think God so highly glorified by casting out their brethren, and putting so many to beggerie, making roume through such depositiones to yong youths, who are oft miscaried with ignorant zeal, may be made, through their aune experience, to feel what it is, which now, without pity, is executed upon uthers."[63] In this Spang was to be proved an excellent prophet in the 1660s. Robert Baillie bravely protested in the general assembly at the number of depositions; they were carried out "to the pitie and griefe of my heart; for sundry of them I thought might have been, for more advantage every way, with a rebuke, keeped in their places; but there was few durst professe [as] much; and I, for my ingenuous freedom, lost much of my reputation, as one who was inclyning to malignancie." The 1649 assembly itself deposed seven ministers, as well as approving the deposition of ten others.[64] New commissions of visitation "for the full purgation of the church" were set up "with most ample power. On these committees the most zealous men are put, that some few can choyse, even of very young men lately admitted ministers, for deposing of such as Presbyteries and Synods does spare." This again aroused protests from Baillie: "I acknowledge the disinclination of my mind to so frequent depositions of ministers. . . to me so severe ane action."[65]

58. Guthry, Memoirs, pp. 299-300.
59. Another two (in the Presbytery of Kilmore) were supporters of the earlier royalist risings.
60. Scott, Fasti, 1:70; 134; Baillie, Letters, 3:92.
61. Balfour, Historical Works, 3:419.
62. J. Kirkton, The Secret and True History of the Church of Scotland, ed. C. K. Sharpe (Edinburgh, 1817), p. 48.
63. Baillie, Letters, 3:81, 82.
64. Ibid., 3:91-92. W. L. Mathieson, Politics and Religion (Glasgow, 1902), is thus wrong in claiming that the assembly deposed seventeen ministers. Peterkin, Records of the Kirk, pp. 555-559.
65. Baillie, Letters, 3:97.

James Kirkton was more enthusiastic; the assembly "by sending abroad visitors into the countrey, made almost ane entire change upon the ministry in severall places of the nation, purgeing out the scandalous and insufficient, and planting in their place a sort of godly young men, whose ministry the Lord sealed with eminent blessings of success."[66] In fact there were not enough such zealous young men to go round; many parishes were left for many months without ministers, since it was thought better that they should have no minister than have a malignant one. Alexander Case (Polwarth: Duns) complained that in Duns Presbytery so many ministers had been silenced that "the few Brethren remayning are gravlie overcharged with more then double burthens making vs groan vnder them." He therefore asked that three suspended ministers be restored if nothing further could be proved against them.[67]

The new commissions of visitation appointed by the 1649 assembly were for the Presbyteries of Stirling and Dunblane; for Ross, Sutherland and Caithness, and for the Presbyteries of Duns and Chirnside. Evidently the previous visitations of these areas had not been thorough enough. In addition the Synod of Angus and Mearns was to be visited.[68]

It was the last of these visitations which proved the most severe. Angus and Mearns had largely escaped purging since the troubles had begun; only two ministers are known to have been deposed in the synod in 1638-1648. But by the end of September 1649 James Hamilton (Old Kirk: Edinburgh), one of the members of the commission, in reporting on the progress of the visitation, wrote "We have walked with als much tenderness as we could yett have found necessitie to depose sixteen and suspend two ministers—and the commission still had to investigate the Presbytery of Arbroath which was "thought the grossest of all."[69] By the time its work was complete the commission had deposed eighteen ministers, suspended five more and silenced two expectants (candidates for the ministry). Two further parishes "wich had old failed men, they ordained to be prowydit of new ministers." [70] Eight other of the 1649 depositions were in the Synod of Perth, again an area which had previously escaped severe purging. Thus half the 1649 depositions took place in these two synods; the rest were widely distributed throughout the country, though as usual the Synod of Glasgow and Ayr (with seven depositions) proved a center of purging.

Undoubtedly the great majority of the fifty-two depositions of 1649 resulted from the kirk party purging its opponents, but the figure probably also includes a higher than usual proportion of men deprived simply for insufficiency, as this was now seen as almost as dangerous as positive malignancy. Thus Andrew Allan (Oathlaw: Forfar) was said to show "greatt weaknesse in ministeriall giftes." He preached twice to the commissioners for visitation, who found him "altogether confused, ignorant of the purpose of his text, and that in his wholl discourses he spake for the most parte nonsense, and litle or nothing fitt for edifieng." He was also found to be ignorant in catechising, void of the gift of prayer, and guilty of swear-

66. Kirkton, The Secret and True History, p. 48.
67. National Library of Scotland (hereafter NLS), Wodrow MS Folio 25, no. 57, A. Case to R. Douglas and J. Smith, 2 July 1649.
68. Peterkin, Records of the Kirk, pp. 557-558.
69. NLS, Wodrow MS Folio 25, no. 59, J. Hamilton to R. Douglas, 30 September 1649.
70. Balfour, Historical Works, 3:430; J. Lamont, The Chronicle of Fife (Edinburgh, 1810), p. 12.

ing.[71] If these charges were substantially true, then clearly he was not fit to remain a minister. Deposing such a pathetic old man might be ruthless, but the argument that the well-being of his parishioners made his replacement necessary was a strong one. Moreover some charity was shown; orders were given that Allan should be paid his stipend for the following year, 1650—this certainly would not have been done had he been deposed for malignancy.[72]

Purging continued in 1650. At least three of the twenty-eight depositions resulted from ministers' conduct over the engagement, and another three were on vaguer charges of malignancy. But most of the depositions followed the failure of Montrose's final campaign. Late in 1649 his forces had occupied Orkney, and in 1650 he invaded Caithness, only to meet with prompt defeat. For welcoming or failing to denounce Montrose "the most pairt of the ministers of Orkeney [Kirkwall Presbytery] were deposed"—at least nine of them.[73] Six ministers in the Presbytery of Caithness suffered the same fate, which evidently left only one minister in the presbytery, since several parishes were already vacant.[74] Thus in 1651 it could be said that "there is not now a Presbyterie there." [75]

These purges in Orkney and Caithness were the most intense in the whole 1638-1651 period, in that more than half the ministers in these presbyteries were deprived almost simultaneously. But they were the kirk party's last fling. The arrival of Charles II in Scotland, English invasion and defeat at the battle of Dunbar led to a great moderate and royalist revival, partly provoked by the excesses of the kirk party. The kirk itself split. The majority of ministers, in spite of the kirk party's attempt to purify the ministry by purging, proved ready to accept the need for compromise and to work with the king and his supporters if the English were to be resisted. This faction, the resolutioners, were opposed by the remonstrants or protesters, a minority of extremist ministers who refused to submit to the majority. Consequently while 1651 saw at least two depositions of malignant ministers, the other three depositions of that year were of a very different character. Patrick Gillespie (East Kirk: Glasgow), James Guthrie (Stirling) and James Simpson (Airth: Stirling) were deposed by the resolutioner-dominated general assembly. All three had been leaders of the kirk party and were now deposed as leading protesters who refused to accept the assembly's authority.[76] The tide had turned. These were the first ministers deposed for being over zealous in the cause of the covenants; it seemed that, as Spang had predicted, the young zealots of the kirk party were to suffer what they had inflicted on others.

In fact, however, these depositions could not be enforced. All three men continued as ministers, and the Synod of Glasgow and Ayr in which the protesters had a majority elected Gillespie their moderator. The kirk was now split by schism, and with English conquest complete there was no state to help the resolutioners enforce their will. In any case the resolutioners had little stomach for purging, which seemed to have achieved so little in the past. The protesters on the other hand were still convinced of its necessity; after all, was not the victory of the reso-

71. W. M. Ogilvie, ed., *Extracts from the Records of the Presbytery of Brechin* (Dundee, 1876), pp. 8-9.
72. Scott, *Fasti*, 5:300.
73. Lamont, *Chronicle*, p. 26.
74. Scott, *Fasti*, 7:119.
75. *RCGA*, 3:404.
76. Scott, *Fasti*, 3:462; 4:289-290, 318-319; Lamont, *Chronicle*, p. 40; T. McCrie, ed. *The Life of Mr. Robert Blair* (Edinburgh, 1848), pp. 239, 278.

lutioners in itself proof that purging had not gone far enough? A protester pamphlet of 1653 denounced "the suffering of many giftles and unprofitable Ministers not gifted of God, to edifie his People, to continue in the Ministry," leaving it "yet in a great measure unpurged," for "there hath been so many diversions from, and interruptions of endeavours to have a purged Ministry in this Land."[77] Only by a great new purge could the protesters regain control of the kirk; but of course without that control purging could not be imposed. Deadlock was thus reached.

It emerges from this study that deposition of ministers under the covenanters had two peaks, 1638-1639, when the covenanters first gained control of the kirk, and 1648-1650, when experience seemed to have proved that purging had not been thorough enough. The latter purge was the larger of the two. 1649 saw the largest number of ministers ever deposed in a single synod in one year (in Angus and Mearns); 1650 saw the only cases of over half the ministers in presbyteries being deposed in one year (in Kirkwall and Caithness). These two peaks of purging hardly come as a surprise, though the extent to which 1639 and 1649 stand out is perhaps greater than expected. What is surprising is the geographical distribution of the depositions. At first only Scotland south of Forth and Fife was thoroughly purged—areas where support for the covenant was already strong. Even after the royalist risings of the mid-1640s, purging in the North as much less intense than it had been in the South. Only after the engagement were the Synods of Angus and Mearns and of Perth purged: only after Montrose's 1650 rising was the far North purged, while the Synod of Aberdeen (the third largest in the country) never suffered severe purging. The name Aberdeen is usually associated with episcopalian and royalist sympathies, yet only in the remote Synod of Argyll and the strongly covenanting Synod of Dumfries (from which, incidentally, no relevant synod or presbytery records survive, which may have led to several depositions being overlooked) was purging less intense (the intensity being calculated by comparing the number of depositions in the synod with the number of ministers in it). Over the period as a whole, Fife and the five synods south of the Forth, which contained almost exactly half the approximately 900 ministers in the country, saw 123 depositions. The synods north of this saw 113. Considering that there undoubtedly were far more ministers in the North than in the South who lacked enthusiasm for the covenants, it is clear that persecution was least severe in royalist areas, especially in the early years of the troubles. This unexpected leniency of the covenanters probably primarily arose simply from calculations of expediency, from the wish to avoid stirring up trouble in the North. It has been remarked that in the purges after 1688 "popularity gave a large measure of immunity to the episcopalian clergy" of the Northeast;[78] the same was evidently true in 1638-1647, and even to some extent in 1648-1651.

What happened to the ministers involved in the 236 depositions which have been identified in 1638-1651? At least 38 had been reponed (declared capable of exercising the ministry) by the end of 1651, though many of them had not by that time found parishes and presbyteries willing to accept them. However, 10 are known to have been restored to their old parishes, 9 to new ones, while one became an army chaplain. Many more were restored by the resolutioners in the 1650s, while many,

77. [A. Johnston of Wariston?], *Causes of the Lords Wrath against Scotland, Manifested in his sad late dispensations* (1653), pp. 34, 84.
78. W. Ferguson, *Scotland: 1689 to the Present* (London and Edinburgh, 1968), p. 104.

334

perhaps most of those who survived, returned to the ministry after the Restoration of 1660. It was the restoring of deposed ministers which made it possible for some to be deposed more than once in 1638-1651; 7 were deposed twice, one three times (thus the 236 depositions involved 227 individual ministers). It was James Douglas (Douglas: Lanark) who suffered three times. He was forced to demit, or resign, the parish of Douglas in 1640 after showing lack of enthusiasm for the covenanting cause by expressing sympathy for army deserters, but was allowed on repentance to become minister of Carnwath. He was deposed in 1646 (probably in connection with Montrose's rising) but by 1648 was again a minister, this time at Kirkwall. Trouble pursued him even to this remote corner; in 1650 he was among those deposed in the Orkney purge.[79]

Of the 227 ministers deposed, 27 are known to have fled the country, some entering the ministry in England or Ireland. Of those who remained in Scotland the kirk gave financial help (or at least ordered such help to be given) to at least 13 former ministers or their families; the proportion of the total is small, but probably many other such cases have gone unrecorded; a minister deposed for insufficiency or some uncharacteristic moral lapse seems to have had a reasonable chance of receiving some kind of help.

Charity and restoration to the ministry mitigated the suffering of some deposed ministers, but most must have experienced considerable hardship. What happened to most of them is unknown; most disappear without trace, permanently or until restored. Branded as enemies of church and state, they can have had little hope of finding alternative employment unless they had influential relatives or patrons.

Loss of many church records makes the total of 236 depositions a minimum figure, but it seems very unlikely that the full figure was more than 10 per cent above this total. Thus the covenanters' purging was on about the same scale as that which took place after the Restoration, when about 270 ministers were deprived in 1662-1663.[80] This was a much more intense purge than that of 1638-1651, being completed in a much shorter period, but the average number of depositions per year in 1638-1651 (17) was similar to that of 1660-1684 (15: 375 in 25 years).[81] Neither of these periods of purges approaches in scale that carried out after 1688, when over 500 ministers were deposed,[82] and the 664 depositions in the twenty-eight year period 1689-1719[83] represent an average of about 24 a year.

Up to 1638 the reformed kirk in Scotland had contained both episcopalian and presbyterian elements, and the great majority of ministers had accepted this, though some reluctantly. The rule of the covenanters saw the first successful attempt to exclude completely one element, the episcopalian, and the purging of ministers who would not accept this change (or were reluctant to do so) was a major part of this process. The experience of the years 1638-1660 made many presbyterian-inclined ministers reluctant to accept the reintroduction of episcopal elements; this led to the second great purge of the kirk, which was in turn to be reversed in the 1690s. The three great purges of the seventeenth century, each more

79. Scott, *Fasti*, 3:289, 300; 7:222; [J. Robertson, ed.], *Selections from the Registers of the Presbytery of Lanark*, (Edinburgh, 1839), pp. 22-24; *RCGA*, 1:28, 102.
80. Donaldson, *Scotland*, p. 365; W. C. Dickinson, G. Donaldson and I. A. Milne, eds., *A Source Book of Scottish History*, 3 Vols., (London 1958-61), 3:162.
81. Drummond and Bulloch, *The Scottish Church*, p. 5.
82. G. Donaldson, *Scotland: Church and Nation through Sixteen Centuries* (Edinburgh, 1972), p. 93.
83. Drummond and Bulloch, *The Scottish Church*, p. 9.

intense than the last, marked the gradual development in Scotland of episcopalianism and presbyterianism as mutually exclusive systems of church government.

TABLE

MINISTERS DEPOSED IN SCOTLAND IN 1638-1651[84]

SYNODS	'38	'39	'40	'41	'42	'43	'44	'45	'46	'47	'48	'49	'50	'51	Total
Lothian & Tweeddale (115)[85]	1	12		3		1	2		1		4	5	1		30
Merse & Teviotdale (70)	3	9	1	1							1	2	2		19
Dumfries (50)	1										1	1	2		5
Glasgow & Ayr (115)	6	12	2		2		1	5	5	1	4	7	1	1	47
Galloway (35)		7			2										9
Argyll (50)						1	1		1	1	2	1			7
Perth (80)							2	3			5	8	1	3	22
Fife (70	2	5		1			1	1			1	1	1		13
Angus & Mearns (85)		2										18			20
Aberdeen (100)			5			1	1				3	4	1		15
Moray (66)	1	1	3	1	1					2	5		1	2	17
Ross (50)	1	3									2	2	1	2	11
Sutherland & Caithness (20)		1										1	6		8
Orkney & Shetland[86] (30)									1			2	9	1	13
National total (910)	15	52	11	5	7	3	7	10	9	12	20	52	28	5	236

84. In a few instances it is not certain within a year or two when a minister was deposed; in these cases the deposition has been assigned to the most likely year.

85. Figures given in parentheses after the names of synods indicate the *approximate* number of ministers in each in about 1645. It must be emphasized that these figures can only be approximate since the information in the *Fasti* is not sufficient to enable a full list of ministers at any given time to be calculated. To avoid giving any false impression of precision the figures have been rounded up or down to the nearest five.

86. In 1646 the Synod of Orkney and Shetland was merged with that of Sutherland and Caithness, but in 1648 the Presbytery of Scalloway (Shetland) was declared to be immediately dependent on the general assembly, belonging to no synod. For the sake of convenience these changes have been ignored in the Table.

XV

A Revolutionary Regime and the Press: the Scottish Covenanters and their Printers, 1638–51

T HIS PAPER attempts to do two things: first, to look at the use the covenanting authorities in both church and state made of the printed word, and at their attempts to control or censor it; and secondly, to examine their relations with individual printers.[1] A very crude guide to the development of printing in Scotland is the number of works listed in Aldis for each year.[2] Figure 1 plots the numbers of entries for each year from 1598 to 1652. Splitting the period into decades, 1598–1607 sees an average of about thirteen works listed each year, the following decade about sixteen. In 1618–27 this rises to nineteen per year. Thus the three decades up to 1627 see slow growth. This speeds up notably in 1628–37, with an average of thirty publications a year listed, and the decade of rule by the covenanters sees a further big jump, to fifty publications a year.

These figures are clearly open to a number of objections. Many items which were printed have undoubtedly disappeared without trace. Some works printed outside Scotland are included by Aldis either deliberately (as they were printed for Scottish booksellers) or in error. A crude count of entries gives a single sheet proclamation as much weight as a major book hundreds of pages long; and very small editions are given as much weight as large ones. None the less, counting Aldis entries does give a reasonably accurate indication of the way in which printing was gradually becoming more common, and it is notable that the peaks in the 1598–1652 graph occur exactly where they might have been predicted. The dated peak years on the graph all coincide with major events in national life — the Union of the Crowns in 1603; royal visits to Scotland in 1617, 1633, and 1641; the National Covenant and Solemn League and Covenant in 1638 and 1643; and above all the Engagement controversy in 1648. The collapse that follows reflects the impact of English invasion and conquest. The distribution of the

---

[1] This paper was read to a meeting of the Bibliographical Studies Group, University of Aberdeen, in March 1984.
[2] H. G. Aldis, *A List of Books printed in Scotland before 1700, including those printed furth of the Realm for Scottish Booksellers, with brief notes on the Printers and Stationers*, second edition (Edinburgh, 1970). The seventeenth-century publications mentioned in the article are identified wherever possibly by their Aldis number, together with STC or Wing number (using the revised volumes where appropriate); some works listed in Aldis are not in STC or Wing, and vice versa, and this is indicated by a dash at the appropriate point in the reference.

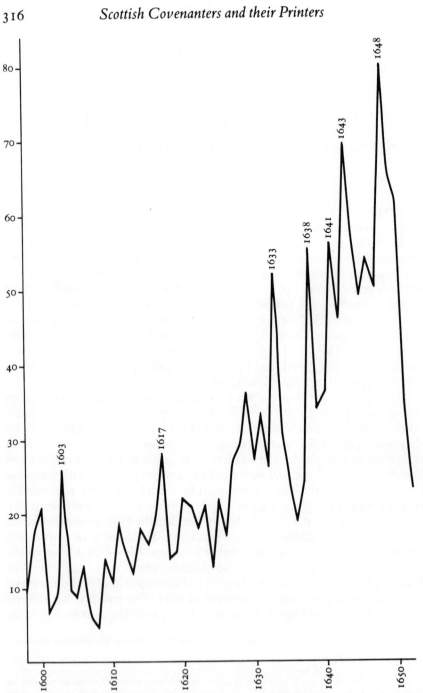

Numbers of entries for each year (1598–1652) in H. G. Aldis, *A List of Books printed in Scotland before 1700* (second edition, 1970)

peak years, and the extent to which they stand out from surrounding years, also suggest something of the nature of printing in Scotland; it is dominated by occasional and ephemeral works reflecting notable events, topical controversies, and intense government activity in times of crisis.

In these decades there were several printers active in Edinburgh, but the sole representative of the provincial press until 1638 was that eccentric Englishman in Aberdeen, Edward Raban, the self-styled 'laird of letters'.[3] Making a living from printing must have been difficult, for Scotland relied on foreign presses for the vast majority of academic and literary works. Of course in relying on the Continent for most Latin academic works Scotland differed little from England; but Scotland had an additional dependency on English presses, which hampered the growth of native printing. The Scottish home market was small, and Scottish scholars seeking to make a name for themselves would want an English or Continental imprint on their works.

Looking at the numbers of works printed in the early seventeenth century, it is hard to see how the various printing businesses managed to survive at all. Even the holding of a privileged position as King's Printer was not a sure way to profit. In or shortly before 1622, Thomas Finlayson, his Majesty's Printer for Scotland, complained that the free sale in Scotland of works printed in England was a great hindrance to Scots printers. To restore his own fortunes he asked that he be given the sole right to sell Scottish books in England.[4] Finlayson's plea met with no immediate response, but in 1626 Charles I agreed that something should be done about the printing industry in Scotland. Nothing was more requisite for the maintaining of true religion than the increase of learning; and nothing more advanced learning than 'plenty of all sorts of good books'. But the king had been told that printers 'will hardlie adventure to advance so much moneyis as necessarlie is requisite for establisching of constant printing works' in Scotland unless they were granted not only the right to print all sorts of books 'bot lykwayse the power to sell such of them in England as comodiouslie cannot be sold' in Scotland. Charles therefore ordered Patrick Lindsay, the Bishop of Ross, to negotiate with such printers as he thought most fit, assuring them not only of rights to print books in Edinburgh or St Andrews but also to sell them in England for thirty-one years.[5] The king's action may have resulted from the complaints of Scots printers, but the outcome suggests that it more probably resulted from the ambitions of

---

[3] J. P. Edmond, *The Aberdeen Printers: Edward Raban to James Nicol, 1620–1736* (Aberdeen, 1886), p. xxix.
[4] *A Companion to Arber*, edited by W. W. Greg (Oxford, 1967), pp. 61, 208. Finlayson's petition is undated, but a related, clearly later document is dated 1622.
[5] *The Earl of Stirling's Register of Royal Letters relative to the Affairs of Scotland*, [edited by C. Rogers], 2 vols (Edinburgh, 1885), I, 72.

318 *Scottish Covenanters and their Printers*

some English printers, frustrated by monopoly rights affecting printing in England, who saw Scotland as a back door into the English market. Finlayson died in 1627,[6] and the office of King's Printer remained vacant until 1632. It was then granted to an Englishman, Robert Young, for twenty-one years. Scots printers protested at this, and Edinburgh asserted that only resident burgesses could set up presses in the burgh. Young therefore agreed to become a burgess, to bring his family to Edinburgh, and to reside there. In the event, though he became a burgess, he probably never lived there.[7] The grant had been made to Young alone, but he was in fact the front man for a triumvirate of highly successful English printing entrepreneurs led by Miles Flesher. In the 1630s Young and his two colleagues bought up three London printing houses, and obtained patents to print canon law and grammar books in England; they also had printing interests in Ireland.[8] In gaining the Scottish patent Young evidently had the patronage of Sir William Alexander, later first Earl of Stirling (the king's Scottish Secretary), and the Scottish bishops.[9] According to Chalmers, in 1628 Alexander had supervised the publication of James VI's translation of the Psalms, of which Young was probably the printer.[10] It is possible that in undertaking this Young already had his eye on the Scottish patent and was seeking official favour. He doubtless pretended an interest in Charles I's advancement of learning in Scotland, but the later assertion by a Scottish rival that his only real interest in being King's Printer for Scotland lay in the rights it gave him to sell his books in England is probably true.[11] Certainly Young was soon busy printing 'Psalm Books' in Scotland and exporting them to England, thus breaking the monopoly of the London Stationers' Company. Some of these works were simply editions of the Psalms,[12] but they also included 1633 and 1634 editions of the English Book of Common Prayer[13] (Prayer Books which included Psalms are frequently referred to

---

[6] Aldis, *List*, p. 112.
[7] *The Acts of the Parliaments of Scotland* (hereafter *APS*), edited by T. Thomson and C. Innes, 12 vols (1814–75), V, 52–53; *Extracts from the Records of the Burgh of Edinburgh, 1626 to 1641*, edited by M. Wood (Edinburgh, 1936), p. 109; [Robert and James Bryson], 'Information anent His Majestie's Printers in Scotland', in *The Spottiswoode Miscellany*, Volume I, Spottiswoode Society (Edinburgh, 1844), p. 299 (the 'Information' was written in 1641, but not then printed); *Earl of Stirling's Register*, II, 776.
[8] C. Blagden, *The Stationers' Company. A History, 1403–1959* (London, 1960), p. 139; H. R. Plomer, *A Dictionary of the Booksellers and Printers who were at work in England, Scotland and Ireland from 1641 to 1667* (London, 1907), p. 199.
[9] Bryson, 'Information', pp. 299–300.
[10] W. J. Couper, 'George Chalmers's *Historical Account of Printing in Scotland*', *Records of the Glasgow Bibliographical Society* (hereafter *RGBS*), 7 (1918–20), 62–89 (pp. 80–81 — where the date 1628 is misprinted '1828'). The earliest extant edition of this translation, now thought to have been largely the work of Alexander, recorded in STC is that printed by W. Turner at Oxford in 1631 (STC 2732; DMH 452).
[11] Bryson, 'Information', 299.
[12] Aldis 863 (STC 2722).
[13] Aldis 798, 831, 831.3 (STC 16394, 16394.3, 16399, 16399.7, 16400); G. Donaldson, *The Making of the Scottish Prayer Book of 1637* (Edinburgh, 1954), p. 43.

simply as Psalm Books). It is very surprising that just a few years before the introduction of a supposedly 'English' Prayer Book sparked off revolution in Scotland, the English Book of Common Prayer was freely printed in Edinburgh without, so far as is known, arousing any hostile comment.

Already by 1634 the London Stationers' Company was penalizing Young and his partners for importing 'Psalms' printed in Scotland, and in 1636 their stock of Scottish Psalms in England was seized. Their activities were denounced as 'of very evill Consequence and tended in a great parte to the ruine and destruction of the Companyes Grant of the said Psalmes'.[14] Young also flooded Scots printed Bibles into England, breaking the monopoly of the King's Printer in England.[15]

Young thus exploited some aspects of his Scottish privileges for maximum profit, and probably neglected his other responsibilities. This soon lost him the favour of both church and state. When the Scottish Book of Canons appeared in 1636 it was printed 'With Royall Priviledge'; but it was printed by Raban in Aberdeen, not by the King's Printer, Young.[16] Either Young's standards were not sufficiently high for him to be entrusted with the Canons, or he was too busy churning out cheap Bibles and Prayer Books for the English market. But, perhaps as a result of his not printing the Canons, it had already been decided that Young must be made to live up to his responsibilities as King's Printer. The Canons were to be followed in Charles I's religious reforms by a new Scottish Prayer Book. Young was to be forced to print it. Thus, ironically, it came about that Young, a printing entrepreneur whose only interest seems to have been profit, printed the ideologically inspired 'English-Popish' Prayer Book which led to the destruction of the king's power in Scotland and to the temporary ruin of Young's business there.

On 15 September 1635 a royal order instructed Young to repair to Scotland at once to dispatch by himself 'or others' such duties as King's Printer as the Archbishop of St Andrews entrusted to him; 'whereof faile not as you will be answerable'.[17] Young's task, Archbishop Laud of Canterbury revealed, was 'to make ready a blacke letter' and have his servants ready to produce the new liturgy.[18] The history of the printing of the Scottish Prayer Book is complicated. Much of a first version was evidently completed by

[14] *Records of the Court of the Stationers' Company, 1602–1640*, edited by W. A. Jackson (London, 1957), pp. 263, 280, 311; *Calendar of State Papers, Domestic, Charles I*, vol. x, *1636–1637*, edited by John Bruce (London, 1867), p. 267; Blagden, *Stationers' Company*, p. 140.
[15] Couper, 'George Chalmers's *Historical Account*', p. 81; Greg, *Companion*, pp. 102, 325–26, 344–45.
[16] Edmond, *Aberdeen Printers*, pp. 57–58; Aldis 868 (STC 22055).
[17] British Library, MS Add. 23112, Register of the Secretaries of State for Scotland, fol. 5ʳ (the order is mentioned in J. Dowden, 'Archbishop Laud's Prayer-Book', *Publications of the Edinburgh Bibliographical Society* (hereafter PEBS), 1 (1890–95), Session 1893–94, paper v, pp. 1–8.
[18] Robert Baillie, *The Letters and Journals*, edited by David Laing, Bannatyne Club, 3 vols (Edinburgh, 1841–42), 1, 436–37.

the end of 1635, but this was scrapped — partly because textual alterations were made,[19] but probably also partly because the quality of Young's original work was not regarded as adequate. The king saw this very much as a prestige publication. In February 1636 the Earl of Stirling had pointed out some errors in Raban's edition of the Canons, adding 'and therefore have the more care in looking to that in printing of the Service-Book, for Young the printer is the greatest knave that euer I dealt with; and therefore trust nothing to him nor his servants but what of necessity you must'.[20] If Stirling had originally been Young's patron, he now clearly regretted it!

Young eventually produced a Prayer Book of high quality, much superior to most Scottish printing of the period. But it is ironic to find an eighteenth-century writer hailing him as a 'Good and Great Master' as a result, when we know Young produced the work only when closely supervised and compelled to do so.[21] Work on the Prayer Book must have affected Young's profits even before it appeared, and the riots and rebellion which followed the first attempt to use the new liturgy in 1637 quickly made his position in Scotland untenable.

With the outbreak of the revolt against Charles I, access to and control of Scotland's printers became of great significance. The covenanters first gained access to the printed word through George Anderson, who had begun printing in 1637 in the College of Edinburgh.[22] It was Anderson who produced the first edition of the National Covenant in 1638, and he produced several other papers for the covenanters in the same year. Meanwhile Robert Young's presses served the king, issuing his proclamations and other denunciations of the covenanters. In Aberdeen the stand of the 'Aberdeen Doctors' against the covenanters was aided by their access to Raban's press. When a delegation of covenanters arrived to debate the issues with the Doctors, the latter had Raban print their *Demands* — but not distribute them. They thus decided not to take the initiative in widening a date between scholars into a public controversy, but were ready to do so immediately if the covenanters made the first move. Their planning paid off. The covenanters made public (though not at first in print) their answers to the Aberdeen Doctors' *Demands* without fully revealing the *Demands* themselves, hoping to gain a propaganda advantage; but the Doctors were able to counter this at once by distributing Raban's edition of the *Demands*. There followed a complicated exchange of papers between the two sides, with Raban printing the papers of both.[23]

---

[19] Donaldson, *The Making of the Scottish Prayer Book*, pp. 148–59.
[20] Baillie, *Letters*, I, 439.
[21] J. Watson, *Preface to the History of Printing, 1713*, edited by J. Munro (Greenock, 1963), pp. 7–8.
[22] Aldis, *List*, p. 108.
[23] J. D. Ogilvie, 'The Aberdeen Doctors and the National Covenant', *PEBS*, 11 (1912–20), 73–86. Raban's edition of the *Demands* is Aldis 911 (STC 64); Aldis 899, 909 (STC 68, 79?) record related materials.

The Aberdeen papers were soon being reprinted both in Edinburgh and London, and the controversy must have brought home to both sides the importance of access to the press.[24] The Marquis of Hamilton had been sent to Scotland by the king to try to reach a settlement with the covenanters and he issued an order prohibiting printing without warrant. His order proved impossible to enforce, but the covenanters may have been particularly alarmed by this attempt to deny them access to the press as a General Assembly had been summoned to meet in Glasgow in November 1638, and Glasgow lacked a printer. If they concentrated their supporters in Glasgow to dominate the Assembly, might the king's supporters be able to seize complete control of the Edinburgh presses? The covenanters' answer, it seems, was to take a printer with them to Glasgow. Moves may have already been made by Glasgow to persuade George Anderson to settle there — both the burgh council and the college subsequently agreed to support his press — but the timing of the move, coinciding with the Glasgow Assembly, is surely not merely coincidental. The value of having a printer in Glasgow was quickly proved. Hamilton ordered the Assembly to dissolve in the king's name; it refused, and was able immediately to issue in print a *Protestation* justifying its action — the first work ever to be printed in Glasgow.[25]

In other ways as well the Assembly's actions indicated the importance the covenanters attached to printing. The Assembly's acts were printed, the first time this had ever been done. This was justified on the grounds that there was not enough time to make the many copies required in manuscript, and that failure to print acts in the past had made it easier than it would otherwise have been for kings to ignore, and suppress correct knowledge of, previous acts. Had previous resolutions to print acts been carried out 'our defection through the almost invincible ignorance of the proceedings of this Kirk, had not proven so dangerous and deplorable'.[26] Once hundreds of printed copies had been distributed it would be impossible for the king to suppress knowledge of what they said.

Royal efforts to deny the covenanters access to the press had failed; and the covenanters were ready to reverse the process. By this time they had formed what amounted to a provisional government, and this supported the kirk's right to control printing relating to religion — which, needless to say, could

[24] See, for example, Aldis 899.5, 912, — (STC — , 67, 66).
[25] For evidence of the failure of Hamilton's order forbidding unlicensed printing, see *Miscellaneous State Papers, from 1501 to 1726*, [edited by P. Yorke, Earl of Hardwicke], 2 vols (London, 1778), II, 111. For the *Protestation* (Aldis 923–24; STC 22047–47.5), see W. Stewart, 'The Protestation of the General Assemblie of the Church of Scotland made at Glasgow in November, 1638', *RGBS*, I (1912–13), 106–17 (pp. 107–09).
[26] *The Principall Acts of the Solemne Generall Assembly of the Kirk of Scotland* (Edinburgh, 1639), 'To the Reader', sig. π2ʳ (Aldis 936; STC 22049).

be defined to include anything relating to the quarrel with the king. An act of the Assembly of 20 December 1638 related that the kirk had sustained great prejudice through 'the unwarranted printing of lybels, pamphlets, and polemicks, to the disgrace of Religion'. Therefore 'by vertue of their ecclesiastical authority' the Assembly forbade printing of any acts of Assembly, covenants, papers concerning present controversies or treatises concerning the kirk without a warrant signed by Archibald Johnston of Wariston, the Clerk of the Assembly and Advocate for the Kirk.[27] Wariston's ability and fanaticism had brought him to the fore of the covenanting movement, and this setting him up as an ecclesiastical censor added to royalist hatred of him. A declaration issued in the king's name commented sarcastically 'A pretty act, that We must print nothing concerning Ecclesiasticall policie and government, unlesse Johnston give Us leave'.[28] Wariston combined his dedication to the cause with an indifference to money which periodically left him in debt and looking round in bewilderment for signs of how God was going to provide for him. In this censorship act he saw such a sign, and gave thanks for 'God's particular caire of me', the act being 'for the Kirks use and to my benefyte';[29] he could charge fees to those who sought licences to print. However, he soon decided that he had misunderstood divine intentions. As usual, he lamented, 'the Lord gaive me a check and a rub in the entree of everything I lipned for gayne' — everything he attempted to do to make money.[30] He had appended a Latin imprimatur to the Assembly's *Protestation* and this had evidently been denounced as smacking of popery.[31] Wariston also found his responsibility for seeing the acts of the Assembly through the press troublesome. He had been ordered to sign all copies before sale to authenticate them, and it had been left to him to fix the price. 'I pray God direct me anent their prices', he wrote 'and if that be the way of his releiving my burthens I craive his blissing thairto'.[32] Unfortunately it is not known whether Wariston succeeded in making a godly profit from the acts.

The acts of the Assembly were printed in Edinburgh by the Heirs of Andro Hart. This was the last work to appear with that imprint, for the press was taken over by the Edinburgh bookseller James Bryson. The

[27] *Records of the Kirk of Scotland, containing the Acts and Proceedings of the General Assemblies, from the year 1638 downwards*, edited by A. Peterkin (Edinburgh, 1838), p. 39; James Gordon, *History of Scots Affairs*, edited by Joseph Robertson and George Grub, Spalding Club, 3 vols (Aberdeen, 1841), II, 167; Baillie, *Letters*, I, 176.
[28] *A Large Declaration concerning the Late Tumults in Scotland. . . . By the King* (London, 1639), pp. 323, 415 (STC 21906).
[29] *Diary of Sir Archibald Johnston of Wariston, 1632–1639*, edited by G. M. Paul, Scottish History Society (Edinburgh, 1911), p. 404.
[30] Johnston, *Diary*, p. 409.
[31] J. D. Ogilvie, 'A Bibliography of Glasgow Assembly, 1638', *RGBS*, 7 (1918–20), 1–12 (p. 11).
[32] Johnston, *Diary*, p. 410.

following year, 1640, the imprint of Robert Bryson, another bookseller, appears. And in 1641 R. & J. Bryson produce some works with a joint imprint.[33] The two Brysons acted as the covenanter's main printers in 1639–41; indeed they were the most active of all Scottish printers, for Robert Young had disappeared from the scene. Late in 1638 or early in 1639 he had given up the attempt to continue as King's Printer in Edinburgh in such turbulent times, ordering his servants to sell their equipment and return to London.[34] This they did, thus helping equip the businesses of both George Anderson and Robert Bryson; both are afterwards found using Young's former types to serve the covenanters.[35] But Young continued to be King's Printer for Scotland, and used that imprint for works produced for the king by his London presses which were directly related to the controversy with the covenanters. Sometimes, as with the 1639 *Large Declaration*, London is given as the place of publication, but other works give no place, and in 1638–39 it is not always certain which were issued before Young ceased printing in Edinburgh and which after. Presumably the king, though he had lost control of Scotland, felt it useful in the propaganda war to have his works appear with the imprint of his Scottish printer.

The propaganda war was, however, clearly won by the covenanters — and not just in Scotland. They well knew that they could not hope to defeat Charles in the war which was approaching if opinion in England rallied behind him. They therefore aimed an intense propaganda barrage at England, stressing that they had no quarrel with the people of England; indeed, as their grievances against the king were the same as those of the English, the people of both nations were urged to co-operate to gain redress. Printed pamphlets formed a major part of this propaganda offensive. As early as February 1639 a royal proclamation to be read in all English churches denounced the 'multitude of printed pamphletts or lybells, stuffed full of calumnyes' produced by the covenanters and spread through England. Other forms of propaganda denounced included private letters sent to individuals in England, and the activities of Scots agents who held private meetings in England. By this the covenanters 'wer begunne to stricke at the roote of princely government, assuming the princely power: *First*, By printing what they please, though he forbid, and to prohibite what they please, though he bidd'. Second, they had dismissed the printer established by the king (Young). The importance the king gave to this paper war is indicated by the fact that the first two invasions of princely power by the

[33] Aldis, *List*, p. 110; *Roll of Edinburgh Burgesses, 1406–1700*, edited by C. B. B. Watson, Scottish Record Society (Edinburgh, 1926), p. 85. Aldis suggests that James was 'probably a relative' of Robert Bryson; Chalmers, that the two were 'probably brothers' (Couper, 'George Chalmers's *Historical Account*', p. 82).
[34] Bryson, 'Information', p. 300.
[35] Aldis, *List*, p. 124.

covenanters which he lists both relate to printing; only then does he list such things as raising subjects in arms against him. In reply the covenanters issued a pamphlet denying the charge that Robert Young had been dismissed and asserting innocently that for a church to have power to control printing where religion was concerned was nothing new.[36]

Once Young had left, the king's supporters had no printer to serve them in Edinburgh. But in Aberdeen Raban ventured to produce a few royalist works in 1639 — the formal refusal of the bishops to accept their deposition from office by the Assembly; a moderate royalist pamphlet; and a prognostication which included royalist verse.[37] In the summer a truce was made with the king, but it collapsed before royalist printing could revive. It was said that the king's declaration of peace was printed but suppressed by the covenanters before publication, and the printer punished.[38] It is possible that Raban was the printer involved; certainly we know he was soon in trouble with the covenanters. At the end of 1639 he and his wife were convicted of involvement in a brawl in which they had been 'Injuring and dinging' others 'under selence of night'.[39] The incident took place on Christmas Eve, so perhaps Raban had been trying to celebrate Christmas in defiance of the covenanters' suppression of the festival; but it may be suspected that his activities as a royalist printer had led local covenanters to be on the look-out for some offence which could be used as a pretext to make life difficult for him.

The following year, 1640, the General Assembly met in Aberdeen, and Raban again found himself in trouble. As the offence of which he was accused dated back to 1625 it again looks as if a careful search for possible offences had been made. In that year he had printed a 'Psalm Book' — in this case an edition of the Book of Common Order which included the Psalms. He was now accused of having slightly shortened some prayers so as to omit anti-Catholic passages, including a reference to 'the Romish idol'. Raban was interrogated as to why he had done this; had any local ministers told him to? His explanation was a simple one — lack of paper. Had he printed the prayers complete this would have involved printing just a few lines on the first page of a new sheet of paper; to avoid this he had made a few minor cuts — cuts which he had not made in any other edition. Eventually he was let off

[36] James Gordon (*Scots Affairs*, II, 198–200, 240–46) summarizes the content of both the February proclamation (STC 9135) and the *Remonstrance of the nobility, barones, burgesses, ministers and commons within . . . Scotland, vindicating them . . . from the crymes, wherewith they are charged by the late proclamation in England, Feb. 27. 1639* (Aldis 954; STC 21907). The latter bears the imprint of James Bryson, Edinburgh, 1639, and the same imprint appears fictitiously in two editions of the *Remonstrance* (one a Dutch translation) printed in Amsterdam in the same year (Aldis 955–56; STC 21908–908.5).
[37] Aldis 942, 945, 949 (STC 22059, 12493, 11501); Edmond, *Aberdeen Printers*, pp. 69–71.
[38] Couper, 'George Chalmers's *Historical Account*', p. 81n.
[39] Edmond, *Aberdeen Printers*, p. xxiii.

with a rebuke.[40] But he probably got the message of these incidents — that he had better watch his step in future. So far as is known his press remained silent throughout 1640, either through some formal ban or his own prudent inactivity.

In 1640 the covenanters, tired of waiting for the king to invade Scotland, decided to force a showdown by invading England. In the count-down to the invasion propaganda aimed at England sought to persuade the English not to regard the invasion as an act of hostility — it was a defensive invasion which would help the people of England against the king. The covenanters later acknowledged a debt of £877 18s. od. Scots owed to Robert Bryson 'for the pryce of ane number of Bookes and declaratiounis sent in to England be publict orders before the armie went yr in anno 1640'. These doubtless included such works as *The Intentions of the Army of the Kingdome of Scotland* and *The Lawfulnesse of our Expedition into England Manifested*.[41] And Robert Bryson's services were not confined to printing. The covenanters also owed him £166 13s. 4d. Scots 'for his expenss service and hazard in goeing in throghe England with the saids bookes'.[42] Thus Bryson had risked his life by acting the part of a secret agent distributing propaganda in enemy territory.

The successful invasion of England forced Charles I to compromise, and in 1641 he came to Edinburgh to make his peace with the covenanters. Robert and James Bryson hoped the triumphant covenanters would reward their services by having them appointed King's Printers — and their establishing a joint imprint at this point may have been designed to enhance their credibility. But they were quickly disappointed. On 30 June 1641 the king appointed Robert Young and Evan Tyler or their assigns joint King's Printers for thirty-one years.[43] The covenanters accepted this, though parliamentary ratification did not come until 1644.[44] The Brysons protested indignantly. They had loyally served the covenanters, and through their efforts and expenditure they had attained 'to such perfection in the airt of printing' that they could serve as his Majesty's Printers more cheaply than any foreigners. It was 'not agreable to reasoun' that Young, the avowed enemy to the covenanting church and state, the publisher of anti-Scottish propaganda, should be appointed. Yet Young's son and a servant had

---

[40] Aldis 635.5, 636 (STC 2709); Edmond, *Aberdeen Printers*, pp. xxiv–xxv, 19, 192; Peterkin, *Records*, p. 169; Gordon, *Scots Affairs*, III, 238–39.
[41] Aldis 970–71, 972, 972.5 (STC 21919–20, 21923).
[42] Scottish Record Office (hereafter SRO), PA.14/1, Register of the Committee for Common Burdens, 1641–45, fols 156ʳ, 157ʳ. James Bryson was owed £275 Scots for his printing and 'uther furnishing' (perhaps stationery) on 12 July 1641, SRO, PA.14/1, fol. 47ʳ.
[43] *Register of the Great Seal of Scotland. Registrum Magni Sigilli Regum Scotorum*, vol. IX, *1634–1651*, edited by J. M. Thomson (Edinburgh, 1897), no. 967.
[44] *APS*, VI, i, 257–58.

arrived in Edinburgh with presses and types and were preparing to print the acts of parliament.[45]

The covenanters were probably reluctant to open a new argument with the king about a relatively minor matter like the appointment of a printer when he was virtually surrendering to them in major constitutional and religious affairs. Moreover it seems that Young made efforts to ingratiate himself with the covenanters. Having triumphed in Scotland, the covenanters were now anxious to help bring about religious and other reforms in England, and had been actively campaigning in London to this end. Young may have suggested that if he was appointed King's Printer in Scotland he would be willing not only to serve them in Scotland, but to give them access to his London presses. In 1639 and 1640 the London imprint of Young as King's Printer for Scotland had appeared on anti-covenanter propaganda; now, in 1641, it appeared on a reprint of the First and Second Books of Discipline, which the covenanters regarded as outlining the structure of a true kirk such as that which they sought to establish in England.[46] Clearly the king would never have approved such a publication by Young, and the only explanation of its appearance seems to be that he was trying to gain favour with the covenanters.

The joining of Tyler with Young in the 1641 grant probably indicated that Young did not intend to take an active part in printing in Scotland, though he would retain a financial stake. In 1641 Edinburgh imprints of the King's Printer his name appears alone once, but the usual imprint is 'Young and Tyler'. The joint imprint continues into 1642, though the imprint of Tyler alone also appears; with Young's death in 1643 the joint imprint vanishes and thereafter Tyler's name alone is found.

Like Young, Tyler was an Englishman. He may have been in charge of Young's Edinburgh business before the troubles — certainly he was involved in selling the disastrous 1637 Prayer Book.[47] From 1642 to 1650 his imprint dominates Scottish printing. But though the imprint remains the same, ownership of the business changes hands. The 1641 grant was to Young and Tyler, but they had partners with a stake in the firm, including Miles Flesher (one of Young's 1632 partners). And as before the troubles, the main interest of Tyler and his partners lay in the rights of the King's Printer to export to England and thus evade monopoly restrictions. As a result the Court of the London Stationers' Company set up a committee in

---

[45] Bryson, 'Information', pp. 300–01.
[46] *The First and Second Booke of Discipline*, and *The Doctrine and Discipline of the Kirke of Scotland* (Wing C4224c, C4224). The two works are identical except for their title-pages. The former gives no printer, the latter Robert Young.
[47] See pp. 319–20 above. Aldis, *List*, pp. 122, 124; Baillie, *Letters*, I, 441. See also Jackson, *Records*, p. 324 and *A Transcript of the Registers of the Company of Stationers of London, 1554–1640*, edited by E. Arber, 5 vols (London 1875–94), III, 688.

1644 to consider the Scottish patent and how to suppress it or buy it up, as it was of such evil consequence to the Company. The confusion of the English civil war probably delayed action, but a new committee set up in 1646 reached an agreement (in 1647) with the three partners who then had an interest in the Scottish grant — Tyler, Flesher, and John Parker. The three partners would sell their rights and equipment to the Company for £430 sterling. Thomas Pape was sent to manage the Edinburgh business for the Stationers' Company, but he died within a few months and was replaced by John Twyn. Running an Edinburgh branch from London in a time of civil war and political confusion was difficult, and at one point it was decided to close it down and ship the type to London, but in the end this was not done.[48] The covenanters would have opposed the closing down of their main printer, or would have appointed a new King's Printer. It was not within the Stationers' Company's power simply to abolish the post of King's Printer for Scotland, so they had to be content with running the Edinburgh business in such a way that it did not interfere with the interests of the Company in England.

Even after the Stationers' Company took over the business of King's Printer for Scotland the imprint remains Tyler, and he remained active in Edinburgh alongside the Stationers' representative, John Twyn. The majority of work undertaken, both before and after the Stationers' takeover, comprised Bibles and printing done for the covenanting church and state — acts of parliaments and assemblies, proclamations, declarations, papers relating to negotiations with the king and the English parliament. The expanding administrative machine of the revolutionary regime provided plenty of such work for Tyler and he was evidently the first printer to produce in Scotland those symbols of the triumph of modern bureaucracy, printed forms with blanks for completion in manuscript — bonds to be filled in showing how much an individual was prepared to lend to the regime, and loyalty bonds swearing obedience.[49]

After Charles I's visit in 1641 and his compromise with the covenanters, power at first lay in the hands of a regime which included moderate royalist elements as well as covenanters. But once the English Civil War began in 1642 the compromise began to collapse over how to react to the English war. Should Scotland intervene? And if so, on which side. At one point in the debate the touchstone of loyalty became the question of which papers should be sent to Tyler for printing. In December 1642 the Privy Council was presented with a declaration of the English parliament appealing for military help, and an indignant letter from the king denouncing the

[48] Blagden, *Stationers' Company*, pp. 141–42.
[49] See, for example, Aldis 1131, 1132, 1215, 1263 (none listed in Wing), and the 1649 loyalty bond (not listed in Aldis or Wing) in SRO, PA.12/4, Warrants of the Committee of Estates, 1649.

declaration. After a furious argument the royalists prevailed, and Tyler was ordered to print the king's letter, but not parliament's declaration. The covenanters then organized a petition demanding the printing of the declaration, and this was met by the royalist 'Cross Petition' demanding the opposite. These were not printed, but the Commission of the Kirk was so enraged by the Cross Petition that it ordered Tyler to print a denunciation of it. Under this pressure the Privy Council gave way, and in January 1643 agreed that the English Parliament's declaration should be printed — though it later added that the fact that it ordered something to be printed did not indicate approval of its contents![50] This confused controversy over what to print proved to be a turning point; in the months that followed the covenanters managed to strengthen their grip on Scotland and commit the country to helping the English Parliament. Justification for such policies poured from Tyler's presses, and the fact that some official publications of both church and state in 1643 appear over Robert Bryson's imprint[51] may indicate that Tyler's presses had insufficient capacity to meet the demands made on them. When the new Solemn League and Covenant appeared Tyler produced an edition of 1,000 copies, but Bryson and even the royalist-inclined Raban also printed it.[52]

Once the regime had decided to support the English parliament, the Scottish presses were again closed to the king and his supporters. Such Scottish royalist publications as appeared were published in England, often in the royalist headquarters at Oxford. There was only one exception to this. In September 1644 the royalist Marquis of Montrose occupied Aberdeen. Up to a few days before Raban had been publishing the proclamations of the covenanters' Committee of Estates which had been meeting in the burgh; now he printed a royalist declaration by Montrose.[53]

It was perhaps this example of a press falling briefly into royalist hands, together with worries about royalist propaganda from England, that led the covenanting state to pass its first act to control printing. On 29 November 1644 the Committee of Estates considered 'the prejudices that do ensue throw the uncontrolled libertie that printers take to themselves to print and publish books and papers at their pleasure', and that 'in all weele governed kingdomes it is expresslie prohibit that anie subject take upon hand to print or publish anie bookes of quhatsoever discipline or science but speciallie libells or chronicles Concearning the state of the kingdom or ages past

[50] J. D. Ogilvie, 'The Cross Petition, 1643', *PEBS*, 15 (1930–35), 55–76 (pp. 56–65); Aldis 1037, 1077.5, 1078, 1080 (Wing C2386, D517 = S1007, D522 = S1007, E1448); *A Bibliography of Royal Proclamations of the Tudor and Stuart Sovereigns . . . 1485–1714*, edited by R. R. Steele, 2 vols (Bibliotheca Lindesiana, vols 5, 6) (Oxford, 1910), II, Scotland, nos. 1770, 1774.
[51] Aldis 1074, 1099b, 1099c (Wing C2098, —, —).
[52] Aldis 1107–09 (Wing —, C4265 = S4441, C4260 or 4261).
[53] Aldis 1134.5, 1149–51 (Wing —, S1193, S1348, S1989).

without Warrant or allowance for that effect'. In future no such works were to be printed or imported from abroad without licence from the King's Secretary, though this was not to prejudice the Kirk's 1638 act for controlling printing relating to religion.[54] As the King's Secretary, the Earl of Lanark, was working with the covenanters at this point, the tradition that he was the correct official to censor the press could be maintained.[55] The state also stepped in to support the Kirk's control of religious printing. In February 1645 the General Assembly was considering a new censorship act to replace that of 1638;[56] it seems that what the Assembly was worried about was not the prevention of the printing of heretical works, but the protection of copyright of works published by ministers. It ordered that a number of such works which were being printed should not be reprinted or imported, and asked Parliament to give civil sanction to this. Parliament agreed, granting copyright for fifteen years.[57] A few months later the Kirk was worried that unrevised versions of, or extracts from, the new Directory of Worship would be printed, and again successfully appealed to the state for support.[58] A general act of Parliament upholding the Kirk's right to censor religious printing followed in 1646.[59]

Though Tyler's presses were kept busy by the patronage of church and state, getting payment for such work proved difficult. In 1647 he petitioned for payment of his work for the state since 1642. The Commitee of Estates ordered that his accounts be audited,[60] and this was done in October. The account then audited, covering December 1642 to October 1647 survives, giving us not only the titles of a number of works of which no surviving copies are known, but also information on print runs — which vary from fifty to 1,500. In all Tyler had printed 130,110 sheets for the state. He claimed payment at two shillings Scots per sheet, but the auditors recommended that he be paid the round sum of 10,000 merks (£6,666 13s. 4d. Scots), which was just over one shilling Scots per sheet. Moreover even this was not paid — in September 1649 he got a recommendation to the Commitee for Moneys to pay him, but it is doubtful if he received anything.[61]

Tyler's presentation of his bill in 1647 may be related to the sale of the business to the Stationers' Company that year. Perhaps if he had received

[54] SRO, PA.11/3, Register of the Committee of Estates, 1644–45, fols 119ᵛ–120ʳ. The act was ratified by parliament in 1646, *APS*, VI, i, 551.
[55] See the censorship act of 1599, *APS*, IV, 187.
[56] SRO, CH. 1/1/9, Acts and Proceedings of the General Assemblies, 1642–46 (1646), p. 175.
[57] Peterkin, *Records*, pp. 432–33 (unprinted acts nos. 51–52, 97–99); *APS*, VI, i, 323–24.
[58] SRO, PA. 11/4, Register of the Committee of Estates, 1645–46, fol. 46ʳ⁻ᵛ
[59] *APS*, VI, i, 551.
[60] SRO, PA. 11/5, Register of the Committee of Estates, 1647–48, fol. 23ʳ.
[61] SRO, PA. 11/8, Register of the Committee of Estates, 1649, fol. 162ʳ; SRO, PA. 15/2, Inventory of Worke done for the State by Evan Tyler, His Majesties Printer: since December anno 1642. A printed edition of the *Inventory* was published in Edinburgh, 1815.

payment of what was due to him he would have left Edinburgh at this point; even if he recognized that his hopes of ultimate payment if he continued to serve the covenanters were slim, he would have known that there would be no hope of payment at all if he left their service and returned to England. Moreover, the final instalment of the Stationers' payments for the business were not due until 1649, and he may have wished to remain in the business until this was paid; or, of course, there may have been some agreement we know nothing about whereby he was to remain in the business as a servant of the Stationers' Company.

Whatever his motives, the events of 1648 must have made Tyler regret his decision to stay in Edinburgh. Bitter quarrels arose between Scotland and England, and between church and state within Scotland, tearing the covenanting movement apart. Moderate covenanters allied with moderate royalists in supporting the Engagement, an undertaking to intervene in England to help the king against the now triumphant English parliament. This Engager party won majority support in the Scottish parliament and the Committee of Estates. But majority opinion in the Commission of the Kirk and the General Assembly denounced the Engagement as a betrayal of the cause of God. In these circumstances the position of the printing business which served both church and state became distinctly awkward. The Commission of the Kirk drew up a declaration denouncing the Engagement and, on 8 March 1648, ordered that it be printed. Parliament requested the Commission to delay publication, and the intention was evidently to suppress the declaration entirely, for its printer was ordered to appear before Parliament. The printer who appeared was John Twyn, which confirms that the Stationers' Company representative was managing Tyler's presses by this point. He appeared on 10 March, but stated that though he had only received the order to print the declaration two days before, he had already completed printing of 2,000 copies and delivered them to the Clerk of the Kirk. Clearly the Kirk had insisted on haste to avoid suppression, and a few days later it distributed the pamphlet with orders that all ministers read it to their congregations.[62]

The Engagers were furious, but the printers were not punished and for the moment the Engagers made no further attempt to bar the press to the Kirk. Both anti-Engager papers commissioned by the Kirk, and Engager ones printed for the state therefore continued to issue from Tyler's presses, though it is notable that the Kirk's appear without his imprint. In June, however, the Engagers resolved to make a more determined effort to close

---

[62] Aldis 1316, 1316.5 (Wing C4217, —). Aldis 1317 (Wing C4215), is not another edition as Aldis states, but a declaration of 5 May; *The Records of the Commissions of the General Assemblies . . . 1646–1652* (hereafter *RCGA*), edited by A. F. Mitchell and J. Christie, Scottish History Society, 3 vols (Edinburgh, 1892–1909), I, 373–82, 384–86, 389–90, 589; *APS*, VI, ii, 9, 11–12; Baillie, *Letters*, III, 35, 36.

the press to their opponents. The Kirk's opposition to the Engagement was seriously interfering with the levying of a new army which was to invade England. On 12 June the Commission of the Kirk agreed the 'Causes of a solemn Humiliation and Fast' devoted to denunciations of the sinfulness of the Engagement.[63] It was presumably fear of the effects this might have that made the Engagers act, on 16 June, by passing (in the Committee of Estates) an act which prohibited 'all and whatsoever printers or others haveing chairge of printing Irnes or presses' from printing 'anie books, declarations or other paipers whatsoever untill first they present thame befoir the committee of Estaitts, under the paine of death'. This was to be proclaimed at the market crosses of Edinburgh, Glasgow, and Aberdeen — the three burghs with printers — and 'other places neidfull'.[64] Subsequently the Kirk's supporters denounced as 'impious usurpation' the 'calling in' of the causes of the fast while it was in the press — or perhaps after it was printed.[65] Thus, at their second attempt, the Engagers were successful in enforcing censorship. Rumour may have led to fears that the Kirk, foiled in Edinburgh, would try to get its paper printed in Aberdeen, for a few days later the Committee of Estates wrote to the Provost of the burgh instructing him to seize any papers he found in the press there and inform the Committee.[66] Later the Provost was given power to license the printing of school books without troubling the Committee — provided they did not deal with public affairs.[67] George Anderson in Glasgow also seems to have taken the censorship seriously, for it was evidently he who submitted a list of six books (none of which concerned public affairs) for licensing — at least the only one of them ever actually published came from his press.[68]

When the General Assembly met in July 1648 it was loud in denouncing the act 'made for the restraining the liberty of printing from the Kirk',[69] but it apparently made no attempt to defy the act, confining itself to supplicating that it be annulled.[70] Needless to say the Assembly had no objection to censorship as such; while appealing for its own liberty of printing it found time to ban the reprinting, selling or using of a catechism printed in Edinburgh in 1646 for sale in England, as it had been found to contain very gross errors.[71]

---

[63] *RCGA*, I, 567–68.
[64] SRO, PA. 11/6, Register of the Committee of Estates, 1648, fol. 26ᵛ, summarized in Steele, *Proclamations*, II, Scotland, no. 1962.
[65] *APS*, VI, ii, 135–36.
[66] SRO, PA. 11/6, fol. 35ᵛ.
[67] SRO, PA. 11/6, fol. 113ᵛ.
[68] SRO, PA. 11/6, fols 101ʳ, 183ᵛ; Aldis 1383 (not in Wing).
[69] Peterkin, *Records*, pp. 498, 500.
[70] Peterkin, *Records*, p. 508.
[71] Peterkin, *Records*, p. 498; Aldis 1204.3 (Wing O A36c).

XV

The Engagers had succeeded in silencing the Kirk where the printed word was concerned. But they could not prevent its use of a much more widely influential branch of the media, the pulpit. It was perhaps the realization of the need to try to counter the power of the pulpit that led the Engagers to experiment with an extension of printed propaganda in a way unprecedented in Scotland — by establishing a news sheet, Scotland's first known periodical. On 5 August 1648 the Committee of Estates appointed a subcommittee to consider how news of the affairs of the kingdom and its army (which had now invaded England) could be published regularly each week, to counter hostile propaganda. Instructions were sent to the army to dispatch its news to reach Edinburgh each Saturday night, so that the paper could then go to press for publication the following Monday — thus the Engagers were to add to their sins the encouragement of sabbath-breaking by printers!

The first issue of the journal appeared on Monday 16 August 1648 with the title *Ane Information of the Publict Proceedings of the Kingdom of Scotland, and their Armies*. The following day copies were sent to the army in England; but at that very moment the army was ceasing to exist, for this was the day that Cromwell destroyed it at the Battle of Preston.[72] Thus the first issue of Scotland's first periodical publication was also the last — if that is not a contradiction in terms.

When news of the defeat of the Engagers reached Scotland, their opponents the 'Kirk Party' rose in arms, seized Edinburgh, and set up their own regime. The Commission of the Kirk immediately demanded that 'the restraint which wes putt vpon printing . . . may be taken of',[73] but this was really unnecessary. The new regime acted from the first on the assumption that all actions taken in furtherance of the Engagement had been invalid, and in January 1649 Parliament annulled all their legislation.[74]

As Evan Tyler must have realized, the declaration that all that the Engagers had done was illegal had implications affecting him. None the less, he hopefully petitioned the new regime for payment of his 1642–47 bill, and also submitted his bill for work done in 1647–49. He emphasized his services. Sometimes his three presses had been working night and day, and he had had to employ extra servants. His predecessors as King's Printer had not had a twentieth of his expenses, yet they had been granted yearly fees as well as payment for work done; he had had neither. In March 1649 Parliament ordered the Committee of Estates to look into the matter,[75] but nothing was done until October — and what happened then must have

[72] D. Stevenson, 'Scotland's First Newspaper, 1648', *The Bibliotheck*, 10 (1981), 123–26.
[73] *RCGA*, ii, 35, 41.
[74] *APS*, vi, ii, 135–36.
[75] *APS*, vi, ii, 341.

confirmed Tyler's worst fears. The Committee accepted that between October 1647 and September 1648 Tyler had printed 37,900 sheets for the state. But all except 900 sheets had been papers connected with 'the late unlawfull engagement against England' and he would not be paid for them. Thus the English printer of an English-owned printing business was penalized for having helped the unlawful Engagement 'against England'! Since the Kirk party had come to power Tyler had printed 54,086 sheets, to which the 900 from the earlier period were to be added in calculating what was due to him. For this it was agreed he should be paid 4,000 merks (£2,666 13s. 4d. Scots) — just under one shilling Scots per sheet.[76] In the event it probably made no difference what it was agreed to pay for and what not, for though the Committee of Estates ordered in March 1650 that he be paid by the Committee for Moneys it is very unlikely that he ever received any payment.[77]

Two fragments of evidence in 1650 indicate the control over Tyler's presses by the Stationers' Company. In January the Committee of Estates ordered the printing of 2,000 copies of a declaration denouncing the renewed plots of the royalist Marquis of Montrose, 'And gives warrand to Evan Tyler or to Master Twine his majesties printer for that effect'.[78] Thus Twyn was regarded as being King's Printer as much as Tyler. And in July when another new army was being raised eight Edinburgh printers, all described as Englishmen and as printers to his Majesty, were exempted from the levy.[79] Twyn's name heads the list, but Tyler's does not appear and he may have left Scotland by this time, leaving Twyn and his seven servants to continue to produce works carrying Tyler's imprint.

A new war with England was now approaching, but the English employees of the London Stationers' Company were exempted from the levy not out of consideration for their nationality but so that (as in 1648) they could concentrate their attention on producing anti-English propaganda as well as other official papers. In this, incidentally, may lie an explanation of why the Stationers' Company continued to use Tyler's imprint. At a time when relations between the kingdoms were fequently strained and some-times led to war, for the Company to have advertised through its imprint its ownership of the Scottish state printer could have led in Scotland to demands for a Scottish takeover, and in England to demands that the Company stop its Scottish branch printing anti-English propaganda. The

---

[76] SRO, PA. 11/8, fols 178ᵛ–79ʳ.
[77] SRO, PA. 12/5, Warrants of the Committee of Estates, 1650, minute of 12 March 1650.
[78] SRO, PA. 11/9, Register of the Committee of Estates, 1649–50, fol. 46ᵛ.
[79] *Extracts from the Records of the Burgh of Edinburgh, 1642 to 1655*, edited by M. Wood (Edinburgh, 1938), p. 252. In fact all eight printers may not have been Englishmen; 'Daniel Written' may have been the brother of John Wreitton who had printed in Edinburgh earlier in the century (Aldis, *List*, p. 189).

problems of the multi-national company in times of international tension are nothing new!

After the battle of Dunbar on 3 September 1650 Cromwell's army occupied Edinburgh. The army was equipped with its own press,[80] and now it had access to the Edinburgh presses as well. Before the end of 1650 the Tyler imprint was gracing English instead of anti-English propaganda, doubtless to the relief of the English printers involved.[81] The Scots regime holding out north of the River Forth naturally denounced such treachery. The young Charles II had joined the covenanters in an attempt to regain his thrones, and on 4 December he declared Evan Tyler to have forfeited his office as he had 'not onlie maid his residence in England and joyned himself with that rebellious partie thaire who have rejected governement But also have joyned to that partie who have invaded this kingdome And by himselfe and his servands printed and published diverse seditious rebellious and sandalous papers'. It was necessary that some printer should be available to serve both church and state, and Charles had been informed of the qualifications of Duncan Mun, bookseller in Edinburgh 'whose studie and endeavour hes bein all his tyme for the knowledge of the science of printing and so is become able and qualified thair for'. Mun was therefore appointed King's Printer in Scotland for life — though the precariousness of the military situation was indicated by the stipulation that Mun was to 'follow' the king and estates wherever they went.[82]

How Mun (or Mond) gained the appointment is unknown. He is presumably the man of that name who was described as a bookbinder when he married in 1639 and when he became a burgess in 1641 — and was to be so described again when he remarried in 1657.[83] He had displayed his loyalty, it seems, by fleeing from Edinburgh when the English occupied the burgh, and no doubt he had an interest in printing. But he lacked one necessity for a printer — a printing press; thus his appointment remained his dead letter. As a result he was evidently soon deprived of office, though one commentator in March 1651 remarked that 'If Duncan Munne had keeped his gift of printing, we had gotten a presse long ere now',[84] suggesting that some believed that, given time, he could have acquired a press.

One would have thought that the sensible thing to have done after Dunbar would have been to appoint to the post of King's Printer, at least

[80] J. D. Ogilvie, 'Papers from an Army Press, 1650', *Edinburgh Bibliographical Society Transactions*, 2 (1938–45), 420–23.
[81] Ibid., p. 423; Aldis 1413, 1416, 1434.5 (Wing K572, O715, —).
[82] SRO, PS.1/116, Register of the Privy Seal, fols 179ᵛ–80ʳ. This is printed from a later transcript in Couper, 'George Chalmers's *Historical Account*', pp. 86–87.
[83] Couper, 'George Chalmers's *Historical Account*', p. 86n; Watson, *Roll of Edinburgh Burgesses*, p. 367; *The Register of Marriages for the Parish of Edinburgh, 1595–1700*, edited by H. Paton, Scottish Record Society (Edinburgh, 1905), p. 502.
[84] Baillie, *Letters*, III, 134.

temporarily, the only printer established in the northern parts of the country (which were free from occupation by the English). This was James Brown, who had taken over Raban's Aberdeen press the previous year.[85] The Kirk had been the first to turn to Brown's press after the loss of Edinburgh, sending him the causes of a fast for the defeat at Dunbar to print.[86] The state seems to have made little effort to use Brown either before or after the fiasco of Mun's appointment. When in January 1651 it ordered the printing of a remonstrance from the Kirk and its own answer, it asked the Kirk to see to the printing.[87] But the Kirk was worried that Brown's press might turn out to be not completely under its control, for later in January the Commission of the Kirk considering 'the great prejudice rebounding to the publict by want of a presse . . . whereby the people want information how to carry on the publict businesse' decided to send an 'intelligent, able man' to Aberdeen to supervise the printing of 'Public resolutions' and stay there 'while the worke be done, oversee the presse, and correct the impressions'. He was also to try to arrange for one press to be moved 'with workmen and instruments' to Dundee or somewhere else convenient. Later the Provost of Aberdeen was requested to provide the minister sent on this mission with enough money to pay the printer.[88]

What was it the Kirk was so worried about? Certainly the Aberdeen press was inconveniently far north; but this was not the primary reason for the Kirk's concern. The real fear was that Brown's press might fall into hostile hands — not those of the English, but of the minority Remonstrant faction within the Kirk itself. The Remonstrants had virtually disowned Charles II and the war against England as ungodly, and the paper the majority party was trying to get printed was the one which was to give that faction its name of 'Resolutioners'. The English, happy to encourage dissension among the Scots, had begun printing Remonstrant papers in Edinburgh (with Tyler's imprint).[89] The Remonstrants were generally very weak in the north of Scotland with a single exception — several ministers in the Aberdeen area were staunch Remonstrants. If they could somehow gain control over Brown's press in Aberdeen they could deny it to the Resolutioners, thus destroying their last hope of getting their side of the dispute in the Kirk printed. However, the panic was probably unnecessary, and the Public Resolutions duly appeared with Brown's imprint.[90]

[85] Edmond, *Aberdeen Printers*, p. xxxiii.
[86] *RCGA*, III, 48–52; Aldis 1398 (Wing C4201c); J. D. Ogilvie, 'A Bibliography of the Resolutioner-Protester Controversy, 1650–1659', *PEBS*, 14 (1926–30), 57–86 (pp. 59–61).
[87] *RCGA*, III, 183–89; SRO PA. 11/10, Register of the Committee of Estates, 1651, fol. 8^r; Aldis 1450.5 (Wing C4254a).
[88] *RCGA*, III, 265–66, 285, 286.
[89] Aldis 1451 (Wing R1009).
[90] Aldis 1436 (Wing C4199); Ogilvie, 'Resolutioner-Protester Controversy', pp. 62–64.

While the Kirk thus remained intensely interested in the power of the press, the state (as already indicated) lapsed into apathy. The Committee of Estates did indeed order the printing of the description of Charles II's coronation at Scone — but only after the Kirk had issued similar orders.[91] The only other official civil document produced by Brown was a declaration by Charles dated 5 August and addressed to the people of England.[92] The long-awaited English advance into northern Scotland had begun, and the king and the Scots reacted by undertaking the despairing invasion of England that met with almost inevitable disaster at the Battle of Worcester. The declaration, sent back to Aberdeen for printing as Charles moved south, can barely have been printed and dispatched after him in time to arrive before the final defeat. The last printed manifesto of the covenanting Kirk before English occupation overwhelmed it was dated 12 August.[93] By that time the Commission of the Kirk had reached Forfar on its retreat northwards before the English, and only the fact that Brown's press had remained in Aberdeen and had not been moved to Dundee made possible this last-gasp access to a printer; and within a matter of days even Aberdeen was in English hands.

This paper has demonstrated that the covenanters were quick to realize the value of the press, and in general exploited it skilfully in their own interests during their years in power. One aspect not touched on, and which would be well worth investigation, is their use of London presses for propaganda when relations with England were sufficiently relaxed for this to be possible. The sharp rise in numbers of publications under the covenanters reflects their concern with propaganda and the increased activity of a revolutionary administration. It is not a sign of any increased cultural or literary activity in Scotland, and there is no equivalent to the extraordinary richness of publications and opinions which flood from English presses in this period as the result of the breakdown of censorship, and political confusion. Instead, whichever regime was in power in Scotland managed to control printing more or less successfully. The country had no great urban centre like London in which printers could evade surveillance, and there was only a handful of presses in the entire country for the regime to keep an eye on.

Another theme which emerges is that by far the largest printing business in Scotland was English-run and English-owned; and it was mainly interested in printing in Scotland as a means of gaining access to certain areas of the English market. We know that the Union of the Crowns led to increasing

[91] *RCGA*, III, 266; SRO, PA. 11/10, fol. 69ᵛ; Aldis 1441–44 (Wing D2026–29).
[92] Aldis 1437 (Wing C2982); Steele, *Proclamations*, I, no. 2939.
[93] Aldis 1453 (Wing D2038).

Anglicization of Scottish life and culture in the course of the seventeenth century. Did English involvement in the Scottish printing industry help to hasten this process? Certainly men like Young and Tyler were unlikely to have much interest in reprinting older Scots literary works, or in printing new specifically Scottish works, literary or otherwise, unless they would appeal to the English market (like some Scottish religious works in the special circumstances of the 1640s). But much further work needs to be done on the extent and significance of English involvement in Scottish printing in the seventeenth century as a whole, before such questions can be answered.

Scotland's First Newspaper, 1648

A S W. J. C O U P E R long ago pointed out in his work on *The Edinburgh Periodical Press*, the answer to the question of what was Scotland's first newspaper is partly a matter of definition.[1] Two issues of an English newspaper were reprinted in Edinburgh in 1642;[2] and in 1651-59 various newspapers were published in Scotland but were written by Englishmen and for Englishmen — for the English troops and administrators stationed in Cromwellian Scotland.[3] Couper therefore argued that *Mercurius Caledonius* (1661) was the first truely Scottish paper, published and edited in Scotland by Scots, mainly concerned with Scottish news and addressed to Scottish readers. Wisely cautious, however, Couper added that the claim of *Mercurius* would only stand 'until some periodical of earlier date, yet unknown, has been discovered'.[4]

Such a discovery has now been made, *Ane Information of the publick Proceedings of the Kingdom of Scotland . . .*, published in Edinburgh in 1648.[5] The existence of this work has long been known, but it has not been recognised for what it is, a government-sponsored newspaper.

Why should the Covenanting regime, in power since 1638, suddenly decide in 1648 that it needed a newspaper to sell its policies to the country? The answer lies in changing political conditions. From the first the Covenanters had appreciated the power of the printing press, and had used it to distribute their official statements and other forms of propaganda; but no need had been seen for newspapers of the type which developed rapidly in England in the 1640s — though the English example doubtless influenced the 1648 decision. Important as the press was to the Covenanters, they had at their command a far more powerful propaganda machine for influencing public opinion; the Covenanting Church and State worked hand in hand, and the Church had willingly used the pulpit to exhort obedience to the State's policies and to spread the official interpretation of news and events. In 1643 for example the Commission of the

Kirk had offered the services of the Church's ministers in spreading news throughout the country, to counter rumours and false information.[6]

In 1648, however, Church and State became bitterly divided. The moderate Covenanters and royalists known as the Engagers resolved to intervene in England to help Charles I against the English parliament, and they won a majority in the Scottish parliament and the Committee of Estates (through which the Covenanters ruled the country). The majority of the General Assembly and the Commission of the Kirk, on the other hand, denounced the Engagers' policies, arguing that the King's concessions over religion were not sufficient to justify supporting him. Thus the Engagers found the unrivalled power of the Kirk's propaganda machine employed against them. They furiously denounced the Kirk for interfering in politics, and an increasingly bitter pamphlet war of declaration and counter-declaration developed. On 16 June 1648 the Committee of Estates threatened death to any printer who produced books, pamphlets, or papers without its consent,[7] but this attempt to muzzle the Kirk had little effect — in spite of the fact that both Church and State used the same printer, Evan Tyler!

On 5 August the Engagers, realising that they were losing the propaganda war, decided to try to regain the initiative by adding a new dimension to the conflict; the State would produce its own newspaper. The Committee of Estates appointed the Earl of Lanark, the Laird of Tulliebodie, and Archibald Sydserf (burgess of Edinburgh) to be a sub-committee to 'considder and provyde for the fittest way how the publict conditioun of the affaires of the kingdome and of our Armie may be weiklie represented to the kingdome'.[8] By this time the army of the Engagers had invaded England under the command of the Duke of Hamilton (Lanark's elder brother), and the committee wrote to him on the same day announcing its decision. Because of the 'many false scandalls and reports that ar vented and spred throu this kingdome against the proceidings and success of our Armies, to the disheartning, if it war possible, and deceving of his majesties good subjects from their dueties in this great work', it had been decided to counter such hostile propaganda. The committee had resolved 'to send out in print an weikly informatioun to the kingdome of the proceidings of our armies and of the publict conditioune of effaires both at home and abroad'. Hamilton was therefore asked to appoint someone to send news to Edinburgh of what was thought 'fitt to be communicated' about the army's progress and affairs in England. This news should arrive by each Saturday night, as the paper would then go to press and appear in print the following Monday. 'The publict has suffered much be want hereof in tymes past, And theirfore the more Care is now requyred'.[9]

On Monday 16 August the first issue of the new paper duly appeared, headed by the slogan 'God save King Charles' and by the royal coat of arms. As was usual in this period the full title was long and rambling: *Ane Information of the publick Proceedings of the Kingdom of Scotland, and their Armies. In pursuance of This most necessar and pious Engadgement for Religion, King, and Kingdoms.* There was no indication that this was not just an isolated pamphlet but the first issue of a periodical — it appears to have been assumed that the reader would know this, for the last sentence of the main text closes with the words 'We have this week been forced, to exceed the bounds of one sheet which hereafter we intend to limit our selves unto'. Thus it had been planned that the paper should have eight quarto pages, which would require one standard sheet of paper; but the first issue, with a backlog of news about the Engagement to convey, had required two sheets, or sixteen pages. In fact the text fills only fourteen of these pages, page fifteen containing only the prayer 'Give deliverance O Lord unto the King, And shew mercie to thine Anoynted, Even to King Charles and his seed for ever', and page sixteen being blank.

The news content of the *Information* corresponds exactly to what the Committee of Estates had ordered: military news (of the skirmish fought with opponents of the Engagement at Mauchline Moor in June, and of the progress of the army that had invaded England), a few official letters, news that the Prince of Wales (the future Charles II) had been invited to Scotland, and reports of events in England. The tone and purpose of the paper are indicated by its opening words: 'It hath been in all ages the constant endeavour of the Enemies of Religion and Government, to maligne and mis-represent the proceedings of those entrusted with the managing of publict affairs: Neither ever was this seditious way pursued with more cunning and care, then at this time, by a number of dis-affected and dis-contented persons. . . .' The *Information* did not include, as had been hoped, any dispatch from Hamilton himself about his army in England. A letter to him by the Committee of Estates on 17

August, the day after the *Information* appeared, reveals the reason for this. The Committee recounted that it had received letters dated 12 and 14 August from the Duke, and continued: 'Wee have receaved in your Graces letter ane not[e] of the proceedings of the Army. Bot befoir it came to our hands we had printed ane information to the kingdome', copies of which were to be sent to him with the committee's letter.[10]

The *Information* came too late to restore the flagging fortunes of the Engagers, for its first issue proved to be its last. The day after it appeared, just as the Committee was sending copies to Hamilton, his army was being routed by Oliver Cromwell at the battle of Preston. The Engager's regime in Scotland then quickly collapsed as Cromwell marched north and the supporters of the Kirk rose in arms and seized Edinburgh.

Obviously the *Information* proved a complete failure as a newspaper, its acceptance as a periodical resting on intention rather than on the existence of issues produced periodically. Nonetheless it does qualify as Scotland's first newspaper, and deserves attention for that reason; or at least it is Scotland's first newspaper so far as is known at present, for it is possible (though unlikely) that some earlier claimant remains to be discovered, confirming for a second time the wisdom of W. J. Couper's caution.

---

[1] W. J. Couper, *The Edinburgh Periodical Press*, 2 vols (Stirling, 1908), I, 56.

[2] Couper, I, 56-57, 163-66.

[3] Couper, I, 57-58, 167-78.

[4] Couper, I, 58-63, 178-83. See also J. M. Buckroyd, '*Mercurius Caledonius* and its immediate successors, 1661', *Scottish Historical Review*, 54 (1975), 11-21.

[5] H. G. Aldis, *A List of Books Printed in Scotland before 1700* (Edinburgh, 1904; reprinted with additions Edinburgh, 1970), no 1334. The title page of the *Information* has no imprint but it was evidently the work of the King's Printer for Scotland, Evan Tyler. The text is dated 'Edinb. 16. August' at its close on p. 14. Aldis also lists (no 1336.5) under 1648 *Mercurius Calidonius presenting . . .*, which sounds like another claimant for the title of Scotland's first periodical. But this is an anti-Scottish propaganda pamphlet clearly (from internal evidence) published in England.

[6] Couper, I, 79-80.

[7] Scottish Record Office, PA.11/6, Register of the Committee of Estates, May-September 1648, f.26v; *A Bibliography of Royal Proclamations of the Tudor and Stuart Sovereigns*, edited by R. R. Steele, Bibliotheca Lindesiana, 2 vols (Oxford, 1910), II, no S.1962.

[8] Scottish Record Office, P.A.11/6, f.104r.

[9] Scottish Record Office, PA.11/6, f.105r-v.

[10] Scottish Record Office, PA.11/6, f.121r.

INDEX

The index has been confined to personal names, as the individual chapter titles give guidance to subject areas covered